The Enterpris City Centre

The re-emphasis on city centres as part of the wider agenda on urban renaissance and sustainable development has increased policy concerns in the field. *The Enterprising City Centre* is a welcome addition to the current discourse. It focuses on urban development processes and the dynamics of changing city centres within the context of the emergence of urban entrepreneurialism as a driving force in delivering urban development. It looks at the role of new modes of governance and the political economy of partnership working.

The devastation caused to Manchester city centre as a result of the bombing of its core in June 1996 wass to have a major physical, economic and cultural impact on the city and its key interests. The robustness of established public–private partnership arrangements enabled community leaders and key stakeholders to highlight the opportunities that this afforded to drive through a very ambitious renewal programme, and to enhance the city centre's competitiveness and quality. The dynamic redevelopment challenges presented to Manchester city centre have provided an ideal case study for research into the issues of regeneration, and the lessons learnt for masterplanning, programme development and implementation can be applied to any city-centre regeneration project.

The Enterprising City Centre reveals exemplars of local partnership working, the development and delivery of realistic implementation plans, and the range of instruments available to create both an improved quality to the urban environment and enhanced commercial and cultural competitiveness of our major city centres. That this was largely delivered in Manchester within a five-year period of intensive development and renewal activity amply demonstrates the value of such experience for wider dissemination.

Gwyndaf Williams has spent the past 30 years at Manchester University teaching on aspects of urban and strategic planning and on the management of urban development. He is Professor of Urban Planning and Development at the School of Planning and Landscape, and his current research concerns relate to strategic planning and development, urban regeneration policies and partnership working, and housing and land development policies. Complementing his university activities has been a long-term interest in professional and community fora relating to urban development concerns within the Greater Manchester conurbation, and the emergence of a regional agenda within north-west England.

Other titles available from Spon Press and Routledge

Towards an Urban Renaissance
The Urban Task Force

Urban Future 21
A Global Agenda For Twenty-First Century Cities
Peter Hall and Ulrich Pfeiffer

The Chosen City
Nicholas Schoon

Cities for the New Millennium
Edited by Marcial Echenique and Andrew Saint

Forthcoming:
Transforming Barcelona
Edited by Tim Marshall

Remaking Birmingham
Edited by Liam Kennedy
For further information and to order from our online catalogue visit our
website at www.sponpress.com

The Enterprising City Centre

Manchester's development challenge

Gwyndaf Williams

Spon Press
Taylor & Francis Group

LONDON AND NEW YORK

First published 2003 by Spon Press
11 New Fetter Lane, London EC4P 4EE

Simultaneously published in the USA and Canada
by Spon Press
29 West 35th Street, New York, NY 10001

Spon Press is an imprint of the Taylor & Francis Group

Typeset in Univers by Bookcraft Ltd, Stroud, Gloucestershire
Printed and bound in Great Britain by TJ International Ltd, Padstow, Cornwall

British Library Cataloguing in Publication Data
A catalogue record for this book is available from the British Library

Library of Congress Cataloging in Publication Data
A catalog record has been requested

ISBN 0–415–25261–X (hb)
ISBN 0–415–25262–8 (pb)

Contents

Contents

Preface

The devastation caused to Manchester city centre as a result of the bombing of its core in June 1996 was to have a major physical, economic and cultural impact on the city's residents and employees, and on its policy makers, businesses and investors. Thankfully no one was killed in this atrocity, and whilst the wider impacts of this event initially dented the city's confidence, the robustness of established public–private partnership arrangements enabled community leaders and key stakeholders to highlight the opportunity that this afforded. The mobilisation of institutional capacity at the local level aiming to enhance the city centre's competitiveness and quality, and to drive through a very ambitious renewal programme, is a testament to the capacities of local leadership and the enterprise and trust established between key interests. It provides an excellent example of good practice in collaborative planning, and a focus for detailed understanding of regeneration programmes and project management frameworks. In terms of urban management concerns, that this was largely delivered within a five-year period of intensive development and renewal activity amply demonstrates the value of such experience for wider dissemination.

My arrival in the city in the early 1970s coincided with the final stages of the core's redevelopment, a process that had taken over two decades to achieve. Whilst relatively successful in commercial terms it was heavily criticised for its impermeability and poor accessibility, its lack of respect for its historic context, and for its failure to inspire in terms of its regional role and international aspirations. The aftermath of the bomb was to provide the touchstone for a new and innovative commitment to address such concerns, and I became interested from the outset in attempting to understand and evaluate the major process of redevelopment activity involved. The aim was to provide a permanent record of the recovery and enhancement process that was to be unleashed, and to gain a greater appreciation of the complexities of the renewal programme. Manchester now possesses a distinctive, vibrant and permeable city centre that has made a substantial contribution to an improved quality of life within the core, and has fuelled the city's regional capital profile both within Britain and internationally.

That I was able to document and discuss this process of renewal was entirely due to the research award made by the Leverhulme Trust to enable me to undertake such a study. However, I am also indebted to a range of other organisations and individuals who gave me their support. In particular, I am appreciative of the MML Task Force, who allowed me to access a range of documentary information, and without whose support much of the detail of this book could not have been written. I am also grateful to MML's core team of officers and retained advisers who remained accessible and supportive throughout. This was to be reinforced by a range of interviews and focus group discussions undertaken by the research team, involving a host of local politicians, central and local government officers, development professionals and private sector interests. Their views and ideas did much to flesh out the documentary evidence, and to provide a focus for my understanding of the wider issues involved, and many of them are reproduced in this volume.

A number of individuals were to play a central role in delivering the research from which this book was written. In particular Stuart Batho, who was the main researcher on the project, played a crucial role in helping to bring together and to organise the main body of information, in undertaking interviews with the key interests involved, and in coordinating the focus group element. His commitment and drive in delivering the research agenda, alongside a renewal programme that was both dynamic and pressured, is a testament to his research skills and capacities. He was centrally involved in the initial drafting of core elements of Part 3 of the study (chapters 6–10), for which due credit is given. Other researchers were also important at different stages of the research, with Lynne Russell providing a central input in the run-up to and the early period of the research, and Alan Disberry playing an important role in coordinating a range of project information at the mid-stage of the research. Their contributions are appreciated, and they helped define the project and bring it together.

In preparing the manuscript, the support of a range of individuals was to prove critical. In particular, Margaret's unflagging support was often taken for granted, and the opportunity is taken here to record my appreciation in full. Within Manchester University, the support of my colleagues in enabling me to have a period of research leave in order to draft the much-delayed manuscript is gratefully recorded. Heartfelt thanks are also due to Abigail Shaw, who without complaint word-processed the bulk of the text and its numerous iterations, and who generally kept me in line. Thanks must also go to Mary Howcroft who, as always, was fully supportive when editing crises arose. Finally, the support of the School of Geography's Cartographic Unit in relation to the figures, and Matthew Ludlam for the use of photographic images, is gratefully acknowledged.

As an independent researcher 'looking in' at a dynamic process of renewal at a particularly significant period in the city centre's development, it is inevitable that, since the research team were not privy to discussions and negotiations over detailed aspects of the renewal programme, that I have limited appreciation of many of the nuances of programme development and implementation. Whilst most of the work recorded here is by now essentially archival, at the time of the original study the research team were aware of a range of political and commercial sensitivities connected to programme implementation, but were outside the fora where these were discussed. Thus, any factual inaccuracies and weaknesses of interpretation are entirely mine, and whilst I have attempted to elucidate the arguments honestly, omissions and mis-interpretations have inevitably occurred with such a complex story. I take full responsibility for such views, and they do not necessarily coincide with the interpretation of the former MML Task Force, Manchester City Council, or the range of other agencies, organisations and individuals whose help with this research was gratefully received.

Finally, I would wish to record my appreciation to the city of Manchester, its residents and its public servants, who have provided an excellent context for my academic activities over the past 30 years, and to the publishers for their support and indulgence during the lengthy period of translating the research into the final manuscript.

Introduction

Dramatic changes affecting the structure and organisation of the modern state over the past couple of decades have been explained at the macro level by the twin forces of globalisation and neo-liberalism. These have resulted in the unleashing of new competitive forces, and have had the consequential effects of 'hollowing out' the established apparatus of government. Such broad influences have had a dramatic impact on the structure and functioning of our major urban areas, seen thematically in terms of economic globalisation and the impact of the informational economy, the experience of increasing cultural diversity and widening social inequality, and on concerns relating to environmental quality and sustainability. Central to this debate on the changing urban realm has been a concern with the continuing competitiveness of urban areas and the sources and outcomes of such competitiveness for urban futures (Begg 2002).

Such developments have stimulated the redesign and restructuring of urban politics and the nature of institutional relations concerning the governance of urban areas, increasing the importance of the 'local' scale in the development and implementation of public policy. As the narrative of the city has changed to reflect an increasing interest in competitiveness, so has the deepening dissatisfaction with established theories and explanations, and there has been a shift in concern to the 'new' politics of urban governance (Oatley 1998; Hall & Hubbard 1998; Jessop 1997a). At the heart of such concerns has been a preoccupation with the increasing entrepreneurialism of urban politics, and a fundamental questioning of the nature of local governance and its mode of operation. This debate has utilised concepts of markets and networks as key features of contemporary governance, focused on the institutionalist basis for collaborative action, and concerned itself with notions of partnership and public–private interaction in delivering urban development (Healey 1997a).

Within such a context of broader socio-economic and political processes, this book attempts to provide a wide-ranging analysis of the local capacity to deliver a competitive response to current urban change processes and concerns. Focusing on city-centre renewal and change in Manchester, and based on the local response to a dramatic event and set of circumstances – namely a major city-centre bombing – it aims to provide a context for an understanding of local capacity and leadership, and to utilise the specificities of this experience for wider application. Manchester city centre was devastated by a 1,500-kilogram terrorist bomb in June 1996, and whilst its immediate aftermath had a dramatic impact on the city and its wider environs, the realisation by community leaders and key stakeholders of the opportunities that this afforded for enhancing the urban quality and competitiveness of the city centre led to the mobilisation of institutional capacity at the local level to establish and drive through an ambitious recovery programme. That this was largely accomplished within a five-year period of intensive development and renewal activity was a testament to the capacities of local leadership and the enterprise demonstrated by the range of key interests. As such, this has proved an exemplar of good practice relating to collaborative planning that is worthy of much wider debate.

Focus of the study

The study on which the book is based was funded by the Leverhulme Trust – 'Managing Urban Development Partnerships: The Recovery of Manchester City Centre' – with the overall aim of evaluating the experience of collaborative working in response to the damage caused by the bombing, and the opportunities afforded by the trauma to enhance the city centre and its economic and social competitiveness. In terms of overall justification the study aimed to address the following issues.

- The scope for urban governance to respond to unexpected crises is centrally influenced by the nature of local leadership, and modes of established partnership working.
- The capacity of cities to capture opportunities for innovative and creative development is dependent on the provision of a clear vision, the existence of trust between all parties involved, and confidence in the delivery of an appropriate strategic response.
- Successful urban regeneration is predominantly dependent on the establishment of appropriate institutional and organisational structures to deliver the necessary vision, and local ownership of policy and programme implementation.

Within this broad framework, the specific objectives of the research were to:

- evaluate the role of local partnerships and policy networks in Manchester in facilitating the establishment of both an agenda for, and a commitment to, the process of city-centre rebuilding;

- appraise the nature of the rebuilding process in relation to all the stakeholders involved, the efficiency and effectiveness of policy and programme delivery, the performance of project management procedures, and the main *outputs* of the regeneration process; and
- evaluate the means by which 'added value' was captured as part of the recovery programme for the city centre as a whole, and the extent to which such an *outcome* has enhanced both the city's competitiveness and local community confidence.

The research involved four complementary phases of work:

1 *The commitment to redevelop* Setting the framework for the study as a whole, this aspect focused on a preliminary baseline study of the city centre's physical, commercial and cultural competitiveness prior to the bombing, the emergency planning response to the trauma, and the process of developing the agenda and local commitment to rebuild.

2 *From policy to programme* This element of the study evaluated the process by which the resulting masterplan's main strategic objectives were translated into policies and programmes of action, with focusing on the translation of the masterplan into development parcels and programmes.

3 *From programmes to projects* This element focused on programme and project implementation experience, being concerned in particular with the management and control of public realm projects, and influence on and the coordination of private sector investment projects. As part of this evaluation a sample of individual development projects were appraised in detail.

4 *The impact of recovery* The final element attempted to assess the relationship between the rebuilt core and the rest of the city centre, and to provide an initial view of the outcome of the renewal process. This element considered the city centre's evolving role in terms of form and function, the impact of the bomb and recovery programme on policy integration and partnership working within the city, and the vitality of the city centre as a whole as a result of the recovery experience.

Following a contextual review of evolving modes of city governance and the contribution of public–private partnership arrangements, the work focuses on aspects of masterplanning, visioning and strategic management, before finally reviewing established literature on programme and project management. Such themes were applied to the experience of Manchester, with detailed content analysis being undertaken of a variety of primary and secondary documentation, both that within the public arena and that internally held by the main agencies involved. This included information held by Manchester City Council, by Manchester Millennium Ltd Task Force (MML), and by MACE (programme managers), some of which was commercially sensitive at the time, but which by now is largely archival.

In terms of empirical work, a total of around 50 interviews were completed by the research team, focusing on aspects of programme development and implementation, and involving discussions with key participants in the renewal programme. The focus of such interviews lay both with evaluating experience in terms of the development of the original masterplan and of its delivery, and with reflections on specific project management and implementation processes. This involved semi-structured discussions with local politicians, local/ central government officers, MML board members and officers, development professionals and advisers, private sector and development interests, and with wider community concerns (Appendix 1). The final stage of the project involved running a series of focus groups to debate the wider impact of the renewal programme on the function, vitality and competitiveness of the city centre as a whole, and to consider the city's future direction. Sessions took place that dealt with economic competitiveness and commercial outcomes, the impact of physical change on the built environment, and concerns relating to access and mobility within the city centre, with these discussions providing an informed framework for tentative initial evaluation of the outcome of the programme, and of future challenges relating to the city centre's continuing competitiveness.

The work has stimulated continuing research on town- and city-centre partnerships relating to development masterplans, to city-centre management practices in England's 'core cities', and has provided a sound conceptual framework for more wide-ranging research on the management of urban development processes.

Structure of the book

The key themes of cooperation and partnership, of local capacity and leadership, and of entrepreneurialism and competitiveness inform the structure of the book, which seeks to understand the essence of delivering an urban quality agenda within a city-centre context. These themes are developed in four main parts, with the initial section setting the governance and policy context for the study. It is concerned with the challenge for urban areas of increasing competitiveness within cities, the emergence of entrepreneurial urban governance approaches, and of the growing interest in the role of city centres within an evolving urban policy context. The second part of the book focuses on the local framework to such issues and concerns, discussing in turn Manchester's response to current challenges facing urban governance, the city's initial response to the bombing of its city centre, and the mobilising of local capacity to develop a comprehensive renewal strategy. The next part of the book, at the heart of the empirical study, focuses on the processes involved in delivering the renewal strategy. It is centrally concerned with programme delivery and project realisation, and deals in turn with the bomb's impact on the city centre's commercial competitiveness, the quality of the emerging urban form and the diversity of its urban consumption patterns, and the contribution of the strategy's delivery for enhancing city-centre access and mobility. In the final part of the book, the study reflects on the lessons learnt for adding value to competitive city centres, the challenges raised for the wider urban arena, and the role of local entrepreneurial approaches for tackling emerging urban policy concerns.

Part 1 of the book, encompassing the first two chapters, attempts to set a framework for the study as a whole. In the first chapter it explores contemporary themes relating to recent urban change processes, emerging urban system relationships, and the challenges raised for urban governance procedures and policies. The role of urban competitiveness and the responsive nature of urban entrepreneurialism are then discussed, with particular attention being paid to the scope for collaborative action and local partnership. The second chapter concentrates on the relevance of such debates for city centres, focusing initially on the legacy for core areas of dramatic changes to urban development pressures over the past half-century. It considers the ramifications for central areas of an emergent competitive urban policy agenda, and considers the policy focus of urban cores in attempting to promote the vitality and competitiveness of their areas. The centrality of sound spatial and programme management approaches to delivering increased competitiveness are stressed, as is the delivery of appropriate operational frameworks.

Part 2, encompassing chapters 3–5, sets out the local policy and action framework within the city of Manchester for delivering city-centre renewal, focusing in particular on local institutional capacity and resources following the bombing of the core. Chapter 3 establishes the main principles behind the city's governance and its emerging policy focus and framework from the early 1980s to the mid-1990s. It pays particular attention to the established vision of the city centre, evolving patterns of policy development and delivery, and the main development and management challenges faced by the core. Chapter 4 focuses on the local mobilisation of key interests and regeneration capacity following the physical, commercial and psychological crisis unleashed by the bombing. This is initially concerned with the emergency planning response, and the development of a discursive framework relating to the commitment to establish a recovery strategy. This was to culminate in the formulation of an initial masterplan, and the establishment of appropriate delivery mechanisms. The final chapter in this section traces the refinement of the initial vision as part of the process of drawing together an all-embracing delivery and implementation focus for the core's renewal. It pays particular regard to an emerging programme management strategy, culminating in the development of the initial implementation plan, the focus for commitment by all the key agencies involved.

Part 3 sets out to detail the experience of delivering the vision for rebuilding and revitalising the city centre, focusing in particular on programme and project delivery. Chapter 6 is centrally concerned with the core management approaches developed to deliver such programming of development activity, being initially concerned with the working arrangements of the key agencies involved, the nature of public entrepreneurship and private sector commitment, and the form of inter-agency working developed to ensure the successful delivery of the renewal programme. It appraises the detailed arrangements put in place for managing programme delivery, and for implementing detailed project proce-dures. The following four chapters (chapters 7–10) take such concerns forward with regard to a number of the key dimensions that together mark the overall success of the city-centre renewal programme – ensuring commercial competi-tiveness; a robust and quality-driven building and refurbishment programme; deliv-ering cultural vitality and diversity in relation to city-centre consumption trends; and enhancing city-centre access and mobility. These chapters provide the main opportunity for detailing project management and project realisation experiences that in total exemplify the key features of the renewal programme. As well as establishing their immediate context within the wider programme, attempts are made to consider their broader impact on the functioning and vitality of the city centre as a whole.

Part 4 of the book, focusing on the final chapter, sets out to reflect on the wider impact of development achievements within the city centre during the period 1996–2002, and its contribution both to the nature of urban entrepreneurialism and to the competitive city. It then establishes the current agenda locally for delivering city-centre management and enterprise, and the local capacity for continuing to deliver leadership for the challenges that lie ahead. It finally broadens out the study's findings to consider the wider ramifications of the work for continuing city-centre competitiveness, and the consequences of enhanced city-centre vitality for the urban realm as a whole.

Part 1

The governance and policy context

The contextual framework for the book is concerned with emerging challenges for urban governance arising from increasing competition for resources and policy innovation, both between and within cities. Indeed the search for novel responses to the challenges set by increased competition has focused on the contribution of collaborative action and partnership by key local stakeholders, and the emergence of new approaches to the political economy of the city. Within such an urban framework, a specific interest in city centres – traditionally the focus of agglomerative economies, but currently faced with major challenges arising from the fragmentation of commercial and social production and consumption – has proved of inestimable interest to both academics and policy makers, and has been at the heart of recent debates on 'urban renaissance'.

The initial chapter briefly focuses on exploring the nature of recent urban change processes and emerging urban system relationships, both between cities and within urban areas. It proceeds to consider the issues raised by such changes for established principles of urban government, and the emergence of a new political economy of the city that focuses on current concerns with the nature of urban governance. Finally, it traces recent developments that debate the nature and form of urban competitiveness, and the scope for local collaborative action to deliver enterprising responses to the problems and concerns of both policy makers and citizens.

The second chapter takes on board a number of these themes, examining the role of city centres within this broader concern for the future of our urban areas. Focusing initially on concerns relating to the development legacy of urban cores, and its impact on both form and function, it considers the nature of recent commercial and societal developments that have affected the viability of town and city centres in the face of 'edge city' development pressures, and finally reviews public policy responses to such concerns since the 1980s. This is considered in terms both of the continuing role of the city centre and of changes to the wider urban realm. Finally, it considers the contribution of government and other key interests in responding to the challenge, and in attempting to positively influence the viability and vitality of town and city centres. It attempts to reflect on the nature of pro-active policies and programmes for the core, and the emergence of town-centre management as a stimulus and focus for enhancing city-centre competitiveness.

Chapter 1

Urban governance and the entrepreneurial city

A set of economic, technological and social forces are currently operating to profoundly influence the role and function of our urban system, interaction and competition between individual cities, and the internal structure of our major urban areas. The challenges of globalisation and neo-liberalism have significantly affected our approach to urban management, this being accompanied by the 'hollowing out' of the state apparatus and a shift from government to governance, a reformatting of political capacities at both sub- and supra-national scales, and an increasing preoccupation in strategic terms with our international competitiveness.

This complexity and dynamism associated with the urban arena thus provides an appropriate base for investigation, and this chapter briefly aims to explain recent urban change processes, and to introduce a number of contemporary concepts relating to the political economy of the city. It then proceeds to consider a diversity of views currently being advanced concerning the restructuring of the local policy arena, before reviewing the contribution of current debates on collaborative action, partnership, and the entrepreneurial city.

Explaining urban change processes

Globalisation and the informational economy

A range of economic and political forces are currently operating to create a global market in goods and services. The explosive nature of technological and informational diffusion and deregulated trade barriers has resulted in the expansion of new technologically sophisticated industrial spaces, increased global competition, and facilitated new more flexible relationships with producers. When combined with the growing internationalisation of investment flows and the accentuated competitive pressures on business, our major cities have increasingly sought competitive advantage.

Reinforcing economic globalisation has been the shift in all advanced economies from the production and handling of goods to the processing of information and knowledge. The networking of these technologies has resulted in secondary, much larger impacts on cities, fundamentally testing established assumptions about urban economies and lifestyles, as cities develop lattices of advanced telecommunications networks as nerve centres for the new technologies. This new locational logic is governed by access to information and knowledge, with major cities being the focus for specialised information, key nodes for national and international interaction, and the locus for improved telecommunications. As a consequence, our understanding of the contemporary city requires that we should grasp the complex interactions between urban places as centres for economic, social and cultural life *and* as electronic spaces (Graham & Marvin 1996).

The impact of new technologies on industrial production and communication systems has increased the spatial scale of markets, enabling the development of new specialised services and goods. Connectivity and integration of network nodes are critical to this process, generating additional synergy for growth and development. Freer entrepreneurial attitudes, access to venture capital and to technological expertise, and public policy promotion of new enterprise formation have all combined to transform geographical space in the search for entrepreneurially innovative environments (Castells & Hall 1993). The impact on cities of modern transport technologies has been spectacular in recent decades, further reinforcing urban decentralisation processes and the growth of new activity centres in suburban nodes. Further improvements in communications are likely to have important impacts on the competitiveness of urban areas, with cities as consumers of high-quality communications technologies enjoying investment in the most advanced applications as central features of their economic competitiveness.

Cultural diversity and social inequality

Cities are not only central to wealth generation but also act as the focus of cultural differences and social diversity. Indeed, whilst their fortunes may depend heavily on their economic and institutional competitiveness, their success will also depend on the existence of social cohesion.

> Achievement of social cohesion is no longer seen as merely a costly redistributive activity, but one which contributes to competitiveness through the mobilisation of skills, creativity and active citizenship.
>
> (Oatley 1998: 3)

The increasing emphasis of urban governance on explicit economic development agendas rather than on social redistribution, reinforced by selective migration, has meant that the cores of our major agglomerations have come to exhibit the hall-marks of social polarisation and exclusivity (Jencks & Peterson 1991). Such uneven development is an inherent characteristic of globalisation, and the mosaic of inequality at all geographic scales, providing the basis of the urban management challenge.

Environmental quality and sustainable development

A central focus of the debate relating to the functioning and long-term prospects of cities has been the rapidly growing concern for environmental sustainability and urban quality of life, both perceived as critical components of society's cultural adaptation to rapid technological change. In discussing the rearrangement of urban governance the key aim has thus been to improve the degree of congru-ence between levels of administration and scales of human activity, whilst reducing their negative environmental impacts. However, real definitional issues remain over the nature of sustainable urban environments, and the credentials of both the compact city and the dispersed multi-modal city region are actively promoted (Jenks *et al.* 1996; Breheny 1992).

Emerging urban system relationships

As a result of all these influences acting on cities as network nodes, both externally and internally oriented shifts in urban system relationships have taken place. This has resulted in changing international hierarchies, and variations in the economic performance and well-being of cities within national urban systems. Externally, a global city system has emerged with premier locations transacting a substantial part of their business internationally, with both other global cities and other nationally significant centres (Simmie 2001; Knox & Taylor 1995). They provide the key sites for specialised financial and business services, and the electronic facilities neces-sary for the implementation and management of global economic operations. A small number of very important provincial cities generally operate at the secondary level, effectively serving as regional capitals, but increasingly attempting to perform international functions. They may serve as administrative and higher-order service centres within their national urban system, may demonstrate considerable dyna-mism and rising per capita incomes, but generally lack access to global networks and higher-level producer services so characteristic of global cities. The search for agglomeration economies and regional competitiveness is becoming particularly important in such cities, however, as the global marketplace reduces the role of the nation state and increases the importance of the city region.

Internally, decentralisation and deconcentration trends within the modern conurbation have facilitated the process of suburbanisation, and a slow but reac-tive acceptance by those with responsibility for urban management of the need for policy frameworks to adapt to the poly-centric and multi-nodal nature of the city region (Barlow 1997). In such circumstances, city cores have remained highly attractive to a wide range of services, and they have been actively transforming their economic capacities, often facing more competition from the central areas of other major cities than from their own suburbs. Thus specialisation of higher-value information-intensive producer services, conversion of redundant commercial space and the construction of residential units, and the expansion of urban leisure and cultural facilities have been the backbone of city-centre revitalisation programmes in recent years. Critics have argued that such developments are increasingly externally oriented, with such core redevelopment becoming segregated from the city's own residents. The increasing duality of economic opportunities and urban quality of life within urban areas thus provides the major urban management challenge for the present and for future policy making.

A question of governance

Since the 1980s, in the wake of such broader economic and political processes, the narrative of urban politics has been substantially modified (Jessop 1998, 1997a). The shift towards the 'new politics' of urban governance, focusing more on process than on institutions, 'refers to the development of governing styles in which the boundaries between and within public and private sectors have become blurred' (Pierre & Stoker 2000: 32). Its primary focus lies with how the challenge of collective action is met, and the issues and tensions associated with policy interactions that operate at a variety of scales, involving networks and webs of relationships, and with increasing significance being attached to local institutional capacity (Table 1.1).

Hierarchies, markets and networks
More generally, governance has been explained in terms of the minimal state, a new public management ethos and the central role of self-organising networks, and related to broader trends associated with post-Fordism (Rhodes 1997). In reality, concepts have evolved from the hierarchical notion of government associated with the post-war expansion of the Welfare State, a market-driven reappraisal arising from neo-liberalism tendencies of the 1980s, and a current preoccupation with the governance of policy networks.

> The process of governing is no longer assumed to involve a single, homogenous all-powerful government, but rather a shifting combination of public departments and agencies, quasi-public bodies, private and voluntary sector organisations, operating at different but interdependent levels.
>
> (Leach & Percy-Smith 2001: 22)

Table 1.1 Modes of governance: markets, hierarchies and networks

Key features	Hierarchy	Market	Network
Normative basis	Employment relationship	Contract – property rights	Complementary strengths
Means of communication	Routines	Prices	Relational
Methods of conflict resolution	Administrative fiat-supervision	Haggling – resort to courts for enforcement	Norm of reciprocity – reputational concerns
Degree of flexibility	Low	High	Medium
Amount of commitment among the parties	Medium to high	Low	Medium to high
Tone or climate	Formal, bureaucratic	Precision and/or suspicion	Open-ended, mutual benefits
Actor preferences or choices	Dependent	Independent	Interdependent

Source: Adapted from Powell 1991

Indeed, market principles and the advocacy of 'public choice' theory have had a significant impact on management practices in today's public sector, centrally influencing the move from a concern with 'government' to the new style 'governance'. Yet whilst the language of 'enabling' has become almost universal, the variation in possible interpretation from the 'residual enabling authority' at one end to the 'orchestrating and community enabling' focus at the other end is real (Wilson & Game 2002). Moreover, whilst the enabling role can clearly be linked with the increasing competition and choice involved in the extension of free-market ideas to public service provision, it has also been associated with partnership, cooperation and collaboration, and the development of local policy networks (Leach & Percy-Smith 2001).

Networks are perceived as the defining characteristics of the new governance agenda, focusing on relations between organisations rather than on internal decision-making capacities. The key features of such networks are that cooperation and trust are formed and sustained, horizontal relationships between individuals are promoted, and the benefits and burdens of problem solving are shared (Rhodes 1997; Lowndes *et al*. 1997). Whilst the concept of policy network is not new, it is particularly compatible with a system of governance involving extensive institutional fragmentation. The rise of policy networks does not of necessity, however, signal a diminished role for government, since such networks don't appear fully formed, and government (central or local) can dominate networks by determining their operational parameters and objectives, imposing their own value preferences through control of financial resources, legislative powers and political legitimacy (Taylor, 2000).

Restructuring the local state

Within this wider context, an interest in local government – particularly in terms of the relationship between the state and the city – has become the basis of recent theoretical perspectives on urban political economy. Early interest in a local government-based analysis of the process of government focused on central–local government relations as the fundamental channel for managing the dual polity of policy initiation (centre) and policy implementation (local), which saw a functional and political separation of the national from the local (Cochrane 1993). The development of empirical and theoretical accounts of local government in Britain was, however, strongly conditioned by the period of radical reform under successive Thatcher administrations (1979–90). This saw the highlighting of increasing central control over local finance, the commodification and privatisation of public services, loss of local state autonomy over remaining public services, and the expansion of non-elected 'governance' and business influence (Leach & Davis 1996).

Literature on urban politics and the local welfare state grew out of a dissatisfaction with the paradigm that had emerged during the 1960s, which focused on the exercise of power by local officials as urban gatekeepers (Dearlove 1973). Castells (1977) in particular argued that urban power reflects the interest of local and national capital, with only limited autonomy for the local state apparatus, these views being reinforced by the development of a body of work on local state theory (Cockburn 1977; O'Connor 1973). This led to subsequent analysis of changing central–local relations in terms of the social relations of the state (Saunders 1980). There were attempts to define a functional specificity for the local state in terms of social/class relations, the possibility of 'local autonomy', and the importance of the 'locality' in terms of wider processes of uneven development (Duncan & Goodwin 1988). A large body of work emerged on leftist local government, rooted in the belief that the local state was more accessible to popular and community-based pressures, and an obstacle to national restructuring strategies for capital (Boddy & Fudge 1984). By the late 1980s this fairly clear theoretical treatment of restructuring had itself been altered by the comprehensive defeat of municipal socialist ideas, and the replacement of critical research on the local state by a concern with 'localities' (Cooke 1990). The search was thus on for a broader theoretical framework that could explain the move to a concern with 'governance', a post-Thatcher move to a partnership-based urban competitiveness, and the perceived move from urban managerialism to urban entrepreneurialism (Harvey 1989c).

The 'Thatcherite' analysis of the local state focused on 'neo-liberalism and authoritarian populism', a radical and strategic project that 'effected a fundamental structural transformation of the institutions, practices, boundaries and perceived responsibility of the state' (Hay 1996: 151). The key elements of Thatcherism were perceived to be the institutional and discursive dissolution of corporatist governance; abandonment of a Keynesian policy paradigm; wholesale rebalancing of governance in favour of the private sector; recommodification of state welfarism in line with a shift from universalism of provision to a 'safety net'; radical centralisation of government power; and a concerted erosion of the autonomy of local authorities (Jessop 1998, 1997b). Such changes to political philosophy led to a review of local government from within, and the espousal of the 'new public management', a philosophy taken further by the Blair government's commitment to the 'third way' as a way of renewing social democracy (Giddens 1998). This is clearly part of a wider process of transforming the state in the direction of more complex multi-level governance, of which local governance is an important element.

Political economy of the city

The breadth of recent changes to the functioning of cities and the patterning of government has seen the periodisation of political theories concerning urban development, involving initially the reworking of pluralist and elitist traditions, through to the promotion of notions relating to 'growth machines', a 'regime' based analysis and to the more recent articulation of 'regulation' based parameters. All such concepts have in turn attempted to provide the explanatory basis for the 'new urban politics' (Holden 1999).

The theory of the 'urban growth machine' attempted to rework elite theory and community power concerns to a political economy account of the local social construction of urban places (Logan & Molotch 1987). It developed this through a local analysis of the role of property and development interests in the local politics of growth, focusing on the struggles over commodification between community interests concerned with the use value of the built environment, and the interests of capital which sought to maximise the exchange value of urban development (Cochrane 1996; Harding 1995). Logan and Molotch focused on place-bound entrepreneurs concerned with physical growth, who facilitated local coalitions of interest around urban development. Such 'growth machines' were, however, unable to achieve their goals alone, and attempted to facilitate a coalition of key players, who either individually or collectively could dominate local urban development strategies. Despite attempts to present such advocacy as de-politicised, the prioritisation of exchange value over use value was seen to threaten both local neighbourhoods and the broader concerns of local authorities.

Critics have argued that the growth machine model has limitations in explaining the process of urban development in that it understates the role of central and local government and local institutions central to the delivery of local services, and the role of the state as a driver of local political processes and of the

9

formation of local interests. It fails to examine how places are produced unevenly within the broader political economy, and, by focusing solely on the commodification of property and land, fails to connect this with wider processes of urbanisation. Additionally, capital investment is not as footloose as suggested by the theory, and it understates the significantly autonomous role of British local government, which is not largely dependent on local tax-raising powers (Jessop 1997a; Stoker 1995).

> In the case of the UK it has been necessary to construct business involvement from above. It has not simply been generated as a result of local pressures from existing business groups. Instead, national and local states have taken the lead in creating institutional space for a local politics of business.
>
> (Cochrane 1996: 9)

Urban regime theory was seen to provide a stronger methodological basis for investigating the politics of business and place, in that it sought to locate the social production of urban governance within a broader political and economic context (Stone 1993). However, as with growth machine analysis, it proved difficult to separate the theory from its American origins, even though it is possible to agree that 'people', 'policy' and 'politics' do matter in responding to economic change, and that these features lie at the heart of the urban governance debate (Jessop 1997b; Judge et al. 1995). Stone accepted the systematic domination of certain interests over urban development processes, but rejected the idea that the governing coalition could fully control the wider community. He argued that different kinds and sources of power were mobilised through networks of participation, and were contingent on specific local circumstances. Thus the local political leadership emphasised the management of key interests as a way of achieving specified goals, and recognised that existing institutions must be negotiated with and coordinated in order to achieve governance (Ward 1996). Regime members were mobilised through self-interested cooperation and through a network of joint interests that, together with active integration with the machinery of local state, could help achieve and maintain a capacity to govern (Painter 1997; Collinge & Hall 1997). Holden argues, however, that active mediation between the 'politics of business and the business of politics' effectively measures the failure of governance.

> In the British case, it may be best to move beyond the discourses of enterprise, urban renaissance and opportunity, to consider the rapid diversification of partnerships and institutions in terms of governance failure.
>
> (Holden 1999: 58)

Serious questioning of the limitations of regime theory outside the US context has raised concerns relating to the characteristics of regimes, the explanatory basis of regime formation, and the extent to which they can be sustained at the local level. Much of the analysis fails to take full account of wider structural processes influencing local contexts and capacities for action, and fails to consider specific supra-local factors that may have driven the creation of regimes, specifically the national policy programmes that have created the incentives and space for active local collaboration (Cochrane *et al.* 1996).

Recent preoccupations amongst urban theorists with 'regulation theory' represent an interesting development of neo-Marxian debate relating to processes of capitalist growth, crisis and reproduction. Its basic appeal rests with the possibilities offered by the framework for examining the transformation of political economy across time and space, and has sought to explain how various modes of regulating capitalism may moderate, but not remove, its internal conflicts and tensions (Jessop 1997b). It has recently been used to study the transformation of local governance, considering the 'new' urban governance in terms of social regulation and the production of a corresponding 'regulatory effect' (Jones 1998, 1997; Painter & Goodwin 1995). Criticisms of regulation theory focus on the fact that whilst it may offer a fairly complete structural interpretation of Fordism, the current realities of post-Fordist restructuring make it difficult to apply (Goodwin & Painter 1997).

Collaborative action and partnership

The increasing failure of traditional models of government to cope with the rapidly changing policy environment of the last decade has led to the search for a more collaborative model of activity as a centrepiece of contemporary developments in local governance. The search for collaborative action has sought to demonstrate the need for integration in the activities of stakeholders, involving diverse interests and actors engaged in interactive and interdependent activity, and 'the prioritising of collaborative rather than competitive advantage' (Lowndes & Skelcher 1998: 317).

Collaborative planning

The decision of agencies to collaborate is usually based on a combination of multiple determinants that may include a sense of common purpose, but with resource dependency and legal/regulatory requirements critical features of such collaboration, together with the search for organisational legitimacy and prestige. At best this is perceived as multiple stakeholders working together to determine a specific policy focus, and an acceptance of the collective vision required to determine the necessary response, involving both reciprocity and synergy and a transformation of interests. With such an approach each stakeholder brings something that may help other participants, and each has resources that others need; they jointly search through interactive learning for actions and strategies that none could achieve alone (Healey 1997a). Indeed, the relative openness and transparency of the process may generate more stable and legitimate policy outcomes (Meadowcroft 1998).

Healey (1998b) puts an emphasis on formal arenas for mediation and resolution of diverse perspectives, and is concerned with the transformative influences of such an approach on existing institutional structures. She argues that institutional redesign is taking place, reflecting wider change processes associated with more diverse and dispersed welfare delivery systems and enabling governance. This approach emphasises the centrality of networks as a mode of governance, whereby the various actors are able to identify complementary interests, with the development of interdependent relationships based on trust and reciprocity. Knowledge and information thus flow through such networks in order to implement common purpose (Thompson *et al.* 1991). Problems may arise with such networking arrangements, however, in terms of the challenge of working across the cultural boundaries of individual organisations, the resource implications of membership, and the difficulties of building 'vertical' networks (Bogason & Tooney 1998; Skelcher *et al.* 1996).

Healey (1997a) makes reference to three key attitudes of particular concern to urban planning and development:

- the extent to which place, territory and locality displace sector and function as foci of governance activity;
- the extent to which the range of stakeholders in governance activity in a locality expands beyond traditional local power elites; and
- the extent to which changes in institutional capacity increase the ability of urban governance to exercise a degree of pro-active planning of the diverse driving forces relating to urban quality of life, and to local economic opportunities.

Within this institutional paradigm concepts of institutional capacity and capital are central organising principles, with a focus specifically on processes that facilitate institutional capacity building. Amin and Thrift (1995) note that at the locality level a plethora of civic associations and a high level of interaction between social groups, reinforced by flexible coalitions that cross individual interests and that possess a strong sense of common purpose, are necessary preconditions for 'institutional thickness/richness'. Within such a context it is particularly important to understand how institutional capacity building is facilitated, since the building of new kinds of governance capacity is often a key objective of government initiative (Healey 1998a).

The notion of institutional capital focuses on a 'stock' of assets based on relationships formed around reciprocal trust and on relational webs and networks that bind people together in terms of social capital (Putnam 1993). Innes (1999) distinguishes between three forms of capital deployed in an interactive governance context – intellectual (knowledge of resources), social (stock of trust) and political (capacity to act collectively) – which have been adapted by Healey as knowledge resources, relational resources and mobilisation capacity. The concept of knowledge resources is focused on the socially constructed nature of knowledge, which is often diverse and based on a variety of assumptions, requiring both the renewal of established ideas and reflection on new frames of reference. Relational resources lie at the heart of social capital concerns, with individuals embedded variously in several webs/networks of social relations, tied together by bonds of rights, obligations and mutual trust. Such web-based relationships have differing morphologies and opaqueness. Healey argues that the quality of such webs is centrally influenced by the breadth of stakeholders it reaches and the bonds that bind the networks; a web-like pattern but with clear nodal points and variable access; sufficient network integration channels that facilitate connections; and the possession of good links with regulatory and resource allocating powers, characterised by open, sincere and trustable relationships. Much of the empirical work on urban regeneration partnerships in Britain, however, notes that the strengths of such linkages are often limited, and that the main actors in such bodies have to devote considerable energy to maintaining and enhancing the quality of their relationships with key players.

Finally, mobilisation capacity focuses on the potential to build a sustainable institutional base for pro-active place making, and the effective mobilisation of 'change agents' or 'brokers' who can facilitate the collective force for change, and position it in policy significant arenas. Mobilisation capacity requires the necessary structural shifts that:

- create opportunities for change and agreement on arenas to target;
- have the capability to identify and target the source of key resources and regulatory power;
- possess a repertoire of mobilisation techniques that facilitates action; and
- have access to change agents that operate at critical nodal points.

Critics of the collaborative approach have raised questions as to how common values can be forged in different policy contexts, with varying power relationships amongst the key players (Tewdwr-Jones & Allmendinger 1998). Particular concerns have addressed how stakeholders sharing a common purpose can be identified and encouraged to get involved; the extent to which such processes undermine local democracy by facilitating 'pressure group cartels'; and the extent to which the outcomes are more a reflection of the 'lowest common denominator' rather than the implementation of a shared vision. Indeed, whilst some outcomes may be immediate and direct, others may be deferred and indirect, and may influence the continuance of collaborative activity.

Partnership development

Central to the notion of collaborative planning has been the contribution of 'partnership' as an instrument for policy implementation, and the concept has been used loosely with reference to a variety of recent urban policy initiatives (Bailey 1995). However, theoretical frameworks for understanding partnerships are not well developed, with such applications containing a 'high level of ambiguity' (Mackintosh 1992). Briefly, it can be envisaged as a coalition of different organisations – public, private and voluntary – impermanent by nature, but conjoined to achieve a common purpose and a shared vision to respond to a particular policy concern (Huxham 1996). Though based on organisational relationships, such partnerships are not generally underpinned by any specific regulation, nor are they characterised by distinct fiscal regimes, organisational structures or modes of operation. An effective partnership limits the scope for domination by any of its member organisations, and the existence of partnership doesn't affect the statutory powers and obligations of such organisations. Whilst partnership working inevitably involves elements of all three modes of governance – hierarchies, markets, networks – this approach has a particular affinity with networking, since it is based on the synergy of collective action and the transformation of the debate through cooperation (Lowndes & Skelcher 1998). Indeed, 'local policy networks' are essentially a conceptual response both to the limits of markets and hierarchical arrangements, and to the large increase in the type of organisation involved in policy making (Table 1.2).

In comparison to networking, which is generally based on an individual set of relationships, partnerships focus on organisational relationships based on formal agreements within clearly defined boundaries. Partnerships normally deliver programmes through a range of member partners that may include public, private and community sectors, coordinated by a facilitating body that is generally

Table 1.2 Partnerships and networks

	Partnership	Network
Focus	Organisational relationships	Individual relationships
Motivation	Voluntaristic or imposed	Voluntaristic
Boundary	Clear	Indistinct
Composition	Stable	Fluid
Membership	Defined by formal agreement	Defined by self and/or others
Formalisation	High	Low

Source: Adapted from Lowndes *et al.* 1997

a limited life body or working group. Such partnerships provide the basis for collaborative action, bringing stakeholders together for a common purpose, and have been at the heart of urban policy implementation over the past decade.

> Partnership processes seem well suited to this restructuring of cities, by integrating capital, leading sectors and favoured social groups in specific locations. In addition to this vertical integration of projects, partnerships also fragment decision making across space and can be argued to be better suited to such selective restructuring than older forms of territorial management.
>
> (Newman & Verpraet 1999: 488)

Partnership working is thus widely accepted as a suitable instrument for tackling complex urban problems that provide a challenge for collective action in a situation of fragmentary public management, and where the need for policy cooperation and coordination is seen as crucial (Stoker 1997). This is particularly the case with the coordination of infrastructural investment, and the unlocking of development resources. In theorising the characteristics of partnerships a number of key features are generally identified.

- *Synergy* whereby more can be achieved by the various sectors working together, than separately. Added value from sharing resources and from joint effort may increase the effectiveness or efficiency of policy outcomes, and involve less government coercion than do other modes of public sector intervention (Hastings 1996). Additionally, being largely based on voluntary agreement to cooperate, partnership may result in widening the basis for interest participation (Peters 1997).
- *Transformation* involves a challenging of the aims and operating cultures of other partners. Thus partnerships become arenas for bargaining, lobbying and negotiation about purpose, objectives and likely outcomes. Indeed, partnership may provide an executive capacity for collaborative effort that could not be achieved through normal political and bureaucratic processes (Bailey 1995).
- *Budget enlargement* may secure more accessible resources by building commitment through leverage. They can be cost effective when compared to other possible means of achieving the same goals, and can be a useful tool through which to gain access to the resources and the skills of other agencies (Hutchinson 1995). Indeed, evidence of partnership formation is now required in order to bid for funds for regeneration and development purposes, with partnership working being 'the key to unlocking competitively allocated resources' (Peck & Tickell 1994: 254).

- *Confidence building and risk minimisation*. In a situation of tight constraints on public expenditure, and the instability of development investment outside the strongest market locations, developing mechanisms for stimulating local confidence is critical. Thus collaboration between sectors can build confidence in long-term planning beyond normal political or budgetary horizons, with potential flagship projects clearly linked to broader community benefits.

In consideration of partnership typologies, Bailey (1995) identified a diversity of partnership arrangements, it being generally accepted that partnerships may operate differently in practice. Indeed, the extent to which they foster short-termism and facilitate a lack of transparency in the balance of power have often raised questions relating to issues of coordination, accountability and control (Bogason & Tooney 1998).

Partnership working is undoubtedly influenced by the geographical locations in which the partners operate, the nature of the activities they undertake, and their membership and organisational structure (RTPI 1998). In addition, given its impermanency, different modes of governance may be required at different stages of the partnership life cycle (Lowndes & Skelcher 1998). Four key stages in a partnership's life cycle have been identified, each stage characterised by a differing mode of governance.

- *Pre-partnership collaboration* is characterised by informality and a stress on personal relationships based on a network mode of governance. The quality of relationship is linked to the level of trust between actors, and the extent to which interaction is seen as leading to mutual benefit and a common purpose. Through such informal networks, information may pass relatively freely, but may still prove difficult in terms of broadening group involvement – given the unwritten roles or informal codes of conduct already in place through established network contacts.
- *Partnership creation and consolidation* is characterised by an increasing importance of hierarchy and a formalisation of roles for ensuring probity, accountability and reporting, and effective implementation structures. This increased formalisation is seen to be necessary since the partnership is moving from a concern with exchanging information and viewpoints to a focus on collective action and programme implementation. It also involves negotiation across organisational boundaries and cultures to establish partnership structures, and to sustain reliable networks for formalised decision making.

- *Partnership programme delivery* requires systematic coordination between hierarchies (regulation and supervision of programme implementation and of contracts), markets (bids and management of expenditure programmes) and networks (informal agreements to negotiate the complexities of programmes and projects). The market mode of governance is particularly central to inter-agency working at this stage, since competitive bidding requirements aim to stimulate partnerships to develop innovative and cost-effective programmes of work, and to ensure the delivery of programme effectiveness and value for money. The tensions between market and network modes of governance are clear at this stage, threatening to undermine trust, mutuality and cooperation.

- *Partnership termination or succession* aims to reassert network coordination as a means of sustaining agency commitment for future collaboration following the termination of partnership arrangements. Indeed, a network mode of governance may well continue to linger following partnership termination and the dissipation of its strategic significance, so as to continue the role of established and valued relationships, to oversee the delivery of specific elements of partnership output not delivered within its specific timescale, and to continue to tackle a range of problems not solved by the specific funded initiative (Sullivan & Lowndes 1996). The termination of formal partnerships may nevertheless aim to empower communities to build and continue local capacity, seeking support from mainstream local budgets for the coordination of focal points of activity in the locality arising from the continuation of informal networks.

One final area of partnership working that has received increasing academic interest relates to the characteristics of the organisations that seek to collaborate in urban governance, and the ways in which those characteristics facilitate or constrain productive partnership. Hastings (1999) argues that a host of issues concerning the nature and fit of the institutional building blocks of partnership working have still to be explored, and suggests that such issues can be understood as dimensions of 'institutional coherence'. This is made more urgent by the increasing complexity of urban governance, the proliferation of partnerships, and the growth of multi-level and overlapping partnership activity. She argues that urban development through partnership and the capacity for strategic decision making require two main types of institutional coherence: intra-institutional coherence (internal cohesion) involving a level of connectivity and mutual adaptability within partner organisations, and inter-institutional coherence (congruity, consistency) between the different partners across various aspects of their operation. Consequently, there is a need for institutions involved in partnership working to recognise that such interaction may require them to change internally so that they are more effective corporate actors, but with greater flexibility and adaptability.

Competitiveness and the entrepreneurial city

The acceleration of economic globalisation and the internationalisation of investment flows since the 1990s have led to the concern by governments in developing both the competitiveness of business activities within the core and the competitive edge of cities, in terms of improvements to physical, cultural and socio-economic resources (Oatley 1998). Thus place marketing has become an important part of economic development strategies, raising tensions amongst policy makers concerning the relationship between growth and competitiveness, and social coherence and cohesion. These basic tensions underpinned the work of the research programme funded by the Economic and Social Research Council (ESRC) – 'Cities: Competitiveness and Cohesion' (1997–2002) – with the recognition that urban performance may be inextricably linked with the performance of the economy as a whole (Begg 2002; Simmie 2001). This has been accompanied by an increasing shift in urban policy concern from an orientation focused on urban decline to concerns over growth and competitiveness.

The programme promoted the need to consider the significance of new technologies and knowledge-based production systems for urban competitiveness (Lever 2002; Graham 1998), the centrality of the linkages between social cohesion and competitiveness (Potts 2002; Boddy 2002) and urban quality of life (Rogerson 1999), and the role of regulatory environments and property markets as 'shaping factors' in helping to explain divergences in urban performance (Gibb et al. 2002; D'Arcy & Keogh 2002; Bramley & Lambert 2002). Empirically, in terms of the measurement of urban performance, demands by policy makers for techniques to benchmark competitiveness measures as an input in formulating regeneration and development strategies have also become evident as a way of capturing the 'distinctiveness' of individual cities (Deas & Giordano 2001). Specific attention has also been paid to the measurement of urban innovation and its impact on the competitiveness of urban regions (Simmie et al. 2002). Finally, in terms of the choice of appropriate strategies and policies to promote urban competitiveness, the notion of clustering and networks between cities is perceived as critical, with the tensions between growth and sustainability being moderated through the operation of urban networks, pooling expertise and funding (Cooke et al. 2002). Questions still remain, however, regarding the extent to which such approaches to governance can improve the prospects of the least promising cities and their constituent neighbourhoods (Urban Studies 2001).

Urban competitiveness

Whilst there is now a wealth of literature on the concept of competitiveness in relation to national economic performance and the trans-national nature of such activity (Porter 1998; Rapkin & Strand 1995), little has been written until recently on the competitiveness of individual cities. This is in spite of a growing realisation of the centrality of urban regions for the competitiveness of national economies. In terms of the arguments for urban competition, two contrasting views are evident in the literature. Porter (1995) argues that, whilst cities and regions do compete, it may be in different ways from those exhibited by either the nation state or the individual enterprise. He argues that economically successful places have concentrations of specialised knowledge, support institutions, and clusters of related and rival enterprises, all providing powerful incentives to innovate. Tapping the assets of cities is thus the product of public and private sector cooperation and the support of community institutions. Lever and Turok (1999: 791) argue that the central tenets of such an approach focus on urban accessibility as a locus for mobile investment and public resources, a commitment to provide an efficient and modern infrastructure of human and physical resources, flexible land and property markets and the promotion of local quality of life, and a responsive system of local governance. In this latter context, the promotion of public choice models of local governance perceives competition as central to allocative efficiency, for responsiveness to public preference, and as representing best value for taxpayers.

Krugman (1996), on the other hand, argues that cities as such do not compete with one another; they are merely the locale for firms and enterprises that compete. He argues that the sets of assets which cities develop according to this formulation – and which may be necessary conditions for competitive success – do not facilitate inter-firm competition, which is fundamentally based on such factors as cost efficiency, innovation and marketing, all operating internal to the firm. Within the literature, the issue of urban competitiveness has focused on three dimensions, namely the processes of competition between cities, including the management process by which assets and performance are moulded; the assets that contribute to urban competitiveness, and the outcomes in terms of competitive success or failure; and the spatial dimensions of such competition between international and national urban systems (Begg 1999). The concerns of this book relate primarily to the first of these approaches.

It is clear that many factors that influence urban performance are internationally or nationally driven, and that the individual city can do little to effect such variables. Equally, the performance of cities within a national urban system will centrally influence overall success, and the efficiency and well-being of its urban system are of national concern (Kresl 1995). We need to consider, however, what makes some cities more competitive than others within this wider context, both in terms of efficient resource utilisation and in the institutional management of urban assets (Figure 1.1). Local policy makers do not benefit from passivity, however, with progressive policy making helping to equip cities to adapt and to foster a dynamic economic and cultural environment, whilst ill-judged policies can deter investment and trigger cumulative negative forces. In assessing appropriate policy environments, it is critically important to accommodate two emergent trends. On the one hand, globalisation limits the freedom of manoeuvre of governments at all levels, obliging the moderation of regulatory and financial demands, and a recognition that social and economic policy must act in concert. On the other hand, changes in the organisation of production blur the boundaries between bundles of assets that comprise separate firms and facilitate the clustering of opportunities (Porter 1998).

The persistence of disparities in key economic indicators implies that there are systematic differences in the relative attractiveness of cities that transcend relative cost differentials. Non-price factors will be much more diverse than the direct costs of business operations, with the importance of the 'local environment' – human and physical resources; governance, regulation and facilitation – all being key assets for urban performance and attractiveness. This explains the increasing competition seen between cities in recent years to gain investment, and to promote and market distinctive urban assets (R. Griffiths 1998). This upsurge in spatial competition can be explained in a variety of ways and takes place across a wide range of policy arenas, with a dichotomy between 'economic' determinants that are generally quantifiable (factors of production, infrastructure) and 'strategic' determinants (institutional design, local policy environment) that are broadly qualitative (Kresl 1995). Recent work on long-run trends in British cities (Begg *et al.* 2002) stresses the importance of capacity building, capacity utilisation and institutional coherence at both the level of the city and the urban system as a whole, but stresses that a 'one size fits all' policy approach is unlikely to be either desirable or feasible in addressing urban competitiveness issues. Further work on the benchmarking of competitiveness by Deas and Giordano (2002) accepts that inter-city comparisons mask processes of competitiveness within cities that are highly intricate and not amenable to quantification, and that it is difficult to determine why strong endowments of assets have been ineffectively harnessed.

The competitive ethos is increasingly affecting cities, obliging them to be more active in marketing themselves, attempting to identify and reinforce their assets, and focusing on a 'structured coherence' based on place image and quality-of-life dimensions. Indeed, the marketing of places with its emphasis on the projection of deliberately crafted images has been the defining feature of the entrepreneurial mode of governance, and has been at the heart of inter-urban competition

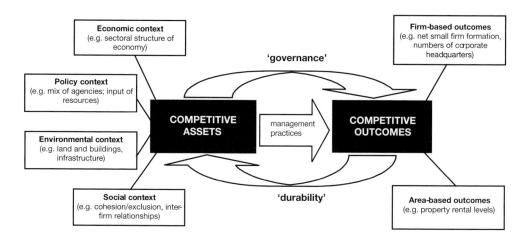

1.1
The competitive process: the assets and outcomes
Source: Deas and Giordano 2001

(Hall & Hubbard 1996). There has been an upsurge in such competition, with the struggle for advantage aiming to attract investment, stimulate the expansion of local economic activity, and to focus on the capacity to deliver through multi-sector partnerships and local coalitions. The shift towards competitive bidding systems in urban policy, and the implicit shift in urban management culture, has meant that the capacity to deliver has threatened to supercede local needs as a central criterion for support, and to challenge its lasting benefits (Loftman & Nevin 1998; Stewart 1996). Such approaches, it has been argued, have frequently aimed to embrace incompatible objectives. In terms of external audiences, they have been concerned with attracting a commensurate share of mobile investment, consumer spending and skilled human resources, whilst for local audiences they have attempted to legitimise local development policies, cementing solidarity and fostering morale and social cohesion (Jewson & MacGregor 1997).

Whatever view is taken of urban competitiveness agendas, the main scope for action by urban policy makers to boost competitiveness is to enhance the local business environment, facilitate training and skill development to foster innovation and learning, improve the quality of the built environment, foster social inclusion and ensure social cohesion, and facilitate multi-level governance that looks beyond traditional policy instruments (Duffy 1995). Coordination between groups with very different institutional arrangements and policy positions remains a key issue at the local level, and underpins the advocacy of collaborative planning and action, and of successful partnership working.

The entrepreneurial city

The shift of concern from urban managerialism to urban entrepreneurialism reflects the changing role of cities 'as subjects, sites and stakes in economic restructuring and systemic competitiveness' (Jessop 1998: 3). The rise of the entrepreneurial city and the resonance of its discourses are, it is thus argued, underpinned by discursive and institutional processes that exceed the local context, but fundamentally involve the 'redesign' of local governance. It has been argued, however, that the concept reflects a retreat of the nation state as the guarantor of social and economic development, the limitations of local state action, and the restructuring of the local state apparatus in the interests of the central state's organisational response to complexity.

> The distinctive feature of 'competition states' and 'entrepreneurial cities' is their self image as being pro-active in promoting the competitiveness of their respective economic spaces in the face of intensified international … inter- and intra-regional competition.
>
> (Jessop 1997a: 28)

Whichever view is taken, the notion of the entrepreneurial city has evolved since the early 1990s in an attempt to understand the current transformation of urban politics and the emergence of distinctive local political cultures (Peck & Ward 2002; Hall & Hubbard 1998). It can be defined by two basic characteristics, namely a political prioritisation of a pro-growth and outward-oriented stance on local economic development strategies, and an associated organisational and institutional shift from urban government to urban governance. The consequence has been a major change in the way cities are governed, and the way that the political process operating in cities impinges on the lives of urban populations. Such notions fit within the broad contours of the 'new urban politics' and the claims of dynamism, flexibility and innovation that are a feature of the self-representation of city and governance elites (Holden 1999; Peck & Tickell 1995).

> Urban management … is not about ways of delivering local government services fairly, efficiently … [but] how people … with shared interests … can come together to identify common concerns, develop strategic ideas, and generate the momentum to bring forward investment.
>
> (Healey *et al.* 1995: 283)

Harvey's (1989c) seminal contribution on the emergence of this debate focused on the process of urban governance centred around the city, which at its heart was a political strategy based on four key concerns:

1   the exploitation of local competitive advantage for the production of goods and services, respecting the changing international division of labour;
2   the competitive position of the city or urban region with respect to the spatial division of consumption (investment for infrastructure and externally oriented rhetoric of urban quality of life);

3 acquisition of a city portfolio of command and control functions (business, media, government); and

4 ability to compete for an increased share of surplus value redistributed through the state (discretionary grants; research and development investment).

Such discourses of entrepreneurship argue that this is the only way cities can compete in an increasingly unpredictable and globalised economy, advocating, 'togetherness in defence against a hostile and threatening world', and with such specific pro-active strategies opening up the possibilities for new strands of local leadership that create a sea change in the political cultures of cities.

> Coalition and alliance formation is so delicate and difficult a task that the way is open here for a person of vision, tenacity and skill to put a particular stamp on the direction and nature of urban entrepreneurialism, perhaps to shape it even, to particular political ends.
>
> (Harvey 1989c: 7)

More generally, the diverse literature currently available on urban entrepreneurialism shares a common concern with three trends concerning urban development and politics, namely the fostering of entrepreneurial cultures in community, business and urban governance networks; the acceptance of, and strategic mobilisation around, the primacy of inter-urban competition; and the reflexive development of 'place-based' growth strategies, where the imagined community of interest is represented at the level of the city or city region. Jessop presents the measuring of the entrepreneurial city in relation to three themes, namely the re-imaging of localities in and through discourse of an optimistic city narrative; the redesigning of urban governance mechanisms as a consequence; and the emerging primacy of geo-economics over geo-politics in the restructuring of capital. He identifies the emergence of 'entrepreneurial cities' within 'competitive states' as a contested outcome of political and economic transformation, and argues that the role and status of the city has been actively re-ast in light of a general concern with the relative competitiveness of places within the space economy (Table 1.3).

> The entrepreneurial city or region has been constructed through the intersection of diverse economic, political and socio-cultural narratives which seek to give meaning to current problems by constructing them in terms of past failures and future possibilities.
>
> (Jessop 1997a: 30)

The focus of such urban development strategies has been on place marketing and civic boosterism; the promotion of hallmark events and festivals;

Table 1.3 Characteristic forms of entrepreneurialism

- The city as an arena for entrepreneurial activity, including the production of new urban places for living, working, producing, servicing and consuming.
- Enhanced entrepreneurialism among the changing mix of city residents, including the attraction of new residents and the reskilling of existing workforces.
- A shift from public to private sector activity in both the political governance and physical design of city space.
- Business as a defining framework for the values and meanings of urban living, with the agenda and interests of city politics having an overriding concern with growth.
- A shift away from the management and provision of local welfare services towards the promotion of economic competitiveness, place marketing and the support of indigenous private sector growth.

Source: Adapted from Painter 1998; Jessop 1998

renovation of the urban fabric and investment in prestige buildings; investment in distinctive consumption spaces; and the promotion of regeneration based on leisure, culture and sport. In short, the fundamental aim is to change the image of localities, but has often resulted in paradoxical tensions between the veneer of inter-urban diversity in the nature of entrepreneurial strategies, and the reality of outcomes that has seen the replication of similar local policies.

Critics have argued that such regimes of interest are potentially fragile, and that coalition partners frequently become disillusioned, marginalised or redundant as the promised rewards of entrepreneurialism fail to materialise. In particular, the volatility of property markets can expose how fragile the basis of major entrepreneurial policies can be (Imrie & Thomas 1993; Turok 1992). In addition, it has been argued, the failure of urban entrepreneurialism to alleviate the social and economic problems of cities, and the neglect of social equity in favour of the prosperity of elite groups, has hidden the 'real' costs of such policies and has exacerbated social and territorial disparities within cities (Loftman & Nevin 1996; Peck & Tickell 1995). Indeed, Hall and Hubbard (1998) argue that what is lacking in the literature is a failure to adequately consider local variations and the 'lived culture' of entrepreneurial cities, and the need for a heightened awareness of changing textures and rhythms of everyday life as they are affected by (and effect) entrepreneurial governance. In short, there has been a paucity of attempts to distinguish what cities are actually being entrepreneurial for and about.

Place promotion, requiring increased investment by local authorities (much of it wasteful), and which may raise tensions for broader welfare spending, necessitates that cities present positive images of themselves to the outside world as part of the narrative of urban entrepreneurialism, whilst underplaying the social reality that necessitates renewal and regeneration programmes in the first place.

Entrepreneurial capital and cultural symbols often entwine in public space to create a visually seductive city centre, masking the real geographies of decay and neglect.

(Hubbard 1998: 201)

The cities shaped by entrepreneurial urban policies, and significantly those parts of the city which are excluded from this 'new' urbanism, involve significant redrawing of the geographies of social, economic and environmental disadvantage.

(Hall 1998: 106)

Thus, the defence of entrepreneurial cities and of enterprising actors has become a powerful ideological tool in city governance, with interdependent interests sharing risks in attempting to cope with uncertainty, reinforced by dense institutional networks involving wider social forces. Overall, the success of such networks and strategies is rooted in the collective ability to 'add value' to broader economic and political processes by developing forms of governance, modes of regulation and configuration of strategies under an entrepreneurial narrative.

Chapter 2

The city centre as a focus for policy concern

The previous chapter discussed the main characteristics of the changing urban realm arising from the effects of globalisation, neo-liberalism, growing social inequality, and concerns over sustainability. New patterns of governance have evolved as a result of increasing concerns with urban competitiveness, resulting in the rapid extension of collaborative action and partnership at the local level, and the emergence of the 'entrepreneurial' city, reflecting new institutional and managerial frameworks. This chapter takes forward some of these ideas within the context of town and city centres, being concerned initially with the legacy for such central areas of broader societal processes, reflecting on the range of policy responses that have evolved, and focusing in particular on city-centre policy frameworks within the wider urban context. It proceeds to consider the scope and processes involved in devising appropriate town-centre strategies, and the rapid growth of a pro-active town-centre management agenda as an instrument for stimulating the vitality and continuing viability of city centres. It finally discusses the prospects for city centres within the rapidly changing urban realm.

In defining town centres, a diversity of distinctive views is evident, each putting a different emphasis on their physical, economic, socio-cultural and institutional make-up. The most straightforward approach has focused on the mix of land uses and the morphological character and nodality of the central business district, in an attempt to establish the relative commercial importance of town centres. Less narrowly conceived and less physical in orientation has been the explanatory power of a concern with the economic utility of land, expressed in terms of land values and rents, and encompassing both existing use and investment value. Sociologists have placed greater emphasis on the cultural significance of city centres, seeing them as places of collective consciousness and civic identity arising from the concentration of public cultural assets. Besides being valuable in their own terms, town centres are thus significant because they promote social interaction, raise personal awareness of civic society, and offer universal access irrespective of personal circumstances. Others have associated city centres with the commodification of urban society around the consumption of retail goods, leisure and entertainment services (Table 2.1).

In sharp contrast, political scientists have focused on institutional behaviour and the distribution of power and influence between the main agents of change within city centres – property owners, developers, investors, built-environment professionals, local government – being concerned that the concentration of power in fewer hands has raised tension between externally based elites and local civic interests. Such key interests have broadly involved three categories of stakeholders. Pre-eminent are the 'producers' of city-centre environments – property owners, developers, investors, retailers, construction and design professionals – consisting of heterogeneous groups and with often very differing agendas. A second group of 'users' – employees, shoppers, residents, visitors – have aspirations that may relate to consumption, socio-economic background, cultural values and preferences, with this diversity often creating representational and ownership problems. The final group relate to 'intermediaries' – local and national government and public agencies, exchange professionals, and community organisations – whose precise role may differ from that of custodian or guardian of particular interests, enabler, coordinator or advocate of change and development, or as a mediator striking bargains and reconciliation between diverse interests (Ambrose 1994).

Table 2.1 The functional base of town centres

- *Market places* retailing forms the heart of most centres, including comparison, convenience and specialist goods.
- *Business centres* providing workspace and employment in financial and business services, administration and distribution, as well as 'incubators' for new enterprise.
- *Educational, health and fitness resources* most centres have schools, colleges and training centres, and there are universities in larger centres as well as doctors, dentists, clinics and hospitals, gyms, sports clubs, swimming pools and health clubs.
- *Meeting places* whether in the open air or in pubs, cafes, restaurants, clubs of all kinds or more formally in societies, conferences, community or religious groups.
- *Arts, culture and entertainment zones* with libraries, museums, galleries, theatres, cinemas, concert halls, amusement venues and stadia, possibly supported by a series of festivals or other events..
- *Places to visit* often having historic or specialist buildings, unique views or well-known sites or events.
- *Transport hubs* providing interchange and connections to local, regional, national and in some cases international services.
- *Residential areas* with town-centre accommodation often most suited for students and single professional people, the elderly and those in transitory employment.

Source: Adapted from URBED 1994

In terms of the distribution of power between these three categories, the network of relationships both between and within each category reflects a constantly shifting set of liaisons and tensions. Historically, producers have dominated user interests because they control the key assets and initiate physical change – particularly in prime areas of town centres – and users are in a weak bargaining position since they often have fragmented constituencies and diverse views. In non-primary locations, however, a much closer working relationship has often been possible between producer interests and intermediaries such as local authorities, given the more limited economic potential of established uses in such areas. Over the past decade the position of intermediaries has strengthened as the concern over the qualities of town-centre environments has grown, and as government at both central and local levels has belatedly realised that town centres are a major economic, social and cultural asset. Of clear benefit to this process has undoubtedly been the steady economic growth and stable property markets experienced by most city centres over this period.

Although these perspectives portray the complexity and multi-faceted nature of city centres they are not mutually exclusive. Indeed, central areas are continually evolving in response to the pressures for change, and have over the past half-century provided a focus for considerable public policy concern. Whilst they have been in receipt of unremitting pressures arising from extensive decentralisation processes within urban society, and from the new centres of activity within the urban realm, they have fought to sustain their continuing viability as a result of economic diversification, their enduring social and psychological significance, and the extent of capital investment in such areas as a result of past commitments. Thus, many public and private interests share a common concern for ensuring that town and city centres remain at the heart of urban activity and of governance.

The city centre legacy

For most of the past century, urban areas have been significantly affected by processes of decentralisation and counter-urbanisation, with the consequent shift in purchasing power from the centre to the periphery draining town centres of vitality and investment. This has been due to a combination of population shift, employment changes and increased personal mobility, reflecting the wider dispersal of economic activity in a predominantly urban society. Whilst town centres contain by far the largest share of total investment value within urban areas, over the past two decades they have gained a smaller share of new development investment, and this has undoubtedly affected the flow of funds into the maintenance and modernisation of town-centre building stock. Thus, whilst major investors have attempted to protect the value of their historic commitments to town centres, they have also enthusiastically spread their risks by investing in out-of-town locations.

> Traditionally, town centres have been the heart, even the apotheosis of our urban civilisations, where a multitude of commercial, retail, cultural and governmental activities and functions are uniquely concentrated. Recently, however, a series of powerful economic, demographic, social and cultural trends have cast doubt upon their pivotal role.
>
> (Evans 1997: 1)

The commercial dimension: retailing

Until the 1960s the distribution of retail activity was relatively stable, with a hierarchical distribution of facilities and with shops concentrated within the most accessible areas of towns and cities. Most retail outlets were small and privately owned, complemented in central areas by a number of larger departmental stores. Shopping was multi-trip and public transport dominated. All this was to change with the growth of disposable income, increased personal mobility, improvements in infrastructure, decentralisation of population and economic activity, and dramatic changes in retail practice and behaviour. The dominance of central areas was to be challenged by three distinct waves of retail behaviour. The development of free-standing supermarkets/hypermarkets during the 1970s with significant car-parking capacity enabled infrequent bulk-buy shopping at predominantly cheaper, more spacious edge-of-town sites. Retail warehousing and retail parks appeared in the 1980s, dominated by DIY, discount furniture and carpets, and electrical goods, and focusing on edge-of-centre sites or adjacent to ring road and motorway junctions. Potentially the most damaging development has been the construction (particularly between the mid-1980s and mid-1990s) of out-of-town regional shopping centres selling the full range of comparison goods and providing support/financial services. Whilst this latter very threatening activity has been tempered over the past decade as a result of a recasting of central government retail policy, pressures on town-centre retailing persist, with current developments in e-commerce, home shopping and designer outlets.

Within town centres there has been a series of changes, all accompanied by physical restructuring. The 1950s–60s were dominated by post-war reconstruction and the implementation of comprehensive development and redevelopment initiatives. The 1970s were dominated by the completion of shopping precincts and covered shopping centres, whilst the 1980s and 1990s have focused on the development of specialist outlets, and the refurbishment of earlier schemes to improve design quality and to introduce new fashionable uses. Currently the focus of town-centre restructuring is on re-imaging, marketing and management initiatives. More generally, progressive developers and retailers alike realise that the continuing commercial success of town centres has increasingly to be seen as a multi-dimensional experience, involving shopping, cultural and leisure activities.

The appearance of town centres has also been transformed by a series of internal forces based around the concentration on a limited number of dominant retail groups (often resulting from corporate restructuring and mergers), with vigorous competition for market share being particularly marked within the food sector. As a consequence, smaller retailers in town centres have responded by moving into specialist niche markets, and have collaborated to increase their buying power and to protect their interests. However, competition from town-centre multiples and out-of-centre superstores and retail warehousing has increasingly squeezed the margins of the smaller retailers. This restructuring of retailing activities has had major physical consequences, with 'anchor stores' frequently cutting across the previous fine grain of commercial activity. As a consequence, town-centre property markets have increasingly polarised between 'prime' locations in demand from large retail chains, and increasingly less attractive 'secondary' areas where smaller shops struggle to remain in business and are under constant threat from financial, professional and leisure services outlets. Whilst retailers have invested heavily in corporate imaging and marketing to boost sales, the concentration of ownership has standardised façades and interiors, and reduced the variety of streetscape. Indeed, relatively little attention has been given to making the most of the architectural character of host buildings and the distinctive design quality of established parts of town centres.

In attempting to explain the dynamics of retail change and the inter-face between town centres and out-of-centre locations, it is clear that the debate represents a mix of responses to competitive commercial behaviour, shifts in life-style and consumption patterns, and reaction to national retail policies and to local action (or inaction). In terms of competition for market share, retailers and developers alike have preferred out-of-centre locations since they yield higher returns (being less costly to develop), are easier to service, and are located in areas of expanding demand. By contrast, established town centres are often too cramped to accommodate modern retail layouts, retailers have less control over perceived environmental conditions, and the opening of out-of-centre stores may be necessary to pre-empt competitors capturing their trade. In spite of such pressures, major retailers and institutions remain committed to urban cores in order to retain market share and to protect existing investment, this largely accounting for major central area refurbishment alongside out-of-centre developments, and retailer support for the rapid development of a town-centre management agenda.

Retailers argue that out-of-town trends have been successful, not only because they are more suited to modern retail requirements, but also because they have anticipated changing patterns of consumption. Push factors discouraging patronage of town centres are perceived to include concerns about the wider decline of the urban economy, the dispersal of population and jobs, environmental and transport problems, an increasingly mobile population, and a failure of standards of customer provision to live up to modern expectations. Pull factors are associated with the range of goods on offer, 'leisure retailing' aspects of regional shopping centres, and the change in customer values that places a premium on the spaciousness, convenience and safety of such facilities for car-based shoppers. Some commentators have suggested, however, that the growth in leisure retailing and rising consumer expectations may engender public frustration with the predictability of such provision, the absence of a sense of place and the lack of visual interest, and the failure to accommodate ethical and environmental concerns. In terms of the future of town-centre retailing it is clear that the face of such activities continues to evolve, with fiercer competition between retailers consequent on the more uneven growth in consumer expenditure, pressures for a greater diversification of product ranges and activities in out-of-centre locations, and the growth of new retail formats. Indeed, town-centre success in the face of such pressures is largely dependent on whether the town-centre shopping experience continues to appeal when compared to the alternatives, and whether retailers can specialise in offering both distinctive goods and a quality service.

The commercial dimension: offices and leisure

Town centres have traditionally contained the largest concentration of office employment due to the agglomeration of public, professional and financial services. This led during the early years of the twentieth century to the construction of purpose-built office blocks within city centres, a growth feature that was to be sharply curtailed by the property crash of the mid-1970s. The return to stability of property markets in the 1980s led, however, to uneven trends in office developments, with town centres perceived to lack room for expansion, to have high overhead costs, poor environmental standards and traffic congestion. The late 1980s saw for the first time the significant concentration of office development in out-of-town business parks, near to airports and major road networks, this being further stimulated by an evolving rationalisation of the financial and business services sector.

The principal push factors accounting for the decentralisation of offices relate to overhead costs and the growing inaccessibility of core areas due to congestion, the unresponsive context of large mono-functional buildings for changing accommodation needs (modern office footplates and controls on building heights), and business requirements for more flexible space on flexible terms. Pull factors include telecommunication advances that have enabled the movement of 'back office' staff to cheaper locations, decentralisation of customer base, and the greater adaptability of new office and business park developments to reflect changing market demands. This was reinforced during the 1980s by a deregulatory environment and a market-led planning policy focus that accelerated the decentralisation of office activity. The collapse of property markets in the early

1990s, and the subsequent recession, led to a rapid contraction of business services employment, and slowed decentralisation trends until the second half of the decade. Thus, whilst overall prospects for office employment appear reasonably healthy, town centres will remain vulnerable to continued waves of rationalisation and restructuring within existing firms.

Within town centres changes have also taken place, with office development investment focused on prime city-centre properties capable of attracting prestigious and financially secure tenants generating good long-term returns, and with a secondary market of property increasingly difficult to let, much of it prey to conversion for other uses. The dramatic restructuring of the banking and finance sector in the 1990s as a result of an attempt to reduce overheads by new technology, has led to the relocation of main office functions to cheaper locations, retaining only the sales function in prime locations. The impact of these pressures on town centres has altered the accommodation needs of the financial services sector and reduced the number of outlets. This has affected the patronage of neighbouring shops, led to a retrenchment of town-centre property markets, and affected the character and feel of town centres. Nevertheless, town centres have inherent advantages in their centrality to serve large catchment areas for service companies, the ready availability of a pool of labour and back-up services, and the availability of inter-personal networks so central to business.

Town-centre interests will have to struggle much harder in future to retain, let alone attract, office developments, as out-of-town business parks now offer an increasingly sophisticated range of business services. The key to this will be the improvement of accessibility and comfort for doing business within city centres, and to make use of redundant business space for social, recreational and residential uses (Coupland 1997; Rowley 1996). Thus the segregation of land uses, encouraged in the 1960s–70s, has lost its resonance, and city-centre policies for the past couple of decades have stressed the centrality of mixed-use development for meeting such challenges.

> The degree to which town centres maintain and develop a distinctive cultural and leisure appeal, and become more popular places to live, will crucially influence their ability to compete successfully with out-of-town locations.
>
> (Evans 1997: 75)

Central to such a prospect is the increasing interest both in building conversion and in new residential developments on vacant city-centre sites, and of diversifying the town- and city-centre experience in terms of leisure resources. Particularly dramatic changes in both these dimensions have taken place over the past decade, with the buoyant market for development of city-centre living and an explosion of leisure-related developments aiming to extend the trading hours of town centres, focusing in particular on the evening economy.

Increased personal mobility and the transport dilemma

Town centres lie at the heart of extensive transportation networks, their centrality explained in terms of their accessibility to consumers and employment sources. Increasing tensions have arisen, however, between personal mobility and quality of life, with the future of town centres dependent 'on how far transportation systems can support commercial activity without sacrificing environmental quality and decent living conditions' (Evans 1997: 43). Without the necessary expansion in transport infrastructure, cars have been utilising scarce urban space in an unsustainable manner, and it has proved impossible to reconcile the differing demands of business, commuters, consumers and residents. The economic cost of such congestion has proved a major constraint in terms of servicing town centres, accommodating car users, and increasing costs related to the movement of goods. The commercial decline of town centres, arising both from decentralisation pressures and as a direct consequence of traffic congestion, has also resulted in deteriorating patronage and standards of public transport. This process has had major environmental impacts in terms of pollution concentration and inefficient energy use, and has had significant social impacts on inner-city neighbourhoods where infrastructural programmes and congestion have reduced their attraction as residential environments.

Transport policy has fuelled such developments arising from subsidy levels and investment criteria, and the political strength of the car and road 'lobby'. Government has shown faith in the transport industry's capacity to resolve issues of congestion and pollution, but has struggled to significantly support alternative modes of transport, this being reinforced by the fragmentation of control arising from the deregulation of public transport in the 1980s. In relation to town centres, the problem of integrating different forms of transport, and the historic under-investment in transport infrastructure, have provided the main problems for modernising and sustaining the competitiveness of such central cores, and for improving their environmental qualities. In future, the management of both infra-structure and traffic demand will be critical for ensuring the health of city centres, and this will inevitably involve a fundamental change of attitude towards car use.

> ... ultimate irony that the government which deregulated public trans-port and liberalised planning policy in the 1980s, encouraging massive private sector investment in edge of town retail, service and leisure developments and the build up of developers peripheral land banks, are now championing town centres and car restraint.
>
> (Evans 1997: 59)

Deterioration of the public realm

City centres represent the most significant concentration of public space within our urban areas, and their diminishing significance as an arena of public life and as a common property resource has raised concern. Additionally, a growing professional awareness of the social significance of the public realm has renewed interest in the cultural importance of town centres as a focus of civic identity. The quality of the public realm is largely dependent on the effective management of its streets, squares, green spaces and other informal areas, and the interface between private development objectives, civic responsibilities and public and community interests (Worpole & Greenhalgh 1999; Tibbalds 1992). The public realm is a critically important aspect of the relationship between urban morphology, design and social behaviour, where the physical qualities of public space interact with social processes to produce the qualities of place so central to the urban experience (Hayward & McGlynn 1995). Thus the social well-being of town centres hinges most critically on the condition, design and feel of shared, universally accessible public spaces, compromised in recent years by their vulnerability to issues of public safety and anti-social activity. The main features that account for the quality of public spaces relate to traffic considerations, the nature of business activity, the extent of anti-social behaviour and crime, the often conflicting and uncoordinated roles of responsible bodies, and the effective privatisation of much of the public realm (Williams & Green 2001). Negative traffic impacts on the qualities of the public realm are clear, and there is evidence that high traffic volumes have detrimental effects on their social function. It has also been suggested, however, that traffic exclusion has some negative impacts, particularly on commerce and safety, this being partly obviated by contemporary 'traffic calming' measures. With the restructuring and modernisation of town centres being dictated by powerful retail and commercial interests there has been some erasing of traditional street blocks and the effective usurping of public space for private ends. Additionally, the increasing commodification of the town-centre environment has often substituted 'character' for 'placelessness', promoting a narrow consumerist mentality.

Actual and perceived rates of crime and anti-social behaviour in town centres have had a serious impact both on the design of urban development and on the use of the public realm, with attempts to 'design out' perceived problems commonly dealt with in authoritarian ways. Indeed, it could be argued that the formal defence of such public space acts against safety, in that attractive and usable spaces are undoubtedly safer – 'if the city centre's attractions are undermined by crime, the fear of crime and the perceptions that it is unsafe, then the decentralising forces ... will be stronger' (Oc & Tiesdell 1997: 20). However, it is generally accepted that design has a major impact on the public realm, both at the local level in terms of detail, and strategically in terms of the integrative qualities of public space. The public realm can also be undermined by conflicting roles, particularly in mixed-use areas such as city centres, where a requirement for ease of movement can conflict with servicing or conservation requirements. This has been exacerbated in town and city centres where public space has traditionally been publicly owned and managed, serving a variety of functions. The increasing trend for privatisation of the public realm, particularly exhibited in shopping centres and malls, has the principal objective of ensuring retail consumption rather than enhancing the quality of the urban experience, and is highly managed with security and image projection being central.

In terms of the management experience unfavourable international comparisons are made, with the decline of management standards perceived to be based on a variety of factors (Rogers 1999). Curbs on local authority spending have meant cut-backs in capital investment for improvement, planned maintenance programmes, and management resources; the capital expenditure cycle downplays the significance of maintenance programmes; and the development process fails to relate the intrinsic link between initial design and subsequent management. It is characterised by fragmented policy delivery in an area of cross-cutting policy concerns, this being reinforced by a lack of management strategy. The lack of an integrated transport and land-use policy, a preoccupation with motorised transport, and a breakdown in the intrinsic relationship between public space and public transport have also been apparent. The lack of a clear set of responsibilities for private development, reinforced by the tensions for private investment between within-centre and out-of-centre developments, has also been underpinned by deregulation and the privatisation of statutory undertakers and utilities, and the contract culture of much urban public realm maintenance.

A host of central government guidance, advice and initiative does exist, but this is reinforced by uncertainties over legal responsibilities and powers available and necessary for a coordinated management framework, a diversity of financial mechanisms for specific elements, and a growing separation between management and maintenance concerns. However, growing professional awareness of the significance of the public realm has renewed concerns for the cultural importance of town centres, with heightened competition from new retail locations prompting town-centre interests to work in partnership to improve standards of management and maintenance, a central feature of the rapid development of town-centre management in the 1990s (ATCM 2000).

The public policy response: a historic perspective

Having considered the legacy and deficiencies of established town centres as a result of wider societal processes, it is now appropriate and opportune to reflect on the evolving policy response. This section will briefly consider the evolution of such a policy framework in the period up to 1990, setting emerging town-centre policies within the wider context of urban policy initiation.

Emergent inner-area agendas

Identifying the nature of the urban problem associated with urban economic decline and social disadvantage has been at the forefront of British urban policy since the 1960s, with the Urban Programme taking over from established concerns with physical obsolescence – 'dominant values underpinning policy were those of the post war consensus of universal welfare rights, public planning and the pursuit of redistribution and equity, prioritisation of social needs and one nation politics' (Parkinson 1996). By the mid-1970s, however, the limitations of policy that was not focused on an understanding of changes in the structure of global economic and strategic relationships were all too apparent, and the Inner Cities White Paper (1977) laid the foundations of a major shift in policy and a new understanding of urban change processes. It recognised the inter-relatedness of economic decline, physical decay and adverse social conditions; the scale and intensity of the problems described; and the collective dimensions of resident experience. It accepted the need to create wealth in cities to form a platform for urban regeneration, with the twin aims of both strengthening inner-city economies and reversing the drift of the better-off population from such areas. Whilst retaining its commitment to deliver welfare services to those left outside the economic mainstream, it expected local authorities to 'bend' established mainstream programmes to reinforce Inner City Partnership and Programme designations. However, by the mid-1980s the initiative began to falter, lost the political support of central government, and ceased to be the primary instrument for achieving urban renewal. It ultimately failed to sustain a strategic approach to urban regeneration, assumed a national consensus between national and local players in terms of problems and responses, and underestimated the difficulties of getting public sector agencies committed to the same strategy and to bend their mainstream resources. It underplayed the problem of defining and involving local community interests, did not provide sufficient resources to make an impact on the scale of the problem, failed to engage the private sector at the heart of discussions, and provided insufficient flexibility and autonomy for partners.

Within this wider context of urban policy development, a range of specific town- and city-centre initiatives were launched. Prior to the 1960s, town centres that had not required major reconstruction due to bomb damage had evolved gradually. However, growing prosperity, the demands of modern offices and the growth of retailing, and the extension of car ownership all made the existing town-centre fabric obsolete. The Buchanan Report (1963) argued that without intervention town centres would be unable to cope with such changes, and a process of comprehensive redevelopment was promoted. This aimed to extend retail and office areas, segregate pedestrians and vehicles through the introduction of subways and high-level walkways, and improve accessibility through road construction and public transport improvements. Utilising compulsory purchase order (CPO) powers, idealistic local authorities progressed in partnership with developers (often involving major developer–politician trysts) to demolish and redevelop inner-city residential areas, to extend town-centre ring roads, to develop purpose-built shopping precincts as a response to growing consumerism, and to introduce major land-use zoning frameworks. The over-development of central areas by such processes, far from creating 'modern' symbols of civic pride, destroyed town-centre landmarks and extinguished many long-established businesses. In the process they replaced mixed-use areas with mono-functional land-use zones. Indeed, such design solutions were often wrongly conceived, saddling many town centres for a generation with the negative consequences of misplaced idealism (Holliday 1973).

With the property market collapse of the early 1970s and the increasing fiscal crisis of the public sector, the emphasis on comprehensive redevelopment of town centres was replaced by a more reflective period of management. Office development was slow to recover, and the focus of retail policies aimed to protect established town-centre hierarchies. Limited amounts of pedestrianisation and public transport priority lanes appeared, whilst concerns began to emerge on the extent of car parking restraint required. There was little awareness at this time of the link between town-centre policies and the emerging inner-city agenda, the increasingly run-down nature of city-centre fringes, the extent to which established commercial space was becoming outmoded due to contemporary developments in retailing, or of the need to link the economic potential of town centres as locations for expanding business services. Overall, policy making in the 1970s lacked a grasp of the emerging economic dynamics of town centres, and the means to fashion commercial revival in a positive manner, this being reinforced by a lack of public sector leadership or resources. There were, however, some positive developments in that greater provision was made for maintaining a mix of employment functions, and the growth of the conservation movement facilitated building refurbishment and environmental enhancement within city centres.

The advocacy of urban entrepreneurialism

With the election of a Conservative administration in 1979, the tenets of post-war public policy were fundamentally questioned, and new institutional and policy frameworks were established. During the 1980s urban policy became part of the broad political and economic programme associated with Thatcherism. It was characterised by five basic processes, namely:

1   the displacement or transfer of local powers;
2   deregulation of controls and the encouragement of property-led regeneration;
3   the encouragement of bilateral partnerships between central government and the private sector;
4   privatisation, contracting and service-level agreements; and
5   the centralisation of power through quangos and executive agencies.

Government increasingly centralised policy, convinced in its view that to regenerate the British economy it had to reduce public expenditure, enact a reduced role for local government, and sharply increase private sector involvement. The focus of the established Urban Programme shifted significantly towards economic development projects that targeted resources on capital rather than revenue expenditure, and the introduction of a number of high-profile initiatives direct from central government that focused on the needs of business and commerce Urban District Councils (UDCs), Enterprise Zones, City Grant). Reviews of the urban policy framework for this period concluded that it was marked by the limited resources targeted on cities as a dimension of total government expenditure, with declining mainstream resources for inner-city public investment (Robson *et al.* 1994). Whilst smaller cities benefited positively from targeted investment, the larger cities and metropolitan areas didn't share in this relative progress, experiencing both absolute and relative decline. Insufficient attention was paid to creating linkages between different policy sectors, and the coordination of central government department priorities. Whilst the building of strong private sector-led partnerships was mooted, the contribution and commitment of the private sector to the partnership process was exaggerated. Finally, limits had been put on the powers and resources of local authorities to play a constructive role, and too little attention had been paid to strengthening the capacities of local communities (Shaw & Robinson 1998). Such research identified a number of major lessons for the future (Table 2.2). Local authorities should be given an appropriate framework to play a significant role, and local communities should be given greater opportunities to influence as well as participate in urban policy. Greater coherence was needed between the programmes of different government departments and there was a need for greater flexibility of expenditure. Finally, there should be a single urban regeneration budget that should be administered at regional rather than national level.

By the early 1990s it had thus become apparent that the approach to urban policy pursued over the previous decade had not reversed urban decline, and that new ways had to be found to address deep-seated economic problems, and to improve the capacity of the state to respond to them. Indeed the recession of 1989/ 93 exposed the over-reliance on property-led regeneration (Imrie & Thomas 1993; Turok 1992), and demonstrated that a broader holistic approach was required to tackle urban decline, along with a need to address the consequent processes of

Table 2.2 Lessons and policy learning within urban policy

- Physical transformation of declining urban areas is only one part of the wider process of regeneration.
- Everything is inter-related, and a 'patchwork quilt' of disparate initiatives compartmentalises urban problems.
- 'Trickle-down' effects do not work, and the realisation of policy fails to reach the needs of disadvantaged communities.
- Regeneration is too important to be left to non-elected quangos, who both exacerbate the alienation of local communities and fail to build capacity.
- Partnerships are vital but need to be 'sustainable' beyond the flow of resources, and need a commitment to share power locally.
- Resources are never sufficient; spatial initiatives and complementary forms of resource distribution are not a substitute for wider governmental policies for cities through mainstream budgets.
- It is important to have clear aims and realistic objectives that are capable of monitoring and evaluation, and to be more concerned with measuring outcomes rather than programme outputs.
- Image matters in providing visible symbols of change.
- Regenerating people rather than places is difficult to achieve and needs to demonstrate community benefits as well as physical renewal.
- Sustainability is the key, with the short-term nature of urban initiatives militating against the development of coherent medium-term objectives and progressive succession strategies.

Source: Adapted from Shaw & Robinson 1998

social polarisation and exclusion (Lawless 1991; Audit Commission 1989). Thus a fundamental change began to appear in the early 1990s, with a commitment to learn and innovate, and a determination to pursue policies that worked, rather than those of necessity limited by ideological considerations (Lawless 1996).

In terms of evolving town-centre policies during this period it was argued that the deregulation of public sector controls was necessary to facilitate private sector investment, with the presumption in favour of development being at the heart of the land-use planning system (Thornley 1993). Government believed that overly burdensome planning controls, local government 'interference' in the market, and inadequacies of public infrastructure had constrained private sector confidence, and it set out a more permissive attitude to development and investment, regardless of location. Many central government policies in this field were only tangentially related to town centres, however, and central areas were not treated as distinct entities in policy terms. Circular 22/84 marked the beginning of this policy shift by advising local authorities that they should not attempt to regulate competition between retailers, stifle new types of provision or prescribe limits for new floorspace, and indicated that it was only necessary to assess the impact of large-scale out-of-centre retailing upon the prospects of the town centre as a whole. It became increasingly clear that government was prepared to take a permissive line towards retail development in most locations, and this deregulatory approach seriously damaged town centres. The retail industry sensed a change in central government attitude, this being reinforced by a lack of imagination by local authorities over their retail policies (PPG6, 1988). The latter half of the decade thus saw an investment boom in out-of-centre developments, with most local authorities following the government's more permissive line. Indeed, some welcomed the relaxation of controls as an opportunity to improve local facilities, to generate employment, or to obtain planning gain, and even those hostile to the concept were sufficiently pragmatic to ensure that they did not lose development opportunities to neighbouring authorities. Many urban authorities were becoming aware, however, of the need for more interventionist local economic-development strategies to support urban economic performance, and were beginning to grasp that their town centres were a major asset requiring comprehensive rather than piecemeal management if they were to remain competitive.

By the late 1980s it was obvious that the commercial dominance of city centres was being seriously challenged by out-of-town retailing and by business parks, even if the booming economic conditions at the time effectively suppressed concerns about the shift of activity away from the core. The prevailing optimism also obscured the fact that modernising town and city centres in order to challenge such developments could only be brought about by major investment. This was reinforced by the increasing fragmentation of urban transport as a result of deregulation, and a failure to integrate emerging economic development perspectives with investment in transport infrastructure. Local authorities, as a consequence, struggled with limited resources to find new ways of managing increasing traffic congestion, which further increased the attraction and the support of government for out-of-centre locations for commerce. The social significance of town centres was similarly ignored, and the qualities of the public realm declined in most town centres as a consequence of public expenditure cuts and competing priorities.

Thus, town centres largely existed in a policy vacuum for most of the 1980s, and only with the collapse of national economic performance did the realisation emerge that aspatial policies had fuelled out-of-town development at the expense of the viability of established centres. It was finally accepted that if city centres were to prosper in the face of such competition, more concerted support and management was required to enhance their economic health, social meaning and cultural diversity. Additionally, as environmental issues became more important in the early 1990s, demand grew for traffic restraint measures and the encouragement of more environmentally friendly modes of transport in such core areas.

Competitive urban policy: the current agenda

By the early 1990s it had become apparent that the approach to urban policy pursued since 1979 had not reversed urban decline, and that new ways had to be found to address deep-seated economic problems. This period was to be marked by changes to the process of urban funding, a reorientation of the substantive aims of policy, and a restructuring of policy delivery (Lawless 1996; Stewart 1994). The pressures of globalisation, affecting both cities and business, were to lead to an overt policy emphasis on competitiveness, this being reinforced by the introduction of bidding initiatives aimed at encouraging localities to address such issues through collaborative working. This involved fundamental changes in urban governance, and in processes of policy formulation and implementation. Cities were opened up to market influence and the business ethos in a way that moved beyond the subsidy approach of the 1980s, to a more pervasive role for private sector interests in influencing local regeneration strategies.

Regeneration initiatives encouraged localities to develop forward-looking strategies based on public–private partnerships, and to improve their structural competitiveness by enhancing infrastructure and local factors of production. Competitive bidding and the contract culture became pervasive as government sought to promote enterprise, vision and opportunity, and the 'creation of entrepreneurial cities which have the capacity to compete nationally and internationally for public resources and private investment' (Oatley 1998: 18). A defining feature of this new ethos was a competitive environment for urban regeneration in which winners (and losers) were decided on the basis of the quality of bids, replacing notions of 'need' and redistribution with a greater emphasis on 'economic opportunity' and the creation of wealth. Advocates argued that such an approach gave better value for money and encouraged more corporate and strategic approaches to regeneration, both of which would have a galvanising effect on localities and would stimulate local leadership. Critics argued, however, that it was a distraction used to mask a rationing and decline of regeneration resources, which undermined the avowed aim to encourage local empowerment, and reduced the scope for inter-authority cooperation. Such 'contractualisation' focused on a culture of procurement rather than on grant aid, with performance indicators used to define funding agreements. Operating characteristics focused on multi-year programmes and multi-agency participation and funding, seen to better promote the development and delivery of integrated development strategies, with these being reinforced at central government level by changes in policy management. The City Challenge initiative was seen as a way of 'piloting' this new approach, embodying a shift in urban policy from a concern with efficiency, economy and effectiveness to cooperation, competition and concentration (Burton & O'Toole 1993).

A range of new principles were unleashed by this process that highlighted the fact that 'need' was a necessary but not sufficient condition for regeneration funding; agencies must demonstrate competence to spend public money in ways central government considered appropriate; public expenditure on regeneration should be targeted on areas of development potential; and that bids for public funding should be subject to competition (Blackman 1995). This new approach was developed further with the introduction of the Single Regeneration Budget (SRB), with the mid-1990s being marked by a variety of implementation frameworks as different policy phases overlapped (Wilks-Heegs 1996). Implementation and the phasing-out of policy initiatives introduced in the late 1980s was overtaken by an entrepreneurial approach to urban policy involving new forms of intervention and new institutional relations. At the same time competitive bidding for government funding had become the dominant element, and was seen as the most effective way of demonstrating efficient governance.

The return of a Labour government in 1997 did not, in the short term, radically change the format of urban policy even if a higher profile was given to it by the restructuring of government mechanisms, and the commitment to 'urban renaissance through design excellence, economic strength, environmental responsibility, good governance and social well being' (Rogers 1999). The government believed that to solve urban problems power would need to be shared with a range of agencies and communities, and in the short term it extended the social dimension of the SRB programme, attempting to bring community issues back into the heart of regeneration projects. In its approach to regeneration it sought to enhance economic development and social cohesion through effective regional action – within a framework set by the Regional Development Agencies – and integrated local governance. It attempted to show that urban deprivation is multi-faceted, and sought to channel investment and to coordinate action in targeted neighbourhoods. Such 'joined-up' governance was perceived to be at the heart of the New Deal for Communities (NDC) programme, the coordinated implementation intrinsic to the Urban Regeneration Company (URC) approach, and the mixed economy of service provision implicit in the Neighbourhood Renewal Fund (NRF).

In its commitment to decentralisation, empowerment and the reform of local democracy, it has promoted a 'modernising' agenda in local government, with the 'enabling' authority working in partnership with other agencies to produce co-ordinated action and responsive service delivery. The driving force for this has been the search for plurality of service providers – emphasising quality and consumer satisfaction – within the context of central–local government cooperation, and the need for strong relationships with both local businesses and communities. It has introduced legislation making it a duty of local authorities to promote the economic, social and environmental well-being of their area, in the process strengthening their powers to enter into partnerships (Local Strategic Partnerships and Community Strategies). Its current priority is to make Britain a more inclusive society, bringing those on the margins of opportunities back into the mainstream of debate, the focus of its National Strategy for Neighbourhood Renewal (2000).

> Urban policy depends for its success, government now argues, on urban politics that operates collaboratively through networks of inter-locking agencies, and which works for the needs of local communities, leading them and giving them a real voice in decisions.
>
> (Hill 2000: 206)

Thus urban policy currently envisages setting priorities to reverse social divisions and deprivation, involves collaborative ways of working across the boundaries between services, with an emphasis on policy networks and multi-agency working as a dominant conceptual framework. At its heart has been the launch of the Urban White Paper (2000), the first major policy statement on the future of our towns and cities produced for two decades. It sought to present a new vision for urban living that served people's needs, was based on partnership and the integration of policies, involved the modernising of local government and local leadership, and the channelling of increased resources in a more directed and efficient manner. Its vision focused on getting the design and quality of the urban fabric right; enabling all towns and cities to create and share prosperity; providing good-quality services meeting people's needs; and equipping people to participate in developing their communities. Stocktaking of progress with this policy framework was undertaken through the Urban Summit (October 2002), and in the detailed monitoring of the implementation of the White Paper. Of relevance for the concerns of this book has been the establishment of a Cabinet Committee on Urban Affairs; commitments to improve public transport so as to improve integration and access to town centres, jobs and services; a consideration of the establishment of Business Improvement Districts; a commitment to improve town-centre environments, security and crime reduction through local partnerships; reduction of the disruption caused by utilities networks; improvements in the management of the public realm; and the promotion of strategic approaches to the development of local cultural policies.

With regard to the policy environment for town centres, the early 1990s were marked by increased private sector frustration at the lack of strategic planning frameworks (particularly with regard to infrastructural investment), and a reaction against market-led development and the minimalist nature of public intervention. Government began to see town centres in a new light as it became apparent that out-of-centre developments were diverting commercial investment from established centres, exacerbating car-based travel, and undermining the government's apparent sustainability agenda. It was finally appreciated that promoting reinvestment in existing town centres through a wider mix of uses would prove a more environmentally sustainable course of action, and the stimulation of local authority–business partnerships that aimed to adopt more comprehensive approaches to the management and maintenance of town centres

became politically defensible. This commitment unveiled a new orthodoxy in relation to town-centre management, with emerging central government advice
recognising the need to plan and to actively manage town-centre environments,
and marking a rehabilitation of integrated land-use and transport planning
approaches, perceived to be heretical in the 1980s (PPG13, 1994; PPG6, 1993).

Current policy guidance provides a focus for the use of the planning
system as a whole in meeting the needs of a growing and competitive economy, for
achieving sustainable development, for promoting mixed-use developments
(particularly in urban cores), and for enhancing urban design quality. In terms of key
policy objectives it stresses the importance of town centres, promoting the government's commitment to sustain and enhance their vitality and viability; to maintain an
efficient and competitive retail sector, and to focus development in locations where
the proximity of business facilitates competition from which all consumers are able
to benefit; and ensure the availability of a wide range of shops, employment and
services to which people have easy access by a range of transport choices. Local
authorities are thus encouraged to adopt a sequential approach to site selection that
involves key town-centre uses, with development proposals for an out-of-centre
development being promoted when other alternatives have been considered – 'the
onus will be on him, to demonstrate that he has thoroughly assessed all potential
town centre and edge of centre options' (PPG1, 1997).

The most significant piece of government guidance for the emerging
town-centre agenda was, however, the revision of advice on 'Town Centres and
Retail Development' (PPG6, 1993), which stemmed from a realisation that their retail
functions were pivotal to their viability and vitality, and that a better balance had to be
struck between central and peripheral locations. It placed much greater emphasis on
the benefits of diversity and mixture of land uses within town centres, and the importance of such central areas in facilitating multi-purpose trips and minimising travel
demands, and advised that the impact of any future out-of-centre retail proposals
upon existing centres should be carefully assessed. Finally, it commended town-
centre management as a way of raising commitment and joint working, and for
enhancing the appeal of town centres. This refocusing of government commitment
to the future health of town centres was restated in the revised guidance issued in
1996, which emphasised a plan-led approach to promoting town-centre development, both through policies and by the identification of locations and sites for development. It reaffirmed the centrality of a sequential approach to selecting sites for
development for retail, leisure and other town-centre uses, and also argued for the
importance of local centres in relation to the hierarchy of central areas. It did nevertheless state that – 'it is not the role of the planning system to restrict competition,
preserve existing commercial interests, or to prevent innovation' (PPG6, 1996).

The circular promoted mixed-use developments and the retention of
key town-centre uses; emphasised the importance of good urban design and the

promotion of a coherent town-centre parking strategy; and the critical role of active town-centre management in developing clear standards of service and improving the quality of the town centre for its diversity of users. Finally, it set out a framework for the assessment of retail proposals, assessing the key tests in relation to the impact of such developments on the vitality and viability of town centres, accessibility by a choice and means of transport, and impact on overall travel and car use.

At the same time as central government was refocusing its town-centre policies, a substantial revision took place in government thinking concerning transport policy – as part of a wider policy framework for sustainable development. This sought to channel development into urban areas where there exists a choice of transport modes; closer juxtaposition of employment and residential uses; intermixing of retail, leisure and entertainment uses; locating superstores at edge-of-centre locations that are accessible on foot; and traffic calming and parking controls within urban areas, supplemented by better public transport provision (PPG13, 1994). Thus by the mid-1990s wholesale changes were put in place to encourage compact urban development by the same government that had encouraged decentralised investment in the 1980s. It is undoubtedly true, however, that the impact of this policy focus on urban cores will only be felt in the medium to longer term, and that in the short term car restraint and active traffic management may further restrict the attractiveness of town and city centres.

This emerging policy focus was taken further by the present government in its Transport Act (2000) and the issuance of revised transport guidance (PPG13, 2001). This reinforced a commitment to place less reliance on the private car and to reduce the length and number of motorised journeys; to give a greater priority to pedestrians, cyclists and public transport in central areas; to increase integration both within and between different modes of transport; and to link such policies to wider environmental and social policy concerns. It sees the land-use planning system as having a key role in managing and shaping the pattern of development, and in influencing its location, scale and density, and land-use mix and design. This guidance argues that urban development and transport strategies at the local level should be complementary, and that development plan allocation policies and transport priorities are closely linked, so as to ensure a more intense and sustainable pattern of urban development.

Commending the concept of 'town-centre management' as a way of raising commitment and improving joint working between public and private sectors, the harnessing of resources and ensuring the coordination of physical improvements, government advice has at the same time signalled and stimulated greater interest in wider management concerns. Town-centre management has assumed a variety of organisational forms – ranging from the traditional local authority-led bodies and consultative groups, a fora of key organisations, and formal public–private partnerships – all aiming to build trust and to ensure the collective ownership of improvements. Initially perceived as a janitorial role (managing public facilities, environmental services, policing), town-centre management has quickly expanded to include aspects of forward planning and the management of physical improvements, facilitated the enhancement of cultural activities within town centres and stimulated the evening economy (Grail 2000). The formation of the Association of Town Centre Management (1991) to issue guidance on initiatives and to promote and exchange good practice has provided further consolidation. It has produced a number of research reports and policy statements that can be adapted to address local conditions – traffic and parking, integrated transport, business improvement, tourism, business rates, sustainable funding – and has advocated the need for a national 'town centre improvement zone' programme (ATCM 2002, 2000, 1996, 1994).

It is generally agreed that as the degree of local joint working between stakeholders has improved and become more pro-active, multi-disciplinary approaches to management have been better orchestrated, and that more attention has been given to accelerating physical improvements. Town-centre participation in best-practice networks has also resulted in more rapid and widespread dissemination of ideas. Funding, however, remains a problem, with local authorities under tight fiscal regimes providing the majority of public funding, with local management of national chains possessing little local financial discretion, and with investor institutions remaining detached from the process (Hillier Parker 1994). Indeed, the removal of local control of business rates and strict restrictions on the extent to which they can participate in joint schemes with private developers has undermined the stake of local authorities in the commercial success of their town centres. Moreover, town-centre management initiatives have often struggled to engender a true sense of collective ownership, with private sector interests committed to concentrating on tangible short-term projects – with tensions often portrayed between retail and other town-centre uses – and local authorities more concerned with policy issues and with a more long-term consultative consensual style.

Overall, however, changes in central government policy and local practice in the 1990s suggest a greater inclination to support existing town and city centres, with clear evidence of more progressive thinking being advanced by all those involved. However, the tools for guaranteeing the long-term success of such centres are still lacking (legal and financial), and it is unclear at this stage whether the remarkable physical improvement and distinctive appeal of town centres can be sustained, or be likely to be undermined by developments in other policy arenas.

Responding to the challenge

Two significant studies have considered the response of city centres to the myriad of challenges they face, namely the URBED (1994) report and the study undertaken for the Civic Trust (Evans 1997). The URBED report argued that with increasing pressures on town centres and the limited public resources available it is important to establish a baseline for considering the vitality of the urban core, to ensure that appropriate monitoring can be undertaken of the centre's capacity to cope with change, and to assess whether proposed development may challenge agreed plans and improvement strategies. This the authors termed a 'city centre health check', now commonly used by local authorities to audit changes within town centres and to monitor progress in relation to wider strategic frameworks. The report noted that the key concerns relate to property yields with regard to different size and locations of investment, and the nature of pedestrian flows both spatially and temporally. Supplementary indicators were perceived to include the demand for commercial property, space in use and vacancy rates, demand by national multiples and corporate commercial users, the quality of the public realm, and aspects of the development pipeline relating to commercial, residential and leisure activities. Policy makers additionally needed to monitor the overall quality profile of town centres over time (through trader/shopper/user surveys), and the extent to which public policy and the attraction of private investment could be coordinated. A clear view of the strengths and weaknesses of the central core – and the opportunities it offered to enhance its position in relation to competitor centres – also needed to be considered.

The URBED report argued that there are four dimensions that are necessary in order to ensure the prospects of a healthy city centre, namely *accessibility*, *attractions* and *amenity*, together with an appropriate *action framework* that is dependent on organisational capacity and committed resources (Table 2.3).

Table 2.3 City centre health check

Criteria	Components
Attractions (diversity, critical mass)	Business space, residential, retailing, services, arts, culture and entertainment
Accessibility (mobility, linkages)	Car, public transport, service vehicles, pedestrians/cyclists, special needs
Amenity (identity, security)	Public space, private space, streetscape, townscape
Action	Strategic programmes, development partnership, continuous monitoring

Source: Adapted from URBED 1994

In devising appropriate town-centre strategies the report argued for the need to make appropriate strategic choices that related to the set of particular local circumstances, and that not only considered land-use issues but also served the needs of its wider community of interests. Thus a clearly defined strategy had to be realistic, positive and shared; one that created a climate of confidence in the meedium to longer term, and which was able to counter perceived weaknesses and threats in the shorter term. It should present both a profile and a positioning strategy, with assessment of the current performance of the centre being critical in devising an informed and appropriate strategy. A clear understanding of its function, user characteristics, accessibility and competitiveness in relation to neighbouring and similar centres was perceived central to its profiling and ultimately to its positioning in relation to urban competition more widely. There should be a shared vision and a clear set of priorities that built on issues of attraction, accessibility and amenity. Such visioning should be widely shared and convincing, establish an agenda that accommodated the main opportunities and realistically appraised the main threats, and clearly provided the basis on which success was to be measured. Strategies and action programmes would need to be produced and regularly reviewed so as to coordinate efforts and to attract resources. Indeed, whilst visioning exercises were excellent ways to involve key stakeholders, the preparation of strategies focusing on implementation timescales and agencies was central to delivering more competitive city centres. Finally, dedicated management was seen as central to the delivery of a more vital and viable city centre, and for ensuring the detailed implementation and effective management of action programmes and the promotion of town-centre competitiveness.

Evans (1997) argues that to survive and prosper key interests have to ensure that town centres focus clearly on issues of quality of life, economic competitiveness and social engagement. Thus achieving change on the ground will require collective attitudes and targeted policies:

- *Balance* the need to maintain a delicate balance between economic viability and distinctiveness, social cohesion and environmental sustainability goals. Additionally, town-centre strategies need to demonstrate compatibility with policies and programmes for surrounding inner-area neighbourhoods.
- *Variety* a much wider range of uses and activities should be promoted to facilitate a positive quality of life for investors, employees and users, with a particular focus on re-urbanisation policies within city centres and their fringes.
- *Flexibility and innovative thinking* the need to adjust town centres to new economic, lifestyle and socio-cultural realities, and the demand for an increasingly flexible use of urban space.

- *Customer care* in terms of the need for enhanced concern with the public realm, and the quality of the city-centre experience that exploits its indigenous assets. This to be reinforced by the specific appraisal of the distinctive needs of city-centre customers/users from service providers.
- *Accessibility* the need to focus on the diversity of public transport provision and to vary the financial incentives/discentives of other modes of transport more transparently to reflect their economic, social and environmental costs in full.
- *Employment creation and the distinctiveness of local production* developments in information technology have eroded traditional town-centre employment in retail and financial services and there is a clear opportunity to expand service industry employment in socio-cultural and lifestyle activities, and to cater for the distinctiveness of local tastes and produce.
- *Local accountability* the transparency of the activities of institutions and commercial interests within city centres needs to be recognised, and it is crucially important that town-centre management fully reflects informed public opinion and needs. This is the key protection to ensure that city-centre developments and change don't solely reflect the interests of the key commercial interests.

Evans argues that the prospects of putting these basic principles into practice are difficult, given the traditionally fragmented nature of town-centre governance and the economic pressures on commercial activity. Reform is necessary in relation to the generation of more resources specifically targeted at enhancing city-centre environments; a range of institutional powers are required in order to experiment with different organisational approaches; and there is a need to redress the balance between 'big' and 'small' business activity within city centres and their fringe environments. He notes that the key ingredients for creating and maintaining competitive city centres remain multi-dimensional – involving a mix of land uses; housing, social and economic elements; issues of transport and accessibility; arts and culture, heritage and amenity; and concerns for sustainability, security, design and maintenance – and involve a core town-centre management philosophy (Evans 1997: 154).

Part 2

The local framework

The first part of the book has established the wider framework for the study, providing a critique of the literature on urban governance and the entrepreneurial city, subsequently applying it to the field of urban policy and focusing specifically on town and city centres. Within this context it has considered how urban cores are responding to the challenge of urban change, and the nature of the current agenda relating to the enhancement and continuing vitality of city centres. It is now appropriate to discuss the local dimension, in so far as it builds on this framework.

This part of the book, the next three chapters, attempts to address this concern, looking in turn at Manchester's established governance structure and its distinctive local policy environment, before proceeding to discuss and reflect upon its regeneration capacity and its immediate response to the bombing of its city centre. The initial chapter in this section focuses on the city's physical and socio-economic legacy and the extent of its civic ambition, before considering the emergence in recent years of a distinctive political culture that has facilitated local partnership working around an entrepreneurial narrative. It concludes by looking at specific aspects of policy development and delivery within the city centre, primarily in the decade prior to the bombing.

The next two chapters focus specifically on the immediate impact of the bombing on the city centre, and the mobilisation of regeneration capacity for collaborative action. Looking initially at the emergency planning response to the disaster and the discursive framework leading up to the decision to renew and enhance the core, it proceeds to discuss the institutional structures and procedures put in place. The establishment of a specialist task force and the promotion of a masterplanning process and framework highlight the involvement of a range of key interests, and the coordination of collaborative effort. Following the establishment of an initial masterplanning vision for the renewal strategy, the discussion then focuses on the processes and procedures involved in translating an initial outline into an implementation plan that was to guide the renewal programme for the next five years.

Chapter 3

Manchester's governance and emerging policy framework

Manchester was the world's first city of the industrial revolution and it is today preoccupied with civic attempts to reposition itself both internationally and post-industrially. It lies at the heart of a metropolitan area of 2.6 million people, with a central core surrounded by a number of significant towns which coalesced to form a conurbation at the peak of its worldwide importance, when 'King Cotton' dominated (Parkinson-Bailey 2000; Kidd 1993).The present chapter sets out to briefly explain its pre-eminence as an industrial and commercial centre, track its civic ambition over the past century, and to document its accelerating loss of confidence with economic decline and restructuring. It then proceeds to look at the fight-back since the 1980s, focusing in particular on the city's governance and evolving policy framework, and attempts to explain the growth of its entrepreneurial credentials in the 1990s. Finally, it focuses on the contemporary framework and current challenges facing both the city and its city centre.

Historical development and legacy

Whilst its origins were Roman, and there was a sizeable medieval city, by the second half of the eighteenth century Manchester had attained the status of a major provincial centre. However, as the world's first industrial city it was to be propelled to prominence during the period 1750–1850, becoming 'the symbol of new ways of working and living'.

Socio-economic development

Machine-based manufacture of cotton was the driving force for this expansion, with red brick mills and their towering chimneys transforming both Pennine fringe valleys and existing residential areas in the core into busy commercial quarters. The resulting urban sprawl created the first industrial city, an economic marvel of its age, and the basis of new social relationships. The 'Manchester Men' of the second half of the nineteenth century – the business elite that largely operated outside formal politics – provided the driving force behind the Free Trade Movement, when the city was 'the foremost commercial banking and transport centre in what was the most commercially advanced country in the world' (Kidd 1993: 103). The social brutalities of the period were the price of the city's economic success, as it became one of England's most overcrowded and unhealthy places, a situation that did not improve until the coming of by-law housing.

From the mid-nineteenth century, while cotton remained the essential driving force of the city's economy, an increasingly diverse manufacturing base and complex labour market behaviour was stimulated, and the city became the focus of a network of industrial communications. This enabled specialisation of the core, resulting in the rapid expansion of the city's financial and commercial services. Economic activity was further boosted by the opening of the Manchester Ship Canal (1894) and the creation of the world's first major industrial estate (Trafford Park 1905). The city's spatial area and population increased dramatically, and as its residential core housing and the new middle classes began to be replaced by warehousing and commerce, the process of outward migration to South Manchester's leafy suburbs began, extending beyond the city's limits with the introduction of the railways. Thus, by 1880 a city of essentially modern structure had evolved as the focus for a larger metropolitan framework, with the emergence of the surrounding cotton towns facilitating a web of urban development (Table 3.1). The concept of metropolitan government was, however, difficult to apply in such a multi-centred setting, and the various elements of the conurbation had grown into one another long before they were united by local government reform (Williams 1996).

Table 3.1 Metropolitan Manchester's population structure

| | Area (km²) | Pop density (per km²) | Population | | | | |
			2001	1951	1901	1851	1801
Manchester City	116	3710	400,000	703,000	544,000	316,000	77,000
Greater Manchester	1286	2003	2.6m	2.7m	2.2m	1.0m	0.3m

The first half of the twentieth century was to see major decentralisation trends, with suburban growth paralleling inner-city decline in a conurbation whose total population barely changed, but which experienced fundamental internal readjustment. Inner-area housing, consisting of nearly half of the city's stock, was largely defined as 'slum properties' and became the focus of public action as the century progressed (Harrison 1981). In economic terms the city and its conurbation was a place of great change, as employment in textiles halved between the wars and exports of cotton goods fell to a fifth of their pre-World War One level. A catastrophic decline of the cotton industry had thus taken place by 1939, with the final collapse of mill production being experienced by the 1950s. Manchester, at least, was protected by its broad employment base and increasing manufacturing role, a temporary salvation not afforded to its surrounding over-specialised spinning towns. As work was lost on the periphery, but continued to expand at the centre, journey to work linkages became more complex, and the conurbation as an area of almost continuous urbanisation also became more closely integrated as a labour market.

It still remained the view, however, in the late 1950s that whilst declining industries were likely to be phased out that Manchester was on the threshold of new and technologically more advanced manufacturing that would recreate jobs, and reinforce the service role of Manchester as a regional centre. Yet only two decades later such confidence had ebbed as the city and conurbation experienced the final culmination of trends that had been present for most of the century, and that had begun to accelerate in the 1950s as a sustained period of economic and social decline (Peck & Emmerich 1992). Indeed, the period from the 1960s to the 1980s was marked by particularly low levels of industrial and commercial investment, a ravaged post-industrial environment, and the emergence of high levels of unemployment and social marginality. This was to signal a loss of morale locally, both politically and economically (Giordano & Twomey 2002).

Civic ambition and public action

During the late nineteenth century the chief targets of civic policy rested with housing and health concerns. With the establishment of local elected government and the provision of municipal public services the city began to extend its boundaries, and to strengthen its infrastructural ties with its surrounding areas. Communal issues generated by the city's industrial and commercial legacy began to be tackled by a series of new residential environments focused on the creation of a number of 'garden suburbs' (Burnage), and the acquisition by civic leaders of land to provide for the development of a major new municipally owned satellite (Wythenshawe). To address the major problem of housing standards the City Council decided in the late 1940s that its main priority was to undertake the comprehensive redevelopment of its inner areas, and it entered into bilateral

agreements with a score of neighbouring local authority partners to build municipal housing for rehousing Manchester's residents beyond the city's limits. This
period was associated with the demolition of the 'heart' of the city, an increasing
dissonance between new social housing areas and employment opportunities,
and a fundamental loss of morale over the qualities of urban life. The 1970s saw
the onset of a decline in birth rates, economic depression and the rapid expansion
of the middle and outer suburbs, forcing the city to come to terms with new
cultural realities.

In terms of strategic land-use policy, early ambitious attempts were
made by civic leaders to produce a plan for the new city region, aiming to shape
the processes of urban change for social ends, and a visionary if limited
Manchester and District Advisory Plan (1926) was produced. Problems of the
post-war city were approached in a trilogy of studies (1945–47), representing a
significant attempt at metropolitan planning by collaboration (City of Manchester
Plan, Manchester and District Regional Planning Proposals, South Lancashire and
North Cheshire Advisory Plan). While each plan was expected to 'nest' with the
others, each had a different thrust. The city plan addressed problems of the
central area, redevelopment needs and housing renewal; the district plan exam-
ined housing standards, proposed neighbourhood units and made the first
assessment of overspill needs; whilst the sub-regional advisory report analysed
resources, environmental issues and strategic problems. They remain today an
impressive early attempt to construct a logical and integrated basis for shaping
the development framework of an entire city region, and for its structural
adjustment.

The economic dimensions of the plans were perhaps their weakest
characteristic, but they did provide the first estimates of overspill requirements
and density proposals for redevelopment. During the 1950s, Manchester
conducted a desperate search for a site for its dispersal strategy, and an increasingly acrimonious dialogue arose with surrounding county authorities over
possible new town locations. Warrington (1968) was designated as a mid-
Mersey growth point at the very stage at which overspill needs began to rapidly
taper and vanish (Rodgers 1986). Almost overnight the conurbation was made to
consume its own surplus population by urban consolidation, and by the mid-
1970s the preoccupation of planning and regeneration strategies became
focused on problems of inner-city renewal (Figure 3.1).

City governance: the emerging agenda

With the conurbation's industries ravaged by economic decline, the power of
Manchester's urban business elite declined and the local authority became

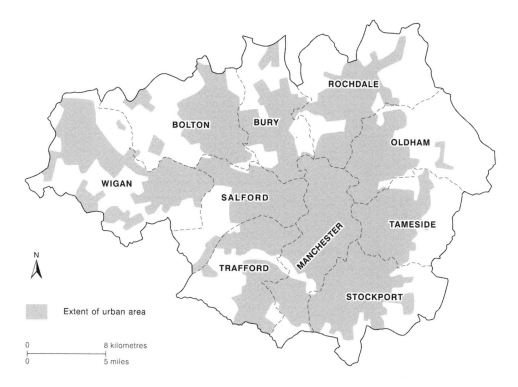

ROCHDALE

BOLTON   BURY

OLDHAM

WIGAN

SALFORD

TAMESIDE

MANCHESTER

TRAFFORD

STOCKPORT

N

Extent of urban area

| 0 | 8 kilometres |
| 0 | 5 miles |

3.1
Metropolitan
Manchester's
urban structure

central to the city's governance. Political power rested with elected members and senior officers, and the early post-war years were a period of 'stability and hope' which saw increased public investment in a period of full employment (Beynon *et al.* 1993). As a consequence, Manchester's politics developed in line with the paternalistic and bureaucratic Labourism typical of large urban municipalities.

The established political culture

Since the 1920s, Manchester's labour politics had been split along two distinct lines, namely the local authority-controlled District Labour Party and a fairly auton-omous trade union movement. Acceleration of the economic and demographic decline of the city during the 1960s–70s sharply reduced the influence of the unions and stultified the renewal of the city's political leadership. Following the reorganisation of local government in 1974, any political radicalism that persisted within the City Council was squeezed out by the increased demands of centralised and professionalised service provision, and the city's Labour Group remained dominated by an ageing body of 'right wing' councillors.

It was within this context that the 'new urban left' began to mobilise, moving from their existing platforms in community and trade union politics into Labour Party activity. They were committed to replacing paternalistic Labourism by decentralisation and participation; had a rhetorical commitment to socialism as opposed to the social-democratic compact embodied in the established welfare state; and were committed to the local state as a key strategic site for economic and political renewal. After decades of relative political inertia, they took over the District Labour Party in 1979, and came to lead the City Council in 1984 under Graham Stringer (Quilley 1995). The decline of the traditional labour representation formed part of a wider process of readjustment within the Labour Party and movement, with the balance of power within the Council chamber not shifting decisively in favour of the 'new left' until the late 1980s. The growing crisis of local corporatism in the face of significant economic collapse and restructuring, and increasing questioning of the welfare state framework, facilitated new policy discourses and the search for alternative agendas. The established leadership, however, proved unable and unwilling to adjust to such pressures, creating a politically charged agenda that the 'new left' both reacted against, and ultimately took over.

The rise of Thatcherism stimulated a dramatic shift in Manchester's political character as the local Labour Party and the City Council leadership became increasingly disoriented, and experienced a progressive decline in morale. The haemorrhaging of party membership combined with an ageing political culture, and a cohort of political activists took up the opportunity to impress their radical agenda on the local Labour Party. The 1980 local authority budget became the focus for a decisive split in Manchester politics, with generational conflicts being fought around issues of the democratic accountability of elected representatives, and the formulation of a strategy to respond to the inevitability of public sector cuts. As a consequence, 13 rebel councillors were expelled from the Council's Labour Group, and were to fight a bitter four-year struggle against the City Council's leadership over spending cuts – the 'Manchester Fightback' campaign. Over this period they forged contacts with a range of grass-root community groups and cultural movements that were to become the basis for the 'rainbow alliance strategy' as it was to emerge within the city.

During this period the incumbent City Council leadership were presented with the task of enforcing public Sservice cuts, and of facing the political consequences of recession in the local economy. There was a gradual but substantial shift towards a more pro-active stance on local economic initiatives within the City Council, even if this failed to penetrate the incumbent political leadership. Indeed, the last phase of the 'old right' leadership within Manchester saw increased demands being made to central government for enhanced funding linked to the local prioritisation of employment and economic development dimensions, and for stimulating community development (CURS 1985). To a significant degree, therefore, the shift to the City Council playing a catalytic role in local economic and social development had been secured before the 'new urban left' ultimately attained power, even if the electoral success of the putsch and the zeal of radical opposition understandably blurred the connection with past practices. The nature of the emerging politics was reflected in the immediate priorities of the incoming Labour Group, choosing to concentrate on consolidating local alliances perceived to have immediate and significant impact – equal opportunities and equality concerns, and decentralisation and democratisation issues. Although the 'old right' persisted as a local political force throughout the 1980s, its grip on the leadership of city politics was loosened irrevocably (Quilley 1997).

The period 1985–87 is commonly understood in terms of the City Council's belated attempts (in comparison with Sheffield and Liverpool) at 'municipal socialism' (Randall 1995). The continuing political tensions between the 'new urban left', a small but influential 'hard left', and the remnants of the 'old right', meant that initially it proved difficult to move much beyond the conservative agenda of the previous administration. In the short term it was marked by increasing centralisation and elite-based decision making, as it sought to manage the financial crisis facing the city, respond to the local strategic vacuum created by the collapse of welfare state certainties, and to develop a radical agenda of opposition to Thatcherism. It eschewed the logic of competition with other cities and local authorities in the name of solidarity. In line with its communitarian objectives it did, however, set up a range of community initiatives and fostered support for a diversity of minority social groups, but is more generally remembered for its attempts to develop an alternative economic strategy that sought to exclude the private sector.

> By 1982 partnership between the local authority and the private sector was mentioned only in a conditional tense, and between 1984–87 the private sector was downgraded as partner and redefined as the opposition.
>
> (Quilley 1995: 228)

However, over the next three years the local economic agenda vacillated between a rhetorical commitment to modernising the economy and to promoting economic democracy, a naive assertion of local economic sovereignty, and the gradual acknowledgement that the local authority could do little to stem, let alone reverse, the process of economic restructuring (MCC 1984a). Fundamental to this was the need to solve many of the intractable features of Manchester's economic problems – creation of new jobs, modernisation of the city's skill base – and an acceptance that its realisation would need partnership with private capital and central government funding. In an important sense, therefore, municipal socialism as a local project never got beyond the drawing board, characterised by rhetoric but involving little radical action due to the dire financial circumstances of the authority. During this period, the external image of the City Council was based on a mixture of radical oppositional politics and the more mundane management of services and the budgetary crisis. In reality, however, the leadership became increasingly engaged in developing a distinctive view of the city's economic prospects, particularly associated with a range of 'special projects', which appeared of greater importance than streamlining service management or ideological opposition to central government. These enabled the leadership to network beyond the boundaries of the town hall and the city itself, laying the foundation for the political and strategic alternative that would emerge with the entrepreneurial turn of the late 1980s (Holden 1999: 96). These 'special projects' were to demonstrate the capacity of local action for strategic renewal, and were focused on the promotion of Manchester airport's development and international expansion; the decision to build the Metrolink light rail system; embarking on the city's nine-year adventure relating to the Olympic 'dream'; and finally, capturing and co-opting Manchester's vibrant popular culture scene. Whilst at this stage there was no clear sense of strategic trajectory, the projects did involve real political leadership based on a small group gathered around the Council Leader and the Chief Executive's office. Over time, these outwardly oriented and essentially anti-municipalist approaches encouraged public–private partnership and a tradition of 'de-politicisation', and came increasingly to define the official goals of the City Council in the 1990s.

The abolition of the Greater Manchester Council (GMC) in 1986 created an institutional vacuum at the level of the city region, but did facilitate a space for the City Council to assert a degree of legitimate leadership within the conurbation and to reinforce Manchester's 'localist' agenda (Hebbert & Deas 2000). In economic terms, the Economic Initiatives Group was established within the City Council in anticipation of the radical (but uncertain) reorientation of national policy consequent on the expected return of a Labour government, and was intended to lay the foundation for the enhancement of the authority's strategic capacity in relation to development and renewal. Faced with the defeat of Labour at the 1987 national election, a profound crisis of leadership and direction ensued at the local level, and the City Council was forced to abandon its largely rhetorical commitment to 'municipal socialism' and to embrace a 'new realism' in terms of its relationship to central government and the private sector.

> After 1987, the City quietly dropped its slogan, which made a rhetorical commitment to 'Defending jobs, improving services', and somewhat reluctantly embraced the politics of 'Making it happen'.
>
> (Cochrane *et al.* 1996: 1324)

Urban development policy

At the conurbation level, the reorganisation of local government in 1974 was a key institutional development for the development and delivery of urban policy, although somewhat uniquely within the conurbation, Manchester's administrative boundaries were largely unchanged. It led to the establishment of the GMC as the strategic planning authority (1974–86), with the metropolitan districts providing the local planning and development framework. The resulting structure plan focused its strategic thinking on four broad themes. Foremost was the emphasis on urban concentration and constraints on greenfield development, reinforced by the intention to redirect development towards the conurbation core so as to make better use of existing infrastructure. It also strongly argued for the maintenance and enhancement of the regional centre, whilst maintaining the vitality of other established town centres within the conurbation; and advocated resource conservation and the enhancement of amenity, particularly in relation to open land and the environment (Williams 1999). Beyond its strategic planning responsibilities the GMC wished to involve itself in urban revitalisation activity more specifically, but was hampered during its existence by a period of low development activity (Law 1992).

Development planning within the city over the past half-century has seen intensive periods of statutory plan making, but with significantly longer informal interludes in between dominated by the generation of non-statutory documents. Whilst the formal phases have proved valuable at the level of broad strategy, the predictive capacity of such documents has proved particularly weak in anticipating issues of economic restructuring and change, and in complementing the increasing diversity of regeneration initiatives. Officers had long valued the speed and flexibility inherent in the development of informal strategies more in keeping with community and political aspirations (Kitchen 1996). Thus, more recently, the main components of the city's approach to development planning have involved a willingness to allow the established statutory plan to fade and not to constrain positive action; active participation in conurbation-wide strategic planning processes so as to ensure that such frameworks did not constrain local-level decisions; a limited role for statutory plans where justified by specific circumstances relating to economic competitiveness and change (airport, city centre); and the promotion of an informal and pragmatic approach at neighbourhood level to reinforce local aspirations.

The unfolding of inner-city policy at the national level in the late 1970s led to the Manchester–Salford Inner City Partnership being launched, but with little inter-authority cooperation, and with such resources being split and administered separately. Within the authority the institutional effects of this programme were diluted since responsibility for partnership delivery was absorbed into the City Council as a whole, filtered through its rigid structures, and with individual departments bidding for particular pockets of money. Whilst such additional resources were to be distributed for economic, environmental and social regeneration projects, as the programme became more established and was to accord closer to central government priorities, economic dimensions began to predominate. As a result increasing pressures were exerted on the local authority to rethink its local economic strategy, with the economic crisis of the inner city leading to criticism of existing policies and discourses (CURS 1985).

One of the most significant effects of this partnership initiative – given the relatively limited extent of resources involved in relation to the city's major economic and social problems, and its established mainstream programmes – was to extend the scope for voluntary sector involvement, in keeping with the emerging political agenda within the city at the time (Williams 1983). It did not involve, however, anything but sporadic cooperation with private sector and business interests, these being essentially focused on environmental improvements and early marketing campaigns for the city centre.

Manchester's neighbours (Trafford and Salford) were politically more pragmatic at the time, successfully gaining Enterprise Zone status in an area impinging on the city's boundary to the west (Law 1988). The City Council was opposed to a similar designation for East Manchester, and resisted the idea of a subsequent development corporation for the area, instead utilising moneys under their direct control arising from the Urban Programme. Its ideological opposition to the main tenets of central government's urban policy agenda of the early 1980s ensured that it did not bid for such initiatives, but the creation of a UDC in nearby Trafford Park (1987) saw the government's agenda of centrally initiated quangos and a property-led 'enterprise culture' beginning to encroach directly on to the city's boundary.

A number of other influences were also beginning to emerge in the mid-1980s that were to provide a core focus for the Manchester 'project' over the next two decades, facilitating the scope for experiential learning by the city's political leadership and senior officials. These 'special projects' created a distinct institutional space through which the elite network within the authority could operate with relative autonomy and at a distance and scale of operation beyond the confines of the town hall. The first of these initiatives was the establishment of the Manchester Consortium (Ringway Developments Ltd) a public–private partnership designed to pursue the commercial objectives of Manchester International Airport in an environment increasingly threatened by the growing radicalism of Thatcherism. This municipally owned airport was transferred to a public–private vehicle to keep privatisation at bay, and in the process increasing the local authority's influence at the city–regional level. The immediate effect of this, however, was to connect the City Council elite to a group of private sector interests, and to expand both the scale and style in which they thought through economic development opportunities. A further initiative relating to infrastructural development in 1985 was the decision to build the Metrolink light rail system through an early 'PFI-style' funding agreement, given the clear absence of alternative funding for transport developments.

At about the same time other prospects emerged which would in various incarnations increasingly drive the development and regeneration agenda beyond the end of the century. The Council leadership agreed in principle to bid to host the 1996 Olympic Games, selling the idea to the Labour Group as a risk-free opportunity that would be led by the private sector. This initial relatively amateurish bid did set in motion a political and populist project that was subsequently to gain an energy and legitimacy of its own, at the core of the city's development strategy in the 1990s. Finally, the leadership's increasing contact and support for the city's rapidly expanding cultural scene was to lead to the gradual deregulation of city-centre space. Over the next decade or so the City Council and local lifestyle entrepreneurs promoted an increasingly vibrant popular culture into its own vision of a modern European city (Taylor *et al.* 1996; O'Connor & Wynne 1996), and in the process created in Manchester a national example of cultural movements (Haslam 1999).

Thus towards the end of this period although the notion of Manchester as an entrepreneurial city was in no way being coherently expressed, these initiatives did provide embryonic foundations for a more ambitious future, and in the 1990s increasingly came to define the official goals of the City Council.

City governance: the contemporary perspective

As a serious attempt to develop a local socialist response the ostensibly economic project of Manchester's agenda during the early years of the Stringer administration was desultory, and the result of the 1987 national election was to propel a 'new realism' of political ambition, focusing on the need to work with other agencies to secure funding. Remarkable political manoeuvring by the Council leadership to ensure their retention of power resulted in the almost seamless shift from the rhetoric of municipal socialism to local boosterism. This was probably Stringer's greatest achievement, reflecting not only changes to political priorities, but also changing perceptions of what was possible in terms of local strategies (Quilley 1999).

> Within the space of just a few years, the city has experienced a political somersault, as under the same Labour administration it has made the transition from a citadel of municipal socialism … to a metropolis of Olympian expedience …
>
> (Peck & Tickell 1995: 56)

'Making it happen' in the entrepreneurial city

The local political and strategic hiatus that followed the general election provided Stringer with an opportunity to reassert his leadership, and proved a watershed for the emergent entrepreneurial city strategy. The Council Leader outlined and won support for the need to enforce a radical reorientation of local strategy in terms of critical cooperation and opportunism, and a series of substantial struggles were to emerge from embracing the 'making it happen' logo. The new order of priorities could be summed up as 'investment, growth and jobs first, (residual) welfare later', with the reassertion of the managerial prerogative being integral to the new economic project being advanced on behalf of the city (Cochrane *et al.* 1996: 9).

The leadership astutely began to promote notions of effective corporate management, espousing a new entrepreneurial model of development that abandoned the principle of solidarity, accepting both the competitive thrust and internationalist framework necessary for successful regeneration (Quilley 2000). This approach represented an increased awareness of economic realities, sought to sanction business coalition and a more cosmopolitan post-industrial environment. The prioritising of investment and job growth ensured that the local party lost its base in community politics and became increasingly centralised. The leader's hold strengthened over both the local Labour Group and the authority's administrative hierarchy, in order to prevent the building-up of alternative local power bases. It was to lead during the mid-1990s to the high-profile resignation of a number of senior officers as the number of chief officers was reduced (Kitchen 1997).

Tensions over the extension of creative accountancy, and the attempts being made to shelter local communities from the brunt of financial restraint were internal to the City Council, and proved problematic for the leadership in both political and institutional terms. In addition, a premium was placed on cooperation between the local political and business elites, and the achievement of a limited number of concrete goals focused on flagship projects and supply side infrastructural initiatives, with these often being insulated from normal democratic processes. Implicit in this was the emergence of new private sector power brokers with interlinking roles, in effect a reconstitution of the 'Manchester Men' of earlier generations, with such elite networks typically spanning the public–private sector divide.

> There are a few people making the decisions, and you have to know who they are … people often refer to the Manchester Mafia … Manchester is small enough to get all the people who count into one room, but big enough to have a cosmopolitan view of itself.
>
> (Development professional)

Externally, the improvement of relations with central government was initially difficult, with latent ideological hostility evident from both parties, but this was eventually to be facilitated by the emergence of a range of public–private partnership initiatives that emphasised the contribution of the private sector, and diluted previous commitments to disadvantaged and marginalised groups. Indeed, a key feature of the period was the increasing ascendancy of a business-led agenda in Manchester, and the leadership's attempts to influence city politics more generally. For left-wing critics the most contentious aspect of this apparent *volte face* involved the abandonment of the principle of solidarity with other local authorities, exemplified by the enhanced profile for place-marketing strategies and the competitive bidding processes associated with emergent urban policy (Quilley 2002).

> The construction of public–private partnerships, it would seem, under the present political climate, is a prerequisite for winning discretionary (and often competitively allocated) public expenditure ... private sector partners are being used by the local state in funding battles with higher tiers ...
>
> (Peck & Tickell 1995: 71)

The end of Thatcher's leadership, and the government's intention to soften and reshape urban policy away from the singularly free-market and property-led approach, provided an opportunity for further improvements in the relationship between the City Council and central government. This was demonstrated in discussions over the launch of competitive urban regeneration initiatives (Hulme City Challenge) and the revival of the city's Olympic dream ('Manchester 2000'), where the very process of bidding was seen to be linked explicitly to enhanced investment opportunities (Cochrane *et al.* 1996). Stringer used the increasingly centralised and elite-based networks within the City Council and beyond to develop a fundamentally different approach to regeneration that stressed the emergence of 'local governance', and the reinvigoration of Mancunian civic pride.

> The formal partnership mechanisms attached to specific projects have been underpinned by a more informal, clubby atmosphere which has brought ... corporate tycoons (AMEC, Co-op Bank) into regular contact with ... lifestyle entrepreneurs (Granada, Factory Records, Hacienda) and a clutch of young architect developers (Simpson Associates, Urban Splash) who have been associated with many of the more innovative and design led developments.
>
> (Quilley 2000: 610)

Common strands in this locally grounded 'high octane' project have been a commitment to increasing the city's 'liveability', the diversification and expansion of the city centre, and the rehabilitation and re-imaging of the city's international credentials. The accompanying 'script' emphasised that the city had embarked on an essentially post-industrial development trajectory focused on flagship projects; that globalisation had created an unavoidable climate of competition and the carving out of both a market niche and a compelling brand image; and that to compete successfully required the subordination of divisive class-based loyalties in the interest of a local 'team effort' (Quilley 2000; Loftman & Nevin 1996).

> The politics of partnership in contemporary Manchester is about leadership without representation ... about finding ... 'people who want to

get things done' and then bringing them together … a virtue is made of cutting the corners of both democracy and bureaucracy.

(Peck & Tickell 1995: 69)

The politics of setting priorities and of deciding who would be winners and losers didn't have an explicit place in the city's new politics of business, with the fragility of such coalitions often leading to the sidestepping of contentious issues (Table 3.2). All this underpinned Manchester's embrace of urban entrepreneurialism, with the 'city' becoming the explicit subject of governance as a way of winning enhanced competitiveness (Quilley & Ward 1999).

… Manchester can claim some measure of success in its enthusiastic adoption of the new ethos of competitive localism. Spurred on by a new cadre of entrepreneurial officers and a pragmatic political leadership, the City Council has been more successful than most in playing the 'partnership' game.

(Peck & Tickell 1995: 76)

I think the more innovative and dynamic local authorities are actually becoming more like private sector players than the private sector … (he) bends the rules, does deals and then works backwards … and intuitively knows that it's the right thing to do. And then he'll sort out the paperwork …

(Private sector secondee)

Having largely fulfilled his opportunistic project, and in the process significantly transforming the city, Graham Stringer resigned the leadership of the Council in early 1996, in anticipation of becoming a Member of Parliament. He was replaced by Richard Leese as Council Leader, at what was perceived to be a point where the possibilities of the city's strategic project and script were beginning to falter, and the nature of the next 'big project' was unclear. He recognised that there were limits to what an entrepreneurial local authority could do, and whilst Leese's interpretation of the city's future role included a much more explicit reference to service provision and social needs, the primacy of regeneration and economic development was unchanged, as was the sustenance of the continuing belief in the abilities of local 'movers and shakers'. The period of readjustment was suddenly brought to an end in June 1996 with the devastating impact of a terrorist bomb on the city centre, but it did in the process open up a range of new opportunities for extending the city's strategic project. Most importantly of all it further demonstrated the reliance on externally produced opportunities (repeated by the award of the 2002 Commonwealth Games), and the fundamentally reactive nature of the evolving strategic framework.

The return of a Labour government in 1997 resulted in a further realignment of central–local government relations and the emergence of a more socially

Table 3.2 Manchester's entrepreneurial city perspective

Corporate logo move from 'defending jobs and improving services' to 'making it happen'	
• Relationship between politics and economics	• Socialist political project subordinated to the economies of selling Manchester in relation to national/European economies and securing discretionary funding.
• Political project	• Reorientation towards the political centre, appeal to middle classes on the basis of economic competence and getting things done. • Partnership as a cross-class growth coalition rooted in a strong chauvinist city identity; acceptance of central role for the private sector.
• Understanding of and response to economic crisis	• Emphasis on local agency and economic self-determination. • Partnership as a 'growth coalition' and a spur to endogenous economic development. • City region competing in a European/global system for investment (and discretionary funding).
• Orientation to urban policy	• Urban renewal seen primarily as a vehicle to relocate the city higher up a putative European urban hierarchy; emphasis on place marketing and flagship developments. • Elitist orientation to 'key player' politics.
• Orientation to manufacturing	• Commitment to a 'post-industrial' script and willingness to abandon manufacturing as the cornerstone.
• Style of decision making	• Orientation to end results and getting things done; executive driven; greatly increased political authority at the centre; 'charismatic' authority.
• Relation to other cities and communities	• Acceptance of institutionalised competition between cities and the inevitability of losers as well as winners.

inclusive agenda, to which the city was in an excellent position to respond. However, the underlying tensions between its enabling and its social role have re-emerged as wider evidence of the extent of local deprivation has become apparent. Indeed, it has been argued that the overriding preoccupation with selling the city to investors has inherently involved the reordering of municipal priorities, thereby exacerbating problems of social polarisation and economic exclusion (Mellor 2002).

> Notwithstanding the propinquity of the city centre and inner city areas ... interaction between the two are nothing like as strong as they ought to be ... in many ways the city centre is an oasis ... on the whole the problem of deprivation in the inner city is getting worse.
>
> (Kitchen 1997: 142)

Urban development and regeneration policy

As already noted, the return of a Conservative administration for a third term did lead to a fundamental reappraisal of the city's political and development priorities. This was based on a more realistic appraisal of the capacities of the city's main-stream programmes and development strategies, the experiential learning gained by senior politicians and officers as a result of engaging with a range of specialist agencies involved at the local level, and the final maturing of the entrepreneurial project in the mid-1990s.

Following the abolition of the GMC and the progressive loss of statutory policy relevance at the conurbation level, the city played a central role in establishing a guidance framework for strategic thinking, which aimed to ensure that its own policy flexibility was not constrained. Its politicians were less parochial and not constrained by the limitations of the city's boundaries, and possessed both strong views and a capacity for strategic thinking (Williams 1999). At the local authority level, the Unitary Development Plan (UDP) process that emerged in the early 1990s saw the city build upon such established planning perspectives and development networks, and took the form of a 'structured debate' with key stakeholders around particular themes. The final plan aimed to improve the city's 'liveability' and to revitalise the local economy, this being reinforced by the goal of enhancing the city's role as a regional capital (MCC 1995a). From the outset, however, there were concerns that the plan would rapidly date due to the extent and pace of physical and economic transformation taking place within the city, and it was clear that such a framework would need to be integrated with the handling of major regeneration and development initiatives. The issuance of informal guidance – City Development Guide – was thus a clear attempt to bridge land-use planning objectives, wider regeneration initiatives, and design quality (MCC 1996a). In terms of economic strategy the city began to act more creatively in linking its economic development objectives to specific and tangible areas where local authority action could have desirable effects, and to respond to economic realism in its various policy and economic programme objectives (MCC 1992a). A similar coherence became obvious in its approach to local housing strategies, where a corporate focus that linked housing policy objectives with other areas of mainstream local authority programmes was clearly evident (MCC 1995b).

The entrepreneurial nursery

Whilst the 'special projects' initiated by the city's political and managerial elite in the mid 1980s gave a hint of the scope for entrepreneurial approaches, at the heart of the initial experiential learning stage were specific central government initiatives. Three of these – Central Manchester Development Corporation, Hulme City Challenge, City Pride – were particularly important in helping to launch this new agenda (Robson 2002).

As previously noted the City Council initially opposed the possible 'imposition' of a development corporation locally, due to its perceived lack of electoral mandate and likely domination by business people, its assumption of wide-ranging planning and development powers and the curtailing of local authority influence, and its emphasis on property development rather than wider distributional goals. Political attitudes began to change, however, with the perception of the relative wealth of such agencies at a time of local authority budgetary retrenchment, and the city's political and business leadership succeeded in steering the location of the UDC towards an existing project – the Phoenix Initiative, a public–private investment vehicle – seeing it as a way both of securing additional funding for regeneration, and building upon genuinely local interests.

> If this was going to happen it was better for the Council to be attempting to shape this in ways that it saw as being in the long term interests of the city, than to stand off from the process.
>
> (Kitchen 1997: 38)

The Central Manchester Development Corporation (CMDC, 1988–96) successfully brought together a number of the projects and development aims of existing agencies. Its main objectives were to facilitate and bring back into use existing land and property; the development of new property sympathetic to existing buildings; to attract private sector finance, and to facilitate environmental enhancement. To these were added two more strategic objectives, namely to increase the geographical extent of the city centre, and to fundamentally alter the functional characteristics of a southern swathe of land and property (CMDC 1990). CMDC was also premised on an expectation that it might dislodge deeply ingrained local attitudes to regeneration, and open up the City Council to the influence of local business.

Negotiations over board membership and the choice of chairperson were particularly significant in explaining the subsequent success of the development corporation. The inclusion of the Council Leader and another senior councillor on the board, and the appointment as Board Chair of a businessman who was politically well connected but had no party political affiliation were both central to explaining the gradual development of good working relationships. The agreement to work within the established local planning framework and the decision to use the local authority as agent for development control responsibilities led to the two bodies developing an increasingly interactive working relationship, with its benign approach enabling the Council Leader to use it as a conduit to assert his own agenda (Deas *et al.* 2000).

CMDC undoubtedly played a valuable role in helping to initiate a major series of flagship developments that fuelled the economic health and dominated the development agenda of an increasingly entrepreneurial city centre, this being reinforced by a continuous programme of environmental improvements, and a major increase in the city centre's marketing and promotional budget. It additionally provided the impetus for the rapid expansion of city-centre housing. All these were enduring legacies for the city centre and facilitated the cultural appreciation by the main stakeholders of what might be achievable through partnership (CMDC 1996). It contributed to the appeal of the entrepreneurial city strategy by putting the city centre at the heart of regeneration, boosted the role of the business elite and property professionals in the political process, and provided a symbolic focus for action. The demise of the agency left a number of challenges for local interests, particularly in relation to the problems of promoting the city in the absence of CMDC's significant marketing budget; how to maintain the momentum of expectations within the area, complete unfinished projects and develop further the relationship with established partners; and how to maintain sufficient revenue budgeting to sustain the substantial environmental improvement programme.

> During the course of CMDC's existence, Manchester City Council … became increasingly at ease with the notion of utilising private finance to fund public sector capital development projects … it became more sanguine about contracting out regulated public services … it came consciously to involve the private sector in local economic regeneration projects, and it became more sensitised to the collective 'business voice'.
>
> (Deas *et al*. 1999: 219)

The confidence gained from this experience, and its stimulus for elite network development was transferred to the Hulme City Challenge experience, where the Council leadership was able to intercept a putative central government initiative and sell the scope for a major regeneration project to the Secretary of State (Michael Heseltine). Focused on an area of social housing south of the city centre that was comprehensively redeveloped in the 1960s, its concentration of physical and socio-economic problems became nationally symbolic of policy failure. The combination of housing deterioration, social deprivation and inequality, high unemployment and socio-cultural alienation meant that the area was always top of the authority's list of priority areas in the 1980s, a period marked by the frustrating search for practical solutions. Inevitably, the different agendas and priorities of the various stakeholders meant that no satisfactory formula could be found and all parties entered the 1990s seemingly settling for a series of ad hoc improvements rather than a comprehensive programme of physical, economic and social renewal. However, a breakthrough was made in terms of an agreement involving a consortium of housing associations that envisaged a comprehensive programme of renewal, just at the time that a major new national regeneration initiative was announced.

City Challenge aimed to support an integrated package of economic, environmental and social regeneration projects in specific areas, and Manchester was particularly well placed to launch this initiative, both due to the breakthrough in thinking about housing solutions in Hulme, and due to the emerging consensus within the city concerning urban regeneration priorities and forms of delivery. Hulme City Challenge (1992–97) was launched as a major regeneration project that would bring together elements of the new urban governance, expand cross-institutional relationships whilst giving a central role to the local authority, and facilitate the rise of partnership with business (particularly AMEC) and the local authority elite (senior officers and members). The notion of partnership of key stakeholders was central to the launch of a programme that attempted to ensure the recreation of a vibrant and stable community, linking it directly to developments in adjacent areas, and in reconnecting it to the city more widely.

It was also a clear attempt to link public and private sector agencies already working in the area, with the overall structures of management and delivery systems being determined by the City Council. Hulme Regeneration Ltd (HRL) – a joint initiative between the City Council and AMEC – was established, mandated to direct and deliver the strategic regeneration framework, accommodating a dedicated project team of secondees and specialist appointments. The City Council additionally established the Hulme Sub-Committee, with full delegated powers to ensure that the local authority was able to respond speedily and positively to those parts of the action plan requiring decisions from the authority in relation to its statutory responsibilities and financial management. The Hulme Economic Assembly and Hulme Social and Community Forum were established as voluntary bodies accommodating key interest groups, whilst Hulme Community Homes was created to oversee social housing development and management.

The City Challenge programme, although ambitious in the Hulme context, largely achieved the outputs set for the five-year programme, brought in a level of external investment needed to realise the bulk of the programme's objectives, largely satisfied local aspirations and realised much of the 'end state vision' established at the start of the programme (Harding 1998). Although the programme could not realistically deliver all the task requirements originally identified, it undoubtedly helped establish confidence in the future of Hulme that enabled the local authority and its partners to build upon significant momentum for further change. It also provided an organisational learning environment for subsequent competitive bidding initiatives elsewhere in the city, and provided real experience and expertise for established and emerging partnership networks in programme and project management activities associated with strategic regeneration. In strategic as well as chronological terms, therefore, Hulme was the centrepiece of the increasing maturity of Stringer's administration, in that it cemented many of the relationships that would come to dominate future partnerships. More importantly it delivered substantial community-centred regeneration in an area that had previously provided a fundamental challenge to the local authority's activities, and that established decision-making processes had been unable to tackle.

Maturing the entrepreneurial project

The selection of Manchester as Britain's bid to host the 1996 Olympic Games, although primarily private sector led, envisaged that the event would act as a catalyst for the renewal of the city and its sub-region. Indeed, the overall tone of the bid, the involvement of CMDC in levering investment, and the element of strong public sector support had significant implications in terms of the overall strategic trajectory of the City Council's wider project. It helped establish key economic development themes, cultivated a new and positive image of the city that focused on the entrepreneurial model of governance ('Driving the Dream'), and was paralleled by the need felt by the leadership to play down the social and economic problems the city faced. The emergence of the bid for the Olympic Games was promoted as 'good news' for the city and its people, placing Manchester on an international stage, whilst building up local expertise and experience. The ultimate failure of the bid, far from being an end to the process, signalled the emergence of a new phase of partnership-based entrepreneurialism, with an immediate decision to bid for the 2000 Games.

The establishment of 'Manchester 2000' as a company to run the bid on the city's behalf (but underwritten by legal and financial guarantees), was to provide an opportunity to extend partnership working within the city region (Law 1994). Its bid placed less emphasis on the Games than was previously the case, with the thrust focused on the scope for regeneration and development that the opportunity would stimulate (particularly focused on East Manchester). The bid proved the apex of the new governance structure and business-led agenda within the city, fuelling a further extension of the role of the local elite. It was also a sign of the progress made by the city in improving relations with central government, demonstrated by the comprehensive financial and legal support subsequently afforded (Cochrane et al. 1996).

The 'Olympic bid period' became an opportunity to mobilise support across all levels, becoming a popular civic project ('We can win!'), and the ultimate place-marketing expression. Within the local authority it also gave opportunities for a cadre of young ambitious officers to get involved in something grand and optimistic, sharpening up the skills of 'regeneration specialists'. The centralisation of power and resources within the leadership and its established partnership support (and legitimacy), meant that local political opposition to such diversionary activity was largely out-manoeuvred. Indeed, as it became clear that the bid was beginning to utilise considerable local authority financial and staffing resources, the justification of the project shifted overtly to the concrete and symbolic benefits of bidding status, with the positive image of the city becoming central to the process (Cochrane et al. 2002).

Whilst Manchester 2000 projected the image of an entrepreneurial approach based on cooperation with the private sector, in political terms it was less about a lasting mode of governance than a concern for short-term partnership to get government funding and to boost the city's image. It additionally underlined the construction of a community of interest based in and on the city, whereby all would benefit from further boosting the profile of the city region. The failure of the bid and the end of the city's Olympic dream (September 1993), led to an adjustment of rhetoric by the city's leadership to emphasising the success of 'just taking part', its value in attracting additional public sector funding into the city, and the benefits and self-confidence generated by opportunistic partnership working with the private sector (Holden 1999). The problem of continuity, and the reproducing of such experience in terms of other major opportunities, was a real one however, and much of the energy expended was subsequently channelled into hosting the Commonwealth Games (Manchester 2002).

The City Pride initiative was announced in November 1993, with the city challenged to prepare a 'prospectus' detailing a vision for its strategic development over the following decade. Manchester felt that its lobbying of central government concerning the capacity of major cities to deliver a 'total approach', together with the city's demonstrable achievements in collaborative working, provided the necessary encouragement for central government to launch this initiative. In addition, the momentum generated by Olympic bidding provided an ideal opportunity for continuing to focus ideas, and to consolidate the process of partnership working. Whilst government did not issue detailed guidance on the form that the prospectus should take, and there was no specific funding regime associated with it, the encouragement of local flexibility and experimentation lay at its heart. The prospectus was conceived in terms of achieving a more long-term unification of the dynamism of partnership working, and competitive resource targeting beyond existing bidding mechanisms (Williams 1995).

The prospectus was given a high-profile launch, reflective of the expansive and ambitious nature of the city's development strategy – a 'flexible friend rather than a project blueprint' – intended to realise the international and local potential of the city (MCC 1994). Interestingly, it was not constrained by Manchester's administrative boundaries, with the conurbation core incorporating the inner areas of Salford and Trafford. It identified a range of strategic projects, along with an indication of possible funding sources, stakeholder partners and target-driven outputs and milestones. However, the three strategic aims – international city for investment and commerce; European regional capital; enhanced local quality of life – clearly demonstrated the extension of the Manchester 'script'. These themes were to be realised through a series of area-based initiatives and projects best felt to build on the core's distinctive opportunities. Central to the progress of such strategic developments were perceived to be the requirement for new institutional arrangements and operational partnerships, and a clearer focus for the delivery of public and private sector investment.

The production of a City Pride prospectus provided Manchester with an ideal opportunity to consolidate the partnership working of the early 1990s through a single piece of collaborative action. It also gave renewed dynamism to the ongoing elite-based project, generalising its ambitions and entrepreneurial strategies at the level of the whole city and beyond (Holden 1999: 234). Following a comprehensive review of the focus of the initial prospectus – disrupted by departmental restructuring, the successful Commonwealth Games bid, and the upheaval caused by the bombing of the city centre – a second City Pride prospectus was launched (MCC 1997a), setting out a vision which focused on four key themes – sustainable communities; the regional centre; international competitiveness and local benefit; and the Commonwealth Games. Interestingly, and reflective of growing local political tensions, a fourth strategic aim was added to the original three – 'an area where all residents have the opportunity to participate in, and benefit from, the investment and development of their city' (Williams 1998).

Internal monitoring reports and an international benchmarking study were to conclude, however, that Manchester's ranking on the basis of investor perceptions was significantly poorer than those based on factual indicators concerning infrastructural provision, labour-market characteristics, and the provision of business-related services. This, together with the recommendations to broaden the partnership base by involving more private sector partners and to provide a more singular focus to some of its activities, was to lead to a number of institutional developments. The establishment of Marketing Manchester (1996) as a promotional agency for the conurbation; the launch of Manchester Investment and Development Agency Service (MIDAS, 1997) to 'attract the highest level of inward and indigenous investment into the Manchester economy, and to maximise the benefits of that investment locally'; and Manchester Enterprises (2000) to facilitate local business support, training and jobs within the City Pride area (MCC 2001). In the case of Marketing Manchester considerable debate and criticism followed as to its capabilities in selling the city, and the justification of its existence to other local and regional players, in a situation where both the local and national political terrain has changed (Deas & Ward 2002; Ward 2000).

The bombing of the city centre and the destruction of its commercial core in June 1996 – the focus of the current study – established a new set of challenges both in terms of the city's capacity to respond to the bombing, and in driving through a renewal strategy. It was to put to the test the emerging confidence of local policy makers and their major private sector partners, as to their abilities to sustain the collaborative momentum already established. Undertaking the comprehensive redevelopment of the city centre whilst maintaining a functioning commercial core represented a significant challenge, seen beyond the local authority's capacities and experience. It was thus determined that a specialist task force – Manchester Millennium Ltd (MML) – should be set up to manage and coordinate the implementation of the rebuilding programme, focus on the coordination of private investment, the development and management of public realm strategies, and overall financial management and funding procurement. MML built up a dialogue on the city centre with all the main stakeholders, stimulating both the capacities and qualities of the local policy culture. The Task Force model, which became a national exemplar, was perceived locally to benefit from 'being independent of the council it has encouraged the private sector to believe that the team operates with credibility and integrity' and to have 'articulated coherently a framework which investors can have confidence in'.

Policy development following the return of a Labour government was to increasingly focus on issues of social inclusion and neighbourhood renewal. This was to create some uncertainty, in that after a decade of establishing a working relationship with a Conservative government hostile in principle but increasingly helpful in practice, the city had to strengthen its connections with a national Labour Party machine that it had largely neglected. Manchester's instinctive political individualism and strategic localism arguably fitted less well with Labour's modernising 'project', and undercurrents concerning the social bi-polarity of the city were to surface, and were seen to cut across the bows of the city's entrepreneurial credentials and its continuing commitment to flagship projects (Griffiths 1998). Fearful that the findings of a poverty report would damage the city's rebuilding process and deter investment, the authority was to effectively suppress the report for a year, fearful that such 'bad news' would deflect the wider agenda (Herd & Patterson 2002).

The increasing focus of development strategy over the past few years has been a strategic commitment to the regeneration of East Manchester. The evolving Manchester 'model' for strategic regeneration is now well embedded, and was perceived to be central to the thinking of the Urban Task Force (1999) report on the development of appropriate institutional structures and working relationships to improve urban competitiveness and regeneration capacities. This report argued that a series of agencies should be established – Urban Regeneration Companies – to tackle regeneration and local development, not as a series of individual bids for resources but as a coordinated and integrated whole. East Manchester was chosen as one of the initiative's 'pilot' areas based on MML's experience and expertise, with key individuals in HRL's work being subsequently involved in MML's activities, and this was transferred directly into the URC's initial framework (Parkinson & Robson 2000).

As such, East Manchester is a strategic priority area for regeneration of sub-regional consequence, with the collapse of employment opportunities and its massive environmental degradation resulting in a huge loss of confidence within its various neighbourhoods and communities (Tye & Williams 1994). It was already home to a variety of area-based regeneration initiatives attempting to tackle the problem of urban decay – namely New Deal for Communities, two SRB schemes, a Sure Start, Health and Education Action Zones and a Sports Action Zone, EU economic development zone – and was the focus of local authority and other agency involvement through targeted mainstream programmes. New East Manchester Ltd (NEM) was launched in October 1999, and formally incorporated as a company limited by guarantee, a joint venture between the City Council, the North West Development Agency and English Partnerships. Its core objectives are to create sustainable communities within the area that focus on quality employment, and residential and service opportunities; and to ensure that the economic benefits of investment are secured for local people whilst at the same time contributing to the sub-regional and regional agenda (NEM 2001). In its complexity and scale it suggests, however, that it will provide a real test for the established experiential learning of the city's elite network.

City-centre development framework

Stressing civic pride and achievement, the zeal of the Nicholson Plan (1945) set out to fundamentally redesign the core of the city – this was reinforced by the much delayed Development Plan (1961), which aimed centrally to ease war damage. Such proposals were only partially implemented, however, due to the massive costs involved in comprehensive clearance and redevelopment. The subsequent City Centre Map (1967) focused on extensive transport proposals and the promotion of commercial activity, giving little weight to the economic and cultural benefits of retaining the Victorian core. It signalled instead the build-up of land holdings to facilitate the creation of a Comprehensive Development Area within the commercial core, the culmination of two decades of earnest activity. This was to provide the framework for the Arndale Centre development of the late 1960s, involving the development of a major shopping centre, associated office development and allied commercial space.

A growing realisation of the size and complexity of the centre and the limited role of local authority land-ownership in influencing change, led the city to seek a more formal set of statutory powers for the area. The City Centre Local Plan (1984) was thus produced to provide such a framework, and it has provided a central backcloth for the launch of a range of recent flagship developments and major physical changes. In land-use planning terms it was ahead of its time, stressing the improvement of accessibility and the need for integrated public transport, the promotion of mixed land uses and commercial balance, the encouragement of residential development and active street frontages, the value of existing waterways and the role of gateway sites in structuring development

Manchester's commercial core immediately prior to the bombing

opportunities. The subsequent launch of CMDC did not result in any significant change to this strategic thrust, with the established framework offering sufficient flexibility for the development corporation's mandate and activities. It did, however, introduce a new 'style' of working within the city that heralded further collaborative initiative in the 1990s.

Its main objectives were to facilitate and bring back into use land and property on the southern fringes of the city centre which appeared immune to the more general resurgence of the city's economy; to develop new property sympathetic to existing buildings and to facilitate environmental enhancement; and to attract private sector investment to enhance the city centre more generally. In complementing the established local plan, the agency launched a Development Strategy (1990) that targeted its work on six major development parcels, with the strategic intent of extending the city centre functionally and geographically, and of promoting its economic diversity. It aimed to promote the centre's international credentials; reinforce the qualities of its built environment, and capitalise on the uniqueness of its central area's waterways; promote the enhancement of the public realm, and encourage further mixed uses within the centre. To reinforce such objectives it additionally aimed to extend the range and choice of housing and to ensure high environmental standards; extend the range of office types and focus on the additionality of office activity; promote the development of speciality retailing and pursue the development of tourism and leisure opportunities. Finally, the strategy aimed to focus on integrated management of transport facilities into and within the central area, and to improve city-centre accessibility.

Whilst the area was partly delimited at the outset to maximise the potential for success, it undoubtedly played a valuable role in helping to initiate a major series of flagship developments. This fuelled the economic health of an increasingly entrepreneurial city centre, and was reinforced by a continuous programme of environmental improvements. It additionally provided the impetus for the rapid expansion of city-centre housing, the resources and quality of marketing that centrally benefited the city centre as a whole, and as a consequence of the process extended it geographically. More negatively, however, arising from CMDC's initial view that its key role was to promote development, during its early years an accumulation of office consents resurrected 'hope' value that the established local plan had attempted to dampen. Additionally, it failed to be very active on the outer edges of its territory that offered opportunities beyond the trajectory allowed for by an avowedly short-life organisation, either in terms of its development shadow effects over non-designated parts of the city centre or spillover effects on neighbouring residential communities (Deas *et al.* 1999).

Manchester's (UDP) (1995) set a context for the role of the regional centre – as an employment, commercial and administrative centre; as a regional shopping and financial services centre; as a focus for city-centre living, and as a concentrated location for health and higher education facilities – with its overall vitality perceived to be critical to the conurbation's broader regeneration concerns. It noted that the established planning framework had served the city well, and argued that a full review of city-centre policies should be 'put on hold' during the operational life of CMDC. Thus its central-area strategy reiterates established policies, albeit for a slightly enlarged area, with consideration of how a changing core might require a different policy mix only now beginning to be addressed as the UDP as a whole is reviewed (Table 3.3).

Whilst statutory planning has so far targeted Manchester's city centre, the issue of the boundaries (and meanings) of the 'regional centre' has risen in prominence. Thus the emerging concept covers areas currently administered by three local planning authorities (Manchester, Salford, Trafford), and for most of the 1990s by two development corporations (Figure 3.2). Whilst it has been impractical to achieve a detailed planning framework for this area as a whole, it has proved important in planning terms not to feel constrained by such administrative complexities. Informal agreements between the three authorities and development corporations provided an input into the early stages of UDP preparation, this being subsequently mirrored in the approach adopted by the City Pride prospectus. Here, the strength of the regional centre was not limited by administrative boundaries, and the management of its policy framework came of age as a high-profile and distinctive activity.

Table 3.3 Manchester's established city-centre policies

- Positive commitment to mixed uses, ensuring active ground-floor frontages, together with the encouragement of residential development.
- Improvement of the city-centre environment for shopping, the upgrading of open spaces and improvements to waterways.
- Promotion of city-centre tourism, and the strengthening of Manchester's role as an international and regional centre for arts and culture.
- Enhancing the city's environmental and historic assets, and the promotion of its main gateways.
- Improvements of accessibility to the city centre, enhancing of pedestrian priority and the creation of new and improved public squares.
- Introduction of positive traffic management policies that remove extraneous through traffic from the city centre, discouraging long-stay parking, providing better access for buses, and improving conditions for pedestrians and cyclists.

While the established statutory framework has clearly been central for the achievement of development realisation, the city centre has remained a focus for a host of non-statutory strategies that have stressed collaboration with key private-sector interests. Central amongst these in setting the parameters for promoting the emergent 'entrepreneurial city' was the launch of City Pride. Its priorities were perceived in terms of the need to repopulate the city centre, reduce physical dereliction, provide an internationally acceptable infrastructure framework, and the attraction of key decision-makers in order to enhance regional capital competitiveness. This was to be reinforced by the broadening of the city's economic base, the achievement of higher levels of employment, and the reduction of poverty. Central to the progress of such strategic developments were the establishment of new operational partnerships, a clearer focus for the delivery of public and private sector investment, and with wider community interests being subsumed (Williams 1998). With specific reference to the

3.2
Manchester's regional and city centre
Source: Adapted from Kitchen 1997, 108, 110

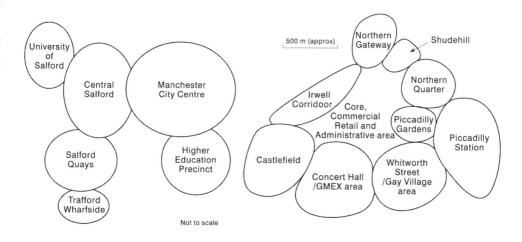

79

regional centre, the prospectus sought to enhance the city's role – involving the expansion of the city's core; greater integration of land uses and regeneration of the city's main gateways; the development of central-area retailing of an international standard; and the attraction of a major international political institution. Thus the regional centre was to be seen as the focus and barometer of the strength and competitiveness of the wider sub-regional economy. Concerns were expressed, however, relating to the effectiveness of its marketing, and success of its re-imaging strategies in 'modernising' perceptions of its urban qualities and opportunities.

Central to the rapidly changing conurbation core has been the host of strategic regeneration initiatives that have come to fruition over the past decade, seen to represent a necklace of development activity around the city centre (Figure 3.3). They signify the city's broadening experience with partnership working, with high-profile political leadership, a strong commitment to networking with government and commerce, and the leveraging of private sector investment. Facilitating such growth coalitions has increasingly made Manchester the national model in transforming the physical character and market potential of urban core areas. Examples have included Hulme City Challenge, Salford Quays and Trafford Park (TPDC); a host of SRB Challenge Fund programmes and projects; the Commonwealth Games; and the variety of emerging initiatives being coordinated by the East Manchester URC. They have provided the backdrop for a host of flagship developments that have been spawned in the city centre and its environs (Williams 2002). Evaluating the significance of such high-profile regeneration activities for the long-term health of the city centre is premature, but they have undoubtedly contributed to its changing form, function and vitality. Concerns are emerging, however, at the

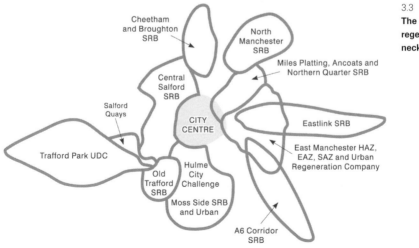

3.3
The city centre's regeneration necklace

core's increasing detachment from its wider area, and the city's bi-polarity in terms of investment priorities. The consequence for economic opportunity, social inclusiveness and urban development quality all impact on surrounding inner-city communities, and provide a real challenge for the city's political leadership within the context of the current modernising agenda for local government.

In terms of development planning two informal strategies presently inform the debate on strategic planning within the city centre, namely the City Development Guide (1996) and the Planning Guidance for the Bomb Damaged Area (1996). The development guide argues that the interplay between the range of factors that create the built environment – sense of place, high-quality design, density and mixed-use considerations, successful streets and sustainable transport policies, stewardship and security concerns – are all at a premium in considering development activity within the core. Concerns by external investors at the specificity of the guide's intent with regard to their commercial interests led to a loss of political will by the City Council's leadership, however, and a significant diluting of the range of technical standards originally included in the draft, effectively reducing its influence on development and business activity. Supplementary planning guidance focused on the commercial core was a direct response to the bombing of the city centre, was produced to set a framework for the renewal programme, and was set within the context of the city centre as a whole.

More generally, a number of other informal city-wide development strategies have had major consequences for the operation and realisation of city-centre objectives, and in providing a climate for investment activity. In particular, the City Centre Environmental Improvement Strategy (1994) aimed to improve the qualities of the commercial core, to contribute to the development of new activity in city-centre fringe areas, and to improve accessibility and linkages both within and between the core and the rest of the city. This has been reinforced by the recent implementation of a central-area CCTV Strategy that has attempted to strengthen aspects of community safety and of emerging public concerns. As part of its Arts and Culture Strategy (1994) the City Council recognised the potential for expanding economic activity within the core, through the extension of activity hours. The opportunities afforded to enrich and enliven conventional commercial areas through the provision of cultural and leisure-oriented commercial activities underpinned the city's review of the regulatory environment constraining the promotion of the '24-hour city', and to attempt to create a more distinctive identity and sense of place for Manchester. All these informal strategies prepared by a variety of local authority departments, but centrally coordinated and with clear political direction, have had as their objective a commitment to ensure the retention and enhancement of commercial opportunities.

The rapidly expanding range of residential developments within the city centre has made Manchester a national leader in such provision, and contributed

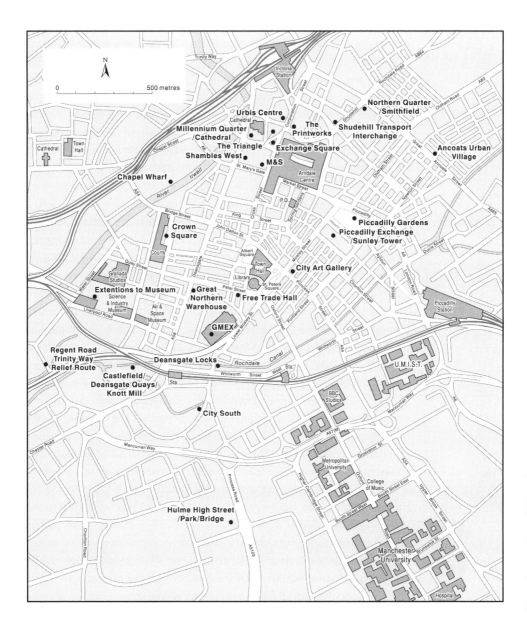

significantly to the economic fortunes and lifestyle characteristics of the core. Such developments are intended to create a sustainable massing of residential use to help support and to expand the provision of local services. Finally, the city's transport strategy aims to improve accessibility both to and within the city centre, and to promote further integration of a multi-modal public transport system (Bus Quality Partnership, Metrolink expansion, enhanced commuter rail investment, Inner Relief Route). Within this context the emergence of a more pro-active traffic

3.4

Manchester's redevelopment map

management system has seen commitments to upgrade short-term parking facilities, improved pedestrian linkages within and between specific areas, and measures to restrict private transport.

Central to the programmed regeneration of Manchester's core has been the parallel promotion of prestige projects on specific sites, both as a means of securing physical regeneration of strategic locations and of ensuring the city's high-profile place-marketing ambitions (Figure 3.4). Existing literature on such flagships argues that they signal the intention to regenerate sites with development potential, act as magnets for further initiative, and are symbolic of a city's capacity to restructure. Critics of such projects note, however, that they encourage the fragmentation of cities by targeting on specific zones and sites, have huge financial costs generally underwritten by the public sector, and often involve 'reverse leveraging' as a result of the private sector's strong bargaining position. They are susceptible to instability within property markets, often being over-ambitious and involving high financial risk. Within Manchester such prestige projects have a long tradition in relation to city-centre modernisation, with the current phase being launched by the G-Mex Exhibition Centre (1986), and with the past decade seeing Metrolink light rapid transit (1992), the MEN Arena (1995) and the Bridgewater Hall (1996), the Lowry Arts Project (2000), the Convention Centre (2001) and the 'Sportcity' initiative (2002) continuing this tradition. Currently, masterplanning activity relating to the Spinningfield development and the remodelling of Piccadilly provide continuity to this element of the 'script'. They undoubtedly form a cornerstone of the city's place-marketing strategy, boosting civic pride and business confidence, and play a catalytic role in reinforcing established facilities.

Chapter 4

Mobilising regeneration capacity

Having established the local political and policy framework that has influenced Manchester's governance over the past couple of decades, it is now appropriate to turn the focus on to the renewal, enhancement and revitalisation of the city centre. This chapter will pay particular regard to the mobilisation of institutional and technical capacity at the local level as a result of the bombing of the city centre, initially focusing on the urban management challenges that this process was to address. Following discussion of the devastating impact of the bomb and the emergency planning response, the present chapter considers the opportunities that this afforded for enhancing the city centre, and the approach undertaken to establish a framework for recovery. It considers, in turn, the organisation of an appeal fund with the short-term objective of offering support for the individuals and small businesses directly affected by the bomb, the establishment of a specialist task force to manage the recovery and renewal process, and the development of a master-planning framework for the development and delivery of renewal.

Manchester City Centre approached the 1990s in a positive and progressive frame of mind, with a robust economy focused particularly on commercial and retail activities; a rapidly expanding residential market; a dramatically enhanced cultural vitality and profile, increasingly being added to by the expansion of popular culture; and an increasingly diverse setting for its people, visitors and businesses. More negatively, however, the central area was constrained by functional and physical limitations and the increasing attractions for business of outer-area locations; by increased concerns over traffic congestion and the lack of an integrated transport policy; by growing concerns over community safety and the central area's contribution to quality of life; and by the increasing separation of the capacities and potential of the city centre from the remainder of the city.

The bombing of the city centre

On Saturday morning, 15 June 1996, the city's emergency planning framework was put to the test when a coded bomb warning was received by the media. The police immediately put into action established emergency procedures, and a suspect vehicle was located at the heart of the city's commercial core. Inner and outer cordons (500 metres and the Inner Relief Road, respectively) were established, and in collaboration with store security staff the police began to evacuate the 80,000 people estimated to be in the centre at the time. The cordons were aimed at preventing further people from entering the city, whilst at the same time allowing people in the centre to leave.

A bomb disposal team arrived but with insufficient time to defuse the 1,500-kilogram bomb. The force of the blast was felt up to 8 kilometres away, with the combination of pressure wave and vacuum sending shock waves down streets and alleys, up elevator shafts and stairwells, and along corridors and building spaces. Amazingly no one was killed, but around 220 people were injured as a direct consequence of the blast (some at evacuation locations, as glass showered down from vaulted ceilings), many of whom were subsequently to suffer shock and trauma. Once the aftershock had cleared, handling casualties became essentially a managed process, but with many 'walking wounded' being moved in public and private vehicles by personal initiative – 'a police woman took people to hospital on a bus – the bus driver wanted paying!' (Local authority Chief

Manchester's commercial core immediately following the bombing

Executive). The movement of emergency vehicles was seriously disrupted, however, by the sheer amount of debris and broken glass.

The damage to property was considerable, particularly for 300 metres along the length of Corporation Street (and for a width of 100 metres), with a total of 1,200 properties and 43 streets being damaged in some way. However, only around a dozen buildings were seriously affected structurally, a number of which were later demolished following discussion with insurers (Marks & Spencer, Michael House, Longridge House, western frontage of the Arndale Centre). A number of key buildings were severely damaged, and needed major repairs following full structural surveys being undertaken – Royal Exchange, Corn Exchange, Arndale Centre. In commercial terms, 672 businesses were displaced; 49,000 square metres of retail space and 57,000 square metres of office space were immediately decommissioned and 1.2 million square metres of property generally affected; the city's central indoor market was closed, as was a major section of the Arndale shopping centre; and residents from housing association apartments above the main shopping centre were displaced. There was major physical damage to the central commercial area's highways, the city's largest bus terminal was to be permanently closed, two multi-storey car parks were temporarily shut, and many key streets (including the city's main north–south link) were to be closed for up to 18 months (Figure 4.1).

In terms of the direct costs of the blast, both tangible and intangible, losses were considerable. It was estimated that the physical damage was of the order of £250 million and with lost or reduced retail turnover being estimated at £50 million, arising from the disruption to trade in the immediate aftermath, or in the relocation of businesses. A third of non-retail businesses suffered a loss of activity, with overall trade in the city centre being down a tenth even six months after the bomb (Gordon 1997). Small businesses that could not absorb the cost of lost trading, and which were either uninsured (a fifth) or under-insured (a third), were particularly vulnerable, this being highlighted subsequently by the small traders who had been located in the Corn Exchange. The other main financial problem faced by business was the loss of stock and the absence of cash flow arising from the disruption to trade. Whilst around 2,500 employees were temporarily laid off, the press noted that hundreds permanently lost employment as a result of the disaster, and the cost of business relocation was conservatively estimated at £10 million. This inevitably raised fears as to the long-term effects on investment and trade within the city centre.

In addition, there was a major cost to the local authority from the loss of rental income, parking fees and market trading licences, and, in the physical aftermath of the bomb, the development and labour-intensive delivery of the emergency plan. The direct losses of the City Council arising from the emergency response were of the order of £5–£10 million – with the existing national

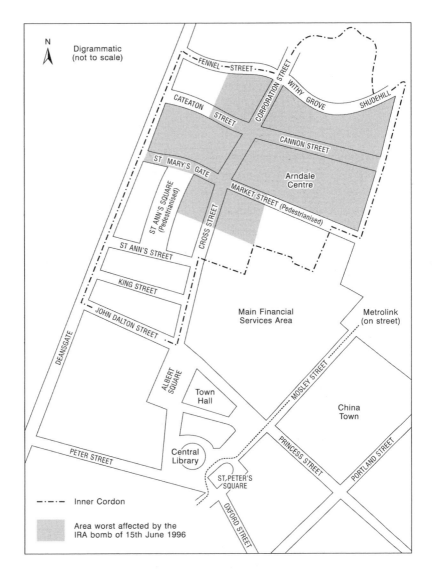

4.1
**The bomb-
damaged area**
Source: Adapted
from Kitchen
1997, III.

compensation scheme, Bellwin Scheme, entirely unsuited for such a situation – with the Council's reimbursement totalling less than £1 million. The total insurance cost of the damage caused was subsequently reported in the financial press as £422 million (in 1996, the world's most expensive man-made disaster), a significant underestimate given the extent of under-insurance evident. This figure was to increase substantially once the loss of business activity in the short and medium term was also taken into account.

Whilst there was no denying the substantial losses felt by the city centre in the immediate aftermath, it was to provide an opportunity to rebuild an enhanced, more competitive and liveable city centre, and was to prove pivotal in terms of the discourse and resources mobilised around the theme of partnership working for urban revitalisation. It offered the scope for modernising the urban fabric on a scale that would otherwise have been impossible within the existing built-up area, enabling contemporary concerns to be incorporated into the rebuilding process (Russell 1998).

The emergency planning response

Manchester was one of the few authorities within the conurbation having direct responsibility for emergency planning, and had well-drilled procedures for contacting key personnel, who cascaded into play the other necessary people and resources. In response to the devastation, a strong partnership was formed between the City Council, the emergency services, and the major private land-owners and occupiers, this benefiting from the remarkable coalition of interests already in place within the city. In addition, valuable lessons had been learned in dealing with a much smaller bombing incident within the city in 1992, and two gas explosions in the year prior to the bomb. The immediate problem for busi-nesses and the general public was one of access, with shop fronts missing and stock destroyed. The priority for the coordination group established in the imme-diate aftermath was to get the city back in business, restore and retain public confidence, and to begin to consider ways of managing the recovery process. This began within 48 hours of the blast, with the City Council becoming the focus of attention and the catalyst for a range of initiatives, focusing in particular on a reoccupancy strategy and business recovery, communication over cordon control and management, and the profiling of media relations (Williams *et al.* 2000).

Reoccupancy strategy

An inner cordon was maintained around the area affected by the blast, initially enclosing 25 hectares of the commercial core. It served a multi-purpose role in that it protected people from physical danger, helped preserve criminal evidence at the disaster scene, and as a management 'tool' was central to the City Council's reoccupancy strategy. It allowed the controlled release of land over time and space, with the authorities keen for owners to resume responsibility for their prop-erty as quickly as possible (Figure 4.2). Reopening of areas within the cordon depended critically on the assessment of damage to buildings and highways; on making the area safe for the general public; clearing debris (building materials, damaged stock, decomposing food); and setting up traffic diversions. The removal of dangerous building conditions was the responsibility of the local authority's Architect's Department, which had a predetermined plan that was originally drafted to respond to the impact of freak weather conditions. This defined a process for establishing priorities in dealing with widespread damage,

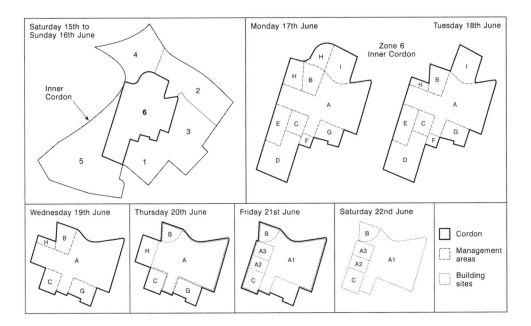

and was put into effect within hours, enabling the necessary local authority staff to be mobilised. These surveyors possessed extensive experience, knowledge and skills in relation to dealing with dangerous buildings, even if the scale and overall urgency to respond quickly presented new challenges.

Communication

Estimates suggest that between 5,000 and 10,000 people descended on the Town Hall (the designated control centre) on the day following the blast, all with their own individual problems and agendas (retrieval of stock or personal possessions, concern over premises and financial security), threatening to overwhelm the volunteers, city officials and emergency planning services.

> On the Sunday morning the Town Hall was crawling with loss adjusters and assessors, demolition contractors and every known glass company, wearing yellow jackets and hard hats … touting for business, and having the appearance of some official status … [there was] frustration by owners and tenants of buildings as it was not always possible for people to accept the severity of the structural impact from the external appearance of the buildings.
>
> (Senior local authority officer)

Since no provision was made within the emergency plan for responding to such numbers, it was decided that area-specific meetings should be held in six committee rooms within the Town Hall (each corresponding to a specific zone). This became the central means of communication, with meetings being held continuously throughout the first week after the blast, providing people with a summary of progress, and answers to immediate questions. Emergency planning meetings between the City Council and the police were held at the start of each day, the results being communicated to the committee rooms, where people were told which areas would be opened up and how to gain access. Some 700 City Council staff were to become involved in one way or another over the next few days, 250 of whom staffed the helpline, which took over 15,000 calls during the first week.

Business recovery
Of central importance for the immediate response stage was the relocation of businesses displaced by the bomb, to facilitate a restart to trading. The City Council's Valuer's Department, in close cooperation with local commercial agents, compiled a database of available property in and around the city centre. The bulk of the work in relation to business relocation, however, was undertaken by a designated business recovery officer who subsequently became part of a team handling the small business response. By the end of the first week, most of the larger businesses, who had both the resources and the emergency planning frameworks in place, were well advanced with their business recovery strategies (C. Graham 1998). However, the range of alternative premises available for larger business relocation was limited, this being demonstrated by Marks & Spencer, who temporarily relocated into two premises. An agreement was secured with the main banks that they would refrain from foreclosure on any business affected by the blast until they had liaised with the City Council. This was important not only for those small businesses directly affected, but also gave the banks confidence that a systematic approach was being taken to business recovery. Furthermore, a one-stop business advice and information service was established with the co-operation of local business development agencies, involving the short-term secondment of representatives from major banks, building societies and insurance companies. It was fortunate that the built form of many of the city centre's more peripheral areas consisted of large Victorian/Edwardian buildings often under-occupied on the upper floors, and there was a ready supply of relatively cheap alternatives available within half a kilometre of the most affected locations. Thus, of the businesses displaced by the bomb, over 90 per cent had been at least temporarily relocated by the end of 1996.

Media relations
A media and public relations strategy was formulated within three days of the explosion, with the City Council taking the lead, but working in collaboration with

other key agencies within the city. Its Public Relations Office worked with established local agencies such as Marketing Manchester, the City Centre Partnership, and the major landowners and traders, to develop and implement a concerted campaign. The aim was to maintain a high national and international profile during the initial period to restore confidence amongst city-centre users; to encourage shoppers, tourists and business users to return to the city centre; to support traders in relocating; and to provide a framework for promoting the city's views to the media on the development of a strategic recovery and renewal strategy.

> The emergency plan served the city well in terms of communication, in its capacity to support, coordinate and liaise between the police and other statutory services, and in responding to some of the immediate needs of the public. It had not, however, anticipated the possible scale of such an event, nor was it geared to facilitate the recovery process.
>
> (MCC emergency planning officer)

By the second week the city was able to start thinking of the longer term, with the launch of the Appeal Fund, a round of meetings with senior government ministers and officials, and the initial acceptance that mere reinstatement of the affected area should be ruled out.

Evaluation of the emergency planning response

The strong partnership formed to handle the immediate emergency response and for initiating the longer-term process of recovery undoubtedly benefited from the coalition of interests that already existed, and was discussed in the previous chapter. A significant amount of institutional capacity existed within the city, and there were people who through previous high-profile initiatives were capable of mobilising this capacity to maximum effect. The Deputy Prime Minister (Michael Heseltine), who had taken an active interest in earlier regeneration initiatives within the city, agreed to give the proposal for a radical regeneration strategy his personal support. This gave the renewal process a high political profile, increased the confidence of central government officials, and was instrumental in securing both EU funding and financial support from central government. Only in a city where many of the key players knew each other, were already working together, and above all trusted each other, could a new vision for the city have been attempted, several different funding streams secured, and a renewal programme delivered with such speed (Kitchen 2001).

> It's a big city, but a very small world. There are a hundred or so people we meet here, there, everywhere … if the bomb had gone off a decade ago, then we would have had total anarchy.
>
> (Senior business leader)

Although the mobilisation of existing strong relational networks within the city was regarded as central to the success of the emergency response and recovery process, a number of other factors were identified as being particularly helpful.

Predetermined strategies
Underpinning the success of the initial response was the City Council's emergency planning process, which depended heavily on lead members from key departments coming together on a cascade principle set out by the existing plan (engineers and building surveyors, operational and building services staff, city catering facilities, the press office). The dedicated emergency control centre in the Town Hall was operational within half an hour of the explosion, operating for 24 hours a day in the initial stages, then 18 hours a day. It would have been impossible to begin opening up the greater part of the area affected by the blast within 48 hours if there had not been predetermined strategies in place for dealing with dangerous buildings, even if modifications had to be made due to the scale of the disaster. Because the incident 'working area' was so large, communications with the emergency services and building surveyors proved difficult to implement comprehensively, this being reinforced by the continuing danger from falling debris. There was a need for an audible warning system for contractors that circumvented the deafening noise of security alarms, many of which continued to ring for days. Furthermore, in order to limit the possibility of looting, all photographs released were centrally vetted. Despite the modifications that were made, experience following the bomb demonstrated the value of the predetermined plan.

Training
All parties involved in the disaster response acknowledged the benefit of training, which helped increase the emergency response capacity within the city. Of paramount importance was the fact that police staff at all levels had the confidence to act without waiting for direction. The City Council had taken part in a nationally organised exercise with the emergency services of neighbouring authorities in the autumn of 1995, and this was felt to have been of immeasurable benefit in familiarising the appropriate people with the control room and the systems which had to be put in place. This exercise had involved many of the departments involved after the bomb, even if it had omitted the City Architect's Department, whose role in the emergency response was to prove crucial. A great deal of 'best practice' was identified, however, and the senior police officers and emergency planning officers involved were to be active subsequently in training courses across the country.

Euro 96
On the weekend of the explosion, the city was host to the European Football Championships (Euro 96), with Russia and Germany destined to play at Old Trafford the

day following the blast, a match that was allowed to proceed. The structures, processes and additional levels of manpower set in place for Euro 96 proved valuable in facilitating the response to the bomb. Arrangements already existed, for example, for local authority officers to meet the police daily, and emergency accommodation reserved at student residences within the city was subsequently used in relation to residents made homeless by the blast, and for some football fans.

Whilst the emergency response to the bomb blast is generally considered to have been successful, with no loss of life and with a city centre that continued to function efficiently if sub-optimally, a number of lessons were learnt from the whole process.

Evacuating the area

In the period immediately prior to the explosion there were potential evacuation problems, with many members of the public assuming it to be a false alarm. The scale and impermeability of the area served only to exacerbate the problems of communication. Whilst the police toured the area in vehicles and a helicopter, and individual stores responded well to their emergency planning procedures, a few people were still in the area very close to the bomb when it went off, and some were badly injured. There were also problems in maintaining the inner cordon once it had been established. Whilst a proposed close-circuit security camera scheme was in the process of being planned for the commercial core, it was not in place at the time, and this hindered police checking of evacuation procedures at street level.

Communication

The City Council's emergency planning officers retrospectively felt the need for improved early liaison with the police, ambulance and fire services to help ensure a fully integrated response. Resource constraints have further encouraged collaboration subsequently, and there is evidence of the local authority emergency planning function being incorporated more fully with the traditional emergency services. Thus, a multi-agency city-centre group was to be established after the bombing, complementing the city-wide group that was in existence prior to the disaster.

Regulating cordon access

Ensuring access for those people who needed to get through the cordons whilst excluding others was a problem on the day of the blast, and during the days to follow. On the day of the bomb individuals with emergency planning functions, as well as building surveyors travelling into the city centre, had difficulty in getting through the outer cordon. To overcome this problem key officials were subsequently issued with police passes to get through roadblocks. In the days following the bomb, the problem of surveyors, agents and contractors having appropriate access into the inner cordon, whilst still having a system which prevented access by members of the public, was resolved by the introduction of a coordinated system of passes. This allowed some control over the unauthorised contractors and loss adjusters in the city, who threatened to further congest the core with their vehicles. There were isolated examples of contractors managing to break through the cordon before being arrested, and a limited amount of looting took place despite the police presence and the real physical dangers involved. Overall, however, the way in which the exclusion zone was controlled and subsequently opened up – allowing access to key holders and contractors to secure buildings, with the City Council undertaking this work where necessary – was critical, and was generally successful in preventing further injury, physical dangers, or looting.

The scale of the disaster
The major constraint to an effective emergency response was the scale of the disaster. The predetermined plan did not envisage the extent of the physical damage or the response by those most directly affected. There were tensions in the immediate aftermath between the need to implement the predetermined plan in order to be able to reopen the city centre core as soon as possible, and the pressure to respond to urgent requests from individuals who needed access to specific buildings. As a result of the scale and impact of the blast, it was not possible to plan in detail for more than a day at a time, and there was considerable scope for rela-tional tensions given the number of organisations involved. In a situation where small businesses in particular were traumatised, often with inadequate or non-exis-tent insurance cover, and with all their resources tied up in unsold stock, appeals for calm in meetings with owners were not necessarily effective.

Lack of structures for recovery
The effect of a large bomb in the retail and commercial centre of a major city demonstrated the need to incorporate the recovery of the area into the emer-gency planning framework. Everything that happened in the first hours after the blast was the result of what were generally felt to be very effective emergency procedures. It quickly became clear, however, that the existing plan had a limited remit, not being geared up to facilitate the recovery process. This became a formal commitment within the first fortnight, and was rapidly followed by the establish-ment of specific instruments that were to deliver the renewal programme.

The discursive response to the bombing
The immediate aftermath of the bomb was dominated by feelings of shock and anger, and a palpable sense of communal loss, with the City Council's primary concern being to deal with the immediate needs of those directly affected; securing, surveying and clearing up the area; and the coordination of established partnership networks to ensure that the city centre functioned effectively at the

earliest opportunity. Two themes dominated local discourse following the bomb. For internal consumption there was the understandable need to stress the resilience of the city and its people, and prospects for renewal; whilst externally there was an emphasis on the need to secure national financial support in order to redress the economic impact and to resist the 'external threat'.

> Manchester is famous for self help, getting on with the job. It is not a city which quits … I know some of my friends already see this as an opportunity to rebuild.
>
> (Chief Executive, Co-operative Bank)

> This is the first time since the Second World War that there will have been the opportunity to plan a major urban centre, and impose some real quality on it. It is a wonderful opportunity, and we must not waste it.
>
> (City Council officer)

> We are not interested in playing a political game. We have a bombed out city centre, they [the government] have the money.
>
> (Council Leader)

Thus a discursive tension emerged between the opportunity for genuine improvement, whilst acknowledging the negative economic consequences of the bomb (Holden 1996). After only a few days, however, the emphasis on 'need' was complemented by the 'talking up' of opportunities for reinforcing Manchester's broader strategic vision, demonstrating once again the nascent politics of opportunity.

> They went for the heart of Manchester, but missed the soul. Together we can rebuild the city.
>
> (MEN poster campaign)

At central government level, rhetorical support for the local opportunity – as a positive symbol of national response – was rapidly backed up by both material and institutional measures. Michael Heseltine's much publicised tour of the city – 'a remarkable individual, a Conservative politician who is both entrepreneurial and interventionist' (Berridge 1997) – led to the announcement of two important measures, namely the 'top slicing' of EU structural funds by £21 million as the first part of a government aid package, and the intention to launch an international urban design competition. The gathering swell of opinion in favour of rebuilding (rather than reinstatement) culminated in a high-profile 'Rebuilding Manchester Debate' (5 July 1996) – organised by MEN, Manchester Civic Society, and BBC North – focused on an invited audience, guest speakers and a discussion panel, with an edited version broadcast subsequently on regional television and radio. A number of themes emerged that highlighted particular problems faced by the pre-bomb city centre, with prospects for the future couched in an often explicit rejection of past 'failures' (design and massing of the Arndale Centre), the tensions between change and continuity and the balancing of short-term needs (keeping the city-centre economy going) and longer-term possibilities (enhancing competitive advantage). In a real sense, therefore, the debate was an opportunity to generate ideas and to mobilise interest groups in terms of a wider strategic agenda.

> What you certainly can't do is suddenly remove the major core of Manchester's shopping … you must keep trade going. We have a very vibrant business in the city's retail sector … and we need to keep it so.
>
> (P&O Director)

> There is a conflict between the sort of redesign of the city centre that we want, and the need to keep businesses going. That's the sort of conflict, a tension, that we have to resolve very quickly.
>
> (Council Leader)

Increasing the permeability of the city centre was seen as a crucial opportunity, with an enhanced public realm, signature buildings and an attractive environment for quality consumption as part of a wider entrepreneurial agenda. In the debate 'positive' suggestions were welcomed, and tensions between commercial and cultural needs downplayed, with the implicit rejection of contributions not seen as 'constructive'. Discourse boundaries were effectively pre-constituted by the previous announcement of the urban design competition and of the intention to establish a specialist task force to deliver renewal, and there was to be no challenge to the underlying institutional delivery mechanism based on the political 'management' of opportunity (Holden 1996: 48). This clearly represented the limited choices faced by the City Council in leading the renewal process, given continuing central government financial controls and political orientation, and the dominant role of private sector interests in the affected area. It did, however, readily connect with the city's recent entrepreneurial agenda and script, which envisaged a local authority coordinating and networking role in relation to public–private partnership developments (Table 4.1). Indeed this slimline and flexible group of public and private sector partners, with its high level of interconnectivity, was seen to hold the key to the process of consensus building (Holden 1999: 249).

> I think the key role of the City Council here will be to bring together central government, the private sector, and users of the city centre, and in particular to make sure that the voices of ordinary people within the city are heard when we are talking about the redesigning and replanning process.
>
> (Council Leader)

Table 4.1 The main theme of the debate

A video made by BBC North was screened in order to prime the debate. This set a discursive context that emphasised the opportunity for redesign. Rebuilding, with a more flexible approach to planning was seen as a way to revitalise and diversify the city centre, and thereby stimulate the economy.

The panel and key experts tended to stress the opportunity to rethink the layout of the centre, but outlined the general conflict between radical change and continuity of trade.

A series of conflicts arose over the plight of businesses. The issue of insurance and compensation from central government caused considerable anger. This led to suggestions that more resources should be provided for the city in both the short and long term.

The Arndale shopping centre became the focus for a debate about the redesign of the look and form of the built environment, and was widely attacked. There was also a rejection of earlier planning practices.

There was a particular focus on improving the diversity and accessibility of the shopping areas, and enhancing the city centre as a place for living, working and playing. The aim was to be a stimulation of the city-centre economy by facilitating a more 'pleasant' centre.

Transport was seen as fundamental for sustained redevelopment, focusing on investment in both pedestrianisation and public transport. The attraction of people back to the city centre would renew its vitality and enhance prosperity.

The need for a strategic vision that would coordinate a wide range of ideas and inputs was stressed.

Source: Holden 1996: 44

> I think we saw the opportunity we all had, and we didn't see that we were in conflict with one another. It all made absolute sense … and it just all looked very deliverable.
>
> (Development interest)

This doesn't, however, detract from the importance of debate as a way of promoting public ownership of the renewal process, and of the benefits of gaining inputs from a wide variety of groups.

> This is a wonderful opportunity, and it would be foolish not to grasp it … and what is fundamental is encouraging people to be part of the solution … by starting this debate tonight … we can create the best solution for the next century.
>
> (Chairman of AMEC)

The urban design competition was to provide the focus for subsequent public consultation, and through this and the communicative activities of MML, the institutional and ideological coherence of the city's strategic vision was to be underpinned. Whilst the original briefing document for the competition, which was produced in early July, reached only a narrow audience, the discourse it mobilised had a broad effect on the scope of the more public debate. It was to lead to two further public fora: 'Rebuilding the City: The Debate Continues' (28 November 1996), organised by the RIBA and the *Guardian*, and 'The Manchester Debate: Rebuilding and Reconciliation' (15 June 1997) on the first anniversary of the bombing.

Establishing a framework for recovery

With Manchester's emergent position as a 'model' for partnership working being put to the test, the process of thinking through the structures necessary for a recovery programme was initiated, and the essential framework was in place within the first month. This was also a critically competitive time for the city centre, with the main threat coming from a 120,000-square-metre out-of-town shopping and leisure centre then under construction (Trafford Centre). The need to retain a functioning and competitive city centre in such a situation – coupled with pressures from insurance companies, landowners and business interests – created a very tight timescale for rebuilding. The aim from the outset was thus not simply to reinstate the urban fabric, but to reinvigorate and enhance the city centre as a whole, with the mechanisms chosen being the rapid establishment of an appeal fund, the creation of a task force to coordinate and manage the rebuilding process, and the launch of an urban design competition to facilitate a master-planning response.

The Lord Mayor's Appeal Fund
Following the dramatic impact of the bomb on the national consciousness, a range of organisations and individuals offered financial support, and the fund's creation was officially announced – The Lord Mayor of Manchester's Emergency Appeal Fund – 'designed to raise and distribute funds to those experiencing hardship, with a principal objective of assisting small businesses to re-establish'. The Board of Trustees met ten days after the blast – senior local authority officers, and Chamber of Commerce and legal practice representatives – with a full-time administrator being in place a week later. A bank account was opened with an initial deposit of £300,000, and a Distribution Committee – with representatives from major business interests within the city – was established to advise the trustees on applications for financial support. For the first four months the trustees and committee met twice weekly to discharge their responsibilities, thereafter meeting weekly, and by February 1997 met only when required.

The Trust administrator was aided by a team of people seconded from the public sector (local authority and the Training and Enterprise Council – TEC) and the private sector (management consultancies, banks, building societies), to help administer the fund. They interviewed all 672 businesses directly affected, providing help to draw up recovery or relocation business plans, administering a series of short-term loans and grants, and providing both practical and emotional support.

> It is through the work of this fund that a vital sector of the city economy – very small and micro firms – has not felt isolated from the grand scale of the redevelopment of the city centre.
>
> (Fund administrator)

Disbursements included grants to alleviate immediate hardship, and a mixture of grants/interest-free loans to help re-establish those businesses directly affected by the bombing. The pressured environment of the fund's administration was obvious in that £800,000 was awarded in the first two months, 462 applications for support were reviewed, and 360 grants and 86 loans were awarded. Whilst the fund had reached £1 million by early September, the trustees were aware of the continuing need for fund-raising in order to establish a sustainable strategy for helping businesses and individuals, and agreed to target individuals with strong attachments to and involvement in Manchester; companies with a strong connection with the area; and professional groups with a local presence. In addition, local authority associations and charitable trusts were contacted, and the local media agreed to arrange fund-raising events.

Whilst the majority of the allocations from the fund were for less than £5,000, a small number were to prove more significant, and the trustees were sensitive throughout to the possibility that it might attract unwelcome publicity. They thus focused their attention on traders temporarily closed but expected to reopen in their existing premises; those displaced and re-established in new and untried locations (from the Corn Exchange to the Northern Quarter), or in locations with poor access as a result of the cordon's continuing operation; and traders who were relocated on a temporary basis who were firmly committed to returning to the city centre when their previous units became available. Initially, subsistence payments to individuals were programmed to end by mid-September, but such awards were subsequently extended in a tapered form until the end of the year.

At this stage it was agreed that whilst the fund was unlikely to be dissolved for a further six months, as its workload decreased the trustees should meet less frequently and that administrative personnel should be reduced. The trustees acknowledged, however, that some form of 'after-care' service was necessary for fund recipients, and that this might become of increasing concern for the future. By the end of 1996 income totalled £2 million and commitments had risen to £2.2 million, and the decision was made to pursue early claims for selective EU funding. It was clear by mid-1997 that the basis of the fund was coming to an end, with over 700 individual applications and businesses considered, and with the vast majority of its mandate met, and the trustees agreed an exit strategy whereby the remaining fund was transferred to Manchester TEC's

Business Link service. They would continue to help businesses still seeking access to financial aid, those aiming to convert established loans to grants, and to offer a small business counselling and advisory facility and an after-care service.

Manchester Millennium Task Force

The enormity of the rebuilding process arising from the scale of the devastation was soon appreciated, and a clear need was felt for a special delivery mechanism to lead that process. Carrying out comprehensive redevelopment in the heart of a major city centre whilst maintaining a functioning commercial core represented a significant challenge, and with verbal guarantees of political and financial support from central government, it was determined that the establishment of a specialist task force – Manchester Millennium Ltd (MML) – involving joint public–private sector arrangements, was necessary. The City Council's role was thus to be that of an entrepreneurial advocate for the process, and the statutory body 'fighting for additional public funding'.

> [The] City Council really took a pre-emptive strike … they took a very strong lead and people looked to them for guidance … amazing how in the face of adversity so many people can work together.
>
> (Senior business leader)

The existence of this cross-sectoral and purpose-constructed agency – which gave further institutional legitimacy to an already powerful elite of 'movers and shakers' – provided the vehicle for quick discussions between the key players about the appropriate form of response to the damage. Attitudes agreed in those discussions in turn became the elements of a common stance in negotiations with government. This also meant that continuity of decision making was provided, with the Task Force intended to lead both the shaping of the response and in implementing the renewal strategy. It initially involved the establishment of a small executive team of local authority/private sector consultees (initially nine people), many of whom had worked together on previous regeneration initiatives within the city, with such past experiences proving critical for its immediate operational effectiveness. Established on 5 July 1996 and launched as a limited company on 17 July, its initial remit was to:

- coordinate the preparation of the recovery programme, to keep it under review, and oversee its effective delivery;
- assume particular responsibility for the creation of a regeneration framework for this core area, facilitate an agreed masterplan, and procure development in partnership with landowners and the City Council;
- secure the resources from the public and private sectors to ensure the implementation of the recovery programme; and

- account to the City Council and to government for public sector resources to support the implementation of the recovery programme.

Working at arm's length from the local authority it was led by the authority's Deputy Chief Executive, seconded to oversee MML's core management team, and was managed and led by a Task Force board, consisting of representatives from the private sector, local authority, and government (Table 4.2). Lacking statutory powers, its initial concern was to promote the refunctioning of the core and to relocate the many businesses displaced by the bomb, whilst at the same time facilitating the bringing forward of a rebuilding strategy that 'balanced urgency with quality'. There is no doubt that the decision to structure the organisation in a way that placed a heavy emphasis on the inputs of development interests had a significant effect on MML's approach to its task, being seen as flexible, politically neutral, and at 'arm's length' from the City Council.

I genuinely believe that the strength of the Task Force is that it is not ridden or constrained by responsibility for the discharge of statutory functions, and as a consequence has an enhanced capacity to deliver. If you have a very close working relationship with the City Council, then this is sufficient.

(Chief Executive MML)

Manchester City Council, however, remained the accountable body for all public resources approved for city-central rebuilding, and retained its planning function for the renewal area, whilst the Task Force's main focus was to facilitate private sector action and to 'articulate coherently a framework which investors can have confidence in'. It is clear however that MML afforded MCC a considerable degree of control over the whole process, whilst ensuring the full commitment and capacities of private sector landowners.

Table 4.2 MML Task Force structure

Board Chair	Chief Executive of AMEC Construction Company ('Northern bluff, but London sharp, a big force of a man who gets things done and wants it done right').
Political	Council Leader and Deputy Leader.
Institutional	Regional Director of the Government Office (GO NW), and regional representative of the Bank of England, together with the chair of Marketing Manchester (a former Minister for Manchester).
Executive	Chief Executive: 'a public servant dynamo behind the city's special projects of the 1990s. Lucky are the cities who get someone with his clout and instincts. A genius at finding funding, he knows everybody in business and government, and they all return his calls.' 'A very innovative person who is always looking for the next challenge, and this is one hell of a challenge.'

The design competition's initial framework

The opportunities afforded to enhance the qualities of the city centre were soon realised, and with the active encouragement of government an 'International Urban Design Competition' was launched on 17 July 1996, with the aim of developing a framework that would provide momentum for positive change in the core and its surrounding area. The initial stage was expected to result in establishing a basic approach (23 August), with those shortlisted for the second stage (4 September to 18 October) expected to develop a comprehensive framework that would provide the momentum for change. The first-stage brief was prepared by the Task Force and City Council officers, in close discussion with the main landowners and GO NW. The whole tone of the document was in keeping with the city's established entrepreneurial discourse, with pressure being put on the fledgling Task Force to manage the process even before its own structure and accounting frameworks were firmly in place. This led to some criticism of the management and adjudication of initial submissions, and of the paucity of information and lack of briefing clarity (*Architect's Journal*, 1 August 1996). This was clearly a product of the special circumstances behind the competition's launch, its timing and timescale constraints.

> The timescale is extremely tight … and will make major demands on tenderers. There was, however, a high degree of consensus amongst all interested parties on what needs to be done, and how we should achieve it.
>
> (MML board member)

The board made early decisions to retain a number of specialist advisers – masterplanning, transport, cost consultancy – to help them in their initial deliberations. For the competition, the Masterplan Adviser was a critical appointment, with the Toronto-based consultant already well known to the MML board and Chief Executive, arising from previous work on the city's Olympic bid and on Hulme City Challenge. His brief was to:

- assist in the organisation of the competition stages, and to participate in the evaluation of each stage submission;
- prepare the detailed competition brief, involving coordination of local officials, professional interests and landowners, and the wider community;
- prepare evaluation reports to fit in with the competition timetable, and to help draft and to coordinate the final masterplan framework document; and
- provide a general masterplanning advice service to MML, and to coordinate activities with the other retained consultants.

Quite clearly the initial and subsequent competition briefs were critical in establishing a design quality statement for the renewal process, clarifying the general and specific aims of redevelopment, and for ensuring the commercial realism and deliverability of the recovery programme. Whilst they centrally involved the Task Force, the local authority and other public agencies, and the main landowners, it proved impossible at this stage to facilitate wider public involvement in setting the agenda.

The initial brief – issued under the imprint of the City Pride Partnership, and thus part of the wider narrative – identified a 'core study area' of some 24 hectares, and a wider area expected to influence the strategic response, but not directly affected by physical damage. It set out the main development areas affected, the very limited range of ownership interests – 'there are a half dozen people or companies that are either going to make or break this initiative' (Development interest) – and the established policy context for the designated area. The proposed framework had to be deliverable, capable of phased implementation that would substantially rebuild the core in three years, and would have to enhance the regional centre's strategic role. Deliverability was to be measured by the framework's ability to ensure continuity of trading, a robust commercial investment plan, and the justification of public sector investment. In environmental and accessibility terms, the framework was intended to preserve, interpret and integrate the city's medieval core, enhance the character and appearance of historic buildings and areas, and improve access to the River Irwell. It was intended to create a pedestrian-friendly environment overall, to reinforce the need to remove through traffic from the city centre, and to sustain excellent public transport links.

It was accepted by the MML board that the selection of shortlisted submissions from the first stage, whilst primarily technical, would also have a subjective element, in order to focus on those aspects offering the renewal programme the greatest potential. Guiding principles included the financial realism and timescale of the proposals; the ambition of the concepts involved and reflection of the requirements of established commercial interests; the adequacy of transport and access proposals; and of the track record of the tenderers with regard to major urban design and masterplanning projects. Final adjudication was undertaken by members of the MML board, its Chief Executive and Masterplan Adviser and a retained Architectural Competition Adviser, and the process eventually involved the consideration of a relatively limited range of submissions (27), from which a shortlist of five teams was selected comprising those that had the competence and breadth required for such an assignment (*Estates Gazette* 26 October 1996).

> We are convinced that in the shortlisted proposals we have the talent, vision and experience to work these schemes into an excellent framework … that the landowners and people of Manchester can move forward.
>
> (MML board member)

The competition's detailed brief

The second-stage brief was drafted by the Masterplan Adviser in consultation with the City Council, the Task Force and the landowners. It was a considerably fuller document, broken down into six sub-areas considered to be crucial in illustrating the scope and level of development. Its intention was 'to initiate the creation of a compelling vision and framework for future development and design … that can guide both immediate and long term reconstruction' in close liaison with MML and the main landowners, and which would solve many of the city centre's inherent problems (Table 4.3). The winner was expected to provide an ongoing masterplanning and urban design service alongside MML's own retained advisers, and help to coordinate the direction of the numerous individual developments. The jury for this stage consisted of the MML Board Chair and Chief Executive, Council Leader and Chair of the City Centre Sub-Committee, regional director of GO NW, MML's retained advisers and a Competition Adviser.

In terms of development and design aspirations the brief stressed that views were not prescriptive, but were intended to raise issues that needed resolving. It argued that the main renewal objective was to strengthen Manchester's role as a regional centre, sustain its retail and business functions, and ensure its competitive advantage in relation to out-of-town developments. The masterplan should provide for additional investment opportunities, enhance the quality of the built environment, and offer functional diversity and increased safety and accessibility. It should offer the potential for increasing the city centre's residential population and add new culture and leisure destinations. Competitors were urged to be conscious of the need to demonstrate a realistic economy of means in proposing elements requiring public expenditure, and be able to justify them in terms of regeneration benefits and value for money. Similarly, elements requiring private investment had to be deliverable and commercially viable. It was stressed, however, that the competition was essentially a masterplanning opportunity rather than an architectural one, since the major landowners involved would retain their own architects, but that clear design guidelines should provide an overall framework for future development.

Table 4.3 The city centre's existing weaknesses

- Medieval core cut off by concrete office blocks and retail outlets, and cathedral isolated by highways.
- Inspiring historic buildings overshadowed by unchallenging supermarkets.
- Huge central shopping area an eyesore, hermetically sealed off from the rest of the city centre, and impermeable.
- Waterfront potential of the core ignored.
- Too many cars driving through rather than to the city centre.
- Central-area streets unsafe at night.

The brief aimed to establish/maintain good overall accessibility and convenient internal circulation for all city-centre users, and to give priority to public transport for access to the centre. Within the central area, the necessity for a pleasant and safe environment for pedestrians was stressed, as was the complementarity of public and private provision. The improvement of bus quality, the long-term operational strategy for the Metrolink system and city-centre rail stations were to be considered, together with the scope for a major new transport interchange within the centre. To improve the core's environmental quality the scope for innovative traffic management should be considered, and the availability of well-located, safe and attractive parking was perceived to be critical to the success of both retail and leisure proposals. In terms of the built environment, competitors were to assume that certain buildings would require demolition, that others would require substantial external and internal refurbishment, and that the associated reconfiguration of other areas would be driven by commercial rather than structural considerations. The masterplan was expected to:

- be bound by sound commercial criteria, and by realism with regard to the availability of public sector resources; and
- provide the basis for bids to government, and the levering in of the maximum amounts of private sector investment.

An elemental cost breakdown of key elements of the masterplan was thus to be demonstrated, and competitors were expected to identify output measures for their strategies.

With the launch of the competition's second stage and the announcement of shortlisted teams – Halliday Meacham, EDAW, BDP, Manchester First, Llewellyn Davies – procedures were set in place to enable the competitors to have direct access to the Task Force and its retained advisers, and to the major landowners. The very process of the competition, in which each of the design firms was given separate working sessions with landowners and key commercial interests, was intended to ensure that a measure of development realism informed their plans, in effect temporarily suspending the real forces of commercial competition.

> These were often tough sessions, with the owners shooting down anything out of the straight and narrow ... constant meetings with the Task Force and competing designers ... growing sense of shared destiny ... realisation that this really could be a win, win situation ... the whole could be greater than the sum of its parts ... the heart of the city could be completely re-imaged, re-designed and re-landscaped.
>
> (Berridge 1997)

Receipt of the shortlisted submissions triggered an intensive period of activities arranged to facilitate the process of technical and commercial appraisal, and public ownership and support, culminating in the final verdict being announced (Table 4.4). In developing an evaluation framework for technically appraising the final entries and in considering the expertise and capacities of the shortlisted teams, a Technical Evaluation Group of local authority and other local agency representatives was established, together with a Commercial Evaluation Group to bring the main landowners and government agencies on board. The former group was concerned with the planning, design and implementability of the fledgling masterplans, whilst the latter group's concern was to assess the extent to which each proposal was commercially deliverable, offer the opportunity to lever in the maximum private sector investment, and justify the anticipated levels of public sector expenditure. This group inevitably faced difficulties in that putative masterplan proposals were by definition flexible, but they did attempt to identify the elements of each submission that were essentially commercial in nature and those perceived to be non-commercial. In addition, the process was to be informed by a variety of informal representations by a host of interests concerned at the evolving development framework, but who were not themselves major landowner/developers (such as Chetham's, the cathedral, and development professionals).

Public consultation and the search for legitimacy at this stage focused on three elements – a MORI opinion poll, a public exhibition of shortlisted schemes, and focus group meetings – these being complemented by a 'Planning for Real' exercise inspired by a voluntary group. Whilst these were seen by MML as a 'comprehensive exercise', it would be misleading to suggest that they were centrally important at this stage to the overall decision-making process, since the focus of the overall design was centrally influenced by the key landowners preoccupied with concerns over commercial realism, and the timescale for consultation was inevitably brief (Myles & Taylor 1998). The commitment to extend consultation beyond the competition stage into the actual implementation phase became very restricted – but was important over specific issues – focusing largely on the publication of a regular newsletter.

Table 4.4 Framework for submission appraisal

- Overall workability of the scheme and the bankability of proposals in terms of the attraction of investment.
- Good mix of land uses and effective transport links with the rest of the city.
- Visual appeal and sensitivity to existing heritage whilst delivering a distinctive vision.
- Meets perceived aspirations of existing landowners and the requirements of traders.
- Reflects and adds to Manchester's character and contributes to the creation of a safe environment.

However, the local media (under the influence of the City Council's Public Relations Office), did play an important role in supporting the public ownership both of the rebuilding process and of the notion of a vision for the millennium.

The MORI poll, based on both 'in street' and 'catchment area' interviews, focused on positive and negative messages relating to the existing city centre, and features that people would wish to see incorporated into the proposed masterplan. The public exhibition of shortlisted schemes – based on models and exhibition boards – was viewed by 3,000 people over one weekend, a third of whom expressed written views, with the clear intention that such considerations would be incorporated within the final design. The eventual winner (and runner-up) proved to be amongst the best- and least-supported schemes in this appraisal, with most public comment focusing on pedestrianisation, green space, safety and public transport, rather than on development sites and buildings. Critics of the shortlisted schemes argued, however, that none of the submissions offered anything stunningly original, and that the competition appeared to have been a missed opportunity (Malone 1997). Alongside such considerations a series of focus groups was established to discuss city-centre perceptions – separately involving groups of children, teenagers and young adults, pensioners, disabled and female groups – and to deliver such views to the Task Force.

On the basis of such consultation and the intense deliberations of the Technical and Commercial Evaluation Groups, a range of evaluative material was prepared for the jury. The jury's final deliberation involved detailed consideration of the five submissions, an evaluation report from MML's retained advisers, comments from a range of public officials and from affected landowners, with the nature of the 'rebuilding settlement' not made clear until the winner was announced.

> There's the normal confusion and chaos preparing the evaluation report, with so many reviews to coordinate. Too much information, not enough judgement, and the clock running out … Howard is pushing us towards a decision; he's three steps ahead, trying to figure out how this is actually going to get built.
>
> (Berridge 1997)

> It fairly quickly came down to two schemes … both, and only these passed the two tests. Could you really get this built in time and to budget, and would the scheme create a place of quality and distinctiveness? One scheme is simple, too simple; the other has richness, perhaps too much. Is it easier to add or subtract; to design up or design down from the original submission?
>
> (Berridge 1997)

In a finally balanced debate between the 'doers' and the 'designers' – involving the short-term horizons of commercial interests set against the longer-term considerations of the design professions – the jury's final decision was announced on 5 November 1996. EDAW – a London-based international design and development consultancy – was declared the winner of the largest city-centre urban development project to be undertaken in Britain since the 1960s. The winning team assembled around EDAW consisted of transport and property consultants (Alan Baxter, Hillier Parker, DLE) and local architectural and urban development consultants (Simpson Associates, Johnson Urban Development). The runners-up – Building Design Partnership (an international multi-disciplinary practice) – were to be retained for a period to work alongside EDAW, who were charged with refining the winning masterplanning framework, taking into account issues raised by the evaluation and appraisal process, and to prepare site-specific design guidelines capable of providing a brief for individual landowners and developers. Thus, to an important degree, the period of the urban design competition was characterised by a suspension of the real forces of competition between city-centre interests, and most crucially by the uncertainty of public and private funding regimes. This honeymoon period – based on trust and a belief that the opportunity would sow its own success – was to end abruptly once the strategic vision had to be translated into an implementation plan.

> The substance of the plan is now fully engaged with the reality of the private owners' intentions and the constraints of the available budget. What was a joy of concept has become a tight game of inches, of positioning for advantage … become very adult … and a huge game of three-dimensional poker. Thank God for Howard … whether he knows what he's doing in detail, I doubt, but he has good instincts and the best poker face of any of them.
>
> (Berridge 1997)

> My legacy in Manchester is not going to be piles and piles of drawings that look wonderful – it's going to be something that works. I make no apology for that.
>
> (Bernstein, in Rattenburg 1997: 57)

Chapter 5

From masterplan to implementation framework

Having considered both the local commitment and capacity to respond to the impact of the bombing, it is now opportune to sketch out the development of a framework for renewing the city centre. This was to be achieved through the development and refining of a masterplan, and the translation of this vision into an implementation instrument capable of ensuring the successful rebuilding of the core. That this was to be attempted within an impossible timeframe and real resource constraints – whilst retaining the functional capacity and continuing competitiveness of the city centre – has proved to be a remarkable achievement worthy of wider dissemination. The present chapter considers the context set by the existing strategic framework, and the emergence of a successful masterplanning vision for the renewal programme. It then proceeds to consider the process of transforming the draft vision (autumn 1996) into a tangible and achievable implementation plan (spring 1997), intended to underpin and set the parameters for the recovery process. As already noted, the competition brief had already set out a clear client perspective, incorporating the interests of both public and private sector stakeholders, and had stressed the importance of producing both a deliverable masterplan and one that facilitated an enhanced city centre and development quality.

The masterplan was expected to help define the 'place' that the stakeholders wanted to create, and to provide a confident framework for investment of both cultural and commercial capital. Given the circumstances, it was intended to assist in managing the considerable uncertainty that persisted as to the future of the city centre as a whole, to meet the aspirations of key development interests, and to deliver the major private and public investment necessary to 'rebrand' the central area. It was also expected to offer the opportunity of a structured approach to land-use distribution and the chance to shape a core area of the city centre; facilitate a wider consideration of issues and impacts that would help shape the basis for dialogue; create a vision that could be signed up to that would be practical and achievable within the timescale set; and to provide a framework rather than a blue-print that would be sufficiently flexible to accommodate change (Table 5.1).

Table 5.1 The masterplanning approach

Steps in the process
- Identify the key drivers of change.
- Understand alternative scenarios through 'foresight' building.
- Facilitate stakeholder consultation and consensus building.
- Select the preferred future vision.
- Define the infrastructure skeleton necessary to realise the preferred future.
- Set the urban design and land-use principles.
- Outline the implementation programme.

Successful masterplan characteristics
- Vision and values driven.
- Flexible to respond to changes in demand.
- Shapes and harnesses market forces.
- Provides flexibility and parity of access to all.
- Promotes mixed uses and increased permeability.

The city centre's established vision

The visioning aspects of the redevelopment brief was, as the previous chapter has already indicated, meant to facilitate a clear, deliverable and achievable masterplan, but was itself likely to be influenced by established visions and strategies (Williams 2002). The city's existing Unitary Development Plan (UDP, 1995) set the land-use policy context for the city centre – as an employment, commercial and administrative centre; as a regional shopping and financial services centre; as a focus for city-centre living; and as a concentrated location for health and higher-education facilities. Indeed, its overall vitality was perceived to be critical to the conurbation's broader regeneration concerns, and as such it was additionally expected to play the role of a regional capital. However, such a framework was based on a long-established vision of the central area (City Centre Local Plan 1984), with the full review of established policies being 'put on hold' during the operational life of the CMDC (1988–96), with scope for the possibility of a different policy mix intended to be addressed in the first review of the UDP as a whole. In the meantime, the City Development Guide (1996) was expected to inform future development by highlighting the core's existing qualities and scope for further enhancement (Table 5.2).

The local authority was also actively engaged in a variety of other facilitating initiatives. In particular, the City Centre Environmental Improvement Strategy (1994) sought to enhance the appearance and quality of the city centre, making it a more attractive place for users, and aiming to improve accessibility and linkages both within and between the core and the rest of the city. An associated City Centre Lighting Strategy was intended to create a positive image of excitement, a vibrant and safe environment that would enhance the attractiveness of buildings and the streetscene. Additionally, as part of an Arts and Culture Strategy (1994) the authority recognised the potential for expanding economic opportunities through an extension of the city centre's hours of activity, in the process animating streets by day and night. This was to be reinforced by a commitment to encourage public art within development initiatives to enhance the quality-of-life experience in the core, and to help create a more distinctive identity and sense of place for Manchester as a major European city. Finally, the overall objective of the local transport strategy was to improve the local environment by making it cleaner and safer, to improve accessibility to and within the city centre, making it more pedestrian-friendly and accessible, and in particular to encourage a switch to public transport.

The Central Manchester Development Corporation development strategy (CMDC 1990) had aimed to promote Manchester as a major international city, reinforce the qualities of its built environment, and capitalise on the unique assets of the central area's waterways. It also sought to promote the enhancement of the public realm and to encourage further mixed uses within the centre. To reinforce such objectives it additionally aimed to extend the range and choice of housing and to ensure high environmental standards; focus on the additionality of office activity and promote the development of speciality retailing; and pursue

Table 5.2 City Development Guide: city-centre focus

- Careful design of buildings and streets – the spaces between should help achieve a strong sense of place.
- Promotion of high-quality environment that combines contemporary design with the city's best architectural traditions.
- Development density and mixed uses promoted as factors that enhance the sense of safety and well-being and encourage a diversity of activity in a '24-hour city'.
- Promotion of successful streets providing both urban patterning and a rich infrastructure for both meeting and trading.
- Promotion of adaptability and flexibility of development, and the reinforcing of public transport priorities.
- Promotion of safety and security through the creation of lively, lived-in urban areas and public spaces.

---

the development of tourism and leisure opportunities. Finally, the strategy aimed to focus on the integrated management of transport facilities into and within the central area, and to improve overall city-centre accessibility (Deas *et al*. 2000).

As previously noted, City Pride's broad aim was to enhance the city's role as a European regional capital and centre for investment; to maintain the momentum for an international city with real cultural, creative and commercial potential; and to facilitate the area's quality of life and a sense of well-being. Within such a context it identified a series of key themes forming the core strategy for renewal and image reconstruction, and perceived to address aspects of comparative disadvantages whilst building on the city's distinctive strengths and opportunities. With specific regard to the city centre the aim was to achieve repopulation of the core; broaden its economic base by the attraction of key decision-making frameworks or institutions; reduce dereliction and provide an internationally competitive infrastructural framework; and in the process enable Manchester to compete effectively with other city regions and other European capitals (Williams 1995).

The initial masterplanning framework

The winning masterplan was expected to provide a simple but dynamic framework that would link design with its capacity for delivery within the contemplated timescale, would represent a robust response to the urban design opportunities, and would provide the appropriate framework for commercial and public funding activities. In short, the key question was – 'which scheme offers the best basis for rapidly moving forward with the city centre's reconstruction' – rather than of necessity being the best urban design or most imaginative urban development solution.

EDAW's submission

In their first-stage submission the EDAW team noted that their basic design principles were:

- to create a 24-hour city centre encouraging a diverse mix of uses;
- to enhance the range of public spaces at both grand and human scales;
- to create pedestrian-dominant transport nodes;
- to sustain places, routes and views respecting the city's heritage;
- to integrate the Arndale with the fabric of the city centre; and
- to provide a major new square as a central focus that would unlock the whole project.

The emerging masterplan's key elements were defined as being concerned with respecting the visual structure of the city, and by featuring the key visual linkages and a clearer articulation of established and new blocks of built form, to create a new city-centre focus. By linking key streets and squares along a clear pedestrian route, it would reconnect the cathedral and the River Irwell to the city centre, and integrate overall transport and accessibility (Table 5.3).

It noted that the most important aim of the reconstruction programme was to restore and enhance the retail core and reduce its present impermeability, and in so doing provide real opportunity for growth by opening up new retail, cultural, entertainment, housing and commercial facilities. Proposals for a new Millennium Centre and a major regional leisure facility were intended to facilitate the notion of a '24-hour city' and reinforce the core's shopping and commercial facilities, this being complemented by middle/upper-market residential developments in order to increase the buoyancy of fringe areas and reinforce the core's vitality. Finally, the proposals addressed the need to improve safety and security through the detail of design considerations, CCTV and an increased resident population. Indicative estimates of the capital costs involved and private-sector investment requirements were presented, and the submission noted that in the phasing and implementation of the proposals due consideration had been given to the need to retain a functioning city centre that was not overly disrupted by the rebuilding process.

All the shortlisted schemes were submitted for both technical and commercial appraisal – involving the competition jury and MML's retained advisers, and detailed discussions with other key partners (the major landowners, MCC and GO NW). In terms of this appraisal, the winning scheme was seen to have a range of positive features (Table 5.4).

Table 5.3 Summary of EDAW's masterplan submission

- A new, bigger Marks & Spencer to be rebuilt on its old site. A walkway through the centre of the Marks & Spencer store will link the Arndale to Shambles Square.
- The Arndale Centre will remain largely untouched, but the Arndale Tower will be reclad and sections of the roof and walls will be replaced with glass to allow more natural light into the shopping centre.
- A pedestrianised route will run from St Ann's Square to the cathedral, incorporating a new public square and a park around the historic place of worship. The Sinclair's pub in Shambles Square will be moved to allow for the new walkway, and residential buildings will be constructed at the rear of Shambles Square.
- Cannon Street will be turned into a covered Wintergarden creating a new shopping street to replace the bus station.
- A new Arndale Food Court will be created at the Withy Grove side of the shopping complex with an expanded market behind it.
- Corporation Street will be reserved for pedestrians and buses only, and a special 'bus loop' will be created around the centre.
- A Trocadero is planned for Maxwell House, with a cinema and games complex. EDAW will also construct a cultural centre on the site of the existing NCP car park with a library and theatre.

Table 5.4 Technical and commercial evaluation of EDAW's scheme

Technical appraisal
The scheme represents:
- a strongly articulated form and structure, the creation of interesting new spaces and linking of spaces having distinctive qualities;
- a sound location of new developments, well-formed frontages, and imaginative remodelling of existing built form;
- clearly articulated development parcels for development activity and phasing of redevelopment; and
- clear pedestrianisation improvements and well-articulated traffic management elements.

Commercial appraisal
The scheme has:
- clear market feasibility, introducing a broad range and mix of uses, and the creation of added value for private-sector investment; and
- commitment to substantial increases in commercial floorspace with a specific focus on quality retail and an enhanced urban leisure experience.

The proposals have a strong commercial logic, the potential to generate very substantial quantitative and qualitative outputs, and represent sound value for money for public expenditure.

Commercially, the scheme underpins the extension of the city core northwards and knits together city spaces, streets and squares in a way that is diverse and likely to enhance the city centre's qualities, this being reinforced by strong public realm improvements that are central to commercial success.

A series of issues needed further consideration, however, and were to be worked upon in the months following the announcement of the winning submission. These included further discussion of the scale of spaces implicit in the winning design and their relationship to surrounding buildings; the prominent arrangement of buildings and uses at a key corner location within the masterplan area (Withy Grove); resolution of potential conflicts between awkward pedestrian and vehicular crossings; and pedestrian access concerns relating to both the River Irwell and within the scheme (Marks & Spencer/Arndale pedestrian footbridge). Further investigation was required of the limited housing opportunities within the recovery plan's core, and the viability of some of the office space and the proposals for the Arndale Tower. Concern was also expressed in terms of transport aspect of proposals that envisaged an increase in short-stay car-parking provision; environmental and congestion issues arising from possible bus routing activities; and the nature of the concept of the metro-shuttle within the city centre.

Winning design

The competition result, announced just 14 weeks after the issuance of the original brief, saw the retention of the EDAW team of consultants to develop their scheme as the basis of an urban masterplanning framework. The second placed team – Building Design Partnership (BDP) – were to be retained, however, as sub-consultants to refine, within the overall EDAW framework, their proposals for the River Irwell and the cathedral/Chetham's School area – later to become an element of the Millennium Quarter – in order to underpin the need for a strong environmental dimension. The key elements of the winning design were defined as respecting the visual structure of the city, featuring the main linkages and maintaining the importance of the key landmarks, and creating a new city-centre focus whilst reconnecting with established elements of the core. It linked key streets and squares along a clear pedestrian route and established proposals for an integrated transport system. It was perceived to best meet the objectives of the rebuilding programme in introducing new uses and enhanced quality, enabling investment to 'grow' the city centre rather than merely redistributing existing activity, and in exploiting opportunities presented whilst seeking to overcome historic weaknesses.

> EDAW went through a very thoughtful process about how to make a quality city. We want a much bigger and better city centre, but in order to get the landowners to do this we need to add value … fortunately, when it came to making the decision, their urban design vision and quality worked commercially as well.
>
> (MML officer)

> Basically BDP's river frontage, park and cross-river solutions were much more ambitious than the ones we'd got. So actually plugging these into the wider masterplan wasn't a challenge … it integrated well … assume that's why the jury and Task Force chose that solution. Here is a good set of interesting ideas that could very simply be applied to the core masterplan that we had put together.
>
> (Development professional)

The details and vision of this nascent masterplan were to receive a great deal of press coverage, ranging from a feeling that pragmatism had reigned supreme – 'City prefers commerce to vision' (*The Times* 6 November 1996) – to a more up-beat perspective – 'Give birth to a new centre on a tight budget and in the shortest possible time' (*Independent* 6 November 1996). Indeed, in many ways the EDAW submission was conservative and cautious, with some commentators arguing that many of the more imaginative, locally sensitive, and radical design elements were being ruled out in favour of deliverability and commercial viability (Malone 1997).

Our plan is a realistic commercial project which will provide things that people really need. In that sense it is very visionary, being deliverable and desirable.

(Averley 1997: 16)

The winning team was to be retained for a further couple of months to refine the putative urban design and masterplanning framework, liaising with the Task Force's retained advisers, and help to provide the basis on which landowners would proceed to define their specific development proposals. The work entailed a review and articulation of the winning scheme's focus through feedback from the various interested parties; refining the scheme in preparation for implementation (public/ private elements, phasing, design parameters, preliminary budget and schedule for implementation); and on the basis of identified development parcels to prepare site-specific design guidelines capable of acting as a brief for site owners and developers. Working with MML's retained advisers, and with close consultation with both land-owners and local authority officials, all this was felt necessary to underpin the produc-tion of an implementation plan that would facilitate delivery of the masterplan. The jury, however, identified a number of areas where further refining of ideas was neces-sary, in consultation with the Task Force's retained advisers:

- major redesign of the riverfront area and the greening of the cathedral/ Chetham's precinct;
- detailed urban design study of the sequence of pedestrian spaces with respect to their volume/scale/definition and the resolution of pedestrian/traffic issues;
- more articulation/recladding of the Arndale Centre's exterior above each of the façades, and of the scale of Market Street; and
- identification in the broader city-centre area of the location of a new bus terminating facility, and the undertaking of further work on the number and location of central-area parking spaces.

Whilst the framework was expected to continue to evolve as the recovery programme moved into its implementation phase, the final broad masterplanning framework was to be adopted by the Task Force, City Council and major landowners in December 1996 (Figure 5.1). This set out the basis for proceeding with reconstruction of the city centre, refining both the themes of EDAW's winning submission, and incorporating elements of BDP's work. The final focus of this work was to establish a masterplan framework within the wider context of city-centre regeneration; to create interesting and active civic spaces, parks and streets, complemented by an integrated central-area transport system; and to promote strong and diverse development parcels within the context of

5.1
**City-centre
renewal
masterplan**
Source: With
acknowledgements
to EDAW

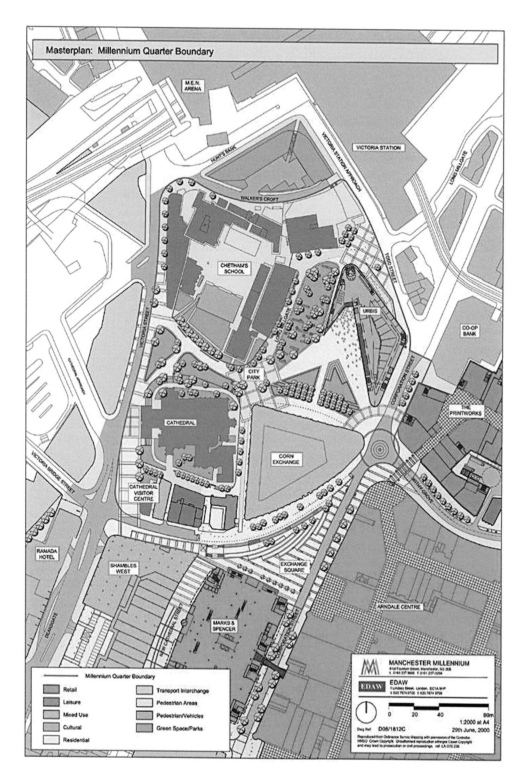

Masterplan: Millennium Quarter Boundary

appropriate development phasing. In terms of the context for reconstruction, the document notes that the bomb-damaged area is only a section of the city's core, and that additional strategies beyond those elaborated in the masterplan framework would help promote the revitalisation of the core as a whole (MML 1996c).

> These benefits will come forward from one of the most radical, innovative and challenging city centre renaissance programmes witnessed in this country for many years.
>
> (MML 1997: 2)

Establishing a framework for masterplan delivery

As the rebuilding was intended to consolidate, conform and build upon the existing policy framework, it is appropriate at this stage to consider the wider management context that was evolving to facilitate programme implementation. A number of key aspects will be considered at this stage, namely the production by MCC of specific development guidance for the bomb-damaged area, MML's preparation of a management framework for programme delivery, the landownership dimension, and preliminary skirmishes over the management of key interest concerns.

Supplementary planning guidance

Since the masterplan would need to be compatible with the city's UDP and its Development Guide, a planning framework was required to support and underpin the successful implementation of the preferred urban design framework. It was agreed that the development of such supplementary planning guidance (SPG) for the city centre would need urgent consideration in order to provide a strong basis to inform development control decisions and negotiations with landowners, and for the discharge of broader statutory functions. Prepared by the City Planning Department, and the subject of consultation with landowners and other interested parties, it was approved by the City Council in late 1996 (MCC 1996b). It set out a number of strategic aims for rebuilding, stressing the need for high-quality, imaginative development. It stressed the centrality of enhancing linkages between the rebuilt core, the rest of the regional centre, surrounding regeneration areas, and gateway locations. This included linkages between areas in terms of uses and overall movement patterns throughout the city centre, together with important urban design principles relating to visual elements within the centre.

The guidance then examines the framework emerging in the refined masterplan, dividing its constituency into five smaller development parcels, and providing guidance principles for new development that would form the basis for detailed planning considerations (Table 5.5).

Table 5.5 Supplementary planning guidance for the renewal area

---

- The *Shambles/Marks & Spencer* development parcel was seen to present a major opportunity to increase prime retail provision, and to expand existing high-quality sectors; provide a major new urban space and improve pedestrian routes through the area; and make a significant contribution to short-stay strategic car parking in the city centre.
- The *Arndale* development parcel focused on the Corporation/Cross Street frontage of the shopping centre, which had borne the full force of the blast and suffered substantial physical damage. The resulting physical upgrading/remodelling required would provide major improved shopping provision of high quality, enabling the Arndale Centre to be much more outward looking, making a greater contribution to on-street retail provision.
- The *Shudehill* development area had the potential to provide a regionally significant leisure complex, being a major visitor attraction in its own right, and to complement the surrounding commercial and residential facilities of the regional centre.
- The *Cultural and Historic Quarter* provided opportunities for the development of a large variety of facilities, and would reinforce positive visitor attractions linking cultural activities with the retail core. It offered significant opportunities to reintegrate the river with the city centre, and to vastly enhance the setting of the city's historic quarter.
- The *Ramada* development parcel presented an opportunity for significant physical restructuring work, offering the possibility of a significant new gateway to the city centre from the north, whilst at the same time exploiting its riverside location to maximum advantage.

As part of the rebuilding process a variety of new urban spaces were proposed which were intended to follow particular design principles in relation to the development of the public realm, and to influence its relationship with surrounding buildings. The active promotion of new uses within such urban spaces should be encouraged, together with pedestrian-dominated streets and squares, both seen as crucial for the vitality of the city centre. Whilst the guidance notes that development proposals emerging as part of the recovery programme would be subject to the usual statutory process – although 'fast tracked' to facilitate delivery – it specifically recognised that changing perceptions of development potential might arise as a direct consequence of masterplan implementation. In such cases, it was expected that proposals would generate a higher level of private sector contributions to public realm improvements and to supporting infrastructure.

Emerging programme management strategy

At this stage of masterplan evolution it became clear to both the Task Force and the other key stakeholders that a programme management strategy would be required to accommodate the amalgam of individual projects envisaged within the overall programme – reconstruction and refurbishment of damaged buildings, new developments, public realm and infrastructural investment. This would help ensure that the process could effectively deliver the integration and interfacing of individual landowner development plans; the development, management and coordination of the detailed design process; project and procurement management, particularly in relation to public realm improvements; and the facilitation of accounting for public funding so that outputs where appropriate were achieved and monitored. A secondee from the private sector (AMEC) was commissioned to create the momentum for establishing an overall management programme, to define proposals for the introduction of a project management system, and to provide recommendations on the administration and delivery of such a system (Table 5.6). This would be delivered through a Programme Manager appointment, to be largely funded by the major landowners.

Since the MML Task Force had no statutory basis, it could only achieve the objectives assigned to it through key interest cooperation. Whilst collaborative and constructive working relationships were patently manifest, it was clear that prior to the initiation of the reconstruction programme that such relationships needed to be placed on a firmer footing, and to be regularised. It was thus proposed that a

Table 5.6 Recovery strategy management responsibilities

Programme level	Task Force	Developers/landowners
Level 1 Master programme	• Establish and maintain master programme. • Develop urban design phasing strategy. • Review and incorporate building owner programmes. • Liaison/coordination with owners and local authority departments. • Monitor and report.	• Prepare/submit outline development programmes. • Identify key milestones (e.g. planning approvals). • Identify primary interfaces (e.g. service requirements).
Level 2 'Project' summary programmes	• Prepare outline infrastructure programmes. • Prepare, maintain, and communicate overall coordination programme. • Prepare and maintain infrastructure design, and procurement programme. • Prepare/communicate coordination milestones/key date schedule. • Monitor and report.	• Develop summary programmes for design procurement and construction. • Identify milestones/key dates for design and construction phases. • Identify all relevant interfaces.
Level 3 'Project' detailed programmes	• Prepare Task Force management programmes. • Review detailed programmes submitted by others. • Prepare detailed infrastructure programmes. • Monitor and report.	• Develop detailed working programmes for all project phases.

Memorandum of Understanding should be prepared, which whilst not legally binding would represent a basis for proceeding in good faith and place a general obligation on all parties. This would define the role and responsibilities of each of the parties and provide the basis for regulating relationships in the future, would become the framework for achieving collective action, and over time could be incorporated in the various legal agreements dealing with specific development proposals.

Such an agreement would effectively underpin the preferred urban design framework with an investment and commercial plan to secure delivery. A draft of this document indicated that the final implementation plan would include not only the agreed masterplan, but would incorporate a phasing and delivery plan, development guidelines and preferred design framework, and specific funding and procurement arrangements. This would require a common understanding of the roles and responsibilities of each of the main stakeholders, and the means by which matters of common concern could be discussed and resolved. However, whilst all parties recognised their long-term commitment to the city centre and the need for this to be reflected in their day-to-day dealings, the memorandum was never formally signed, since the main landowners felt that this would unnecessarily limit their commercial autonomy.

> Once the masterplan was signed off, I said it's going to be really interesting to see if we talk to one another again. And we didn't … we just bashed on with what we had to do individually … and now whenever I want to get any of them together, it's sort of like a shock to the system.
>
> (Development interest)

The land ownership dimension

One of the few beneficial consequences of the city centre's comprehensive redevelopment of the 1960s was the concentration of direct landholding in relatively few hands, with a degree of overlapping ownership, and a focus on major corporations possessing professional management. Whilst this didn't prevent conflict appearing over particular issues, it simplified the basis for consultation and negotiation, and greatly facilitated the coordination process at every stage. Five major landowners (the Prudential, P&O, Marks & Spencer, Frogmore Estates, the Co-operative Society) controlled all the buildings in the main bomb-damaged area (25 hectares), and the fact that the City Council retained most of the freehold within the area affected was a very useful lever in negotiations (Figure 5.2). In addition, the local authority was also the landowner in parts of the affected area, and had statutory responsibilities for the public realm. Finally, NCP owned leases on a surface and a multi-storey car park within the area. This was instrumental in progressing the masterplan process, and an early opportunity was taken by the Task Force to provide a forum for all the major landowners to meet and discuss the general future

1. Cathedral
2. Frogmore Estates
3. NCP
4. Chetham's
5. P&O
6. Prudential / P&O
7. CWS / CIS
8. Bass / Samuel Smiths
9. Chesterfield Properties
10. Marks & Spencer
11. Vector Investments
12. Railtrack
13. Lee Park Properties
14. Prudential
15. GMPTE

5.2
Land ownership in the renewal area

of the city's commercial core, as well as the potential of their individual holdings. All the landowners recognised the opportunity the regeneration presented, and a communality of interest developed between them. The imminent opening of the Trafford Centre, and the expected threat that it posed for city-centre competitiveness, served to concentrate minds. A central role of the Task Force was thus from the outset to work with the key landowners to ensure 'they individually and collectively took ownership of the regeneration plans'.

> The reason we could get landowners like P&O, M&S and the Pruden-
> tial together so quickly was because we had worked with them before.
> The mobilisation of the public and private sector looks very fast and
> impressive, but it's the result of many years of hard work.
>
> (MML Chief Executive)

P&O held the largest property interests, holding a long leasehold of the Arndale Centre and the Ramada block, and a significant leasehold interest in Shambles Square. There was considerable speculation, however, regarding its strategy for investment within the city, since a substantial company reorganisation in the mid-1990s had seen public pronouncements of its intention to dis-invest in property. The speed and extent of this future strategy was unclear, however, and it was difficult to establish whether P&O was a short- or long-term player, even though the Arndale Centre was its largest shopping centre nationally. There was concern that, if P&O intended to dispose of the Arndale Centre in the short to medium term, it might try to maximise its position with regard to insurance/reinstatement, and would not be prepared to invest in solutions which could add value to the centre in the longer term.

> Given P&O's spread of interests in the City, there had to be considerable potential to agree a 'package' of investments, using the City's interests in the Arndale bus station and Shambles Square to secure investment in making the Arndale more permeable.
>
> (MML officer)

The Prudential owned the Royal Exchange, and also held interests in both Shambles Square and the Arndale Centre. Whilst it only held a minority interest in the Arndale Centre, it was a key player in Shambles Square, holding an intermediate long-lease interest. Indeed, the ownership of Shambles Square was particularly complex, with the city as freeholder gaining 20 per cent of the rents received, the Prudential taking 67 per cent, and P&O receiving the top 13 per cent share of rents. After the bombing the Prudential was thus keen to promote a major new quality retail development on Shambles Square, both to improve its investment value and to 'add value' to the nearby Royal Exchange.

The other key player in the Shambles block was Marks & Spencer, which owned a strongly performing store that was topped by an office block (Michael House). Immediately following the bombing the company recognised the opportunity afforded to it by the devastation, and its requirement for a new store with a bridge link into the Arndale Centre was fixed, this being regardless of any future decision to take up space in the Trafford Centre. The rapid decision by the store's board to increase its commitment and investment in the city centre was to be critically important to the emerging renewal programme, as well as for the city centre as a whole. The city, as freeholder of the site, was in a position to facilitate this development, and temporary accommodation was secured for the company to continue trading in the short term within the central area. Adjacent to the Marks & Spencer building was Longridge House, an office block owned by the Royal Sun Alliance, which it had already declared surplus to its requirements prior to the bombing. The insurance company agreed in principle to sell the site to Marks & Spencer (subject to the insurance payment and agreement of a sensible price), giving the retailer an early opportunity to reconfigure the footprint of its development.

The full potential of property north of the Arndale and Shambles Square had never been realised prior to the bombing, due to the physical and psychological barrier created by the Arndale and Shambles developments. This included the listed Corn Exchange, the freehold of which was held by Frogmore Estates, and as it was a high-yielding property the company believed it would benefit from the city centre's expansion. Prior to the bombing it was occupied by a large number of small businesses, including secondary office and retail users, food and leisure facilities, and was a market for craft outlets. Occupational leases within the building all had provisions for the landlord to break, and the bombing was to provide Frogmore with the opportunity to secure vacant possession in order to change the use and the tenant profile of the building, and to tie the Corn Exchange back into the city centre, both physically and psychologically.

By far the most significant landowner in the northern part of the city centre was the Co-operative Society. For many decades, the Co-operative Wholesale Society (CWS), the Co-operative Insurance Society (CIS) and the Co-operative Retail Society (CRS) had occupied the Shudehill area of Manchester as their national headquarters. In 1991–92 CWS and the CIS along with Bishopsgate Properties had set up a joint venture – Shudehill Developments – to redevelop surplus land for a major 45,000-square-metre shopping centre. Planning consent was granted, and CWS/CIS bought out Bishopgate's interest. However, the advent of the Trafford Centre adversely affected the viability of the proposed retail scheme, and at the time of the bombing Shudehill Developments was keen to promote more mixed-use development of the site, driven by leisure but with some retailing and possibly housing.

The City Council had significant freehold interests within the commer-cial core of the city centre, and within the bomb-damaged area it owned the entire freehold of the Arndale Centre, the Ramada Hotel block and the Shambles Square block (with the exception of the two 'stranded' historic pubs). The City Council also owned the freehold of a number of smaller properties and land parcels including sections of the Corn Exchange, and property on parts of Fennel Street, Cateaton Street and Shudehill, together with a section of Long Millgate car park. It was thus in a strong position both as landowner and as freeholder to use its influence to focus and direct the emerging renewal programme.

Interest management and preliminary skirmishes

With the end of the competition, the rebuilding process faded from the public gaze, with the period marked by the difficult and unheralded process of charting the path from the vision to the launch of the implementation phase. The period – November 1996–April 1997 – was characterised by considerable uncertainty and difficulty, as the Task Force and City Council struggled to secure the neces-sary financial and technical support to prepare for the masterplan's implementa-tion involving, detailed bilateral negotiations. It was to be characterised by a change of mood, and by difficult and sensitive masterplan discussions as MML sought to put 'real numbers' against each party's commitments. These bilateral negotiations were at the heart of attempts to keep private sector interests on board during the apparent lull between the published masterplan and the initial implementation plan – 'major projects like these are like wars fought on many fronts in many theatres' (Berridge 1997).

> There's been a strong consensus to date, and now people are actually getting down to the hard realities of negotiating positions … . What was a joy of conception has become a tight game of inches, of positioning for advantage, all becoming very adult.
>
> (MML consultant)

For central government, with a general election only six months away, ministers and officials were mindful of their declared receptiveness to bids for public funding for the renewal programme, but were extremely cautious as to the local authority's capacity to make political capital out of the process (particularly when they had already sounded out the Labour opposition). It adopted a very considered approach with regard to evaluating the cost-effectiveness of public sector funding elements within the wider context of public expenditure arrangements. It also had to ensure that its relationship with GO NW was close and constructive in facilitating government commitment to the orientation of the development strategy.

With regard to the local authority, the new Council Leader's initial attempts to establish a more 'social' agenda for regeneration was challenged by the aftermath of the bomb, the concerns for the city's fragile economy, and the masterplan's 'funding gap'. This central–local tension became even more apparent after the Local Government Financial Settlement 1997/98 was announced, with the City Council threatened with a major shortfall in its resources. Lobbying of central government took the form of special pleading by the authority ('fair deal for the city' campaign), promoting the city as the site of dynamic partnership opportunities, and the centrality of local solidarity. In the end, the city won a concessionary increase in its resources that was more symbolic than financial, but did enable it to sustain and promote the wider entrepreneurial 'script'. At this stage it was also fighting a range of other battles of significance for the city's future – the development of the Stadium in East Manchester; the promotion of the delivery of a second runway at Manchester Airport; and the development of a strategic response to the threat posed by the Trafford Centre – and balancing such effort was particularly critical at this time.

In terms of the renewal programme, the challenges of established statutory procedures (planning/listed building consents) and powers (particularly compulsory purchase orders), and the Council's role as the accounting body for public funding support, was to prove critical. It was centrally involved at this stage in establishing the appropriate legal/financial and management arrangements within the authority in order to handle the demands of the recovery process, and to ensure that the necessary infrastructural improvements required for wider plan implementation could be put in place. Politically, it provided an opportunistic focus for continuing the Manchester script, and the entrepreneurial network of linkages developed within the city over the previous few years. This was, however, to create tensions in terms of the City Council's relationships with some interests within the core, best exemplified by the authority's handling of a particularly aggrieved group of a hundred small traders displaced from their tenancies in the Corn Exchange.

For the MML Task Force, it provided the context for ensuring that its management and delivery structures were in place, and that its working relationship with the major landowners and City Council was properly embedded. It had to demonstrate, from the experience of a fairly positive initial few months, that it had the capacity both to facilitate implementation, and to appropriately harness the necessary resources. Indeed, the small Task Force team and its retained professional advisers had to oversee the development of the overall design and procurement of public realm and infrastructure improvements. It was under pressure to demonstrate that it was in a position to commission and to administer a robust programme and project management system relating to the total rebuilding programme, and to have procedures and fora in place to resolve likely disputes between partners. Finally, it was required to develop jointly with the City Council an agreed approach to an ongoing media and promotion programme, and to be able to sustain the responsibility for promoting public information.

In relation to the private sector, whilst the substance of the plan was now fully engaged with landowner intentions and the constraint of available budgets, commercial realities raised a number of tensions. The difficulty lay in being able to demonstrate that the renewal programme was achievable, that they should take ownership of the concept, and that they would benefit individually as well as collectively. This was made more difficult by the expectation that they would contribute to the cost of the programme and project management system being established and administered by MML and, where justified, to the costs of public realm and infrastructural improvements beyond their own immediate development boundaries.

> There is a mutual dependency – P&O have to trust that M&S are going to do what they say they are going to do – and a mutual distrust – will either of them actually deliver? The City Council probably has the money in the form of public funding, whilst the owners have the time pressures to renew trading.
>
> (Berridge 1997)

It proved a difficult task to ensure that such interests were prepared to sustain and respect the integrity of the preferred urban design framework, and to begin the process of appointing their own design and development teams to initiate the process of designing/redesigning specific development parcels. A good example of such concerns was evident in the frustrations caused by P&O's approach to masterplan concerns. As owners of the Arndale Centre and the Ramada Hotel and joint owners (with Prudential) of the Shambles development parcel, they were a key to masterplan implementation. The Arndale Centre, whilst commercially very successful, was Manchester's least-loved city-centre building. P&O throughout the process of masterplan evolution had preached the gospel of commercial reality, and of their corporate responsibility to protect shareholder interests. However, having borne the brunt of the bomb it had a major redesign exercise to face – 'a hell of a lot of fixing for not much immediate return' – and it soon became apparent that questions were being raised as to their commitment to the vision, and their lack of imagination in relation to the necessary renewal and re-imaging. In short, what leverage and informal pressure could MML, MCC and other landowners exert – existence of Marks & Spencer stores in other P&O shopping centres, possible role of the city's CPO powers – that would significantly change their approach?

> M&S start from the position that they are going to build the finest, state of the art store ever in their company's history, to return in triumph to their Manchester home. P&O start from the position that the Arndale Centre is misunderstood and no earns respect for its ability to generate more cash per square metre than almost any other building nationally. After six months they have barely progressed beyond the most minor of changes. The only thing that they can all agree on is that it would be better to just put it back the way it was (re-instatement), take the insurance money and listen to the sound of cash registers.
>
> (Berridge 1997)

Similarly, Marks & Spencer were experiencing faltering sales figures and a drop in share value, their proposed building was anticipated to cost well over budget, and the imminent completion of the Trafford Centre began to raise questions as to their ability to complete the intended project, and to their additional contributions to land assembly and landscaping costs. This was potentially serious since the rebuilding strategy was formulated on the basis of commercially focusing on Marks & Spencer, both as the key anchor and as catalyst for other developers.

> How much is bluff? How far can we go to keep them happy? If M&S baulk at doing a full scheme then the whole master plan is in serious trouble. One of those gaping chasms of disaster opens up in front of us. Without M&S there is no chance of brow-beating P&O to do something even half decent … at which point there is no chance of attracting the investment we anticipate further north … at which point the master plan comes down to a few trees.
>
> (Berridge 1997)

> It was an amazing task to try and convince the landowners that there would be real value in demolishing their buildings … greatest difficulty was convincing P&O and Prudential … . where one party wouldn't do anything until someone else did it first.
>
> (Development professional)

In the event Marks & Spencer went ahead and completed their flagship scheme, a decision that was to prove the cornerstone of the whole recovery process. P&O sold the Ramada Hotel block to Marriott, who expressed a major intention to renew the building. With the Arndale Centre, P&O's retained architects finally abandoned 'hapless inaction' and begun to demonstrate how they intended to rebuild in a comprehensive manner. As it was subsequently to be realised, the company had decided to move out of shopping-centre development and management, and sold both the shopping centre and rebuilding designs for a reported £315 million to Prudential Assurance, a company that was already a major player in the masterplan area. Whilst such negotiations, together with Marks & Spencer discussions with Royal Sun Alliance, were kept out of the public gaze, the realignment of landholdings in the core of the renewal area was to significantly simplify the coordination of redevelopment.

From masterplan to implementation plan

It is finally appropriate to discuss the focus and orientation of the final masterplan and the initial implementation plan, with these two documents providing the framework for the subsequent five years of redevelopment activity. The competition winners were subsequently to lead a masterplanning team, with the refined conclusions of an intensive period of activity being completed by the unveiling of the final masterplan and model (10 February 1997) and the publishing of the initial implementation plan (17 April 1997).

'Framework for the future'

The masterplanning framework approved by the MML board and City Council in December 1996 focused on creating a '24-hour city centre' offering a diverse mix of retail, cultural entertainment, residential and commercial uses; central public spaces on both a grand and a human scale; pedestrian-dominant transport routes and nodes; and places, routes and views respecting the city's architectural heritage (Table 5.7). It spelt out the proposals for the various development parcels, the creation of a new chain of public open spaces that reflected public aspirations, and elaborated an approach for an integrated transport system. In terms of development parcels it set out to demonstrate how through refurbishment and

Table 5.7 The masterplanning vision

'This vision, shared in partnership with public, private, voluntary and community interests is based on the strong conviction that Manchester's long-term future lies in strengthening its role as the North West regional centre, and as a leading European city'.

'The city centre renewal programme has a much wider significance than the physical boundaries of the masterplan. The programme is linked inextricably with the city's regeneration strategy, and will kick start additional private investment on individual sites bordering the masterplan area, and at the interface with surrounding districts'.

Source: Adapted from MML 1997

development the retail core could be strengthened and expanded, the cultural diversity and entertainment facilities would be enhanced, and additional residential and commercial opportunities would be provided. In terms of civic spaces, the masterplan noted the city centre's deficiencies in this regard, and the strangulation of good-quality street environments by transport congestion. It argued that the city's investment in public realm projects would demonstrate a commitment to urban quality to compare favourably with other international cities, and that this should be at the heart of the renewal process. Finally it noted that, with regard to a transport strategy, the aim of the framework was to produce an integrated system 'to form a balanced, legible and sustainable network'.

During the refining process a whole host of different tasks were carried out which modified the format whilst holding on to the key criteria of the draft. This focused on building footprints and impacts on surrounding buildings and the public realm, and considered floorplates, heights and volumes of buildings and road widths – arriving at technical solutions that arose from a greater appreciation of detailed possibilities than could be accommodated at the competition stage.

> One of the ideas we had was to extend the Arndale out … giving it a new frontage so we could move from the above street trading floor down to street level … [the] idea was that we would just build new units all the way along … looking at the detail of the building we realised that you could do better than that, that you could actually peel off the front of the building and have the existing shops go through.
>
> (Development professional)

Value judgements had to be made about prioritising different tasks, with discussions setting out the principles, philosophy and the vision behind the task before being 'sucked into' the detail.

> Let's get the fundamentals right … let's not disappear into pavement details at this stage, or what the building is going to look like. It would

> be much more important to say … we want active frontages, we want
> doorways, … whether you build out of brick or stone can be left to a
> discussion a few months down the line.
>
> (Development professional)

As a result of this iterative process – 'involving considerable shuffling around the edges, but retaining the fundamental components of the winning design' (MML project director) – a number of key changes were to emerge.

- Two historic public houses were relocated and realigned from Shambles West to a site near the cathedral.
- The detailed execution of the landmark cultural building (Urbis) changed substantially as a result of a commitment to hold a design competition.
- Whilst the fundamental concepts of the original plan stayed in place with regard to the Arndale Centre (active street frontage, Wintergarden, improving functionality), the detail of how these elements were actually going to be achieved was significantly developed.
- The major expansion of the leisure scheme at Shudehill substantially displaced the housing component and the existing proposals for the transport interchange.
- The location and form of the Cathedral Visitor Centre changed substantially as a result of the process of design and consultation.
- The importance of the new public square (Exchange Square) increased as a result of discussions relating to the 'stitching up' of the surrounding area, and the attempt to create a more dramatic solution.

Thus, by spring 1997 the final masterplan was in place, and the apparently quiescent rebuilding process suddenly reasserted its dominance over city politics and the media. The decisive moment came with the announcement that the government's contribution to the rebuilding programme (in addition to the initial 'top slicing' of EU structural funds) would be a 'Manchester Special Grant' of £43 million (with the city having previously had a 'separate line' on the DETR's annual budgetary tables in connection with Olympic bid preparations), reflecting the fact that the city had chosen a plan that would be deliverable and affordable. As a consequence the rebuilding programme would be driven by a holistic strategy rather than simply being project driven, although the commercial and temporal pressures to focus on specific projects had been intense over the previous six months.

> I think they did a good job. I think we got a cohesive plan together that
> made sense, that utilised what we'd got and added value, but didn't
> go into massive redevelopment for the sake of it.
>
> (Development professional)

I think the streetscape that they've tried to get and will achieve is very good ... they've actually done a bit of town planning which I think is great ... linking the north part of the city with the south to make it more seamless ... . with the projects very much the product of the masterplan.

(Development interest)

The quality of the masterplan, the fact that it combined excitement and interest with deliverability made it unique.

(MML officer)

The first implementation plan

This delivery document drew together the various strategies and programmes for the renewal programme, provided the framework within which individual initiatives would be brought forward and phased, and provided the basis upon which performance 'on the ground' could be monitored (MML 1997). It was to provide a clear statement of the strategic goals and objectives of the renewal programme, the Task Force and its partners, and a statement of priorities governing rebuilding. It set out a robust framework to give funding partners confidence in the overall programme, and to provide a context within which individual initiatives could be progressed and funding applications be presented. Finally, it provided a formal basis against which the Task Force and its partners, and the overall success of the renewal programme, could be monitored and performance judged. The deliverability of such objectives was undoubtedly strengthened by the local authority's commitment from the outset to positively utilise its landholdings as a bargaining chip to facilitate development, and through collaboration with others to deliver key aspects of the plan.

As initially conceived, the objective was to have much of the core area rebuilt by the end of 1999, so as to ensure the rapid reinvigoration of the city centre, and to combat the challenge of the Trafford Centre. It set out the strategic vision for reconstruction and gave details on the specific costs and programmed responsibility for implementing individual components. Estimates of private and public investment were provided, along with the sources of such funding, with the projected outputs and benefits of the reconstruction programme being described in detail. In funding terms the clear aim was to optimise the benefits and minimise the costs to the public sector, with public resources intended to help fund infrastructural and public realm improvements linking commercial development parcels. It was made clear, however, that public funds would not be used to improve the profitability of established commercial activities by merely moving development around, but were expected to enhance the city centre's image, appearance and competitiveness. Finally, as part of the forward strategy, a number of key priorities and associated work programmes were put forward for further reports to both the Task Force and the City Council. The implementation

Table 5.8 City-centre renewal: strategic objectives

Strategic objectives	Goals	Projects
Restoration and enhancement of retail core	Reinforce the city centre as a retail heart of the region by timely restoration of retail floor space, and creation of a wider range of shopping opportunities.	Redevelopment of Shambles Square for a quality retail scheme, anchored by Marks & Spencer; and the remodelling and reconfiguration of the Arndale Centre.
Stimulation and diversification of the city's economic base	Secure investment and development of leisure and cultural activities to broaden the interest and attraction of the centre. Seek to maximise the impact of the rebuilding plans to underpin the economic vitality of the regional capital.	The Corn Exchange; the Royal Exchange; the Printworks; and the Ramada.
Development of an integrated transport strategy	Economic accessibility by all modes and users. Remove through traffic from the city centre by the completion of the Inner Relief Road. Provide sufficient, quality short-stay parking which is well signed. Encourage greater use of public transport, and provide a safe and pleasant environment for pedestrians and cyclists.	Inner Relief Road; IRR signing and signalling; Bus Quality Partnership, transport interchange, super bus stops and bus priority, Metroshuttle; Metrolink strategy; traffic and pedestrian Management; access arrangements during construction.
Creation of a quality city core fit for the twenty-first century	Overall 'greening' and enhancement of the quality of the public realm. A series of new public squares, improved streetscape and major open spaces so as to give confidence to private investors and occupiers, enhance the quality of life and create an urban environment attractive to all. Enhance the setting of the architecture and historic urban fabric, and promote greater accessibility for all users.	New Cathedral Street; City Park; Exchange Square; public art; Integrated city centre management and security strategy.
Creation of a living city by increasing residential population	Renewal programme seeks to build upon inherent strengths of the city centre as an attractive place to live, by creating opportunities within the core for potential housing investment; improving the quality of infrastructure and the public realm, and reinforcing strategic links with other parts of the city centre to promote such investment.	Possible developments at Shambles West, Shudehil, and Corn Exchange, and on the fringes of the bomb-damaged areas.
Creation of a distinctive Millennium Quarter	The creation of an integrated package of initiatives based on the city's historic core. The strategy aims to create a distinctive flagship visitor centre sitting within a new green precinct in a largely traffic-free area, linked to the commercial heart by an innovative new civic space.	Urbis Centre; Cathedral Visitor Centre; City Park; Exchange Square (also to involve the relocation of the historic Shambles pub into cathedral conservation area).

Strategic objectives	Goals	Projects
Coordination, delivery and promotion of the rebuilding programme	The effective coordination and strategic management of the planning, design, procurement, construction and cost-control elements of rebuilding; effective public consultation, information and promotional programmes to maintain confidence and vitality in the city centre, and to encourage inward investment.	Programme management teams (design coordination, procurement, and implementation; cost management, construction, and health and safety advice), masterplanning management teams (EDAW, Oscar Faber, Joe Berridge); consultation and marketing (focus groups, presentations, newsletters, market appraisals).

plan was clear that it not only described the intended course of action for realisation of the new city centre, but also acknowledged likely risks and uncertainties – market conditions, competition, funding, timing – inherent in such an integrated, complex and urgent regeneration process.

Lacking a specific statutory remit, the Task Force's focus at this stage was to establish a clear statement of the strategic goals and objectives of the programme, and to state the priorities and management mechanisms relating to the delivery of renewal and redevelopment (Table 5.8). The published masterplan was translated into a series of 'development districts', with a combination of new build, renovation, public realm improvements and transport initiatives – Shambles Square, Exchange Square, Millennium Quarter, Shudehill, Arndale Centre, Ramada block. Whilst proposals for such development areas were area specific, linkages with the surrounding retail and financial core and the city's major regeneration initiatives were perceived as being very important. Indeed, it was argued that the central area's redevelopment must interact with these other areas in terms of uses and movement in order to enhance the whole quality of the city centre. The plan then went on to elucidate the main development and commercial strategy, a delivery framework for the public realm, and the focus of the transport strategy, all of which are evaluated in the next part of the study (chapters 7–10). In terms of the masterplan's implementation, however, it noted that four delivery mechanisms were available:

1 the local authority's statutory planning controls, and its agreed policy framework and instruments relating to development within the core;

2 design guides adopted and managed by the Task Force, which would take the form of individual design briefs prepared for development sites, public realm and infrastructural projects. For privately led projects these briefs would provide the level of detail necessary for owners and their architects to proceed to final design as quickly and securely as possible. For publicly initiated projects they would establish a discipline of budget and schedule necessary to ensure quality standards;

3   procurement strategies adopted and managed by the Task Force, which would focus on procurement method for the final design of public realm projects, undertaken on the basis of negotiation with the Task Force and its advisers, through design competitions or through a competitive tendering process;

4   the continuation of consultation and collaboration with the key stakeholders, being concerned with issues raised by the masterplan and augmented by the retention of additional specialist advisers where required (such as a historic building and archaeology adviser). In relation to public consultation, following the instruments used to facilitate public comment on the initial competition, MML committed itself to a quarterly publication – *Millennium News* – this being complemented by the production of a public information pack. In addition, the media and public relations strategy for the rebuilding programme was intended to dovetail with the Task Force and City Council's wider marketing activities.

The implementation plan proceeded to discuss the overall funding strategy for the recovery programme, focusing on the encouragement of private investment and the justification for public expenditure. Whilst four-fifths of the total cost of delivering the rebuilding programme was expected to be financed by the private sector, public funding was expected to play a mutually supportive and interlinked role. Even at this stage tentative output measures were presented, dealing both with the masterplan's physical delivery, and with wider socio-economic and environmental benefits. Finally, in discussing the management of the implementation framework, the document reiterated the Task Force's overall terms of reference, whilst noting that it would realign its structure to ensure that it could robustly manage implementation. The forward strategy of the Task Force, concerned with the effective delivery of a major investment programme, would thus be undertaken in close consultation and collaboration with landowners, the City Council and central government.

In June 1997, the first anniversary of the bombing was to be marked by a raft of media reflection and boosterism – 'fight back for the rebirth of the city' – providing evidence of the rapid progress being made in beginning to deliver the renewal programme. Translating the original masterplan into an implementation mode had proved the necessity of an overarching commitment to keep private sector stakeholders on board, whilst at the same time involving close collaborative working with other agencies. Indeed, the successful delivery of the masterplan was to be critically dependent on the effective coordination and strategic management of both the overall programmes and an extensive list of projects, putting to the test local partnership and networking arrangements.

Part 3

Delivering the vision

The last section considered the development of a local capacity for policy innovation in responding to the bomb's impact, and in developing an appropriate strategic vision for renewal. It is appropriate at this stage to look specifically at the process of managing programme delivery, and to reflect on the wider impact of the renewal programme on the city centre as a whole. This section consists of five chapters, the first of which is concerned with the overall approach to programme management, with the remainder looking in turn at the delivery of the masterplan's commercial framework, the centrality of improving the quality of the core's built environment, the cultural vitality and lifestyle aspects of the emerging city centre, and the effects of the programme's transport strategy in improving local access and mobility. All these chapters are underpinned by a discussion of project profiles lying at the heart of programme realisation.

The focus on programme management arrangements and procedures initially considers the nature of agency and inter-agency working in relation to those bodies mandated to deliver the renewal programme, and the associational networks of key interests affecting developer and investor involvement. It then proceeds to look in detail at the process of managing programme and project delivery, focusing in turn on masterplan refinement, the centrality of design quality, funding and procurement management, and of overall construction management. Finally, it considers the Task Force's exit strategy and the management of outstanding responsibilities following its demise.

The focus of the renewal programme was to enhance the city centre's commercial competitiveness, and the study proceeds to consider the core's development context and the masterplan's commercial strategy. Reviewing in turn the commitment to restore and enhance the retail core, and the stimulation and diversification of the city's economic base, the chapter considers both the stimuli and the constraints that have influenced the delivery of enhanced competitiveness. Finally it considers the project dimension of the main commercial elements of the programme, and their impact on the wider city centre.

The next chapter is concerned with the commitment to enhance the core's built form and aesthetic qualities as a fundamental attribute of the renewal programme, and the balance between this and the pressures of commercial realism. This is highlighted with reference to the regulating and management of public realm developments, and the extent of such influence in reconfiguring private sector proposals. Finally, it considers the impact of this commitment to a design-driven agenda both, for the renewal programme as a whole and for the wider city centre.

The following chapter considers the strategy's focus on cultural and lifestyle components of the city centre, and the role of the core in satisfying urban consumption needs. The chapter looks in detail at the emergence of a new cultural quarter within the central area, tying in the historic core with the modern city, and the explosive growth of city-centre residential pressures and leisure-related facilities. Finally, consideration of a number of key projects aims to reflect on the wider impact of the renewal programme on the city centre as a whole.

The final chapter in this section considers the programme's contribution to enhancing city-centre access and mobility. An initial concern with established transport policy objectives is followed by a review of the masterplan's transport strategy, considering the extent to which the programme has facilitated and enhanced such objectives. Following a discussion of the particular difficulties associated with project realisation in this field, the chapter concludes with reflections on the consequences of delivering all the transport elements for enhancing the city centre as a whole.

Chapter 6

Managing programme delivery

Within the context of the city's promotion of entrepreneurial partnerships the present chapter reviews the establishment of an institutional framework for delivering the renewal programme, building on the existing experience of collaboration with private sector interests, and focusing on the key delivery agencies. It assesses the approaches undertaken to manage programme and project delivery and the programming of renewal capacity; the realities of masterplan and construction management activities; funding, procurement and performance management concerns; and issues of safety and the management of risk. Finally, it briefly discusses the issues involved in implementing a forward strategy, and the Task Force's exit strategy following the completion of its remit.

Agency structures and operation

The key agencies involved in delivering the renewal programme within the city centre were the Task Force (MML) and its retained advisers, and Manchester City Council as the accountable body responsible for ensuring probity and political legitimacy. The Task Force's retained advisers – particularly MACE (its programme managers) and EDAW (responsible for masterplan management), and a number of other specialist advisers – were central to the implementation process. This was reinforced by the Government Office for the North West (GO NW), whose role was to ensure that central government's commitments and expectations were addressed. There were inevitably limitations as to what could be achieved by these agencies, however, without the full endorsement and involvement of the main private sector interests, and it was the management of relationships with

business, developers and investors that were to prove critical for the success of the recovery programme.

Manchester's commercial core 2000 – midway through renewal

Manchester Millennium Ltd (MML)

Carrying out comprehensive redevelopment at the heart of a functioning city centre within such a tight timescale was quickly seen to be beyond normal local authority's capacities, and the City Council was mindful from the outset of the government's conviction that 'the way forward in turning a disaster into an opportunity ... is some form of joint public–private sector arrangement' (Department of the Environment civil servant). It was agreed that a specialist Task Force should be set up to focus on the renewal programme, and with verbal guarantees of political and financial support from central government a public–private company limited by guarantee was to become operational within the first month. Initial doubts amongst those already involved in city-centre issues of the need for such a body were to disappear following the growing realisation of the size of the task and the imperative for a dedicated team. Such a body was ultimately seen as flexible, politically neutral and at 'arm's length' from the local authority, helpful in giving the renewal programme initial credibility with both landowners and investors.

The Task Force's initial mission was to promote the rehabilitation of the city centre so as to ensure the speediest possible reduction in the scale of the exclusion zone; to relocate the many businesses which had been displaced; and to bring forward a strategy for rebuilding the core. Its organisational structure and operational focus was to evolve, however, as it became more centrally involved with masterplan implementation, overseeing the delivery of the programme, and with securing the necessary resources (Table 6.1). The Task Force was to conclude its remit in April 2000, by which time the core of the rebuilding programme had been completed, with the delivery of the remaining elements being transferred to be overseen by the City Council's Special Projects Team.

Manchester Millennium Ltd (MML) comprised a board and an executive team, and was committed from the outset to provide a 'lean and mean' organisation, encompassing both public and private sector interests. Lacking any statutory basis and beginning life without dedicated resources, it was important to establish its credibility at the outset, and its board was carefully constituted to balance public and private sector interests, even if this was not fully appreciated by all the key actors.

> ... you may say that your actual property owners group, with vested interests, shouldn't vote themselves large sums of money. But somewhere down the line you had to get commercial realism.
>
> (Senior businessman)

For the first six months the board met weekly and thereafter monthly, with the activities of the Task Force being reported directly to the local authority through its city-centre sub-committee. Its executive team was responsible to the board for managing and coordinating the implementation of the rebuilding programme, and in championing the successful delivery of the masterplan. Led by a Chief Executive, the small core team of officials provided a range of skills relating to programme and project coordination, commercial and financial management, and funding procurement. The Task Force's Chief Executive (seconded from the local authority) was to provide the key link and liaison with the City Council and central government, and with private sector interests associated with the recovery programme. The Project Director was given overall responsibility for the development and implementation of all projects in

Table 6.1 Task Force responsibilities

- To coordinate the preparation of a recovery programme, to keep that programme under review, and oversee its effective delivery for report to the City Council and the government.
- To assume particular responsibility for the creation of a regeneration framework for the core area of the city centre, including the definition of an agreed masterplan and the procurement of development in partnership with landowners and the City Council.
- To secure the resources from the public and private sectors to ensure the implementation of the recovery programme.
- To account to the City Council and to the government for public sector resources to support the implementation of the recovery programme.

---

the implementation plan; responsibility that the programme as a whole delivered the strategic objectives and target outputs; that the programme spent to budget and timetable; and that projects would be implemented in accordance with funding guidelines and City Council regulations.

The Task Force was itself restructured to accommodate additional roles as the pace of implementation increased, and it thus sought additional management capacity, particularly in relation to infrastructural and public realm elements, and for specialist technical advice. The core team largely comprised secondees from the City Council and the private sector, all selected for their depth of experience and core skills, and the breadth of their established contact networks – 'we knew how each other worked and what each could contribute' (MML officer). This ensured an understanding of the perspective of landowners and business, and of governmental decision-making processes. This core team was supported by retained advisers on aspects associated with masterplanning, design and transportation planning, construction management and cost control (Figure 6.1).

You have to recognise and understand the decision-making processes within private-sector organisations … to get each of these organisations on board. This would have been missing in a City Council team.

(MML Chief Executive)

6.1
Task Force delivery structure
Source: MML Task Force 1998, 74.

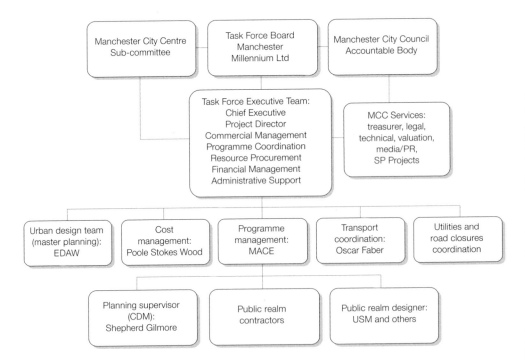

> Without people from the City Council, the Task Force would still be fumbling around … they helped break down the amorphous mass of the town hall, understood where power lay, and could deliver what the Task Force wanted.
>
> (MML Project Director)

The Task Force had no statutory powers in its own right, and whilst such powers would have given the body some armoury in its discussions with investors, the bureaucracy associated with the exercise of such responsibilities was seen as unhelpful to the task in hand. This reinforced and reflected the City Council's prevailing culture as a facilitator of appropriate development, whilst retaining a considerable degree of influence over the renewal process. Indeed, the Task Force was seen as a non-partisan arbiter and broker – 'pushing through, managing and lubricating the wheels to get it all to happen'. Thus, for instance, at an early stage it played a central role in bringing together insurance companies, reinsurers and loss adjusters to explain the regeneration strategy, and facilitated a 'community of interest' amongst key stakeholders, aiming to reduce the scope for future conflict. Indeed, it was to prove easier for the Task Force to develop the necessary external networks, particularly where those relationships with the City Council had historically been poor. It facilitated and integrated focused action, was less likely to be distracted from its task, with its limited operational life serving to focus minds and to sustain momentum.

> You basically have a team that can deliver anything, or at least know who to talk to. The single-minded drive and all the contacts are critically important.
>
> (Masterplan team leader)

During its first year, however, there was some criticism about both the paucity of detailed information available relating to the competition brief, Task Force activities following initial masterplan consultation, and the lack of real external involvement in progressing the final vision. This situation was undoubtedly influenced by the size and complexity of the task in hand, the limited size of the core team, and the pressurised timescale anticipated for regeneration. The attention of the Task Force was inevitably to be focused on private sector projects that levered in the greatest benefits, and the delivery of an imaginative public realm strategy, and both these foci were to be successfully delivered. The least successful component of its work was ultimately perceived to be associated with delivering the transport components of the plan, a complex strategy that was never intended to be fully delivered within the Task Force's timescale.

> You get to one of the most critical issues of all – transport – and they just sidestepped it. It's not a sexy issue, and it's not what they were interested in.
>
> (Senior businessman)

The Task Force's retained advisers

The logistical management of the implementation process was undertaken by a specialist programme management team – MACE – appointed following a competitive tendering process in spring 1997. Working directly to the Task Force's Project Manager, they were expected to develop a detailed management framework for programme and project implementation in liaison with Task Force personnel, the masterplanning team and other retained advisers. As programme managers they were expected to ensure the effective coordination and technical interface of the numerous public and private sector projects within the renewal area, involving direct coordination of public realm works and influence over private development and redevelopment activities. They acted as project managers for a range of discrete public sector projects and public realm works, managing the design coordination, procurement and implementation of such schemes. With private sector activity, this influence extended to detailed liaison with private developers over their proposals, managing interface and coordination issues, and attempting to ensure the integration of private sector projects into the wider rebuilding scheme. Whilst they had no jurisdiction within the hoardings of individual private sector projects (each retaining their own contractors and project managers), they did attempt to develop a culture whereby every interest looked upon the rebuilding process in overall terms.

> ... ensuring individual developers and their contractors became stake-holders, partners in the entire city-centre renewal process ... and generating a level of unselfishness.
>
> (MACE Programme Manager)

MACE was to deal with project management aspects of utility diversions and road closures, and assisted the private sector in putting together the necessary applications and statutory notices relating to individual development projects. Utility diversions had in particular to be coordinated since they often ran through private sector development sites and reappeared at the heart of public realm works. They also exceptionally carried out enabling works for private sector development in a fee-earning capacity. The resulting programme and project management function was to accommodate nearly 50 individual development and redevelopment initiatives, the vast majority of which had been completed by the termination of the Task Force remit and of MACE's contract (Table 6.2).

A close symbiotic relationship was established with the Task Force's other retained consultants, who developed a new range of tasks and responsibilities as the masterplan moved into its implementation phase. The key consultants at this stage were EDAW, who, following their success in winning the design competition and in working up a draft masterplan, were retained by the Task Force to ensure its delivery. EDAW's role at this stage was to safeguard the integrity of the original vision,

Table 6.2 City-centre renewal: project inventory

Development projects
- Marks & Spencer
- Shambles West
- New Cathedral Street (Podium)
- Arndale Centre
- Corn Exchange
- The Royal Exchange
- The Printworks
- Urbis
- Ramada Block
- Ramada Hotel
- Shambles Pubs
- High Street Car Park
- Cathedral Visitor Centre
- Corporation Street Bridge Link

Transport projects
- Market Street Metrolink Station
- Shudehill Metrolink Station
- IRR (Regent Road to Chester Road Stage 2)
- IRR (Addington Street Gyratory)
- IRR (Missing Link) – feasibility study
- Variable message and static signage on the city centre
- Transport interchange
- Bus priority measures
- Bus terminal facilities
- Bus super stop
- Traffic management measures in the city centre
- Highway improvements in the city centre
- Pedestrian/cycle routes and signage

Infrastructure
- CCTV/security measures
- Information/signage

Millennium Quarter
- Exchange Square
- City Park
- Fennel Street
- Long Millgate
- Cathedral Gates
- Cathedral Yard
- Cathedral Street
- Walkers Croft
- Corporation Street (North)

Public realm projects
- New Cathedral Street
- Corporation Street
- Corporation Street/Withy Grove
- Corporation Street/Cross Street
- St Mary's Gate
- Shudehill
- Deansgate
- Cateaton Street
- Market Street

Public art projects
- Millennium Quarter
- Outside Millennium Quarter

Source: MML 1999

and to ensure that the masterplan's strategic objectives were not diluted. Evolution of the masterplan during the implementation stage – when proposals for individual sites were developed in greater detail – was guided by a series of objectives, which the EDAW team used to inform the renewal programme. These objectives aimed to develop the masterplan in a way that reflected the aspirations and policies of both MML and MCC; to ensure that the masterplan's design parameters were safeguarded whilst at the same time being commercially viable; and to provide the appropriate level of design guidance and information to ensure that both public and private sector interests could make informed decisions as to their contribution. In terms of private sector projects EDAW were in a position to provide guidance and coordination advice relating to masterplanning and detailed design issues, whilst in relation to public realm projects this involved briefing teams carrying out detailed design work.

A range of other consultants were retained by the Task Force to ensure the delivery of the recovery programme to time, cost and quality. The original masterplanning and competition adviser (Joe Berridge) was retained for a further period to provide an independent review of the overall masterplanning process, to ensure the maintenance of quality controls, and to review the urban design strategy as the rebuilding programme evolved. In addition, in the design field Urban Solutions Manchester (USM) – a partnership between the local authority engineer's department and a local architect – were retained as a result of competitive tendering, to act as public realm designers on the various publicly funded projects. Oscar Faber were similarly retained beyond the original masterplanning phase to provide transport planning and engineering services advice. Their role was to develop and coordinate the overall transport strategy, and to consider how specific transport projects impacted on public and private sector development activities. Similarly, the Poole Stokes Wood consultancy was retained to provide cost management services, controlling and monitoring project costs over the life of the rebuilding programme, and providing value-for-money calculations. Finally, Shepherd Gilmour were retained to provide a construction planning supervisory role; the coordination of all health and safety aspects and the minimisation of risk.

Manchester City Council and other government interests

The local authority quickly saw the opportunity offered by the recovery process to improve its relationship with central government and to further its entrepreneurial strategy – 'they took a strong lead and people looked to them for guidance' (Development interest) – in ensuring its pivotal position in the rebuilding process. The institutional space created by MML's creation allowed the local authority to appear as an enabler within the local partnership process, managing the wider vision whilst delivering specific benefits to the landowners in terms of their 'enlightened self-interest', and as a statutory body 'fighting' for Manchester's share of public resources.

> … the way the council decided to share power with other structures to deliver change on the ground ensures that the City Council probably represents the most sophisticated structure of government to be found anywhere in the country.
>
> (MML senior officer)

Indeed, in the period between the announcement of the winning design and the launch of the implementation phase it is clear that MML afforded the City Council a considerable degree of influence over the whole process of 'tooling up' for recovery, this coming at a time when a host of other pressures were also present – procuring the resources for the Manchester Stadium, implementing the procedures relating to the development of the airport's second runway, and the construction of the Trafford Centre. This period was also to see the emergence of contradictory tensions inherent in attempting to balance the continuing entrepreneurial city image, whilst being able to demonstrate an increasing concern with the social inclusion agenda of the incoming government. All these concerns were undoubtedly to influence the relationship between the City Council and the Task Force in working up the delivery framework.

The local authority was the accountable body for all public resources approved for the city centre rebuilding programme, and the Council was the applicant for the public resources expended by the Task Force. The management of these resources was handled through the City Council's main financial accounting system so as to ensure financial probity, and the fact that the authority was able to do this reflected positively on its established record of delivering complex regeneration projects. MML's Chief Executive was the designated accounting officer for all such expenditure, and he reported directly to its board, and thereafter to the City Council's city-centre sub-committee.

In addition, having the direct support of the Chief Executive and finance departments, the Task Force worked closely with a range of other Council personnel – planning and transport programmes, legal and valuation services, the media and public relations. Whilst the local authority retained the planning function for the renewal area, the process was streamlined by the 'fast tracking' of planning applications by dedicated authority officers funded from the Task Force budget. In addition, the authority was responsible for the delivery of a number of the highway projects associated with the city centre's transport strategy, which were at the heart of the renewal masterplan. Finally, the Council's Special Projects Team was given responsibility for delivering elements of the Millennium Quarter, a coordinated range of projects programmed to be implemented after the ending of the Task Force's remit.

The return of a Labour administration in May 1997 saw a period of uncertainty in the local authority's interface with government (and indirectly with the Task Force). Its instinctive political individualism and commitment to the entrepreneurial city project could arguably be said to fit less well with the government's 'modernising' drive in relation to the delivery of public services, and to its central concern with social inclusion. As a result, the relationship between the City Council's political leadership and the Task Force approach to recovery was to be acutely sensitised, with consequences for the delivery of the programme.

In delivering the recovery programme a host of other 'interests' were directly involved, the most central being GO NW. As sponsors of the programme they were at the heart of funding and procurement issues relating to discussions with central government, English Partnerships, the Millennium Commission and the European Commission. They were additionally the focus of an annual reporting system relating to Task Force activities and progress. English Partnership's primary contribution was to aid site assembly and demolition work in relation to the

Shambles block, particularly through 'gap funding' where otherwise there would be financial deficits, whilst the Millennium Commission's role was in connection with the funding of the Millennium Quarter. The 'top slicing' of EU structural funds was central to the realisation of the major infrastructural projects, and was to be particularly important at the early stages of the renewal programme. Finally, at the local authority level, Salford was to be consulted on the competition shortlisted schemes, to contribute to the development of the regional centre concept, and to be represented on various Task Force working parties.

Inter-agency working

Given the Task Force's lack of statutory powers, concerns over transparent governance in the delivery of the renewal programme related primarily to issues of legitimacy and accountability. The decision was made at the outset to locate it physically separate and distinct from the City Council, with office space being retained in the city's financial quarter, accommodating both the Task Force and its retained consultants. This 'separateness' and reliance on external consultants caused some initial resentment within the City Council, fuelled by the feeling that the Task Force was perceived to be driving management issues for the city centre as a whole. This was a difficult balancing act to achieve, given that whilst its remit was to focus on the bomb-damaged area, the overall objective of the renewal programme had to be concerned with regeneration of the commercial core as a whole. There was some feeling that local authority departments were marginalised, particularly when the private sector bypassed them, going straight to the Task Force on city-centre issues. Preserving inter-organisational relationships at both officer and political levels was thus a delicate task, and strong working relationships between key people were to emerge. These individual relationships, the role of senior politicians on the board, and the reporting mechanisms to the City Council, all helped to ensure, however, that the Task Force role was rarely controversial. A reasonable balance was maintained, although there was sometimes a lack of clarity as to who had the ultimate say on issues (particularly affecting the public realm). Furthermore, as a key landowner in the renewal area, the City Council through its representation on the board, could have pushed its own interests, thereby facilitating a potential conflict of interest. That it did not do so was a comment on its commitment to the wider agenda, and to bringing about positive change.

> The Council has a seat at the table as a major landowner and this is a key bargaining chip in developing the masterplan … the Council uses this creatively … not attempting to extract maximum value, but to lever in maximum private sector investment.
>
> (MML Project Director)

In its relationships with central government there was always the potential for tension given that GO NW carried out a dual role. As well as being Task Force partners, they were also overseers of the probity and value-for-money aspects of programme delivery. Whilst never resulting in direct conflict, tensions were to be raised at the stage of determining CPOs, funding and procurement issues, and the procedures involved in the annual reporting mechanism.

There were also tensions at times between different emphases in private and public sector agendas. The tenacity of some interests in disputes over relatively minor issues caused problems and delays, with the Task Force 'brokering endless arguments' over specific commercial interests. These have to be seen, however, within the context of the overall level of agreement between the agencies involved, and the remarkable rate of progress made, despite differing organisational cultures and decision-making structures. The degree of consensus reflected not only the gains which organisations would make as a result of the implementation of the masterplan, but also a sense that what was proposed was of greater significance for the city than any one organisation's interests. There was evidence, therefore, of a degree of compromise by interests that might otherwise have sought more favourable positions.

> Everyone is very sensitive about public relations and the emotion underpinning this, and the commitment and determination to deliver. None of the agencies involved is going to want to be seen to be putting the spanner in the works.
>
> (Senior businessman)

Throughout the formulation and delivery of the renewal strategy, the relationship between the Task Force and key landowners and investors was a significantly iterative and collaborative process, whilst for the city's residents and main users, the process was informed through an existing body of consultation on the strategic direction of the city centre, supplemented by opinion polls, exhibitions, and liaison with focus groups. This was really the consequence of the necessary speed and scale of operation, and the need to cultivate private sector aspirations in order to sustain the momentum of recovery. The engagement of parties whose ownership of land or resources could either prevent or promote the furtherance of the public agenda was to involve detailed negotiations relating to precise site considerations, and was to lie at the heart of programme delivery.

Managing programme delivery

Programme management relates to the coordinated management of a portfolio of projects, in order to achieve a set objective, filling the gap between the broad focus of strategies and the intense detail of projects. The main justification for adopting a programme management approach is that the delivery of planned change is implemented in a more integrated way; it provides an effective response to disparate initiatives, and improves resource management and project integration. Finally, it facilitates the improved control of the delivery framework to ensure quality, and the better management of risk and project priorities (Lichfield 2000; Audit Commission 1997; Reiss 1996a).

Interest in this field has grown sharply in recent years due to rapidly changing regulatory environments, the increasing importance of performance scrutinies and value-for-money studies, and the market testing and contract cultures increasingly central to urban development and regeneration policies. As a result we are seeing an increased need for defensible information systems relating to the delivery of multi-project initiatives, the need to coordinate diverse objectives and benefits, and to ensure the coordination of resource procurement and the limitation of cost overruns. This requires a clear appreciation of both public and private sector organisational procedures, structures and cultures; an understanding of the development process in terms of delivery and management; and a sound understanding of how individual projects fit together to produce coherent redevelopment strategies (Table 6.3).

The critical initial decision requires a definition of the boundaries of the programme and its target outputs, with the tranche of projects involved helping to establish a format for reviewing progress in terms of particular milestones or the end of a particular phase. Each individual project will typically enable only a proportion of the total benefits planned for the overall programme to be realised, and when projects are managed as a programme it is easier to coordinate their outputs to deliver all the benefits obtainable from the strategy. Thus any changes to the specification of an individual project will have a knock-on effect on the programme as a whole, and will require management input.

Table 6.3 Rationale for the programme management approach

- *Shared objectives* where there is a need to coordinate several initiatives, with individual projects supporting a broader strategy, or where a set of proposed projects address a common problem or deliver a common set of benefits.
- *Management of complex change* where a set of changes cannot be managed as a simple project due to size/complexity, or cover a much wider range of development skills than do conventional project management structures.
- *Shared resources* where the use of resources from a common pool can be optimised by project coordination.
- *Advantages of scale* where the grouping of projects can give cost savings by avoiding duplication of effort, increases the scale of infrastructural investment and the use of more specialist skills, and can facilitate risk reduction.

Programme management leadership involves directing the delivery of the vision through the appointment of a programme director/chief executive, with overall responsibility for ensuring programme objectives are achieved and the intended benefits are realised. The management of programme integrity and the project portfolio usually lies with the programme manager, responsible for ensuring the continuing coherence of the programme, the monitoring of overall progress and initiation of corrective action. Programme managers also ensure resource efficiency in the allocation of resources, and the management of dependencies and interfaces between projects. The project team, working directly to the programme manager, are essentially custodians of infrastructure plans and designs, and the management of technical standards, and are usually underpinned by support staff who collect, coordinate and analyse management information. This overall framework requires a structure, style and culture, supported by working practices and procedures that encourage the free flow of information across projects, well-defined procedures for change control, conflict resolution and risk management. As will be revealed later, there are always inherent tensions between pressures to complete to time and budget whilst at the same time preserving the full scope of the programme and adherence to policies and standards.

Project management is an essential ingredient of any construction activity, and provides the building block of a programmed approach, helping to identify and deliver over time a range of projects that best meet requirements with available resources (CIOB 1996; Audit Commission 1996). Whilst there are general principles and checklists for ensuring project delivery, each project is unique, requiring the coordination of a wide range of people with different skills (Table 6.4). Projects need to be identified and justified in a disciplined manner within a corporate framework, and authorised at defined stages of programme

Table 6.4 Key stages in project management

- *Inception stage* involving the client, project manager and the project team.
- *Feasibility stage* outline project brief and detailed design brief.
- *Strategy stage* project organisation and control, appointment of a project team, procurement method, site selection, acquisition and investigation.
- *Pre-construction stage* design management and statutory consents; tender list and managing project quality.
- *Construction stage* monitoring design and construction processes, and fitting out.
- *Commissioning of engineering services* transition from a static to a dynamic installation, contract and post-contract phase.
- *Completion and handover stage* continuing project management responsibilities, planning and scheduling, monitoring and supervising completion and handover, post-completion project evaluation.
- *Client commissioning* occupation stage.
- *Post-completion review and project close-out report stage* project audit, cost and time study, human resources aspects and performance study.

delivery. Indeed, successful project delivery requires commissioning parties to adopt a management framework which clearly identifies key roles and responsibilities, allocates and monitors human, physical and financial resources needed at each stage of the project, and sets up management systems that provide all concerned with clear and timely information. There is clearly a need to establish a project system that incorporates all relevant inputs and activities, milestones and constraints, and monitors progress against the programme as a whole. This involves the effective management of project costs, an assessment of the potential impact of identified risks, and puts in place an effective quality management system (Kwakye 1997; Healey 1997b).

In Manchester's case, with the masterplan in place, the effort was subsequently focused on managing the implementation process. This was to be facilitated by the production by the Task Force of the initial implementation plan (April 1997) and its annual updating (May 1998, May 1999). The latter implementation plans were to reflect a maturing of the Task Force position, and the changing political and commercial context of the rebuilding programme. These plans were underpinned by a detailed implementation plan (DIP, September 1997) – jointly produced by the Task Force and MACE – which aimed to ensure that the management framework and established procedures were in place. In addition to the DIP, monitored on a quarterly basis, was a separate project directory, a working document updated and issued independently when project amendments occurred (Table 6.5).

The approach is to establish a quality culture within which high calibre people intelligently apply formal procedures, ensuring that the strategy

Table 6.5 Detailed implementation plan objectives

Mission statement 'to provide a flexible, responsible management team, creating a working partnership that fosters "can do" attitudes; to manage and motivate all parties to achieve the creation of a city centre which will stand comparison with anywhere else in the world, and which will meet the needs of all its users and residents'.

- Provides the framework within which individual initiatives are to be brought forward and is the basis upon which performance 'on the ground' is to be monitored.
- Addresses detailed coordination of major private sector and public realm construction activity.
- Focuses on an audit trail to give full accountability for procurement of design and construction at the best value for money.
- Aims to minimise disruption to the daily life of both commercial and public communities within the city centre.
- Provides for the earliest possible delivery of the Task Force's strategic objectives by using a flexible but robust management approach.
- Delivers the vision of the masterplan in a logical, sensible and well-ordered manner.

Source: Adapted from MML 1999

and quality objectives are met ... The DIP is a key tool in developing and managing the masterplan ... to drive forward the rebuilding programme, and give impetus to the continued regeneration of the wider city area.

(MML 1997)

Organising programme delivery

The whole objective was to communicate activities and progress, to coordinate action and to monitor achievements, and to agree any necessary remedial action. At the heart of this was the development of a 'meetings regime' to facilitate effective delivery of the programme, and the production of key monthly reports – board reports, project status reports, cost reports – issued in an interactive manner (Table 6.6).

The Task Force board, attended primarily by board directors, Task Force Chief Executive and Project Director, had the objective of reviewing policy aspects of the renewal programme, with typical agenda items relating to masterplan update, funding, and key issues needing resolution. The project report meeting involved Task Force team members, MACE, EDAW and other retained advisers, discussing the monthly status report, and providing a forum for strategic decision making. These reports were intended to address critical issues over performance and output, to discuss key milestones and any corrective action required, and to provide high-level feedback to the Task Force from consultees. Cost management meetings, involving Task Force team members and retained advisers, were mandated to review all aspects of project costs in order to ensure that they were managed within agreed cost plans. They were expected to review any specific areas of concern, make proposed design changes, and implement cost management reporting and monitoring. Finally the masterplan and development coordination meetings, involving Task Force team members, EDAW and MACE (and often involving City Council officers), provided a coordinating framework for outputs and actions relating to the overall masterplan, and to site assembly and development procedures. It was also to provide a forum for

Table 6.6 Programme delivery: meetings regime

Weekly	Masterplan and development coordination; detailed public realm design; road closure; MACE team.
Fortnightly	Administration and coordination; public realm design; cost management; utilities.
Monthly	Task Force board; project status report; transport strategy.
Bi-monthly	Health and safety; site logistics coordination.
Ad hoc	Strategic design, private development projects.

consultants to receive client briefings, and instructions from the Task Force in relation to private landowner sites and to other issues of concern.

To manage the recovery process it was inevitable that such discussions had to integrate with key City Council committees. The city-centre sub-committee (of the policy and resources committee) gave the political legitimacy for expenditure. All Task Force reports were reported to this committee (following board approval), which had a five-week meeting cycle. It approved the programme of activities to be delivered by MML, and it developed procedures of blanket approvals/omissions as the need to expend money increased substantially during the 1997–99 period. The finance committee (five-week cycle) was a second-level authority to spend money, effectively ratifying details given to the city-centre sub-committee. Finally, the environmental planning committee (five-week cycle) was responsible for giving formal approval for planning applications and for statutory requirements, and for decisions relating to the public realm, strategic planning matters, and individual development projects.

In order to coordinate all such activity MACE produced short- and medium-term meeting arrangement timetables, updated and reissued as necessary. These documents were circulated widely within the Task Force and its retained advisers, and targeted City Council officers. MACE also established a reporting hierarchy to provide up-to-date information on progress and projects, the essence of the system being short lines of communication, together with a documentation management system for handling multi-project complexity. Finally, the whole reporting system was to involve an annual review process with GO NW, a two-way process accounting for government commitments and facilitating central government advice and assistance seen to be helpful in delivering the programme.

The process of programming

The renewal programme was set out at four levels of detail in the form of a programme hierarchy, reflecting the range of activity from the top level overview down to individual project details relating to specific contractors (Table 6.7). The function of the programming strategy was to deliver the masterplan vision in a logical and ordered sequence, and to coordinate the numerous actions required by both public and private sectors. The definition of 'project parcels' provided the effective control of the implementation process through design, development, funding and construction, and these were amalgamated into agreed groupings corresponding to the renewal area's main sub-districts.

Three levels of programme hierarchy were established – for each private development project, for public realm projects, and for supplementary projects linking multiple parcels and areas. These were fitted within the wider phasing and stages of the masterplan's realisation, with public realm and supplementary projects geared to support the plans of private landowners and developers.

Table 6.7 Programme delivery hierarchy

Strategy	Phasing and strategic programming level
Level 1 (by project)	Overall strategy for the renewal project, regularly updated to reflect phase/stage of masterplan.
Level 2 (by stage of project)	Reflecting the summary programmes at key stages – commercial feasibility, design, procurement, construction.
Level 3 (working level for each stage)	Sequencing each stage of the project for both private development and public realm projects (working documents).
Level 4 (detailed programming)	Detailed documentation produced by specialist contractors and related to individual projects or sub-programmes.

Implementation of public realm dimensions required great care, dovetailing with the completion of private sector-led projects, retaining good access within the city during reconstruction, and ensuring that such improvements were not subsequently damaged or compromised by construction work on adjacent sites.

In terms of programme delivery, the overall Task Force role was split into three areas at this stage. Public realm and utility works were the joint responsibility of MACE and MML's executive teams, this involving gearing up for EU procurement rules, assembling the required legal documentation, appointing designers to carry out detailed design work, overseeing the movement of utilities, and finally appointing contractors. Funding, an onerous and time-consuming exercise, was to become a dedicated area of work as the team sought to coordinate detailed bidding arrangements relating to the diversity of funding sources, to dovetail applications, and to meet delivery criteria. Delivering individual components of the masterplan involved three types of projects. With private sector projects the Task Force was relatively peripheral, helping to facilitate the plans of commercial interests. Public sector projects were led by the Task Force and programme managed by MACE, the majority of which were always envisaged to be non-commercial in nature. Joint venture projects involved the City Council as major landowner, and enabled it to centrally influence the form of the final development. All this information was produced in 'graphical programming' form (GANTT charts), and used as a 'live' tool, which was monitored, updated and amended to reflect the latest situation.

Central to the programme management function was the development of a phasing strategy to coordinate all the public and private sector projects, and the enabling works necessary to carry out individual projects. The overall goal was clearly to deliver the masterplan vision in a logical, sensible and well-ordered manner, thus minimising overall disruption to the city centre. The renewal scheme was inevitably driven by commercial imperatives, with the priority to secure the 'core' programme in order to provide the necessary momentum to bring forward proposals in the wider masterplan area. Clearly the public realm works had to be phased in a way that avoided damage by construction activities on neighbouring sites, and took account of the risks inherent in different projects as they came to fruition. Given the confined nature of the masterplan area and the inter-related nature of individual projects, delays associated with one project inevitably affected the programming of other schemes, and the management strategy was to require constant revision.

It was the role of MACE to manage such knock-on effects, regularly checking the programming of individual projects to determine whether they were on schedule, and if not, to adjust the schedule of other programmes of work accordingly, this particularly affecting public realm interfaces with private sector projects. Thus, for example, programming for the Arndale Centre elevation was changed on a number of occasions, necessitating the revision of public realm programming for Corporation Street. Additional schedules were thus necessary, to monitor on a constant basis such issues as road closures, tendering and other date-dependent processes. Arising from the sensitivities of city-centre renewal, the logistics involved in project delivery was one of the key concerns, being central to the perception by others of the Task Force's ability to manage. Thus the main functions of this process were to coordinate a range of activities relating to all the development projects, involving developer hoardings and scaffolding arrangements; materials delivery and control (including wider city impacts); traffic management of both site and public service vehicles; pedestrian access and safety, and activities within public areas; and signage and advance notice requirements. In addition, the logistics strategy had to accommodate threat assessment and awareness, emergency service integration and emergency evacuation procedures, and crime and vandalism prevention. MACE had also to ensure that contractors undertaking site works had a logistics coordinator with specific duties and responsibilities for establishing an effective site presence.

In terms of monitoring and control the Task Force required effective programme and progress control to achieve not only project completion dates, but also the intermediate key milestone requirements. Software-based comparison of actual and planned progress, combined with regular forecasts of possible variances, revealed areas and issues requiring corrective action. Invariably, in such situations corrective amendments to projects necessitated further amendments, which hopefully would not impact on key milestones and completion dates. The overall renewal programme was updated monthly, using information from the status reports, design progress reports and contractor project reports. This enabled an overall progress summary to be produced, and elucidated the necessity of any corrective action.

Masterplan management

The overall approach to masterplan implementation was founded on a strategy of establishing a framework for individual projects and schemes within which the processes of design, funding procurement and construction could be undertaken and controlled. EDAW's continuing role involved developing and refining the original objectives, with the plan being adjusted in response to the development of more detailed proposals for individual sites. Key objectives in this process were to ensure that the masterplan evolved in a way that reflected the policies of MML and MCC; that liaison with landowners and developers and their design teams safeguarded the design parameters whilst retaining their commercial viability; and to provide the appropriate level of design guidance and information to ensure that all agencies involved in the renewal programme could make informed policy and development decisions. The SPG for the bomb-damaged area, along with the guidance provided during negotiations with developers, public realm design teams and the City Council, provided the framework for masterplan implementation. In addition, there was a series of outputs amplifying the masterplan and providing guidance on design issues. Written descriptions of the masterplan were issued as and when required (for example, for funding issues or as a background for planning applications), and masterplan drawings were updated regularly to reflect changes in development projects and adjustments made to the public realm. A series of documents was produced to support the implementation of the masterplan, outlining design parameters for public realm projects; a materials palette as an aid for public realm design teams; and a design and development framework to highlight issues to be addressed by developers and their design teams. A series of strategy documents formed the basis for the ongoing development of the masterplan and informed the detailed design of the public realm – public art strategy, signage strategy, traffic management strategy. In addition to such outputs, the masterplan team also contributed to the renewal programme's design and development process through liaison and briefing meetings, reflecting the stage of delivery of individual projects (Table 6.8).

The EDAW Project Director in charge of the overall management of the masterplanning team (and of liaison with MML) was responsible for advice on strategic decisions relating to the design of developments, and their impact on the masterplan; on liaison with developers and their design teams; and for reporting on masterplanning issues to MML and the City Council. He was supported by an EDAW Project Manager, concerned with the management of client instructions and the main liaison with other consultant teams, allocating tasks to the masterplanning team and to preparing masterplan documentation. Design coordination relating to specific sites within the renewal area was provided by design team members, in close liaison with specific developers and their design teams. In addition, the team was centrally responsible for coordinating alterations

Table 6.8 Masterplan implementation: liaison and briefing

- *Client liaison/project management* weekly masterplan team meetings and masterplan coordination meetings to review current and future masterplanning activities and to identify tasks and liaison to be undertaken.
- *Strategic masterplanning* relating to key issues, outputs and a programme for delivery, together with consultation with wider interest groups as part of the masterplan process.
- *Design guidance and briefings* for developers and their design teams, involving support from MML/City Council and liaison with other agencies.
- *Design development* liaison with design teams for built projects and public realm, and subsequent adjustment to the masterplan; involvement in specialist studies on specific design issues and specialist consultant briefing as part of the design procurement process.
- *Consultant team liaison* involving design team meetings and the review of draft documentation and plans issued by MML consultants.
- *Design coordination* liaison meetings with landowners and their design teams as appropriate; consultation regarding design outputs with the Task Force, City Council, other agencies; approval of design strategies by Task Force board and the city-centre sub-committee as appropriate.

---

to the public realm, and for the development of public realm design on particular publicly funded projects. The production and control of detailed design drawings were at the heart of the masterplan as a whole, with the knowledge that unresolved design issues were always likely to threaten masterplan integrity.

Other consultancy support

At the heart of this management process was the retention of a range of consultancy services that were to provide a pro-active role in delivering the renewal programme. EDAW were to oversee the detailed implementation of the masterplan, and to continue as urban design consultants until the public realm and private-sector design briefs had been satisfactorily resolved. They were in turn to draw on the services of a number of specialist sub-consultancies in their monitoring and testing of emergent design solutions (architect, historic buildings adviser, public art adviser). The Task Force's own retained advisers were to provide independent authoritative advice, focusing at the implementation stage on design quality. Indeed, a number of the key elements of the masterplan were to benefit from additional creative input in the form of design competitions – Exchange Square, Millennium Centre, City Park, Bridge Link, Art Works – with successful design teams being retained to take their designs through to working documents and site supervision. Each competition had a review panel, this being complemented by a review of the design capabilities of the entries (EDAW, Berridge Associates), compliance review (MACE), and financial appraisal (Poole Stokes Wood).

Transport consultancy advice was provided (Oscar Faber) on a number of highways projects, and on masterplan transportation issues more widely. This was extended to assist EDAW in the development of the masterplan and the issuance of design guidance for the duration of the renewal programme, and for broader discussions with key partners on the wider development of an integrated transport strategy. There was a clear need to coordinate connections and proposed works by utility companies to avoid conflict or, the necessity for repeat excavation and reinstatement, and to produce a commonly agreed policy for future access and reinstatement. The utilities consultancy (Baxter Associates) was retained to carry out a strategic review of utilities, mapping existing structures and reviewing demand against the masterplan, and identifying necessary diversions and alterations. The design team responsible for public realm projects – USM who were under the direct control of MML/MACE – were responsible for developing design proposals in accordance with the masterplan, accommodating design briefs prepared by EDAW, and meeting the requirements of the statutory authorities. They were expected to coordinate design realisation with both utilities and adjoining owners; to obtain the necessary approvals and prepare tender documents; and to assist in the procurement of works and their supervision.

The cost consultants were to provide strategic and detailed advice to the Task Force on the overall costs of masterplan delivery, and to include cost consultancy services for all public realm projects. In this role Poole Stokes Wood provided early cost advice on budget estimates, the testing of alternatives within value management principles, and the monitoring and reporting of costs throughout project development. Indeed, the budget estimates agreed by the Task Force at the outset (March 1997) were to form the basis for comparison against which all future cost plans, cost checks, tenders and final accounts were to be assessed. They were responsible for cost management information – valuation, cost reporting, cashflow, output – and this was all linked to monthly cost management meetings involving MACE and other Task Force personnel.

Construction and contractor management

Contracts were developed in accordance with City Council standing orders, EU procurement rules, and existing CCT regulations. Thus a set of procedures was set out at the start governing detailed contract management, the major difference from the norm being that the external programme managers (MACE) had access to programme documentation for individual development schemes. The cooperation of contractors was to be critical to the overall success of programme delivery, and landowners and developers were to instruct their contractors to work closely with the Task Force and their retained advisers MACE through the instigation of regular contractor coordinator meetings. However, since MACE was not ultimately contracted to them, it could not impose conditions on private sector developers, and given the voluntary nature of these meetings it was inevitable that some contractors only attended when they perceived it to be specifically beneficial. Thus contractors would on occasion flout the access and logistical arrangements devised by MACE for their sites, and programme managers had to work hard to influence the private sector by persuading, cajoling and enthusing them.

Unlike most regeneration schemes the rebuilding of the city centre represented a programme of works at the very heart of the commercial core. Maintaining a functioning city centre, whilst at the same time allowing contractors to enter and exit the city to service the variety of construction projects that converged on a small area of the core, presented a significant challenge (Table 6.9). An access strategy for construction vehicles was thus drawn up, and implemented in cooperation with the major landowners, developers and contractors. Five routes into the city were designated for use by construction vehicles, the number of daily loads calculated, and construction traffic for a particular scheme then given a dedicated route to enter and exit the city. Signage outside the city directed drivers into the centre along their designated routes, ensuring that all the radial routes into Manchester were used to service the full range of development sites. As construction traffic neared the city centre access was based on different contractors gaining entry to their site from over a dozen points on the Inner Relief Road (IRR), ensuring effective access to sites and limiting congestion. Without such a strategy all the construction traffic would simply have left the motorway and entered the city by a key radial route (Princess Parkway), resulting in the highway as well as city-centre streets becoming log-jammed.

As well as ensuring continued vehicular movement into and within the city, it was also important to maintain good levels of pedestrian access. Penetration by pedestrians into areas where construction work was taking place was essential to maintain continued patronage of the centre by customers and visitors throughout the rebuilding process. Thus MACE had to impose an access regime for pedestrians on all private sector developers, in addition to the normal hoardings licences, even if this sometimes restricted their activities.

Devising and implementing the project phasing and construction vehicle access strategies required continual discussion and liaison between MACE and

Table 6.9 Construction traffic routing strategy

Sites A	Marks & Spencer; Arndale Phase 1 Façade; Arndale Phase 1 Boots Fit-Out; Arndale Phase 2 Build-Out South.
Sites B	Exchange Square; Marks & Spencer Access Ramp; Shambles West; Cathedral Visitor Centre; Ramada block; City Park.
Sites C	Printworks; Corn Exchange; Transport Interchange; Arndale Phase 2 Build-Out North; High Street car park; Arndale Phase 3 Build-Out; Urbis; Arndale North; Arndale Wintergarden.

private sector contractors, facilitated through fortnightly contractor coordination meetings. These meetings brought together all the different contractors to discuss with MACE any problems being experienced over interface issues, their programme and update on their activities; and any exceptional loads they were planning to bring into the city. The meetings were also used to 'flag up' special events occurring within the city that would affect access arrangements, with representatives from the police, the City Council's operational services unit and the highways department also being present. These were all people with whom contractors had to discuss road closures and traffic management, and thus the meetings provided a useful forum. In addition, managers from MACE visited individual sites to discuss with project managers the scheme's programming in more detail, and to check whether the progress being reported was actually being made. So long as any problems within a project's programme of events did not impact negatively on public realm interfaces, or prevent the reopening of parts of the city, MACE were not overly concerned however at specific operational adjustments.

A central part of the mechanism for managing the reconstruction process was the successive applications to the Magistrates Court from May 1997 onwards of a series of traffic regulation orders (27), road closure orders (27) in relation to development intentions and to environmental action. In a number of cases the closure order related to development intentions or were linked to CPO procedures (transport interchange), and a number of orders regulating traffic were also subject to the award of planning permission. In addition, eight separate walkway closure orders were initiated for short-term periods, in connection with the redevelopment of the Shambles block.

Funding and procurement management

MML was mandated to spend resources approved for this purpose by the appropriate public funding agencies, and was responsible for programme management and performance, and expenditure monitoring of the rebuilding scheme. However, as already noted, the City Council as the accountable body was the applicant for and recipient of public resources made available for the programme. It was also responsible for ensuring that all projects were implemented in line with grant regulations, that expenditure was properly accounted for, and agreed outputs delivered. The City Treasurer was responsible for ensuring the proper administration of the financial aspects of projects in accordance with statutory obligations and the city's standing orders.

The initial urban design competition was funded from resources provided under the EU Technical Assistance Fund (£1 million) and local authority resources (£1 million), and competitors were advised that their plans had to be developed within the parameters set by sound commercial criteria and realism with regard to the availability of public sector resources. Indeed, each bid was specifically tested in terms of the encouragement of private investment and the economy and justification for public expenditure. The principle of providing the maximum outputs and benefits at minimum cost for public expenditure continued in refining the masterplan during implementation. With over four-fifths of the total cost of delivering the rebuilding scheme to be financed by the private sector, it was inevitable that public funding would largely help fund infrastructure and public realm improvements linking commercial development parcels (Table 6.10). Whilst the extent of public funding initially created uncertainty within government, the extent of requirements was agreed in early 1997, and private development commitments were secured as the renewal programme unfolded. The two were interlinked in that public expenditure was expected to improve the overall functioning and physical quality of the city centre, thereby giving the private sector the confidence to invest. Such funding was not aimed at improving private sector profitability, however, and was expected to deliver the highest urban quality at the most economic use of public funding.

As a consequence of the successful initiation of the implementation plan it became clear that the private sector target was likely to be substantially exceeded as the rebuilding programme gathered pace. This was to be further strengthened by the City Council's commitment to utilise its landholdings and value in the city centre to facilitate delivery of the masterplan, and the commitment of its own resources to underpin the renewal strategy. This commitment fulfilled the Council's obligation to underwrite any additional funding requirements over and above the resource allocations of central government and the EU, and was perceived by Holden (1999: 280) to stand out in marked contrast to limited private sector investment in the broad strategy (their focus being on individual development projects). Indeed, Holden argued, there was a basic separation between the pattern and structure of public (primarily strategic objectives 3, 4, 6) and private sector investment (almost exclusively objectives 1, 2, 5), and limited welding of spend across public–private sector lines despite MML's belief in the synergies of joint and collaborative interests. It could be argued, however, that the synergy came from an agreed masterplan with a consistent quality design approach, and with each partner promising to deliver its element within a timeframe and in a way that complemented and contributed to the success of the other elements, and the delivery of the whole vision.

In terms of private investment leverage, the masterplan was to provide the framework for key commercial components, with the beneficial impact of the rebuilding programme expected to ripple outwards and to act as a catalyst for new investment and development within the wider city centre. The key landowners committed substantial expenditure in developing plans for their individual sites and buildings – land acquisition, project development, demolition and construction activities – using insurance moneys to help fund investigation and repair works. Whilst

Table 6.10 Expenditure plan 1997–2002 by strategic objectives (£ million)

Strategic objective	Central government and Millennium Funding					Other agencies				Total public/private investment
	DETR			ERDF	Millennium Fund	Contributions		Leverage		
	Manchester Special Grant	English Partnerships	Transport			City Council	Private	Other public leverage	Private leverage	
1 Restoration/enhancement of retail core	–	10.5	–	–	–	20.0	–	23.0	257.5	311.0
2 Stimulation/diversification of the city's economic base	–	–	–	–	–	–	–	–	102.0	102.0
3 Development of an integrated transport strategy	–	–	23.0	2.6	–	2.5	–	–	0.5	28.6
4 Creation of quality core	3.1	1.6	–	4.5	–	–	1.1	–	–	10.2
5 Living city through increased residential pop.	–	–	–	–	–	–	–	–	10.0	10.0
6 Creation of a distinctive Millennium Quarter	4.0	–	0.2	11.8	20.1	4.8	0.5	–	–	41.4
7 Managing and delivering the renewal programme	1.0	0.3	0.7	1.2	–	–	0.7	–	–	4.0
Total expenditure	8.1	12.4	23.9	20.1	20.1	27.3	2.3	23.0	370.0	507.2

Source: MML 1999; Task Force Final Report to GO NW, MMC 2002

public investment, by its very nature, was likely to be front-end loaded, given the imperative of landowners to be back in operation quickly, the majority of private investment was expected to be committed over the first three years of the recovery programme. Indeed, the confidence generated by the masterplanning process enabled Prudential to acquire P&O's interest in the Arndale Centre for £325 million (1998), complete the centre's remodelling, and announce the proposed redevelopment of Arndale North in a further scheme worth £125 million (2002).

In terms of expanding public investment, development projects were appraised in accordance with the detailed requirements of various funding agencies, with such project applications being considered at the appropriate level by MML. Following Task Force approval the City Council's resource procurement manager was responsible for final authorisation to commit the necessary resources to the project. The Task Force Project Director had the responsibility for authorising any increases in expenditure as a result of unforeseen cost increases, taking into account any capacity for savings elsewhere and the need to maintain value for money.

Public funding took the form of a grant of £43 million from central government and its agents, £20 million from European Regional Development Fund (ERDF), and £20 million from the Millennium Commission, this being focused on five key elements. These were the public realm strategy and improvements; integrated transport strategy and infrastructure; establishing the Millennium Quarter and the Millennium Centre; underpinning new development where abnormal costs (often arising from the design framework) needed to be met through deficit funding; and masterplanning, programme management and promotion of the rebuilding programme.

In terms of the public expenditure profile the focus of government expenditure varied over the length of the programme (Table 6.11). However, quite clearly its management of differing grant regimes wase to modify over time as the

Table 6.11 Public expenditure profile (£ millions)

Funding source	97/98 outturn	98/99 outturn	99/00 outturn	April 00– Dec 01 (Target)	Total
DETR total	14.8	18.3	7.7	3.6	44.3
Transport	7.1	7.2	6.0	3.6	23.9
English Partnerships	6.6	5.7	—	—	12.3
M/c special grant	1.1	5.4	1.7	—	8.1
ERDF	—	—	6.0	14.0	20.0
Millennium Commission	—	—	5.5	14.6	20.1
Total	14.8	18.3	19.2	32.2	84.4

Source: MML 1999

recovery programme developed, and in order to reflect detailed project 'packaging'. Thus, for example, in the first year (1997/98) DETR expenditure exceeded the original target as a result of a reprofiling of EP expenditure on land assembly in support of the commercial strategy for the Shambles Square project area, and the creation of New Cathedral Street. Similarly, ERDF/Millennium Fund expenditure targets were reduced in the Millennium Quarter following a delay in the final formal decision on the Millennium Centre project application. Additionally, DETR's 'Manchester Special Grant' was accelerated by the reprofiling of investment in the rebuilding programme, facilitated by the progress made in the public realm strategy and the initiation of the Millennium Quarter. Finally, elements of the transport package (DETR/ERDF) were delayed due to the difficulties encountered with the CPO for the transport interchange project.

This strong expenditure performance was to reflect the unrelenting pace of activity by the Task Force, City Council and the private sector in bringing forward development projects, and in preparing the ground for other strategic projects at the design stage. This was also reinforced by the goodwill, flexibility and commitment of MML's public and private sector funding partners.

Performance management: targets, outputs and benefits

Key milestones and outputs were monitored monthly by MACE through its status report, this providing the basis of Task Force monitoring of achievement. Progress was measured against targets on a quarterly basis, being reported to the board and to GO NW. Annual progress reports, approved by MML's board, were also made to central government, and provided the basis for the following year's programme. The gathering momentum of activity on the ground was reflected in the milestones achieved during the first two and a half years, effectively the first and core phase of renewal (completed November 1999), encompassing the opening up of Exchange Square, Corporation Street bridge link, St Mary's Gate, the new Marks & Spencer store, and the recladding and build-out of the Arndale. It was clearly evident by then that the majority of key outputs would be delivered in years three to five as projects were completed.

Whilst total programme outputs appear to have been fully met, there was some variation during the life of the recovery programme as the commercial strategy responded to market conditions, and continuing appraisal of the ways in which developments in the masterplan area added to, rather than competed with, developments within the wider city centre. The main outputs relate to direct physical outcomes concerning space that is new or substantially remodelled/refurbished (Table 6.12). Modal shifts in transport, a reduction in through traffic and enhanced accessibility, together with wider social, economic and environmental benefits, were to appear less tangible but were undoubtedly significant.

Table 6.12 Key outputs from masterplan realisation

	Total programme agreed with GO NW	Completed masterplan*
New quality retail floor space	75,700 m	81,000 m
Damaged retail space back trading	23,225 m	
New leisure floor space	45,107 m	
New quality offices	4,645 m	6,000 m
New hotel accommodation	300 beds	164 beds
New civic and/or cultural space	10,526 m	8,416 m
Enhanced streetscape and/or new squares	30,657 m	34,000 m
New residential units	150 units	450 units
Listed buildings repaired or restored	5 buildings	
CCTV and/or community safety initiative	1 initiative	
New city-centre management scheme	1 scheme	
Missing links in Inner Relief Route	3 sections	
New business start-ups	250 businesses	
Car parking spaces upgraded	1,500 spaces	
Bus priority measures	20 measures	
Traffic calming schemes	10 schemes	
New permanent jobs created	1,100 jobs	1,400 jobs
Temporary construction jobs, person years	6,500 jobs	7,000 jobs
New public parks/green spaces	5,688 m	8,300 m
New trees	240 trees	200 trees
New transport interchange	1 interchange	
Improved Metrolink stations	2 stations	
Private sector leverage	£380m	£490m

*includes Shambles West, Transport Interchange and Arndale North

Source: MCC *Special Projects Group Progress Report 2002*

In normal circumstances a baseline study would have been undertaken, against which additional costs and benefits of implementation would have been measured. However, in a mature city centre devastated by a bomb this was always going to prove difficult to establish, and if the baseline is assumed to be the reinstatement of the floorspace damaged by the bomb, then the real additionality is the investment focused on this area net of insurance money and reinstatement costs. In addition, the broader economic outputs resulting from the implementation of the masterplan would include the positive impact on business confidence and the generating of new business opportunities.

In terms of overall value for money the winning submission was selected, in no small part, on the basis that it offered the greatest benefit and private leverage for the least input from the public sector. Indeed the masterplan as a whole and individual projects were constantly appraised within this context, and the construction process itself was delivered utilising value management approaches. This included issues of capital cost, buildability, life cycle and operating cost implications, and issues of quality, aesthetics and performance. Similarly, the Task Force adopted a strategic approach to enhancing the value of public realm projects, attempting to ensure that the design teams involved were constantly reminded of its overarching objectives and priorities in the design process.

Health, safety and the management of risk

The rebuilding programme was large, complex and timescale ambitious, and the strategy was developed not only to maximise the opportunities but also to accommodate the potential risks within fixed public finance frameworks. The main features of the risks involved concerned potential delays to the delivery dates of individual projects and phases; the possibility of cost overruns to projects serviced in whole or part by public funding; the risk to public health and safety both during and after reconstruction; and risks to the local commercial and physical environment. Because of the extended period of time for the programme to be achieved and the initial lack of detailed specification, it was necessary to give risk management a high profile within the framework of programme management. Thus, for instance, during the early days of programme implementation, the difficulty of obtaining Millennium Commission funding for the Millennium Centre threatened to scale back proposals for the Millennium Quarter, this being reinforced by the need to find match funding from other sources. Similarly, the ERDF commitment was likely to be reduced due to the increasing strength of sterling against the ECU during 1998, putting at risk elements of the public realm programme within the funding's timeframe. In terms of individual projects, risk registers were maintained to ensure that such risks were appraised both for their own effects, and their possible impact on the wider programme. Indeed, project interfaces between public, public–private, and private–private projects proved a major frustration for the Task Force, who were called in to adjudicate in disputes on a number of occasions.

The main areas of risks associated with the rebuilding programme related to public expenditure, private sector investment, and the process of statutory approvals. With public investment, after initial concerns over the securing of necessary funding and detailed approval of expenditure, the main issues related to the fact that implementation of the masterplan was dependent on the coordination of a complex package of funding sources, each with its own priorities, timetable, eligibility rules, and requirements for matched funding. This necessitated the establishing of sophisticated financial management systems to ensure the proper targeting and monitoring of public funding between different projects and funding regimes. Flexibility between grant regimes was required to overcome some of these problems, involving considerable debate with government, with the distinctiveness of circumstances putting established procedures to the test. Similarly expenditure targets had to be flexible between financial years to reflect actual achievements on the ground, and the synchronising of private developments with public realm and transport works.

With private sector investment, whilst it was expected that all the 'core' projects would go safely into the construction phase, the main uncertainty at the outset was whether all elements of private sector outputs would be fully completed on the ground within the five years of the programme, and the final projects are only now being completed (Shambles West). Luckily the period was characterised by relatively buoyant market conditions, both nationally and locally, and benefited from the relatively short timescale of the programme. Additionally, the key players were major international companies already committed to Manchester and the rebuilding programme. The risks to the programme were well demonstrated however, by the collapse in the fortunes of Marks & Spencer in the late 1990s, and P&O's decision in 1998 to divest themselves of their interests in shopping centres.

Whilst all statutory approvals required of the City Council were successfully 'fast tracked', some approvals required to deliver the masterplan were beyond their powers, and had to be referred to a higher authority for decisions. Thus DETR considered scheduled ancient monuments, listed building and conservation area consents, and compulsory purchase orders, whilst the Ministry of Transport (MOT) had to approve road closure and traffic regulation orders. In the case of privatised utilities, the cost/time/practical difficulties of relocating infrastructure necessitated close liaison with various statutory agencies (through a utilities liaison group), and flexibility had to be built into the programme to accommodate this. The main risk, however, was one of delay if objections to proposals had led to a public inquiry over a key project. Undoubtedly there were complex land ownership and acquisition issues related to site assembly, and close working with the major landowners was sought throughout to minimise such risks. The strategy was to relocate and accommodate current landowners and occupiers in the new city centre on a voluntary basis, but given the very complex nature of the Shambles redevelopment the City Council used its CPO powers to underpin negotiations, to mitigate costs and provide certainty of delivery. This threatened to challenge the momentum of the programme in a core location, but did benefit from the successful negotiation of withdrawal of objections prior to the inquiry. Where it was not possible to achieve a negotiated settlement of objections, procedures built into statutory systems were to prove lengthy in relation to the timescale for rebuilding, and delays were experienced as a result. This was particularly the case over the transport interchange CPO, which took nearly three years to resolve, and which put ERDF support at risk. This in turn put back the delivery of the integrated transport strategy (bus priority measures, Metrolink station), and the redevelopment proposals for Arndale North, necessitating a reprofiling of the necessary public expenditure.

An active health and safety management system was set up by the Task Force as a core management principle to be in place throughout the duration of the city's regeneration, with bi-monthly meetings being held involving all relevant parties, and with safety trends reported in the monthly status reports. A project health and safety management plan was produced and monitored by Shepherd Gilmour, and a health and safety accident review implemented following each significant incident.

Implementing a forward strategy

The masterplan proved a robust framework for the rebuilding programme and almost all the key principles and projects were in place (if not completed) by the ending of the Task Force's remit in spring 2000. Whilst the first year's implementation plan annual report was able to demonstrate hard evidence of achievement in terms of both financial commitments already secured and level of activity on site, overall levels of output and value for money improved in subsequent years. Indeed, as the renewal programme progressed there was much evidence to suggest that the rebuilding scheme was acting as a strong catalyst for investment elsewhere within the city centre, creating sufficient momentum to sustain an enhanced level of activity. Initial consideration of an exit strategy was therefore undertaken in spring 1999, this demonstrating that the Task Force had created sufficient momentum for its succeeding body. Completion of works to the core-damaged area had been achieved (new build of New Cathedral Street and Exchange Square, refurbishment of the Corn Exchange (Triangle) and the Printworks, and relocation of historic pubs). It had delivered the majority of the transport programme for which public funding had been obtained (except for the transport interchange, delayed by CPO procedures), and had facilitated the first phase of construction activity on Shambles West and on the Millennium Quarter. Finally, the framework for the redevelopment of Arndale North had been defined for subsequent implementation.

The exit of the Task Force
The Task Force was disbanded in March 2000, following the City Council's approval of forward management plans to support completion of the remainder of the city-centre renewal programme. A detailed 'handover strategy' was developed, reported both to the Task Force board and to the City Council, following which arrangements were agreed with the local authority for all capital projects still underway in spring 2000. This was agreed, both to ensure continued integration of the programme management function, and to discharge any public sector accounting obligations where the public sector fulfilled a client role for works

being undertaken. A final meeting of the MML board (June 2000) was to wind up the formal company structure. Thereafter, residual responsibilities were assumed by the City Council's Special Projects Team, with appropriate functional, organisational and management systems being put in place to ensure that these elements were managed in an effective manner (Table 6.13).

Table 6.13 Masterplan projects completed and forecast

Task Force delivered projects (97/00) (completed prior to its closure)	Completion date	Task Force initiated projects (00/02) (initiated but completed beyond its timescale)	Completion date
Commercial/Economic			
Corn Exchange external repairs/refurbish	05/98	Corn Exchange/Triangle	08/00
Royal Exchange repairs/refurbish	11/98	Printworks	09/00
Boots refurbishment	07/99	Voyager Bridge	10/00
Printworks site demolition	07/99	Shambles West – residential	03/02
Corporation Street Bridge	11/99	Shambles West – retail	03/02
New Marks & Spencer store	11/99	Ramada redesign	03/02
Arndale Phase 1 (recladding)	11/99	Victoria Buildings – residential	04/03
Arndale Phase 2 (build-out)	11/99	Arndale North – retail	05/04
Relocation of listed pubs	11/99		
Deansgate access ramp demolish	11/99		
Shambles West demolition	01/00		
Public realm			
Royal Exchange area (Cross St/Market St)	11/98	Withy Grove	07/00
New Cathedral St (east)	09/99	Market St	12/01
Cross St	11/99	Shambles West borders	03/02
Corporation St	11/99	South side of Withy Grove/Shudehill	06/05
St Mary's Gate (south)	11/99		
CCTV project	03/00		
Integrated transport strategy			
Market St/Metrolink Station	10/98	Shudehill Metrolink Station	03/02
Kingsway bus priority	04/99	Church St bus priority	03/02
IRR Dawson St link	06/99	Transport interchange	04/03
IRR Addlington St gyratory	08/99	Traffic pedestrian management	04/03
IRR signing and signalling	11/99		
Bridge St bus priority	11/99		
Cannon St temporary bus station	11/99		
Cross St bus superstop	01/00		
High St car park	02/00		
Millennium Quarter			
Exchange Square	11/99	City Park/Cathedral Gardens	06/02
Environmental enhancement		Cathedral Visitor Centre	06/02
(relocated pubs area)	11/99	Urbis	06/02

Source: *Task Force Final Report to GO NW* (Special Projects Group, MCC 2002)

The team provides the construction project management arm of the City Council, and was already responsible for a host of other capital projects within the city – Art Gallery extension, Great Northern Initiative and Convention Centre, Heaton Park renewal, Manchester Aquatics Centre, Piccadilly Gardens, Market Street, Sport City. It was additionally responsible for the development of operational management for a number of these capital projects, providing a company secretary role – Manchester Concert Hall Ltd; Manchester 50 Pool Ltd; Millennium Quarter Trust. Overall, therefore, the remainder of the city-centre renewal programme was to be delivered by an experienced unit within the local authority, possessing project management, financial and cost management skills, and commercial valuation experience.

A small team of key personnel and essential consultancy support (drawn primarily from the Task Force) was thus retained by the City Council to coordinate the final delivery and financial management of the rebuilding programme up to summer 2002. These forward management arrangements ensured that there was a dedicated focus of responsibility in place for delivery to cost and to programme of the final elements of the masterplan renewal scheme. Other key tasks formerly managed by the Task Force also continued within the work programme of the retained team, and progress reporting to the City Council, GO NW, Millennium Commission and other partners continued.

City Centre Management Company

A city-centre coordination scheme had been launched by the City Council and key retailers in 1994 that had facilitated partnership working, if only at a relatively low level. However, a concern with the continuing management needs of the city centre following the termination of the Task Force remit led to work being initiated on establishing a more sophisticated public–private partnership arrangement to facilitate continuing progress. Formally launched in autumn 2000 the City Centre Management Company was expected to undertake a range of strategic responsibilities for management, maintenance and improvement of the city centre. Its operating expenditure was to be funded by the City Council and a number of private sector partners, with financial commitments secured on a three-year rolling programme basis. As a vehicle for delivery, it would enable key partners to have a direct stake in the initiative, provide a focus for integrated investment and service plans, and an easily understood channel for attracting private funding to deliver widely agreed priorities. Above all, it was intended to establish a strong client focus for the city centre, formal mechanism for agreeing service requirements, and a basis for monitoring and improving links on the ground. The company's objectives for the centre were to be underpinned by a detailed business plan setting out the mechanisms, resources and responsibilities in relation to a number of key functions – environmental management and maintenance;

Table 6.14 City-centre management scheme objectives

- *Strategic objective 1* Establish a formalised city-centre management scheme that embraces the public, private and voluntary sectors to support and promote a common vision for Manchester city centre.
- *Strategic objective 2* Act as a focus for overseeing the quality and efficiency of services provided to support the operation of the city centre.
- *Strategic objective 3* Encourage, facilitate and maintain improvements to the physical environment in the city centre.
- *Strategic objective 4* In conjunction with Greater Manchester Police, implement a strategy to reduce crime and the fear of crime in the city centre.
- *Strategic objective 5* Improve accessibility into and within the city centre, with particular focus on the promotion of high-quality public transport and the balanced provision of car parking.
- *Strategic objective 6* Coordinate the promotion and marketing of Manchester city centre as the prime regional destination for shopping, leisure, tourism and investment.
- *Strategic objective 7* Foster and develop the economic vitality and diversity of the city centre by supporting, encouraging and facilitating inward investment.
- *Strategic objective 8* Monitor the performance of Manchester city centre by establishing a package of key performance indicators.

Source: Adapted from MCC 2002a

security; marketing and promotion; access and transport – and programme indicators were to be established against which progress and service delivery could be measured, which ensured that the impetus of city-centre investment was maintained (Table 6.14).

Thus, a new management model for the city centre was defined that would provide a strong focus for the effective management of the public realm, and of new public facilities; assume responsibilities from the Task Force for harnessing the commitment of the full range of interests involved in the centre to support its future success; provide a radical edge to the successful marketing of the city centre for investors and visitors; and develop and refine opportunities for improving the safety and sustainability of the city centre. In spring 2002 the City Centre Strategic Plan 2000–2005 was launched, addressing all the key issues affecting the city centre's development. It was to bring together the various strategies that had been developed over the previous few years – planning, transport, management and security, marketing and events, funding and governance – and was intended to provide a focus for the City Council and its key partners.

Chapter 7

Commercial
competitiveness

At the heart of economic change, urban cores have experienced dramatic modification over the past few decades, the result of external processes of globalisation and increased competition, and internal pressures associated with the decentralisation of economic activity. They have had to adopt new approaches to facilitate investment and growth, reduce their dependence on retailing, and facilitate the expansion of other market sectors. More particularly, they have promoted the expansion of leisure and cultural facilities, the provision of more diverse office capacity, and the stimulation of residential development. Increasingly centres for consumption, they have realised that if they wish to continue appealing to investors and consumers they must improve accessibility and provide an attractive and a secure commercial setting. In the process they have had to balance the traditionally short-term objectives of business with the longer-term assessment of the broader social and economic needs for built space.

These challenges were to lie at the heart of Manchester's rebuilding programme, and the present chapter considers the extent to which the implementation of the masterplan vision facilitated enhanced commercial competitiveness. It considers the processes associated with refining the original commercial focus of the strategy and the nature of its subsequent delivery, involving the restoration and enhancement of the retail core, and the diversification of the city's economic base. Following an appraisal of facilitating mechanisms influencing implementation, the chapter reviews project realisation experience – Marks & Spencer, Arndale remodelling, Printworks, Triangle – before finally considering the commercial impact of the renewal programme on the city centre as a whole.

City-centre development context

The current phase of development activity within the city centre began to take off in the late 1980s, the result of growth in retail spending and an office boom, encouraging new stock to be built and old stock to be renovated. One of the main challenges prior to the bombing was the attempt to build on the established strength of the regional centre and to extend and reinforce the existing City Pride 'vision', with such concerns being addressed in the formulation of the commercial strategy for the rebuilding programme.

The retail environment

In the mid-1990s Manchester's relatively compact prime retail area was enjoying good levels of growth and low levels of vacancy, and with evidence of considerable potential for more quality retail space (Market Street £1,750 per square metre; St Ann's Square £1,250; King Street £1,150; Deansgate £500; fringe £200–£300). Although the early 1990s were marked by a national recession, commercial opportunities in Manchester city centre remained buoyant.

> Protected by the city's tardiness in exploring the out-of-town retail concept … retailers saw the changes occurring in the city centre at that time and were happy to reinvest and consolidate …
>
> (Property agent)

Retailer demand was greater than supply in the prime core, and a need for high-quality stores with large floorplates had been identified as a way of enabling the central area to realise its full potential. The retail core focused on two main areas, with each serving broadly distinct customer bases. The prime location was and remains the area containing Market Street and the city's Arndale Centre. It has focused on mass-market retailing, contained all the major high-street names, with Zone A rents standing at approximately £1,700 per square metre in 1996. Such figures had not changed significantly since the early 1990s, however, and fell off dramatically in surrounding areas, due to the inward-looking configuration of the Arndale Centre. Constructed in the 1970s, its sheer scale and mass had long dominated the city's retail core, with recent internal refurbishment activity having little impact on improving the centre's poor internal layout, its impermeability or external appearance.

To a certain extent this shopping centre worked in isolation of the city centre as a whole, and was secured outside trading hours. There was no doubting its commercial success, however, with an annual rent roll of £20 million and an overall valuation of £250–£300 million, even if it had not proved a suitable location for attracting international retailers. Prior to the bombing it was fully let, and ranked as one of the most successful retail locations in the country. As the centre had only one active frontage (Market Street), however, certain parts of it did not trade well, this particularly affecting the northern block (across Cannon Street). In addition, it was felt that Market Street itself was unpleasant and required remodelling.

The second major retail area in the city was and is concentrated in and around King Street and St Ann's Square. By the mid-1990s this area had become the location for quality retail provision within the city (fashion multiples and designer labels), with Zone A rents ranging from £1,100 to £1,400 per square metre. There was considerable pressure from quality retailers to secure space in this area, with demand far outstripping the available supply of units. This had led to the spread of retail into the upper floors of stores and into adjacent areas not necessarily suited to retailing, with former banking halls being given a new lease of life.

> It's too expensive for retailers at the lower end … and at the other end where the growth has really come on, I don't think it's a traditional or sustainable pitch … just features of the pressure in the city centre for more space, actually squeezing retailing into locations which aren't natural.
>
> (Development interest)

For quality retailers, the lack of large floorplates in the right location resulted in the search for accommodation in alternative locations outside the conurbation core and beyond, and the provision of quality retail space was to be a crucial element of the city's evolving and pro-active strategy for the city centre to compete effectively with out-of-centre developments (Trafford Centre, Handforth Dean, Cheadle Royal).

In the mid-1990s the retail core contained four main department stores, the performance of each generally reflecting the quality of the trading area in which they were located. Marks & Spencer (opposite the Arndale Centre) was located at the very heart of the core, being considered one of the top three retailers in the city centre. Kendals (House of Fraser), located on Deansgate, continued to trade relatively well, benefiting from its proximity to the increasingly strong concentration of quality retailing on King Street and in St Ann's Square. The two department stores of Debenhams and Lewis's, both at the Piccadilly end of Market Street, continued to struggle to trade effectively from outdated buildings too large for their requirements. Both stores, however, were to be given new leases of life, if only temporary, with the relocation into surplus floorspace of retailers affected by the bomb. Food retailing remained poor relative to that in other cities of a similar size, with a dated Safeway supermarket in Shambles Square, and the Marks & Spencer's food hall providing the only in-town food shopping, but with a Tesco Metro being constructed on Market Street. Restaurant and cafe provision had also started to improve in the mid-1990s, with a great burst of new restaurant/cafe operators entering the market. Whilst much of this activity focused on Deansgate and Castlefield, it was felt that scope existed for additional growth in this sector, and that there was the potential to attract large international brands.

Whilst inflicting considerable damage on the retail core, and throwing up new challenges, particularly in relation to the ability of businesses to trade effectively in the short term, the bombing did offer the city the opportunity to enhance its retail profile. The damage to Shambles Square opened up new opportunities to develop quality retail space, removing in the process a significant physical barrier to the core's permeability. It also created the opportunity for Marks & Spencer to procure a new store, removing layout constraints that had previously prevented expansion, and which had led it to consider relocating to the Trafford Centre, the retail core's single largest threat. Due to come on stream in autumn 1998, its 100,000 square metres of trading area was an assured commercial success, and there was a general consensus that it would have a far greater impact on mid-market retailers (the Arndale in particular) than on prime niche locations (St Ann's Square and King Street). Thus the city was seeking to diversify and strengthen its overall product in response to market demand for high-quality retailing, and competition both from other major cities and out-of-town developments.

The office environment

Manchester has long been an office centre of national significance, with the 'square half mile' the focus of the city's financial and professional community. The late 1980s was a crucial time for the development of the central area's economy, with requirements for city-centre office space expanding rapidly as the finance and business centre grew, in the process attracting some major relocations. By the recession of the early 1990s, the city's financial community had become increasingly free standing, whilst the continued expansion of the professional sector (particularly accountancy and legal practices) heralded the attraction of major companies requiring larger footplates. The prime office core in Manchester is centred on a relatively small area bounded by Princess Street, Mosley Street, Market Street and Cross Street, but with the Great Bridgewater Scheme of the early 1990s marking a significant break-out of the traditional core to provide quality floorplates as part of a new commercial district. As a result the traditional office core was stretched to incorporate this new development, and opportunities for refurbishment were enhanced.

In the mid-1990s the city's total office stock was around 2 million square metres (net), with prime office rents in the traditional office core being above £200 per square metre, rents for good-quality refurbished space being £150 per square metre and for refurbished space on the periphery of the core at around £100 per square metre. Providing modern office buildings with large floorplates had proved difficult within the tight confines of the historic office core, facilitating such development to the south of the city centre, and with more competition predicted. After a complete lack of new office development in the early 1990s, the city had embarked on a number of major new and refurbished schemes, and whilst tenants had been secured for about one-third of such space, the prospect of oversupply was looming.

Office property in the bomb-damaged area of the city was for the most part older, and considered of secondary value in terms of market activity. Prior to the bombing, the Prudential had invested £7 million in refurbishing 8,000 square metres (net) of office space in the upper floors of the Royal Exchange to provide larger floorplates, but this had not been particularly successful. Indeed, Market Street had traditionally marked the northern boundary of the office market, beyond which few developers had dared to venture, and with the exception of the large Co-operative office complex such activities in this part of the core had always tended to struggle. Longridge House and the offices above Shambles Square had proved unpopular and failed to meet modern user requirements, with rental values as low as £50 per square metre. Likewise, the office tower above the Arndale Centre performed poorly, compromised by the centre's visual appearance and poor access at street level, with prevailing rents in the tower being around £100 per square metre. The Corn Exchange provided further secondary office accommodation at the northern end, but struggled as a small office location, with a significant vacancy rate.

Whilst there was clear demand for office space within the centre, this demand was finite, and it was felt that space was best provided in and around the traditional financial core. Indeed, most established office activity in the core was driven by local occupiers trading up, coming on the back of the expansion of business services in the early 1990s. With competition from out-of-town locations which were maturing as business locations (Salford Quays and Trafford Park), there was a desire not to spread office space within the city centre too thinly. With far better opportunities elsewhere in the core for prime office development (particularly Piccadilly), it was felt that northern gateway sites would be more appropriately developed for a mix of uses supporting and complementing an expanding retail core. Thus the bombing offered the opportunity to demolish a considerable amount of the poor-quality second-hand office stock – Longridge House, Michael House and the offices above Shambles Square. Furthermore, there was the opportunity to improve existing office blocks such as the Arndale Tower, by providing an improved entrance at street level, and of recladding as part of the centre's overall improvements.

The leisure environment

In the early 1990s the leisure and hotel industry represented one of Manchester's greatest success stories, but there was a general perception that the city centre was under-provided in the leisure sector, and that scope for further development existed. Castlefield was emerging as a key focus of leisure and tourism activity, and there was a dramatic shift back to the city centre of restaurants and bars. However, there remained considerable scope for further development, with large breweries and leisure operators actively searching for such opportunities. The main leisure development and anchor in the northern sector of the city was the 20,000-seat MEN Arena (a by-product of unsuccessful Olympic Games bids), which had proved highly successful, but had tended to operate as a discrete trip venue rather than as part of a multi-purpose visit. There was, however, clear potential for extending its economic benefits by developing further leisure and visitor attractions in the area between the city centre core and Victoria Station.

A proposal for a major city-centre leisure- and retail-related development – the Great Northern Warehouse – had been on the drawing board for nearly a decade, and had been one of the major outstanding intentions of CMDC that had not been realised. Whilst it was felt that there was unlikely to be demand for more than one major leisure-led scheme, it was agreed that all such putative schemes should be encouraged. The development of Shudehill was recognised as a clear fulcrum linking both Victoria Station and the Northern Quarter to the city centre. It was perceived as unlikely to be developed as a major retail site due to the construction of the Trafford Centre, and a broader mix of retail, leisure and possibly housing appeared a more realistic proposition. By early 1996 the boom in leisure-based developments became strongly centred on Deansgate, with demand pressures facilitating expansion in two directions, to the north in the direction of the Arena, and south-central towards Great Bridgewater Street.

The success of Manchester as a tourist destination had led to a buoyant hotel market within the centre, and a number of major hotel proposals were in the pipeline. The north/north-west quadrants were felt to be under-represented, however, with the viability of hotel development in this area being questioned without the availability of grant support. Immediately following the bombing, however, the Corn Exchange, Maxwell House and the Arndale Tower were considered as potential hotel development opportunities, but none was to be subsequently progressed.

The residential environment

During the late 1980s initial interest in city-centre living was promoted by CMDC, and in the early 1990s there was a sudden growth in planning applications both for student accommodation and for private sector developments, with nearly 2,500 completed units being delivered during 1991–94. By the mid-1990s there were around 25 completed schemes, with demand for city-centre housing remaining strong, involving both the conversion of vacant disused warehouses and poor-quality office space, and the construction of new-build projects. Under the influence of the CMDC, the corridor along Whitworth Street to Piccadilly Village had provided the main focus of residential activity within the city centre, but locations outside this area were showing encouraging signs of development interest. Within the bomb-damaged area there was limited existing residential accommodation (housing association units and a student hall) but the northernmost area of the masterplan area was felt to offer considerable potential. This was, however, dependent on the creation of a high-quality, secure environment, and the resolution of possible conflicts with commercial activities.

The masterplan's commercial framework

The replacement, diversification and improvement of the city's retail provision was seen as the key to successful rebuilding, with this being complemented by other market sectors in order to broaden the economic base and the appeal of the city centre. Competitive threats, pressure from insurance companies/loss adjusters, and the fixed-term nature of temporary relocation accommodation created a tight timescale for the rebuilding programme, and such considerations drove the commercial strategy. It was also essential that the central area did not become a long-term building site, facilitating disruption and threatening the city centre's competitiveness. Thus from the outset the timing and management of commercial redevelopment was seen as critical.

Restoring and enhancing the retail core was to be achieved through a threefold strategy that aimed, first to respond to market demand and the current lack of space for quality retailers by redeveloping Shambles Square for high-quality 'designer' stores and international retailing, enhanced by a flagship Marks & Spencer store. Second, the aim was to improve the image and functionality of the Arndale Centre, stitching it back into the fabric of the city centre. Finally, the necessity of making the city centre safe, attractive and accessible to shoppers and visitors was promoted as both a community and a commercial objective. Stimulating and diversifying the city's economic base, the second strategic objective, was to be achieved through the development of leisure and cultural activities to broaden the interest and attraction of the centre, and involved the delivery of four key projects – the Corn Exchange, the Royal Exchange, the Printworks, and the Ramada block.

Underpinning the commercial strategy were three core objectives, namely to maximise market opportunities to meet demand for quality retail, leisure and residential uses in the city centre; to use public funding to lever in maximum private investment and public benefit; and to substantially complete the reconstruction within a three-year period. All the key landowners had given support for the underlying principles encapsulated in the final masterplan, and this continuing support remained at the heart of the renewal programme's delivery. The winning submission had credibility because it complemented the aspirations of the city and the major landowners, but of itself this was unlikely to guarantee that the commercial strategy would be realised. Delivering the plan was always going to be difficult, and in the period prior to the launch of the implementation plan the winning design inevitably went through a process of refinement. Whilst retaining the key criteria in the original plan the design team worked up the detail of the individual commercial schemes – determining footprints, heights and volumes of buildings – coming up with technical solutions that in the initial competition environment it had not been possible to specify. It was during this period of time that the masterplanning process was to change from conceptual enthusiasm to a bargaining process, involving constant positioning and repositioning for advantage.

From the outset it was recognised that a central issue in the redevelopment of the retail core was the Arndale Centre, and the degree to which this could be changed, re-imaged and altogether reinvented. Attempting to bring about change was always going to be difficult when the owners had little appetite for large-scale improvements, given that reinstatement would secure its established commercial profitability. Furthermore, given P&O's publicly aired desire to refocus on their shipping activities, there was a fear that their strategy was to sit tight, make as much short-term money as possible, and then sell the shopping centre. It was thus left to MML and the City Council to facilitate their commitment, given the centrality of the Arndale's future for the whole redevelopment programme. Whilst the long-term strategy was clearly a need to break the centre's retail monopoly, with competition forcing its modernisation, in the short term the need was for the company to urgently demonstrate its commitment to reinvest.

> Can we tempt them with offers of Cannon Street and the market site … they assure us they don't see much value in it. Can we threaten them with planning regulation … they don't need much if any planning approval to reconstruct. Can we bribe them … we don't have the money. Can we cause them pain by depriving them of the bridge link … M&S would object. Can we embarrass them … yes, but this would significantly affect the tenor of the city's relationship with its main commercial landowner.
>
> (Task Force adviser)

The difficulty for the Task Force throughout the masterplanning phase was in demonstrating to the landowners that the renewal programme was achievable. In a game where there was a great deal to play for, but everything to lose, MML's masterplanners had thus to engage in a process of confidence building, selling the message that a commercial scheme would be hugely successful for all participants, would retain business in the core and attract new businesses. Fortunately, Marks & Spencer had to make a move, and their rapid decision to commit themselves to a new city-centre flagship store is recognised as the key driving force behind the entire renewal strategy.

They possessed a strong vision of what their new store should look like in such a sensitive setting, and to a certain extent everything else was to fall into place around them. When the renewal programme was being formulated it was the most important anchor a retail core could have, and considerable effort was expended on ensuring their continued commitment to the proposal as the company's overall fortunes waned. It was an important catalyst, and concentrating on their proposals was the logical commercial decision, since this commitment gave confidence to both Frogmore Estates (Corn Exchange/Triangle) and Richardsons (Maxwell House/Printworks), and was an important factor in motivating the Prudential to make an acquisitive move for the Arndale Centre. Inevitably, however, the Prudential in balancing risk and return needed some urging from both MML and the City Council to take the risk in the short term for an enhanced portfolio in the medium term.

Delivering the commercial strategy

Implementation of the commercial strategy was initiated in spring 1997, with the different elements continuing to evolve as project realisation began to materialise. The absolute priority for the strategy was to secure the 'core' programme – the Marks & Spencer store and contiguous New Cathedral Street; a reconstructed and improved retail frontage to the Arndale Centre; and a major leisure complex at Shudehill. It was expected that these developments would then provide the momentum necessary for a much wider programme of new development and investment – Shambles Square, the Ramada block, the remainder of the Arndale Centre, and the Millennium Quarter. The private landowners clearly had a major influence on the evolution and subsequent delivery of this strategy, and were instrumental in keeping the original vision largely intact. Inevitably there were problems along the way, and MML had to use a range of 'carrots and sticks' to resolve conflicts, and to keep the main parties on board. Delivering the key components of the strategy was thus an iterative process, working out detailed building footprints, carrying out feasibility work, modifying plans to respond to market conditions, and ensuring successful project realisation.

Restoration and enhancement of the retail core

The initial strategic objective sought to reinforce the city centre as the retail heart of the region by the timely restoration of retail floorspace and the creation of a wider range of shopping opportunities. Two projects were at the core of achieving this objective: the redevelopment of Shambles Square for a quality retail scheme anchored by Marks & Spencer, and the remodelling and reconfiguration of the Arndale Centre. Both of these schemes proved extremely complex to implement, with the Shambles Square/Marks & Spencer land parcel being continually refined. Land assembly proved particularly complex, with over 60 interests being acquired by agreement, and with a significant number of small businesses being relocated. The relocation of two historic pubs – Old Wellington and Sinclair's Oyster Bar – was a necessary element of the whole scheme, requiring building dismantling and re-erection. In addition, a formal CPO had to be initiated to facilitate land assembly, with the order being confirmed in August 1998. The land was subsequently 'vested' in the City Council, who, following detailed negotiations with Prudential, agreed to commit additional resources to underpin the public realm elements contained within the Shambles West scheme.

The redevelopment of the Arndale Centre was also complex, this being primarily due to the commercial stance of its owners rather than the physical and legal complexities of the site. In an attempt to improve its external appearance and functionality the Task Force was to work assiduously with P&O to define a development and investment plan for the entire centre, with the implementation of the first phase intended to focus on achieving the maximum visual effect. A comprehensive approach was adopted to overcome potential viability problems with aspects of the proposed remodelling, and to agree a phased package of improvements, cross-subsidising the more profitable parts with commercially more marginal elements. Following a design competition a team was appointed to deliver a replacement bridge link between the Arndale Centre and the new Marks & Spencer store at first-floor level (over Cross Street), seen as a necessary element in the commercial enhancement of both sites.

Advancing the commercial strategy for the centre was made more difficult once it became clear in autumn 1997 that P&O was actively pursuing policies attempting to dispose of its shopping centres, and that all the centre's damaged units were repaired and back trading. In order to sustain the masterplan vision MML and the City Council were thus to work closely with Prudential, encouraging and supporting their decision to acquire P&O's interests, this being completed in late 1998. Thereafter the parties worked closely to deliver an improved frontage to Corporation Street; the refurbishment and remodelling of the Boots store; and to define a detailed profile for Arndale North/Cannon Street and the Voyagers Bridge elements. The final element of this strategy – the redevelopment of Arndale North/Cannon Street – is to be implemented in 2004, as a £125-million redevelopment scheme.

This will involve radical remodelling and redevelopment in line with the overall masterplan's intentions, with the key components of the emerging proposal being to redevelop those parts of the Arndale from Cannon Street to Withy Grove for a mix of retail and food uses, involving the provision of a new anchor department store with active frontage on to Exchange Square. The relocation of the main east–west pedestrian links along Cannon Street within a glazed arcade/Wintergarden, with more flexible opening hours than the centre as a whole, is to be reinforced by the creation of active frontages along Withy Grove and a new entrance to the Centre. The reconfiguration and relocation of the market to a single level, the creation of a new entrance to the Arndale Tower from Exchange Square, and the refurbishment of the office block complete the proposal.

Stimulation and diversification of the city's economic base
The second strategic objective sought to secure investment and development of leisure and cultural activities to broaden the interest and attraction of the city centre.

It aimed to maximise the impact of the rebuilding plans both in underpinning the economic vitality of the regional capital, and in the direct creation of jobs, attempting to ensure that local people derived the maximum benefit from such employment opportunities. Four projects provided the core for achieving this objective: namely, the Corn Exchange; the Royal Exchange; the Printworks; and the Ramada block.

As a core element of the renewal programme, delivering a major leisure complex was seen as critical, and the commercial strategy identified an area of land along Withy Grove/Shudehill (focused on Maxwell House) as a strategic site. This was a semi-derelict parcel of land with a history of unimplemented development, with the proposed scheme seen to integrate with proposals for both Arndale North and the transport interchange. It was additionally perceived to be the key for increasing permeability through the northern section of the Arndale Centre. In the early stages of the masterplanning process MML worked closely with the owners and a potential development partner to secure a quality entertainment develop-ment, for what was seen as a major catalyst in turning around a decaying northern gateway. However, it became clear that detailed negotiations between the various parties involved could not be concluded, this threatening to extend the building's uncertain future. Thereafter, the City Council and MML pro-actively sought to secure an alternative development partner, and Richardson Developments acquired the site and worked up detailed plans for a major leisure scheme – the Printworks – seen as a new entertainment district, this being completed in spring 2000. The orig-inal masterplan proposed new residential development as part of the wider redevel-opment of Shudehill, but the scale of the Printworks and the transport interchange subsequently expanded to incorporate the entire Shudehill site.

The listed Corn Exchange and Royal Exchange buildings took the full force of the blast, and meticulous repair and renovation works had to be carried out to both structures. Their refurbishment was intended to add diversity to the commercial core by providing specialist office and retail accommodation, supplemented by the restoration of the Royal Exchange Theatre. The commercial strategy for the Royal Exchange, substantially owned by Prudential, was to maximise private investment in the property; to ensure that the improvements were of a high quality and integrated into the wider rebuilding proposals; and to secure the earliest completion of the works. This was achieved by autumn 1998, focusing on a niche shopping centre on the lower floors, a major theatre complex, and with offices above. In terms of the Corn Exchange, Frogmore Estates terminated all established leases so that a comprehen-sive redevelopment scheme for the building could be implemented. Extensive feasi-bility work was undertaken to establish the viability of future uses and the optional tenant mix, and sensitive repair and restoration of the external envelope was required. A high-quality retail-led scheme, branded the 'Triangle', was created, with a key element being the wish to encourage both day- and night-time activity, intended to complement and make positive use of its interface with the new Exchange Square.

The fourth element of the strategy was focused on the Ramada block, a P&O-owned gateway building for people entering the city from the north, but which had had a long-term negative impact on the Deansgate streetscape. The masterplan envisaged considerable opportunities for upgrading and improving the block's appearance and functionality, but subsequent change of ownership has continued to stultify its intended redevelopment. The commercial strategy for the Ramada block set out to upgrade the hotel and extend it into the vacant Premier House office block next door; relocate the hotel's main entrance to Deansgate; secure the radical remodelling of the building at ground level in order to pull the activity and vibrancy of Deansgate further north; and create a new active and attractive street frontage. Under the ownership of Chesterfield Properties the Ramada Hotel was rebranded and internally refurbished, but commercial arrangements to extend the hotel were not secured, and MML were not in a position to influence the owners in relation to radical remodelling of the building at ground level. On acquisition in 2000, Quintain Estates submitted plans for the redevelopment of existing retail units along Deansgate (opposite the new Shambles West development), and the conversion of Premier House from office to hotel use, but this proposal has yet to be realised.

Driving forward commercial change

Implementation of the commercial strategy has been aided by a number of factors, with three key elements being particularly helpful. First, the city's buoyant retail market and the healthy state of the general economy reduced the risk of investing in the retail core, and bolstered investor confidence in the renewal programme. Second, the threat of the Trafford Centre facilitated the implementation process by helping to drive forward the pace of the agenda, and ensured delivery in a commercially viable manner. Finally, the City Council helped move the process forward where perhaps it could have faltered without the intervention of the authority, both as landowner and as a body with statutory responsibilities. It successfully used its assets to promote and deliver aspects of the renewal programme that left to the private sector would not have come to fruition, with the significant residential component in the commercially driven scheme for Shambles West being one such example.

Given the complexity of the rebuilding process, issues inevitably arose during the implementation phase, complicating programme delivery. P&O's less-than-enthusiastic initial approach to renewal, its interests in a number of key development parcels, and machinations over the possible Arndale sale, were to prove a major barrier to the implementation process. Despite making up ground since the Prudential's acquisition, full realisation of proposals for this block remains behind schedule. Additionally, a major frustration for MML was the speed at which some private sector landowners worked, even when their commercial decisions involved large financial commitments. They, in turn felt that MML sometimes lacked a full appreciation of private sector cultures and investment decisions.

The project dimension

It is appropriate at this stage to consider the project dimension by briefly looking at projects associated with the commercial strategy, a key element of the renewal programme. In terms of the masterplan's main strategic objective – restoration and enhancement of the retail core – this section will focus on the new Marks & Spencer store and the remodelling and reconfiguration of the Arndale Centre. The other strategic objective that was primarily economic – stimulation and diversification of the city's economic base – will be considered through a brief review of development experience relating to the creation of the Printworks leisure complex, and the refurbishment and remarketing of the Corn Exchange.

Case study 1: Marks & Spencer store

The Shambles development parcel is centred on an area with a long history of development activity, originally forming part of the city's medieval settlement, but more recently being badly damaged by bombing during World War Two. The opportunity for comprehensive redevelopment was seized upon as part of the wider rebuilding strategy, with the area being redeveloped in three stages. Longridge House was completed in the late 1960s, and the Marks & Spencer retail store and accompanying office tower was occupied in 1973. During a final phase the store was extended at upper levels fronting on to the Shambles Square development. By the late 1980s, however, the surrounding area was suffering from a poor image and a deficient pedestrian environment. It struggled to compete with the nearby prime retail pitches on Market Street, and this affected trading at the store. Although highly profitable, it was not seen to be delivering its optimum commercial return due to the inefficiency of its basic layout. In the early 1990s plans were made to address this concern, and discussions were held with adjacent landowners over the possibility of delivering an improved footprint. Indeed, informal discussions had already taken place regarding the possibility of procuring the adjacent Longridge House – an office block that had long failed to meet user requirements – a situation readily acquiesced to in the aftermath of the bomb.

Following the bombing, the store found temporary accommodation for its food outlet in Spring Gardens and for its other business within Lewis's department store, with the company back fully trading by November 1996. Detailed analysis of the damaged building revealed that the shock wave had travelled through its entire structure, the building swaying from side to side and being lifted vertically. Marks & Spencer decided that it was more economic to demolish the building than to repair it, and made an early commitment to sponsor an entirely new flagship store on site. The proposal was for a store with a large span, rectangular floor plates over six levels, and with a sub-basement car park. Its principle trading area would be at basement, ground and first-floor levels with a

The new Marks &
Spencer store

customer restaurant on the second floor, and with staff facilities and offices on the
third floor. It would have entrances on all four sides, and with a pedestrian
walkway connecting it at first-floor level with the Arndale Centre. Demolition was
to be complicated by the fact that the building was one of the earliest exponents
of the pre-stressed post-tensioned beam technique, necessitating the whole
structure being cut up and removed in precise sections: an extremely hazardous
operation.

Assembling the footprint for the new store proved to be extremely
complex due to multiple ownership and leasehold interests. With the city as freeholder, Marks & Spencer, P&O, Prudential and Royal Insurance having significant
leasehold interests, and numerous retail and office users possessing various sub-
leases, the redevelopment of the Shambles block was to prove challenging. Half a
dozen different land parcels either fell directly within, or impinged upon, the Marks
& Spencer/New Cathedral Street footprint, and individual land parcels had various
sub-leases. It is not surprising therefore that the Shambles Square area was
served with a CPO, and it is miraculous that the new Marks & Spencer store was
completed and trading fully just over three years after the bomb, in a situation
where the necessary legal agreements would have normally taken a decade to
conclude. This was to be a key feature in the proposal to open up new opportunities for quality retailing in Shambles Square, affording the possibility of larger
floorplates as part of the redevelopment of the entire parcel.

The outline planning application was submitted in December 1996, alongside consultation over a draft commercial strategy for the Shambles block. Agreement 'in principle' with the Task Force, P&O and Prudential was forthcoming in spring 1997, with the full commercial strategy for the wider Shambles Square being approved by the Task Force in May. The full planning application was submitted in July 1997, being consulted upon widely with a range of private and public interests. In September 1997 the application was approved subject to safety and constructional conditions, the nature of external materials and surfaces, and a key condition retaining pedestrian permeability through the store by a route linking Corporation Street and New Cathedral Street. A CPO was pursued alongside to ensure that the necessary land was acquired for the new store, as part of the wider Shambles Square redevelopment.

Changing conditions in the British retail market – increasing competition, the growth in designer labels, and emerging online shopping – were particularly influential on the evolving commercial plans for the store. During construction, concern was expressed that the figure of over 20,000 square metres of retail trading space was too high, given the increasingly straitened position of the company's share price and merchandising position. It was calculated, however, that to reduce the proposed footprint at this stage would prove more expensive. In the

The Selfridges end of the the Marks & Spencer building

event, whilst the company's commercial fortune was to improve, its commitment to a new store nearly twice the size of the previous one was to prove over-optimistic, and was to lead to subsequent redivision of the building.

In terms of the construction process, with most of the necessary building demolition and excavation completed by June 1997, the next 15 months were to see the main core and structural steelwork being completed, and the construction of the podium being commenced. In a parallel area of activity, demolition and enablement works for New Cathedral Street running along the east side of the site were also completed. Cladding and glazing work commenced in November 1998, and the building was fully weatherproofed by June 1999, with the period up to its formal opening in November 1999 focusing on an internal fit-out for the store.

Implementation was to prove extremely complicated – due to the island nature of the site – with live projects on three of the building's elevations, namely Exchange Square to the north, the Arndale build-out to the east and New Cathedral Street to the west, the latter splitting the Shambles parcel in two. Logistics and project coordination were vital to the rebuilding process, and having to work closely with all these projects was to result in a number of setbacks, especially when the plans for the adjacent developments were still evolving. For example, Bovis in undertaking below-ground development to provide the necessary access arrangements for the Marks & Spencer store, were hampered by not knowing what was going to be built above ground, and had to demolish and rebuild a newly constructed ramp access as commercial requirements for Shambles West firmed up. In addition, as plans for the Shambles block were confirmed – of which the Marks & Spencer store was one element – it became clear that, in order to unlock the full development potential of the site, the two historic pubs would have to be dismantled and relocated.

Detailed logistics arrangements for the Shambles parcel was necessitated by the complexities involved in the construction process. Until 1999, only a small strip of Corporation Street was available for site deliveries, and towards the end of the project this was closed as new public realm improvements had to be laid. On site the hoists and tower cranes were booked daily, with access via Deansgate and the underground car park. The internal structure of the store was used as the materials movement and logistics centre, with the internal lifts providing for vertical movement of materials.

In terms of the design solution, the building – designed by Building Design Partnership – is constructed from in-situ concrete and steel, with a footprint of 65 by 100 metres. Industrial glazing panels on the four sides consist of laminated glass, and although this does little to lessen its sheer scale and mass, the building's design incorporates a glass-covered pedestrian galleria running east–west through the store. It has sought to ensure integration with the masterplan's intent, and its corners on to Market Street are rounded for matching with surrounding buildings. Similarly, the curved façade of the new Cathedral Street elevation is intended to help reveal views of the Millennium Quarter from St Ann's Square.

The completed building was to be Marks & Spencer's largest store, undoubtedly acting as a catalyst for the wider regeneration process, and a focal point of the whole redevelopment area. It proved absolutely essential to provide the drive and energy for surrounding projects, but initial misgivings about the possible excess of retail space became clear in April 2001, when Marks & Spencer announced plans to sell off half the store to Selfridges (complementing their presence in the Trafford Centre), in a leased initiative worth £50 million. The existing central mall divides the two stores, with Selfridges opening in September 2002 following refitting. With the recovery of Marks & Spencer's fortunes in 2002–03 their market share has been sustained locally by their opening of a complementary store in the Trafford Centre, occupying the premises formerly taken up by C&A (who withdrew from retail trading in Britain in 2001), an option they had originally rejected in 1997.

Case study 2: Arndale Centre remodelling and build-out

The Arndale Centre is one of the country's largest in-town shopping centres, covering a 6-hectare site and comprising 150,000 square metres of shopping space, and a 22,000-square-metre office tower. The process of putting the site together for comprehensive redevelopment took two decades, with the Arndale Property Trust buying up property from the mid-1950s, and with the remainder being purchased subsequent to the acquisition of the company by Town and City Properties in 1963. In the mid-1970s the leasehold was sold to P&O Properties, who were to manage the development until late 1998 when it was sold to Prudential. The Arndale Centre was completed in three phases, with the first phase of 60 shops and the Arndale Tower being completed in 1976; the second phase accommodating the indoor Market Hall, Boots and the bridge link to Marks & Spencer being completed in 1978; and the final phase including BHS and Littlewoods and the underground bus station being completed in 1979.

> Tthe interior was hot and stuffy, the malls were undifferentiated, and shoppers became lost … But the developers thought they were doing the right thing by providing what was essentially a huge box containing shops.
>
> (Parkinson-Bailey 2000: 211)

After the bombing, the traders and retailers began to return within three weeks, and three-quarters had returned within the first year after the blast. In late 1996, when the commercial strategy for the Centre was being formulated, redevelopment was envisaged to consist of a number of component elements that would involve the redesign of some areas as part of the wider redevelopment of the Arndale Centre as a whole. The fundamental objective that underpinned the company's aspirations in procuring wholesale improvements was that the work involved would need to meet their normal commercial criteria, in order to justify the substantial investment involved:

- extending the Corporation Street frontage of the Arndale by up to 7 metres, replacing the former blank wall with an active street frontage;
- the reinstatement of the pedestrian footbridge linking the Arndale Centre with the Marks & Spencer store;
- a Wintergarden proposal that would result in a covered extension to the building over Cannon Street, and would facilitate new access into and through the Centre;
- the refurbishment of Arndale North to provide a major new shopping development with a glazed frontage on to Withy Grove;
- the remodelling of the Voyagers Bridge and its access crossing over Market Street;
- the redevelopment of the Arndale office tower for possible use as a hotel, residential or commercial project;
- the permanent closure of the space underneath the Arndale Centre as a bus station and the transfer of such activity to the proposed Transport Interchange; and
- the comprehensive refurbishment of the High Street car park (at the north-east end of the Centre) as part of the wider initiative to improve city-centre car parking.

Arndale Centre – long view from top of Market Street

By spring 1997, P&O had formally submitted their proposed strategy and investment plan for the Arndale Centre, alongside a design framework that sought to enhance its contribution to adjacent townscape by animation, pedestrian permeability, and enhanced architectural form. Design activity was to slow down significantly during the latter part of the year, however, as the focus shifted to the negotiations over the Centre's proposed sale. Redevelopment intentions nevertheless proceeded with full planning applications being submitted and approved for the Wintergarden (June 1997), the Arndale build-out (January 1998), the pedestrian footbridge (August 1998), and the redevelopment of the Cross Street elevation (October 1998). Whilst such approvals were subject to specific development timescales, the uncertainty caused by the proposed sale was to seriously threaten the integrity of the masterplan, and ensure slippage in delivery of the eventual renewal programme.

The Arndale Centre was finally sold to Prudential in December 1998 for £325 million, signifying a further stage in its evolution. The single greatest threat to retailing in the city centre was to be the opening of the Trafford Centre in autumn 1998, reinforcing the recent launch of two smaller centres to the south of

Arndale Centre – remodelling/ build-out on to Corporation Street

the conurbation (Cheadle Royal, Handforth Dean), and there was a general consensus that with its 85,000 square metres of retail space and 10,000 free car spaces it would have a major impact on mid-market retailers. Thus the commercial viability and desirability of visual improvements to the centre as a whole was intended to reinforce the 'build-out' on to Corporation Street, and the glazed 'build-over' to the Cannon Street frontage.

The Arndale Tower, despite its size and attraction to a number of high-profile users (ICL, BP, P&O Properties) had been tarnished for a long time by the poor visual image of the shopping centre, and deficient access at street level. It was also increasingly under pressure from major office developments at Salford Quays and the main arterial routes to the south of the conurbation, and the masterplan offered opportunities to increase its competitiveness, both as a result of a refurbishment programme for the office tower and for the centre as a whole.

By the end of 1997 the Corporation Street build-out had become the most pressing issue, and it was considered important to progress quickly in order to achieve trading for Christmas 1998. Detailed discussions were necessary on the funding of both service relocation and the build-out works, and whether from early 1998 it should be Prudential rather than P&O who should be taking the lead on the project. Such intentions were also highly dependent on agreement being reached with the established occupiers, with a premium agreed for major refurbishment with a number of key retailers (Burton Group, W H Smith). In the event the build-out work was not to be initiated until summer 1998, and was not completed until March 1999. Indeed, the Boots 'spin-off' development, involving the wholesale renovation and extension of its store as the chain's flagship, was not to be completed until autumn 1999.

Another key feature of the Arndale remodelling involved the completion of a new bridge link between the Arndale Centre and Marks & Spencer, the result of a design competition. The coordination of this complex project (at differing levels and slanting interface) was to involve detailed negotiations with a variety of parties (Marks & Spencer, P&O, Prudential, MML and the City Council, Arup, Bovis), being built between two live projects being delivered at breakneck speed. This made coordination between the key agencies, private sector constructors, and public realm programmes extremely difficult – 'it isn't every day that you put a footbridge between two buildings that are being built at the same time' (MML project director). However, in April 1999 the bridge collar was firmly put in place, reconnecting once again the two sides of Corporation Street.

Two other major projects – the redesign and renewal of the Voyager Bridge food court (crossing Market Street), and the refurbishment of the High Street car park – were also in place by the end of 2001. However, the proposed refurbishment of the Arndale Tower for office development has been delayed, and the

Wintergarden and Arndale North proposals are still to be initiated. With the completion of the transport interchange in early 2004, Cannon Street's temporary role as a bus station can be discontinued, thereby facilitating the development of the glazed Wintergarden. This 'opening up' of access to Withy Grove has stimulated progress on the Arndale North retail development, and work can progress on the scheme in 2004, thereby completing the remodelling of the entire Arndale Centre block.

In design terms the main focus of the Arndale redevelopment programme was generally to improve the qualities of the retail core, specifically to break up the mass and singular style of the existing building, and to present a new presence and character for the whole Arndale Centre. This was to include new street-level entrances and active frontages, new building lines to facilitate visual and spatial interest, the creation of the Wintergarden as an attractive pedestrian route, and improvements to the Voyagers Bridge and Withy Grove access. Within the façades' depth, articulation was encouraged in order to break up the mass of the building, this being realised by the use of projections and canopy, with the ultimate objective being to remove the entire existing tile-cladding system. The refurbishment of the Arndale Centre was a complex project with many inter-related components, each progressing at different speeds and with varying problems. Whilst individual projects have had a positive impact on the surrounding townscape, some aspects of the plans have been slow to reach fruition due to both commercial realities and difficult landowner negotiations.

Case study 3: the Printworks leisure development

Originally built in 1870, the building was used for newspaper production from 1924, with a new printing plant being installed in the 1960s. It was acquired by Robert Maxwell in 1985 for the production of his own publications, subsequently to be transferred elsewhere, and the building was to stand empty from 1987. At the time of the bombing the site was owned by Shudehill Developments, a joint venture company headed by CWS/CIS, and had been the subject of a number of commercial development proposals, none of which had proved viable. Overall, the deteriorating building complex was beginning to have a negative impact on the northern fringes of the retail core, and an urgent solution was required.

During the first half of 1997 Shudehill Developments was in regular contact with Burford PLC, and agreement in principle had been signed with a megaplex operator, as part of a wider regional leisure and entertainment facility. However, after undertaking more detailed appraisal work and reviewing project costs, it was felt that the development proposal could not support the agreed site value, and Burford revised downwards their offer. Shudehill Developments, disappointed with the progress being made, began to actively market the opportunity to other development companies, and once Burford had lost their exclusive negotiating position, they decided to formally withdraw from the scheme.

In July 1997 the site was bought by Richardson Developments for £10 million, with a full planning application being submitted six weeks later. A mixed-use entertainment centre of 46,000 square metres was proposed – comprising a multi-screen cinema complex; a family entertainment centre and health club; restaurants, shops and nightclubs – associated with a multi-storey car park located at the proposed transport interchange. At the time of the bombing there was a considerable interest in the market for a new leisure development in the city centre, and approval was being sought for a major commercial leisure development in the Great Northern Warehouse (next to G-Mex).

Additionally, the Castlefield area had developed as the main attraction for leisure and heritage tourism, and a number of the city's art galleries and museums had made Lottery bids to extend and improve their facilities. The local authority recognised, however, that the Shudehill site presented a good opportunity to link both Victoria Station and the Northern Quarter to the central core, and were generally supportive of the proposal. This was seen as being particularly urgent given the existing and threatened competition from the Trafford Centre, Cheadle Royal and Salford Quays.

Central to the proposal was a traffic-impact assessment, and the intention of demolishing the building subject only to the retention of its façade.

Printworks development – view from Exchange Square

Printworks development – internal view

There was some concern over the impact of massing of the proposed development, the lack of imagination in relation to the scheme's conservation area location, and its conflict with the City Development Guide, but planning permission was approved in November 1997, subject to conditions over floorspace allocations, advertising controls and construction details. Most importantly, however, it was a condition of the approval that the complex should not be used until the new transport interchange was operational.

Whilst it is essentially a new building complex behind a façade, Richardsons wase keen to retain the site's historic value – 'in our internal street we are trying to recreate an old Mancunian/Victorian warehouse theme' (Developer's agent). Its architects proposed, however, that whilst a themed street would run through the complex, the cobbled area would contain the sounds and smells of an American city of the mid-1920s, a focus that was to be largely adhered to. The developer's first goal was to secure key commercial anchors, and by the end of 1998 it was able to announce secured operators for the cinema complex (UCI), the health club (Holmes Place), a major themed restaurant (Hard Rock Café) and the entertainment centre (Virgin). Thereafter it sought to release the asset value from the development, and sold a majority stake to a pension fund.

Demolition was completed and construction started in July 1998, with a range of construction problems arising, on what was a very restricted site for the volume and configuration of the development proposed. This was to delay completion of the development, and the £55 million scheme was not opened until November 2000, and without the associated car-parking facility.

Triangle – view from Exchange Square

Case study 4: the Triangle development

The listed Corn Exchange was built between 1897 and 1904 as an extension to the exchange building located on the site since 1836. At the time of the bombing it contained a large number of businesses – small-scale retailers, tertiary offices, a craft market and a number of food outlets – and was best known as the city's main 'alternative' shopping centre, with nearly 300 small traders selling crafts, books, records and memorabilia. Following the blast, the building's owners – who had purchased the building for investment in 1989 – terminated the leases of the building's occupants, as they were legally entitled to do, for 'major redevelopment proposals'. Despite being helped by MML to relocate elsewhere within the core, the small traders remained angry throughout at their treatment by the developer.

Triangle – internal view

Throughout the redevelopment process the building was owned by Frogmore Investments, and although the ownership footprint was not to present any difficulties for redevelopment, its historic value and listed status did raise serious concerns. The project comprised three phases, initially focusing on disaster recovery and making the building safe for development (October 1997), the reinstatement of the external envelope (December 1997), and finally the refurbishment and alterations to the building to provide for an 'up-market mixed-use commercial opportunity' (November 2000). The bombing had left the building in an unstable and dangerous condition, with the roof structures being lifted and distorted, partition walls being blown over, load-bearing walls suffering significant displacement and cracking, and with utilities left in a perilous condition. In both securing the building and reinstatement of the external envelope, project managers were constrained by the property's listed building status – '[there have been] many occasions when we have been wanting to do something in terms of betterment for the building, in creating better space for commercial activity, but we have been constrained by English Heritage' (Development interest). In March 1998 the listed building and planning consents needed to begin the external repair and refurbishment work were secured, and in September 1998 full planning permission and listed building consent were granted.

A range of uses were considered for the building, all possessing market opportunities but also threatened from neighbouring developments. In retailing terms, as already noted, the perceived need was for high-quality stores with larger footplates, with such opportunities being offered by the redevelopment of the neighbouring Shambles Square, and with implicit benefits for the Corn Exchange in terms of niche provision. The potential of the Corn Exchange as a major office location was not seriously considered, despite the fact that the bombing had given the city the opportunity to demolish substantial amounts of secondary office space. Much more likely as part of the initial appraisal was its consideration for potential hotel development, with the local market booming and with this area being under-represented.

The main focus of the strategy for the building, however, was to ensure 'the sensitive repair of the building and its adaptation to accommodate an appropriate range and mix of quality users', encouraging longer opening hours as a contribution to energising the new Exchange Square. In May 1997 preliminary plans were released which proposed refurbishment for a mix of retail and informal leisure uses at basement and ground-floor levels, with a hotel on the upper levels. Subsequent market testing and appraisal work was to lead by early 1998 to Frogmore considering bids from three quality hotel operators. Their preferred route was finally, however, to focus on a retail/restaurant development with offices on the upper floors, at a late stage ruling out a possible residential element. The company's board approved the development profile and funding in November 1998, and the 'Triangle' was born.

As with many Victorian buildings, the Corn Exchange was built very solidly, and thus raised significant challenges when structural changes were needed. Adjustments to the basement slab, for example, meant that the construction team had to go below the existing foundations, often requiring significant underpinning. Listed building status also proved restrictive, since nothing could be bonded to mosaic or terrazzo tiles, and floors had to be treated with a floating membrane over which carpeting was laid. Development was to prove logistically challenging given the 'live' projects taking place on all sides – re-erection of the historic pubs, implementation of Exchange Square proposals, the redevelopment of the Printworks, and the initial stages of constructing Urbis – and it was necessary to manage the refurbishment of the building alongside the timescale of public realm enhancement. The consequence of this was that site accommodation had to be moved twice during the refurbishment process, and the inside of the building had to be used as a storage facility for building supplies. In design terms, the historic value of the building placed constraints on development proposals, with the Exchange being built as several different buildings, with numerous level changes within floors. The designers had little choice but to create offices in the upper floors that followed the divisions and natural breakage of the building, even where this left significant areas of potentially unlettable space. The new interior included an additional glass dome to bring even more light into the centre of the building, with a ground-floor atrium and with glass escalators serving the five-floor galleried development.

The building had a staged opening, being fully operational by November 2000, housing 12,000 square metres of high-quality retail space in 55 retail units, and concentrating on 'lifestyle retailing'. The office element is targeted at the creative side of Manchester, with the media, design and marketing industries most likely to be attracted to this type of space.

Commercial impact of the renewal programme

Measuring the added value created by the cumulative effects of the various schemes being implemented is a difficult task given the inability to directly attribute improvements in yield and rental value. The commercial property market within the city centre has undoubtedly improved over the past five years and yields have hardened, but this has only mirrored wider trends in the national economy arising from low interest rates and buoyant consumer markets. It is perhaps still too early to establish the longer-term impact of rebuilding given the fact that the major commercial projects have only recently come on stream (and Arndale North's remodelling is still awaited). However, with a small number of landowners controlling development within the core, it is clear that the investment value of their assets has been substantially enhanced. It is also possible to reflect on the wider impact of the renewal programme on the city centre's commercial competitiveness, and to consider the views of those development interests most centrally involved. Such reflection is possible as a result of focus group discussions held as part of the study.

In broad terms the reconstruction of the city centre following its bombing has not only restored the physical foundation of the central area and improved its permeability and pedestrian flows, but also triggered a new era of urban investment. It has acted as a catalyst for new uses, occupiers and investment flows, and has stimulated an element of redistribution of existing occupiers and economic activity. Whilst the final outputs expected from the masterplan are significant, the main evidence from masterplan realisation has been the 'spin-off' developments both within and beyond the renewal area, and the obvious change in investor perception (Table 7.1). The emphasis of such additional investment has been both on quality and mixed uses, underpinning the enhanced commercial competitiveness of the city centre, and its substantially changed profile – 'international status is all about public perception, and developer and investor perceptions have undoubtedly changed' (Development interest).

Since the initial phase of renewal in 1997, an exciting and innovative retail centre has evolved, the bomb acting as a catalyst for many of the new schemes and flagship projects. The 'ripple effect' of the successful implementation of the renewal programme, and the buoyancy of the national economic climate, has enabled fringe

Table 7.1 The masterplan's final commercial outputs

New quality retail space	81,000 m²
Damaged retail space re-trading	23,225 m²
Retail space improved	18,600 m²
New quality office space	6,000 m²
New leisure space	45,107 m²
New hotel beds	164

areas of the city centre to develop (Smithfield, Ancoats), and facilitated new economic links within the city centre. Thus, for example, the £14-million renovation of the Boots store on the junction of Cross Street and Market Street was to transform the store into the chain's flagship building, seizing the opportunity offered by the rebuilding programme for radical redesign and a contemporary finish.

> This is by far the biggest rebuilding Boots have been involved with. That's a statement of confidence in the city and says a lot about how we view the longer-term prognosis for Manchester.
>
> (Boots store manager)

Much the same sentiments were evident in the redevelopment of The Circus on the corner of Portland Street and Oxford Street on a site that had been denied investment since World War Two. Here a major £20-million mixed-use scheme was completed in 2001 involving the construction of a new hotel, a night-club and a range of mixed retail uses, involving the reuse of listed façades.

It has facilitated the introduction of retail footplates not previously available within the city. With Harvey Nichols opening a store in the Shambles West development alongside a range of niche up-market retail units, the redesign of the Marks & Spencer store to facilitate the sharing of the building with Selfridges, the refurbishment of the Royal Exchange Shopping Centre, and the major investment in the Corn Exchange and the Arndale North developments, it is clear that the area around Exchange Square will provide the heart of the city's retail prospects for years to come. The regeneration of Piccadilly Gardens, which has additionally involved the refurbishment of its two major departmental store locations, together with the recently completed refurbishment and upgrading of the Market Street pedestrianisation scheme, is evident of the buoyancy and confi-dence exhibited in the retail centre's prospects. Indeed, property industry predic-tions are that whilst the Trafford Centre will have experienced five-year retail turnover growth of 20 per cent, by 2003 the situation for the city centre is expected to improve by 60 per cent. Indeed, the Trafford Centre has had broadly a positive effect on improving the city centre's commercial offer – 'keeping the city centre on its toes' – forcing it to reassess the focus of its continuing competitiveness.

The main winners from this process have undoubtedly been the major landowners (Prudential in particular, and Marks & Spencer latterly), and it is clear that corporate enterprise as a whole has used the opportunities afforded to expand, refurbish and remodel its commercial activities. The main losers from this process have undoubtedly been many small businesses with insufficient protection in their leases to the consequences of large-scale redevelopment, poor insurance cover, and displacement to physically and commercially less attractive areas beyond the central core.

In the office sector Manchester has tightly prescribed 'islands' of development that have traditionally centred on the 'square half mile', with developments outside this core only taking place in buoyant periods. As already indicated, the main period of growth in prime rental values within the city centre was seen in the early 1990s, when strong demand for quality office space from professional services was met with limited supply. The completion of the Great Bridgewater Street office development (1994) was seen to meet such demands in terms of quality office space with larger footplates and on-site parking. This extension to the office market location created opportunities for the refurbishing of secondary properties in the traditional core. However, following the bomb there was an initial fall of office stock availability, with a significant amount of secondary office accommodation – 'seed bed for new business' – being lost. Subsequent hotel, leisure and residential development has taken up much of the slack in this secondary market, and has begun to raise questions as to whether too much of this secondary office stock has been recycled.

The bombing created an opportunity to remove a range of poor secondary office accommodation for higher value and more diverse uses. Office rents remained fairly static for the rest of the decade, characterised by a high degree of localism and internal relocation of the professional services sector. It was undoubtedly affected by the changing urban environment within the core, with infrastructural improvements and growth in retail and leisure facilities being the key features in maintaining the city's appeal for investors. This has facilitated the growth of local 'maverick developers', who have strayed away from the traditional institutional core to more fringe locations, often associated with restoring and converting disused buildings. Indeed, such independents as Urban Splash have tended to work in the shadows of mainstream developers, counterbalancing low rental values with a close proximity to the institutional core (Northern Quarter, Oldham Street), and stressing the role of good design in adding value.

It is not surprising, therefore, that the masterplan foresaw the possibilities of only a limited amount of new office floorspace being possible within the revamped bomb damaged area, and with increasing competition from out-of-centre business parks (Salford Quays, Princess Parkway). Particularly marked was the lack of demand for larger footplates or new office space at this time within the central area, the increasing take-over of elements of the traditional office core (King Street) by high-quality fashion retailers, and a healthy continuing demand for secondary properties. Indeed, with the complex redevelopment of the city centre, the growth of mixed-use and multi-purpose development has dominated the commercial property market. This has to be set against the context, however, that never before has central Manchester had so much to offer office occupiers in terms of infrastructural and public realm improvements, retail and leisure developments, and a vibrant evening economy. Indeed, there is ample evidence of traditional out-of-centre office developments competing for space in the 'new' institutional core of the city, on the back of an emerging high-quality regional centre.

The period leading up to the bombing saw the emergence of a consumption- and lifestyle-based city centre that facilitated an explosive growth of a range of prime leisure and lifestyle facilities in the commercial core, initially focused on the Deansgate area. It expanded subsequently to the north in the direction of the MEN Arena and south-central to the Petersfield and Castlefield quarters. Responding to the bomb stimulated interest in the market for major leisure developments, as the masterplan sought to diversify economic activity within the centre. Demand became so great that developers have turned to the conversion of secondary office space into leisure opportunities. With two major developments now completed – Printworks, Great Northern Warehouse – there is some concern that the leisure market may become saturated in relation to Manchester's population, and may have to retrench if market conditions deteriorate.

> The city is trying to run before it can walk, and substantial growth in the city-centre residential market may be the leisure market's main saviour.
>
> (Development professional)

The booming leisure market continues to be sustained by low unemployment and high disposable income, and a vibrant city-centre residential and student market. The explosive growth of hotels within the core since the mid-1990s is a reflection not only of the Commonwealth Games' ability to boost visitor numbers, but the wider regeneration success that has made the city centre a premier short-break destination.

In terms of the city centre's commercial future, it is widely felt that the commercial buoyancy evident in 2003 will need careful management, and a clear vision statement of the core's economic direction, so as to ensure that the present momentum continues. However, it is widely felt that the current mix of markets within the city is likely to be mutually supporting in the face of recessionary trends, which would in the process enhance the competitive tensions between the city centre and the Trafford Centre. Some concerns were expressed, however, as to the effect of technological change on the continuing competitiveness of the core, and the way in which the revamped city centre can continue to be promoted to a wider consumer and investor market.

Chapter 8

Creating urban quality within the core

Town centres play a multi-purpose role in that as well as serving economic functions they are also an important source of civic pride and identity. Promoting the quality of the urban fabric is a central feature of government guidance relating to the integrated management of urban areas. This is advocated for its contribution to sustainable development concerns; in enhancing attractiveness for business and investment; in reinforcing civic pride and sense of place; and in creating safer city centres. In the previous chapter we discussed the extent to which Manchester city centre had been able to meet a multiplicity of challenges through extending and diversifying its economic base and in enhancing its commercial vitality. However, equally important in increasing the centre's competitiveness has been the improvement to its urban fabric. The current chapter attempts to review progress in this field by appraising those elements of the renewal programme that have done most to contribute to the city centre's current vibrancy. Initially concerned with the core's existing morphology, it considers the centrality of design aspirations to the renewal programme, and the balancing of this with commercial realism. It then proceeds to consider the reconfiguration of the core's commercial footprint through block remodelling, before appraising design-led instruments for realising individual projects.

Local development context

Existing morphology and quality

Little of Manchester's pre-Georgian origins survives, being demolished by the Victorians during the city's expansive phase, and today it is the late Victorian and

Edwardian plan and built form that dominate the core. The city's morphological interest lies with the consequence of the cotton industry that dominated its development, and that left a distinct material legacy from an era of mass manufacturing – architecture, physical layout of buildings, defunct tracts of land and spaces, canals, railways, warehouses and mill works (Hartwell 2001; Parkinson-Bailey 2000).

Like other cities Manchester suffered badly from bomb damage in World War Two, with the focus thereafter on salvaging the better-known and dominant buildings (Free Trade Hall, Royal Exchange), and with most Victorian and Edwardian buildings being given scant recognition. In the immediate post-war period there was a chance to rebuild something new, and the Nicholson Plan (1945) envisaged that the 'old grimy, out-of-date, irrational buildings of the Victorian era would be swept away to be replaced with bold, new buildings of the twentieth century' (Parkinson-Bailey 2000: 162). A new education precinct, new cultural and sports facilities, an exhibition hall and a processional way were proposed, together with uniform pavilion blocks of new commercial and civic developments, wide streets and green spaces. For Manchester, however, this new 'nobler and braver' age was a long time coming, with the continuing collapse of the industries that lay at the heart of the city's economic wealth.

It was not until the mid-1950s that the first new commercial post-war buildings were erected, to be followed in the early 1960s by growing pressures for major redevelopment of central-area commercial sites. This was stimulated by government commitment to the strategic redevelopment of war-damaged cities through the Comprehensive Development Areas (CDA) mechanism. The local authority was extremely active at this stage in acquiring central-area land and property (both by negotiation and by CPO), and large-scale authority-led schemes were to radically change the face of the city in the 1960s. The Crown Square developments (currently the Spinningfield redevelopment area), accommodating law courts and the city's education service, were the largest civic development initiative, paying little heed however to the city's historic grain, and facilitating the growing impermeability of the core. Further blight was caused by land and building purchases acquired for new highway construction, and the intention of establishing major multi-level interchanges on the edge of the commercial core. Fortunately little of these road schemes came to fruition, and by the mid-1970s the proposals were replaced by an existing Inner Relief Road plan and a number of smaller schemes. Speculative office building took off in the city centre in the early 1960s, resulting in the destruction of a swathe of Victorian buildings perceived to be unsuitable for modern requirements. Considerable net overprovision was realised by the early 1970s, however, as the city 'intentionally expunged its industrial image', stimulating a growing conservation movement dissatisfied with the quality of new developments. Indeed the local authority had numerous CDAs underway at the time

(Market Street, Shambles, CWS area), and few older buildings were being retained and reused, being replaced by modern buildings with little historic value.

Manchester in the early 1970s was losing both office jobs and retail employment as decentralisation pressures increased, and it was argued that renewal of the retail sector was vital for the city's commercial health. Construction of the Arndale Centre began in 1972 (the culmination of nearly two decades of land acquisition under a CDA), and was to be completed in 1979, creating a 115,000-square-metre retail development of 210 shops and a two-storey market hall. Parking spaces for 1,800 cars, a bus station in the basement, and a 22-storey office block completed the development. This was to have a major impact on the core's morphology and townscape, and on shopping behaviour within the city. When linked with the associated commercial development on the other side of Corporation Street (Shambles North/West) it formed a vast impermeable development that seriously detracted from the character of the commercial core. With only one active frontage (Market Street), the building did little to animate surrounding streets, with an impenetrable wall forming the Corporation Street frontage, facing Marks & Spencer's new retail store and its accompanying office tower.

The Shambles block was redeveloped in the late 1960s, featuring a new civic space (Shambles Square) surrounded by two office blocks and ground-level retail units. Two listed public houses survived the redevelopment, being 'jacked up' within a soulless setting. These twin developments, with their combined retail power, were to result in the gradual commercial decline of the Oldham Street/Piccadilly area. Above-grade pedestrian bridges linked the Arndale and Shambles developments and the Ramada block over Deansgate. The incorporation of shop units into overhead deck structures was also envisaged, with the Voyagers Bridge linking the Arndale Centre with Boots on the opposite side of Market Street.

From the mid-1970s onwards local development attitudes began to change, with environmental quality enhancement becoming a central concern, this signalling the start of an extensive programme of conservation area designation and the listing of historic buildings. The removal or reuse of derelict land and obsolete buildings, and the cleaning up of urban waterways were at the heart of this focus, with the development of the former Central Station as an exhibition centre (G-Mex) and the promotion of the Castlefields Urban Heritage Park being seminal early regeneration efforts in the core. Following a successful promotional campaign for city-centre shopping in the early 1980s, the local authority began to commit itself to public realm improvements, with a pedestrianisation scheme for King's Street, Market Street, Albert Square and St Ann's Square. This aimed to enhance the city's image, and to entice commercial development and retail consumption. Brickclad buildings became the norm, as a reaction to the concrete developments of the 1960s and early 1970s, but there was still little evidence of any radical attempts by developers to enhance the character of city-centre buildings.

The 'modern era' was set in motion by the CMDC, which aimed to bring back land and buildings into effective use, to enhance the environmental qualities of the city centre, and to increase the core's commercial potential. This was particularly difficult to achieve given the recessionary pressures on business in the early 1990s, but it did herald a new vision of the qualities required for success within the core, and was marked by a succession of landmark developments that have contributed a new townscape dimension within the city centre, involving both new build (MMU Library, Bridgewater Hall, MEN Arena, Barbirolli Square) and refurbishment (Castle Quay). Thus by 1996, the city centre's urban character – beyond the monolithic Arndale/Shambles development – was beginning to change quite radically, with developer confidence returning to the city, and with public–private partnership arrangements in full swing.

Established policy guidance

During the early 1990s the key policy framework for considering townscape quality was to be focused on the UDP (1995), City Pride (1994) and the City Development Guide (1996). The UDP was to build upon a fairly flexible and informal planning regime, with established policies felt to have served the city centre well, even if the design elements within the plan were perceived as being relatively weak. Central to achieving the plan's objectives was seen to be the creation of a safe, attractive and accessible city centre, with specific areas being targeted as priority for public realm improvements – land adjoining city-centre waterways, conservation areas within the core, and areas of major pedestrian activity, civic squares and access routes from transport interchanges. Whilst there was clear commitment to mixed-use development, higher development densities, and the planned development of inner-city sites, these were essentially strategic concerns rather than specifically focusing on townscape, with little detail on public realm policies and the qualities of urban space being promoted, and a general feeling that the city was largely reactive in design terms. Indeed, Marshall (1994) argued that Manchester as a landscape had been misunderstood by modern development, and whilst accepting that commercial pressures influence design issues, argued that there was a need to enhance the city's character and individuality in the process of ensuring quality development.

In relation to the City Pride visioning exercise, the promotion of an environment with a strong visual quality and a sense of vitality was seen as essential, perceived as a long-term project which would continue to evolve over the lifetime of the prospectus. The vision rested on the marrying of an enhanced international prestige with local benefits, with a number of the themes – infrastructural standards, building and facility accessibility, strengthening of physical fabric and encouraging higher density – stressing a growing concern for environmental quality within the core.

Finally, an independent panel was established to consider the factors that would create and enhance the city's built environment, and to draft a city development guide. This would promote a strong sense of place, and incorporate guidance on the careful design of buildings and streets, and the spaces in between. The resulting draft guide attached a great deal of importance to the form of physical layout to be achieved within the city centre, with its radical nature raising concerns from property and investor interests (particularly over issues of development density and permeability) (Kitchen 1997). It was adopted in a very watered-down version – guidance on sense of place, especially in the maintenance of the public realm; the importance of high-quality design, density and mixed use; successful streets, sustainability, transport and car parking; and stewardship and security – as guidance to inform future development proposals. Design guidelines for the public realm were outlined in three of the elements highlighted – notably those of a sense of place, the quality of design, and successful streets.

As has already been noted, the damage to property as a result of the bombing was considerable, particularly for 300 metres along the length of Corporation Street and for a width of 100 metres, with the total of 1.2 million square metres of property affected. However, only a few buildings were seriously affected structurally, those taking the brunt being largely post-war additions to the fabric of the commercial core. The majority of the Arndale Centre survived intact, with the opportunity being taken to refurbish and upgrade the facility. The Shambles West block, although badly damaged by the blast, remained structurally sound, and was demolished (and the historic pubs relocated) in response to the intentions of the masterplan rather than as a direct consequence of the bomb. Finally, whilst a number of key historic buildings – Royal Exchange and the Corn Exchange – suffered major structural damage, they were refurbished and remodelled and now provide a vital contribution to the vibrant core.

Balancing aesthetic quality with commerce

Following the decision to hold the masterplanning competition, a two-stage process was launched, with the initial stage expected to define the preliminary approach to be adopted, and with the second stage intended to develop an urban framework which was comprehensive in nature, and which would provide the momentum for positive change in the core and its surrounding area.

The brief and emerging vision
The initial brief noted that the Task Force's intention in launching the challenge was to generate 'imaginative and realistic ideas to complement the needs and aspirations of a great regional capital city', and to provide:

a development and investment framework which creates an architec-
turally distinctive core which is of an urban character ... is responsive
to access needs ... physically and socially integrated with the rest of
the city ... maximises private investment and stimulates economic
activity ... promotes the widest possible range of opportunities ...
minimises the risk or fear of crime ... and where activity can take place
at most times of the day and night.

(Competition brief)

It was expected to enhance the setting of listed buildings and the
character and appearance of conservation areas; improve the appearance and
role of the River Irwell; preserve, interpret and integrate the medieval core of the
old city; and create a pedestrian-friendly environment with attractive spaces. The
framework was also expected to rationalise access requirements, to remove
through traffic and to sustain excellent public transport links.

The second-stage brief was a considerably fuller document, expected to
create an imaginative interpretation of design and development aspirations, to
demonstrate a clear workable approach to phasing and implementation, and to facilitate and justify the required investment. It stressed, however, that the competition
was essentially a masterplanning opportunity, and competitors were to assume that
certain buildings would require demolition, others would require substantial external
and internal refurbishment, and with the reconfiguration of other areas to be driven by
commercial rather than structural considerations. With each of the design firms being
given separate working sessions with landowners and investors, a substantial
measure of commercial realism would inevitably inform evolving frameworks. Thereafter, as already noted in chapter 4, technical design and commercial appraisals of the
submissions were to take place, involving MML and other key interests.

The key features of EDAW's winning submission were based on a set of
basic design principles that, as a result of the jury's conclusions, were to require some
further refinement (Table 8.1). The framework was expected to continue to evolve as

Table 8.1 Design principles underpinning the winning submission

- A 24-hour city that encourages a diverse mix of uses.
- Central public spaces on both a grand and human scale that maintain the importance of existing key landmarks.
- Pedestrian-dominant transport nodes.
- Places, routes and views which respect the city's architectural heritage, visual structure and linkages.
- Integration of both the Arndale Centre and the cathedral with the fabric of the city centre, and brings the centre through to the River Irwell.
- Provides the new Exchange Square as a central focus.

the recovery programme moved into its implementation phase, following the masterplan's adoption in December 1996. During this period, the winning team and MML's advisers worked to review the issues raised by the jury, refine the winning scheme in financial, programming and physical design terms, and on the basis of identified development parcels to prepare site-specific design guidelines capable of acting as a brief for the owners/developers of each site (see chapter 5). During this iterative process 'there was considerable shuffling around at the edges, but the fundamental components of the winning design were very much evident'. Additionally, since the masterplan would need to be compatible with the city's existing policy frameworks, a rapid decision was made to prepare supplementary planning guidance for the bomb-damaged area to support the successful implementation of the preferred masterplanning vision. In physical and built-form terms the key changes that were to emerge as a result of this iterative process were targeted and substantial, and by spring 1997 the final masterplan was in place (Table 8.2).

Creating and delivering the quality core

With the publication of the initial implementation plan, delivery of the masterplan had been translated into key strategic objectives, amongst which 'the creation of a quality core fit for the 21st century' was a central element. This aimed to:

- create a high-quality public realm attractive to private sector investment;
- help to enhance the quality of life and create an urban environment attractive to all users;
- promote accessibility and offer a safe and healthy environment for diverse uses and activities; and
- enhance the setting of the architectural and historic urban fabric.

Table 8.2 Physical modifications to the initial masterplan

- The relocation and realignment of the two historic public houses from Shambles West to a site near the cathedral.
- The detailed execution of the landmark cultural building (Urbis) changed as a result of a design competition.
- With the Arndale Centre, whilst the fundamental concepts of the original plan stayed in place (active street frontage, Wintergarden, improving the functionality) the detail of how these elements were actually going to be achieved was significantly developed.
- The major expansion of the leisure scheme at Shudehill, and the proposals for the transport interchange would substantially displace the housing component.
- The location and form of the Cathedral Visitor Centre changed substantially as a result of the process of design and consultation.
- The importance of the new public square (Exchange Square) increased as a result of discussions relating to the 'stitching up' of the surrounding area, and in an attempt to create a more dramatic solution.

Realisation of this objective in public realm terms was to be achieved by the creation of new public spaces – new square, new street, new park – together with the upgrading of existing streets within the masterplan area in order to increase overall permeability. Emphasis was placed on the use of high-quality materials and finish that would be relatively efficient and cost effective to maintain and repair, and included a commitment to the extension of public art into the fabric of the city. The strategy also envisaged improvements to the quality of private buildings so as to ensure that they made a positive contribution to the city's streetscape.

> Good-quality design must matter more, because my practice and others like it are now working on city-based projects, whereas a decade ago we never would have been. I think it would then have been much more commercially driven, rather than design-led, practices that would have been involved.
>
> (Local architect)

Finally, to ensure that the quality of both the public realm and private sector development was sustained for the longer term, the masterplan recognised that the enhanced core would need to be managed to the highest possible standards, and new agreements to strengthen management arrangements in partnership with the private sector were proposed.

Private interests

The message to commercial operators was twofold: namely that new developments in the city centre would be hugely successful commercially as a result of the rebuilding programme, and that businesses already in the city should be persuaded to stay and to reaffirm their commitment.

> If you had a building that looked on to a space like that, that is so easily accessible in the middle of the country's second city, do you think you are really going to fail? And when you started talking about how easy it was for people to get in there, and why people would want to be there, people bought the message.
>
> (EDAW team leader)

MML's commitment to an enhanced public realm would give them a vastly improved streetscape for commercial activity, and would be largely funded by the public sector. This was clearly in their long-term commercial interest, even if there remained some initial problems.

> We hadn't got all the funding in place, we were still negotiating … we were still clearing up after the bomb … were still demolishing their

buildings. So I think there was a credibility problem in the nicest possible way … 'oh this looks great, but when is it going to happen?'

(MML officer)

Once the commercial benefits were generally accepted, the second task was to persuade the commercial operators of the benefits of spending significant resources on their individual buildings, to ensure that both new development and refurbishment were of the highest quality. The masterplan established the grain around a series of development parcels, and the developers and their professional advisers were expected to underpin this focus in relation to individual buildings.

We said very early on – you have to do two things. Get a range of architects to do your buildings, and get a different range of landscape architects to do the detailed design work on your public realm. Whilst we are not going to do the buildings, we are going to tell you what the components should be, and we will work with these people to deliver these elements.

(EDAW team leader)

Whilst the extent of design oversight on development proposals was significantly different from normal expectations – 'facilitating good architecture by stealth' – and generally acquiesced to by developers in relation to the larger prize, it proved a much more difficult task to convince them of the merits of spending money on the public aspects of their developments. The difficulty lay in the ability to measure quantitatively the commercial benefits derived from such activity, and whilst 'there were developers in there that bought the story, it was bloody hard work with some of them' (Masterplan adviser).

Obviously we were never going to put tiles back, but by the same token, to remove the rest of the tiles would cost around £30 million … and it wouldn't have got us a single extra customer through the doors. Equally, to get rid of the Voyager Bridge, which some people wanted us to do, would have cost £30 million for a view … and MML wouldn't pay for it.

(P&O Shopping Centres, Chairman)

In order to make aesthetic improvements to individual buildings, commercial interests required the financial ability to add value, and were likely to argue this case in relation to the company's responsibility to shareholders, rather than to the arguments relating to enhanced profitability.

They [MML] will say to us 'this is a great idea don't you think?' … and you personally agree … and then they say 'well do you think you could see your way to donating x pounds towards this,' … They look at you

> with a sort of innocence and you say 'well actually no, because until we
> know where we're going, were not in a position to give you money'.
>
> (Prudential representative)

For instance, to fund aesthetic improvements to the Arndale Centre and
to provide money for their interests in Shambles West, P&O originally suggested that
there should be an in-fill retail development on Corporation Street between the
Arndale Centre and the new Marks & Spencer store. This commercial gain and
improved circulation possibilities being offered to P&O would enable it to contribute
to other elements. Similar discussions took place over the Cannon Street/Winter-
garden proposals, and level change requirements within the centre. The City Council
and MML resisted such overtures on the basis of traffic issues, the retention of views
through the Northern Gateway, and commercial consequences for surrounding
areas. At this time there were undoubtedly tensions between the aspirations of MML
and some commercial interests, and a balance had to be struck between aesthetic
enhancement, design quality, and what was commercially achievable. Indeed, some
private landowners felt that the Task Force and its consultants were involved too
much in detailed design issues, whilst EDAW felt that they had to intervene given that
certain landowners were making insufficient progress.

> The owners think that the city's assets are worthless, the city thinks that
> the changes it is requesting to the Arndale Centre are nothing more than
> cosmetic. Who knows? It's a large game of three-dimensional poker.
>
> (MML design adviser)

> The public sector has responsibilities for all sorts of things … and how
> they shape the public realm is very relevant, … but to have all of this
> driven by aesthetics, and their insatiable desire to design everyone
> else's buildings is just ridiculous.
>
> (P&O Shopping Centres, Chairman)

> What happened was that we ended up having quite a large impact on
> some of the buildings because to a greater or lesser degree the archi-
> tectural teams involved weren't coming up to scratch, or needed
> pretty strong guidance to raise their game.
>
> (EDAW team leader)

In the end, however, EDAW were pragmatic about what they realistically expected the private sector to deliver in terms of building enhancement, and
it was inevitable that in some cases economic forces were to constrain design
aspirations. Thus the Voyagers Bridge ended up being upgraded rather than
removed, yellow tiles remained on large parts of the Arndale Centre, and the
Corporation Street bridge link was agreed to and publicly funded.

There's going to be a fight about above-grade bridges ... I'm an agnostic. Don't like them generally, and would prefer people to cross at the street level to keep things active. But, if there's enough energy, enough blood in the street to take two levels, then maybe you can have a go, as long as it's delicate and filigreed.

(MML design consultant)

The two key areas of public–private sector debate relating to issues of urban quality concerned the reconfiguration of Shambles West and the remodelling of the Arndale Centre, both highlighted as project examples. However, it is useful at this stage to briefly discuss the major design dimensions involved. In relation to the Shambles West block, as head lessee, Prudential entered into an agreement with MML enabling the block's redevelopment potential to be realised, and a design brief was prepared in July 1997. This viewed the block as the programme's most important development parcel, since it defined the edge and the character of the extension north of St Ann's Square into New Cathedral Street, making it a central defining element. It was originally considered to offer a range of redevelopment opportunities, these being refined by 'an architectural statement' published in September 1998 that brought such considerations up to date. This envisaged support for active street life by bringing the frontage right up to its boundaries, and defining a new street pattern whilst relating it to its surroundings. At its heart would be a departmental store with its own identity, but without losing the overall sense of continuity along New Cathedral Street as a 'city block'. A complementary residential block was introduced, conceived of as wedge shaped, rising out of the St Mary's/Deansgate elevation, and projecting over the pavement for its full height. This elevation was intended to present an opportunity to express the drama of the tall residential block, and contrast this with the architecture of the departmental store.

In June 1997 EDAW presented a 'design framework' for the Arndale Centre – long the butt of criticism for its external appearance – that attempted to address issues of context, the dialogue with adjacent buildings and spaces, and its permeability for pedestrian movement. Major damage to the Corporation Street frontage caused by the bomb raised the opportunity to significantly redesign, and in some areas redevelop the Arndale Centre, to break up its mass and singular style, and to underpin the aspirations of the key parties involved. However, the work would need to meet P&O's normal commercial criteria in order to justify the substantial investment proposed. The framework thus set a series of principles/ parameters aspired to, whilst allowing flexibility as to exact timing and detailing of individual components. In terms of permeability the framework proposed a build-out with new street-level access to shops; the improvement of circulation within the centre, and the creation of a Wintergarden and an attractive pedestrian route with new active frontages; and major improvements to Voyagers Bridge and Withy Grove. Aesthetic quality would be enhanced by the removal of the yellow tiles, renovation of façades and an increase in street-frontage activity.

Public realm
The creation of a series of vibrant and attractive public spaces was an integral feature of the masterplan, focusing on a new pedestrian boulevard linking St Ann's Square to the cathedral (New Cathedral Street), a major park to provide a more appropriate context for Chetham's/the cathedral/Urbis (City Park); a civic space as a central meeting place (Exchange Square), and an improved pedestrian environment on the main commercial thoroughfares within the core. The creation of a quality core was also to embrace an innovative strategy to introduce public art into the fabric of the city, and gave added impetus to the introduction of CCTV. In a specific sense the delivery of public realm projects was dependent on a completion of key sections of the Inner Relief Road; the programming of road closures and traffic regulation orders; securing agreement with utilities providers to relocate services; the programming of individual private sector developments; and the management of public transport facilities and revised bus-routing arrangements.

Implementation of the programme had also to be carried out efficiently, dovetailing with the completion of key private sector projects, but at the same time minimising disruption. Complex and detailed programme management arrangements were introduced to facilitate this, with the dual aim of maintaining good access to and within the city during reconstruction, and ensuring that completed public realm improvements were not subsequently damaged or compromised by major construction work on adjacent developments.

In July 1997 an 'outline design report' was prepared by EDAW, setting out the design team's approach to the initial phases of public realm delivery, with this document serving as a preview for subsequent detailed design work (Table 8.3). Design was expected to be accessible to all, to promote and accommodate pedestrian movement, and to give circulation priority over vehicular movement. It had to be cost efficient, durable and sustainable, within target budgets, and conceived to help unify the various styles of adjoining architecture. Finally, the public realm had to provide an appropriate level of security for the general public and for business.

The first phase of public realm activity comprised Corporation/Cross Street (from Cannon Street to Market Street); Market Street (from Exchange Street to Corporation Street); New Cathedral Street (with an east and a west phase); Deansgate/Cateaton Street (to facilitate the new access arrangements to Shambles Square); and areas around the Mitre Hotel (to facilitate the relocated pubs). A complex sequencing arrangement of these works was programmed, with the first element around the Royal Exchange commencing in September 1998, and the final element adjacent to Marks & Spencer being completed in November 1999,

Delivering the vision

212

Table 8.3 Design parameters for the public realm programme

- Choice of materials for street surfaces, lighting units and street furniture must be of high quality, easy to maintain and be able to withstand the rigours of heavy use.
- Design of new urban spaces should reflect their intended use and generally be uncluttered, should have a sense of enclosure but not dominance.
- New/existing streets should provide safe facilities for pedestrian walkways and crossing points.
- Use of urban spaces for other purposes such as street cafes and performance areas should be encouraged, and urban art should be incorporated as an integral part of the overall design.
- Development should complement new and refurbished urban spaces, especially in terms of scale, mass and materials.

---

marking the ending of the first phase of the renewal programme as a whole. The timing of the works was inextricably linked to the completion of a whole series of private sector projects – the Royal Exchange, the Arndale–Boots elevation, the installation of a bus super stop, the Arndale build-out, Marks & Spencer, Shambles West – and involved a whole series of managed processes (Table 8.4).

The focus of the second phase was substantively to concentrate on work relating to Exchange Square, but included public realm activity in the neighbouring Withy Grove (south) and Corporation Street (north) areas. The same procedures were adopted as with the initial stage, with the main objective being to coincide with the key opening dates for the private developments surrounding Exchange Square – in particular the Printworks and the Triangle. The third phase of public realm activity focused on the final elements of private sector development projects, the refurbishment of Market Street, and centrally on the work

Table 8.4 Public realm implementation: detailed design processes

---

- Detailed design briefs provided for all work in phase 1, together with a phasing and logistics strategy to underpin the delivery of such works, including agreement on procurement issues and rules.
- Agreement by the Task Force/City Council of a public realm works quality plan, detailed phase 1 design, and the appointment of Urban Solutions, following a competitive tendering process, as the lead public realm design team.
- Finalising of tender documentation and appointment of contractors, following a competitive tendering process, to undertake phase 1 works.
- Negotiations with utilities providers on the relocation or diversion of services, and with private suppliers relating to street furniture, together with the preparation of detailed road closure/traffic regulation order procedures.
- Ongoing coordination programming and site logistics to minimise disruption and to ensure a smooth interface with adjacent projects, including implementation of a construction access strategy.

---

associated with realising Millennium Quarter projects. Whilst largely completed by July 2002 (Shambles West completed in early 2003), the transport interchange (early 2004) and the redevelopment of Arndale North (2005) are still awaited.

Overall, public realm activity was successfully completed around and interacting with major development initiatives. Interface issues did however raise considerable tensions with some of the private sector interests, the main focus for criticisms relating to the development of Exchange Square.

> They sent me a brief for it, which horrified me, because it was all about building palaces … As far as I'm concerned, you could slab the whole thing over in York stone and say: right, over to you, Mancunians. No, they wanted to turn it into something grand, and they also wanted the international thing.
>
> (P&O Shopping Centres, Chairman)

> I think everybody's trying too hard on that. Somebody must have said the competition worked well last time, let's try it again, and I think it was a shambles. Manchester has got enough skill to have delivered that square without the need for international inputs.
>
> (Development company, Chief Executive)

St Ann's Square leading on to New Cathedral Street

**New Cathedral
Street with its
curved frontage**

In complementing public realm activity the importance of art and culture in regeneration was recognised from the outset, seeing it as helping to improve the quality and attractiveness of the environment, encouraging the use and ownership of public spaces, and strengthening the potential of the area. A public art steering group was thus established to consider how artists could best contribute to the reshaping of the city centre, and a professional artist was retained by MML to collaborate with the masterplan design team. A strategy for public art in the renewal area was produced, identifying locations for specific projects, and highlighting areas of future opportunity.

Reconfiguring commercial footprints

This section, by focusing on a specific development parcel, will aim to consider the implications for urban form of reconfiguring an established commercial footprint within the core, and its contribution to the success of the renewal programme as a whole.

Case study 5: the Shambles block

Located at the heart of the city's commercial core, the block consists of a rectangular-shaped site that originally formed part of the medieval settlement of Manchester, and it experienced incremental changes in the period up to World War Two. The area retained a fine-grained street pattern and a good level of permeability, with north–south routes providing links between the cathedral area and St Ann's Square. The small-scale nature of historic development patterns also ensured that buildings within the Shambles block followed the natural topography of the land, which slopes from Corporation Street in the east to Deansgate in the west, and from St Mary's Gate in the south to Cateaton Street in the north.

During World War Two the Shambles block was badly damaged by bombing, and the opportunity for comprehensive redevelopment was subsequently seized, the block being redeveloped in three stages. The first phase took place on the north-east quadrant of the site with the construction of Longridge House in the early 1960s. Planning permission was subsequently granted for a new retail store and accompanying office tower, which was occupied by Marks & Spencer in 1973. The remainder of the site was redeveloped from the late 1960s onwards as a series of schemes around a new civic space known as Shambles Square. Two office blocks with ground-floor retailing (Mackintosh House and Cannon House) completed the northern half of the site. Other developments included a series of shop units on St Mary's Gate adjacent to Marks & Spencer, and a block incorporating a supermarket, retailing units, and a further office block (Adamson House) on the corner of St Mary's Gate and Deansgate.

The new structures radically altered the area both functionally and aesthetically, but failed to respect the surrounding streetscape and natural topography of the area. The fine-grained street pattern was lost, replaced by an impermeable, largely inward-looking series of developments, which served to isolate the cathedral area from the commercial heart of the city centre. Vehicular and pedestrian movement was rigidly separated, with the deck construction enabling the development to include underground car parking and servicing facilities. The historic pubs that had survived the redevelopment process had, however, to be raised 'in situ' to an appropriate grade level, so they could be incorporated within the wider scheme. This meant that whilst the entire Shambles block was at grade on Market Street and St Mary's Gate, it was significantly raised on the Deansgate and Cateaton Street frontages, creating a blank wall frontage, and severely restricting pedestrian movement across the site.

By the late 1980s the development was suffering from a poor image, struggled to compete with adjacent retailing areas, and had rental income significantly lower than that achieved on Market Street. P&O (the main commercial interest) considered major redevelopment of the area impossible, due mainly to the complex arrangement of leases and sub-leases. Proposals for short-term improvements proved relatively expensive, and, with the various parties unable to agree a funding package, the area remained unchanged. Marks & Spencer was trading well but suffered from an extremely poor store layout, a feature that the company had regularly attempted to address. Discussions had already been held with the City Council and adjacent landowners concerning the possibility of delivering an improved footprint (May 1996), with the chain aiming to change the shape of the store and to gain some additional floorspace. Indeed, preliminary discussions had taken place with Royal Insurance regarding the possible procurement of the adjacent Longridge House.

Half a century after the wartime bombing had facilitated the wholesale redevelopment of the Shambles site, the 1996 attack once again offered the opportunity for fundamental redesign. Buildings on the eastern side of the site (Longridge House and Marks & Spencer) bore the full force of the blast, and were subsequently demolished, but the remainder of the block remained structurally sound. The winning masterplan envisaged the reintegration of the area into its surrounding urban fabric, with the Shambles block seen as presenting major opportunities to increase quality retail provision within the city, improved pedestrian linkages between St Ann's Square and the cathedral area, and enhanced short-stay car parking provision within the city centre. Increasing permeability was vital to relink the cathedral area to the city's commercial heart, and was to be achieved by reintroducing a north–south link through the Shambles block in the form of a pedestrianised boulevard, the first new street in the city for 50 years. Development sites on either side of the new street became central to achieving MML's objective of restoring and enhancing the city's retail core, with the redevelopment of the Shambles site being regarded as the most significant priority of the masterplan. However, the plans were highly ambitious given the site's complex physical structure and intricate nature of land ownership interests, and facilitating the proposed development required the commercial footprints of the entire block to be reconfigured.

The multi-project basis of the Shambles block

MARKS & SPENCER STORE

In the first few weeks and months after the bombing, the company was presented with a range of problems focused on the need for temporary accommodation, essential to ensure the chain retained its substantial customer base. A great deal of thought was given, especially within the first few days after the blast, as to whether the Marks & Spencer building was repairable, and discussions continued with Royal Insurance over the possible acquisition of Longridge House. The severe damage to the building, coupled with the desire of Royal Insurance to vacate the building, gave Marks & Spencer an early opportunity to acquire the property. The company pledged its absolute and total commitment to the city, and there was a real desire to create a new landmark building. Whilst the bombing provided the opportunity for change, it was Marks & Spencer's decision to build a flagship store at the very heart of the bomb-damaged area that provided the necessary catalyst for the subsequent commercial renewal of the city centre, and the future remodelling of the Shambles block as a whole.

NEW CATHEDRAL STREET

The creation of a new street through the centre of the Shambles site represented one of the masterplan's key strategic planning objectives. This would create an important new pedestrian 'spine' through the city centre, linking the high-quality retail district of King Street and St Ann's Square with the major new civic space of Exchange Square, the Millennium Quarter and the MEN Arena beyond. The new street would not only provide an important physical link, it would also create a new visual link, revealing a view of the cathedral from St Ann's Square. It was to be a broad space to accommodate large numbers of pedestrians moving along and across the street, and would provide a memorable shopping experience, with pedestrian security ensured both night and day. Built entirely on a deck structure, the new street would span underground parking and servicing facilities.

SHAMBLES PUBS

Although badly damaged, the two historic public houses located within Shambles Square – the Old Wellington Inn and Sinclair's Oyster Bar – survived the bombing largely due to the inherent flexibility of their timber-framed structures. However, the Old Wellington was the most severely damaged of the two, reopening in early 1997 after receiving painstaking repairs and remedial work (costing £500,000). Sinclair's Oyster Bar was more fortunate in that, shielded from the explosion by the Old Wellington, it was able to reopen within days of the blast. The original EDAW masterplan envisaged that the two historic structures would remain in situ, with new developments incorporated around them. But as plans for the Shambles block were further refined, it became clear that the key to unlocking the full development potential of the site was the relocation of the pubs, and a cathedral-owned receptor site was identified as a suitable new location. These were ambitious and controversial plans, with MML involved in difficult and complex negotiations with the two breweries, the Dean of Manchester and other interested parties, such as English Heritage. The breweries were initially unreceptive to the suggestion that their pubs should be dismantled and rebuilt elsewhere, and this necessitated protracted negotiations. For the Dean of Manchester, the decision to allow public houses to be erected on land owned by the cathedral was clearly difficult. In addition, there was opposition to the proposals from conservation groups within the city. In parallel with the delicate discussions with land-ownership interests, there were also complex construction and engineering issues to be resolved. Nevertheless, by the end of 1997 considerable progress had been made, enabling the alignment of New Cathedral Street to be released for redevelopment.

SHAMBLES WEST

Although damaged by the bombing, the properties towards the western side of the Shambles block were repairable, and trading began in earnest once the main phase of emergency recovery had been completed and units refitted. Nevertheless, there was a real desire to see the western half of the Shambles block redeveloped as part of the wider renewal plans, this being seen as central to restoring and to enhancing the retail core of the city centre. It was always envisaged that the redevelopment of Shambles West would form a second phase of the redevelopment process, with the momentum generated by the new Marks & Spencer store helping to drive forward commercial plans for the remainder of the Shambles site.

At the time of the bombing the ownership of Shambles Square was particularly complex, involving the city as freeholder, and Prudential and P&O as major leaseholders. By March 1997 it had been agreed that the Prudential would assume the principal development role for Shambles West, and that P&O's interest in the site would be acquired. As head lessee, the Prudential was to enter into a number of agreements enabling the redevelopment potential of the site to be released, and an outline commercial strategy was agreed. A development brief was being prepared in parallel, setting the framework for the most important land parcel of the rebuilding programme (July 1997). Any development on the site would define the edge and character of New Cathedral Street; redefine the surrounding streetscape in terms of activity and vitality; and form an important gateway feature for those entering the city via Victoria Bridge. Shambles West was considered to be well positioned within the city centre, offering the potential for a wide range of uses – retail, restaurant, residential and office activity – as well as other facilities including potential hotel and night-life functions. A commercial team was thus assembled to prepare feasibility studies and to take the project forward.

Development procedures

Assembling the new footprint for Marks & Spencer, Shambles West and New Cathedral Street proved extremely complex due to the site being in multiple ownership with around 70 interests having to be acquired to facilitate redevelopment. With the city as freeholder, Marks & Spencer, P&O, the Prudential and the Royal Insurance holding significant leasehold interests, and numerous retail and office users possessing various sub-leases, complex layers of ownership interests existed on the site. For example, around half a dozen different land parcels either fell directly within, or impinged upon, the Marks & Spencer/New Cathedral Street footprint, and a number of these had upwards of four and five sub-leases on them.

Shambles Block – commercial elements

MARKS & SPENCER

An outline application for the new store was submitted to the City Council in December 1996, seeking approval in principle for a retail development with basement car parking. The decision to approve was subject to a key condition that, given that the development would lead to the loss of former pedestrian walkways, a route through the Marks & Spencer store between Corporation Street and New Cathedral Street should be made available to the public during trading hours, thus retaining permeability through the site. A full planning application was submitted in July 1997, being consulted upon widely with the landowners and leaseholders directly affected or immediately contiguous to the site, the only significant objections being from conservation interests. The application was approved in September 1997 subject to a variety of construction and layout conditions.

NEW CATHEDRAL STREET

Outline permission for the new street was granted in October 1997. A full application was subsequently submitted in April 1998, with approval being sought for a pedestrian street with a basement loading area directly below, and underground parking at sub-basement level. The application also included proposals for permanent access arrangements to service the Marks & Spencer store and the proposed Shambles West development, which involved an access ramp being located off Deansgate close to the existing junction with Cateaton Street. The application was approved in May 1998 subject to a number of conditions.

SHAMBLES WEST

An outline application for the mixed-use development proposed for the Shambles West site was submitted in August 1997. It sought detailed approval to siting and access arrangements for the mixed-use scheme, included up to 32,550 square metres of space for retail, and food and drink uses, whilst a further 16,740 square metres of space was proposed for office and leisure uses, with the possibility of incorporating residential use also being highlighted. Joint vehicular access was proposed with Marks & Spencer, through the new access ramp. Support for the scheme was generally forthcoming from consultees and established leaseholders (but with some opposition to the relocation of the historic pubs), and the proposals were approved with conditions in October 1997.

PUBLIC HOUSES

In June 1997, Bass Taverns and Samuel Smiths breweries submitted an application for the re-erection of their dismantled public houses on land at the junction of Cathedral Gates and Cateaton Street. In addition to the reconstruction of the two pubs, proposals included a new service extension block, an external eating and drinking area, and associated landscaping. Arising from consultation with key interests the main criticism came from conservation interests, concerned that

Shambles Block –
residential
element

relocation would destroy the structures and medieval plot layout of the core of the
medieval city; that dismantling and subsequent reconstruction of the pubs would
reduce them to a pastiche; that new buildings should fit around old and not vice
versa; and that the pubs were incompatible with a Corn Exchange location. There
was also concern that the de-listing and de-scheduling of the pubs – necessary
for their relocation – would render them vulnerable to demolition. The application
was approved in September 1997, but with a variety of conditions. In addition to
the usual constructional issues it also stipulated that an archaeological study had
to be undertaken of the receptor site, and a permanent display was required to
illustrate and interpret the historic significance of this unique development.

In addition to planning permissions, the redevelopment of the Shambles block involved a variety of other consents. Listed building consent and scheduled ancient monument consent were required for the relocation of the two pubs, requiring the de-scheduling of the Old Wellington and the de-listing of both buildings. A process to be repeated in reverse had to take place once the two pubs were on their receptor site. Walkway closure orders had to be sought for numerous pedestrian routes that cut across the Shambles block, with such permissions being sought in phases. Finally, party wall notices had to be sought in order to facilitate the re-erection of the pubs on their receptor site, with such notices being served on the Mitre Hotel, the Corn Exchange and the cathedral.

In order to ensure the certainty of delivery of the masterplan's proposals for the Shambles block, it was decided in July 1997 that a CPO should be pursued for the purchase of land at Shambles Square. It was recognised that failure to successfully assemble the required land could seriously jeopardise the masterplan's integrity whilst at the same time it was accepted that a CPO would be used only as a last resort. The approach adopted favoured occupier agreement to land acquisition, with a strong emphasis on the relocation of businesses to other parts of the city centre. The land covered by the order was necessary to facilitate the implementation of key elements of the masterplan, namely the building of the new Marks & Spencer store; the construction of New Cathedral Street; reconstruction of the listed pubs on a designated receptor site; delivery of a high-quality mixed-use scheme for Shambles West; and the development of a Cathedral Visitor Centre. As a result of the urgent need to acquire possession of the Marks & Spencer and New Cathedral Street footprints at the earliest possible opportunity, the CPO was split into two separate orders.

Notices were subsequently served on 'Phase 1' occupiers (the Marks & Spencer and New Cathedral Street footprint), which included occupiers of Mackintosh House and St Mary's Gate, with possession required within the following four months by negotiation and agreement. By September 1997 all the interests in Mackintosh House had been surrendered, the level of configuration agreed, and demolition initiated. Securing vacant possession of St Mary's Gate proved more difficult, however, with a number of the tenants unhappy that the arrangements proposed could be justified under CPO rules. To assist negotiations, City solicitors agreed to pursue a part CPO on that area of Shambles Square affecting the Marks & Spencer/New Cathedral Street footprint, and those properties intended for the Cathedral Visitor Centre.

Notices were thus served on these 'Phase 1' occupiers in November 1997, with full vacant possession being achieved in mid-January, and demolition of St Mary's Gate initiated in May 1998. Formal approval was secured from English Heritage for the relocation of the listed Shambles pubs (both dismantling and rebuild packages), and work formally started on site in mid-December. The

CPO for the remainder of Shambles West could only be served once Prudential had agreed to commit themselves to the redevelopment scheme and to share in the acquisition costs, and the CPO for the remainder of Shambles Square was prepared in spring 1998. A total of 14 objectors remained outstanding, and a public inquiry was launched in June 1998. In the end, the inquiry lasted a day with all but three objectors withdrawing after further negotiation, and with none of those outstanding appearing. Of the original 70 tenants in Shambles Square, terms had been agreed with 65, with every effort being made to find them alternative accommodation elsewhere within the city centre. The inspector duly confirmed the CPO for Shambles Square at the end of August 1998. By autumn 1998, most of Shambles Square was vacant, and the end of the year was agreed for final possession. By mid-February 1999 all formal statutory CPO processes had been complied with, and with the land to be 'vested' in the City Council. In turn the authority was to issue Marks & Spencer with a 'holding lease' for the footprint of their new store. Despite further delays, by May 1999 detailed Heads of Terms had been agreed between all the key parties, and the final stages of site assembly and relocations were completed. This facilitated the letting of the contract to demolish Shambles West.

From the outset it was recognised that implementation of the renewal scheme for Shambles Square would be complex, with commercial viability a key concern. Indeed, the complexity of land assembly, the mixed-use content of the development, the need to redevelop the entire complex podium structure, and the relocation of the historic pubs added significantly to the costs of renewal. There was an early realisation that substantial public funding would be required to assist delivery of the wider Shambles development, and that this also involved investment in New Cathedral Street. Funding secured from the City Council, English Partnerships and from the European Commission (ERDF) would be used to facilitate the delivery of the new street, and to meet the 'abnormal' costs of the wider commercial redevelopment (land assembly, demolition, infrastructure/services). English Partnerships agreed to a funding package of just over £12 million, which was used to underpin the delivery of the Shambles scheme, and a further £1 million was procured from public sources for public realm works to New Cathedral Street. The City Council initially committed funds to the programme of works for the Shambles site, but this had later to be increased as additional resources were felt necessary to underpin the delivery of the Marks & Spencer store, and to secure a quality scheme for Shambles West.

Development implementation
The multiple ownership of the Shambles block meant that land assembly had to be phased. With the Marks & Spencer/New Cathedral Street footprint, for example, the separate parcels of land were released to Bovis as agreements were

concluded between Marks & Spencer and the various landowners and lease-holders. Owing to the pace of the rebuilding programme, construction work had to begin before the entire footprint of the site was assembled, with the redevelopment being phased. The Bovis/Marks & Spencer team had to assume that ultimately they would acquire all the necessary parcels of land, and attempts were made to acquire, from the relevant commercial parties, agreement to a critical path on vacant possessions. Inevitably perhaps, legal agreements were never concluded early, and the team had to have an element of flexibility within their programme. For example, to avoid any potential delay caused by the late demolition of commercial units in St Mary's Gate, the phased erection of the steel structure was resequenced.

From a project management perspective the Marks & Spencer scheme presented a number of unique challenges, the most significant being logistics over the development of what was essentially a land-locked site. Whilst the store was being constructed there were live projects on three of the building's elevations – Exchange Square directly to the north, the Arndale build-out to the east, and New Cathedral Street to the west. Restricted access meant that logistical considerations were a very important part in the success of construction. Up until September 1999, for example, only a small strip of Corporation Street was available for all the deliveries to the site, and this access point was subsequently lost as the new public realm improvements for this street had to be laid in time for the 'grand opening'. Access via Deansgate and the underground car park was therefore utilised, and the internal structure of the store was used as the materials movement and logistics centre.

The Marks & Spencer store, New Cathedral Street and the Shambles West developments represent separate projects, each having different owners and funding sources. However, all were inextricably linked, having beneath them underground car parking and servicing facilities, and with shared access arrangements. This arrangement served to further complicate the implementation process, raising intricate issues of coordination. Whilst the Marks & Spencer store was being constructed, commercial plans for Shambles West were still evolving, and carrying out work below ground level without knowing precisely what was going to be built above ground level proved difficult. For example, the Marks & Spencer design for the Deansgate access was initially signed off and the access ramp constructed. However, when Prudential subsequently secured a tenant over the Deansgate access, this required further modification.

The delicate nature of the interface between the Marks & Spencer store and New Cathedral Street resulted in the Marks & Spencer/Bovis team constructing the deck structure of the new street, thus enabling both projects to take place at the same time. The contract for constructing New Cathedral Street was later extended to include the demolition of buildings comprising Shambles

West. Delays in acquiring vacant possession of properties in the western half of the Shambles block meant that MML were unable to demolish the buildings within the timescales Marks & Spencer required. Therefore, to guarantee a cleared site on Shambles West for the opening of the new store and other first-phase developments, the Marks & Spencer/Bovis team undertook the demolition works, and was paid for doing so by the local authority.

MARKS & SPENCER

The external elevations of the Marks & Spencer store are characterised by limestone cladding and extensive glazed panels. As an island site, with major pedestrian routes on all sides, the store unusually has four active frontages. To meet the need for permeability through the store (a condition of the original planning permission) the building's design incorporates a glass-covered galleria running east–west through the site, but this does little to lessen the sheer scale and mass of the development. The integration of the store's design with the wider masterplan involved discussions between the Marks & Spencer team and MML, and ensuring that the public realm works matched the store at ground level was clearly critical. To help the building fit in with the surrounding urban landscape, its cornice is at the same height as that of the adjacent Royal Exchange, and the building's corners on Market Street are rounded. In addition, the curved façade of the New Cathedral Street elevation helps reveal views of the Millennium Quarter from St Ann's Square.

SHAMBLES WEST

Developed as a prestigious mixed-use project incorporating new quality retail premises, a Harvey Nichols department store, and designer retail units, together with a block of contemporary, luxury apartments, the design solution reflects the up-market nature of the scheme. The block contains active frontages on all four elevations, with new shop units accessible from pavements at grade level. Particular emphasis has been placed on the context of each of the building's corners, responding to their interior functions and their wider urban context. To match the new Marks & Spencer block to the east, the masterplan has required the New Cathedral Street frontage to be curved.

NEW CATHEDRAL STREET

The design solution for the street is contemporary, but with high-quality surfacing materials being selected to reflect and enhance the prestigious nature of the adjacent retail developments. Urban Solutions Manchester (the designers of the street) worked closely with designers of the adjacent private sector developments to ensure the innovative streetlights complemented those from adjacent shops. The overall design approach to the street was to ensure a simple and uncluttered solution, to allow unrestricted pedestrian movement, and to facilitate ease of cleaning. This design philosophy also extended below ground level, attempting to ensure the minimum number of pipes and cables were buried under the surface of the street, thus reducing the need for future maintenance upheavals.

Achieving urban quality through competition

Holding design competitions is increasingly regarded as a way of achieving urban environmental quality, with a key recommendation of the Urban Task Force being – 'all significant area regeneration projects should be the subject of a design competition, and funds should be allocated … to meet the public costs of such competitions' (Rogers 1999: 78). The initial masterplanning competition for the renewal area aimed to establish the overall framework for reconstruction within which individual projects could be brought forward, and the success of this approach led to further competitions being held to procure designs for a number of key public sector elements. It is appropriate at this stage to briefly consider the individual projects involved – Exchange Square, the primary public realm project within the plan; Corporation Street bridge, a key infrastructural project; and Urbis, a flagship public building – all considered in terms of the competition process and implementation experience.

Case study 6: Exchange Square

Central to the masterplan was the creation of a series of improved streetscapes and major open spaces, intended to increase permeability within the renewal area, and to improve linkages with other parts of the city centre. The most significant element of this strategy was the creation of a major new civic space. At the heart of the renewal area, its successful design and construction was seen as vitally important to the overall success of the plan, being critical in bringing together a range of public and private sector projects that surrounded the space, as well as facilitating a new focus and confidence to the area north of the retail core. A competition brief was produced by EDAW in consultation with the Task Force and City Council, outlining the context for the project, identifying site opportunities and constraints, and the overall design objectives. It was aimed at producing – 'a space of international stature that brings life and a sense of place to the renewal area' – with the competition intending to procure the initial schematic design.

The area delineated as the site for the new space was an irregular triangle shape, which prior to the bombing was predominantly a road junction. Two major roads, which accommodated significant levels of traffic travelling across the city, intersected the space, and formed the boundary between the retail core of the city centre and the under-utilised area to the north. The new public space was to be created through the closure of the major public highway running east–west through the area, and the placing of traffic restrictions on the

north–south route. A mixture of buildings of different ages and architectural styles bounded and defined the space, with the Arndale Shopping Centre on its eastern boundary; the Shambles block situated on its southern boundary; and a number of historic structures (Corn Exchange and the cathedral area) forming its northern boundary. As part of the wider proposals of the masterplan, the context for the square was to be centrally influenced by the construction of new buildings and the refurbishment of existing structures (Marks & Spencer, Shambles West, Arndale remodelling, Urbis, Printworks, Corn Exchange).

The new square was not only regarded by MML as the most important public realm element within the renewal area, but also envisaged as the main focus for future street-based activity within the city centre as a whole. Aspirations for the space were high, and this was reflected in the effusive language used in the design brief – 'the most innovative and creative public space to be created in the UK to celebrate the Millennium'. It was envisaged that the space should be multi-functional and that it had to be flexible whilst retaining a distinct character (Table 8.5). Whilst the brief stated that the design should ensure 'the creation of an experience associated with places like Covent Garden, or the Place Pompidou', this grand vision was not universally welcomed by surrounding landowners, some feeling that the square was being used to meet a wider political agenda than that necessary to meet the aspirations of Mancunians.

Exchange Square – lower level facing Arndale North

A key objective of the masterplan was to increase permeability within the city centre, and Exchange Square was critical in realising this objective. It would form part of a new pedestrian spine running north–south across the city, linking St Ann's Square and New Cathedral Street to the south, with the new City Park to the north. In addition, the space was to provide a focus for cross-axial routes from the proposed Wintergarden on Cannon Street, Victoria Street Bridge

Table 8.5 Design objectives for Exchange Square

- To create a key public square in the heart of the city capable of encouraging street theatre and accommodating large-scale events.
- To utilise high-quality contemporary design that makes creative and dynamic use of water, lighting, tree planting, street furniture and paving that is both inspiring and memorable.
- To create a safe and efficient public transport route along Cateaton Street and Hanging Ditch; and to efficiently accommodate key pedestrian circulation routes and a series of refuges where visitors can meet and rest.
- To respect the existing stature and importance of the Corn Exchange and character of the existing buildings on the northern edge of Cateaton Street; and to attractively incorporate the reception site for the public houses between the Mitre Hotel and Corn Exchange.
- To negotiate the level change between New Cathedral Street and areas to the north in an accessible and attractive design; and to allow activities within existing buildings to spill out on to the space.

Exchange Square – upper level facing Selfridges

and Cateaton Street. However, whilst providing a focus for movement within the city, it was also recognised that the new square had to establish a strong identity of its own, rather than simply becoming a 'foyer' for the surrounding developments. Ensuring the space had a distinct identity whilst respecting existing views and vistas, and the diverse architectural character of the surrounding buildings, thus represented a significant design challenge.

In order to promote a level of unity across the renewal area and to ensure performance and quality from the finished product, guidelines were targeted at specific elements of the public realm, and such decisions had to comply with established City Council guidance. For example, existing strategies on lighting, management and security, public art, and on disabled access all had to be considered when proposals were being drawn up. Designs were also to be evaluated for their long-term maintenance implications, essential to the continued success of the renewal programme.

The area was a difficult space to work with, and posed a number of design challenges. Its irregular shape, the large number of ingress/egress points, and significant level changes (the levels dropped by 2.5 metres at the junction of New Cathedral Street and Cateaton Street), made it difficult to reconcile the inevitable complex pedestrian movements in the space, whilst ensuring access for all. Furthermore, the continued use of Corporation Street by vehicular traffic, albeit at reduced levels, meant that issues of pedestrian safety had to be carefully considered. The brief offered substantial guidance on how pedestrian movements should be accommodated within the space, but argued that pedestrians should not be allowed to dominate the design.

The intention to use the square as a venue for temporary events meant that support facilities – water, power and waste points in access chambers; rails and barriers; appropriate changes of level; and multi-use surfaces – had to be accommodated within the design solution. Additionally, as part of the wider masterplan's transport initiatives the new traffic circulation system had design implications for the space in relation to service vehicles and taxi access, bus routes and stops, and pedestrian crossings. Furthermore, a complex network of utilities had to be considered in the design solution which facilitated the movement of some but not others, and access points had to be incorporated.

A two-stage design competition was launched in June 1997, with initial expressions of interest resulting in five teams being invited to submit more detailed designs. The deadline for such submissions was mid-September, with the jury comprising representatives from the Task Force, the City Council and key landowners, together with two independent designers. They evaluated the entries in terms of their design approach and qualities, functional appropriateness and understanding of the design context and constraints, construction and maintenance costs of the design, and the relevant experience of key team members.

However, the jury decided that they were unable to proceed with any of the submitted designs, arguing that none had achieved the mission statement of creating a world-class design that was contemporary and innovative.

In order to address this potentially serious situation, which threatened the delivery of the entire masterplan, it was decided that, rather than procure a winning design, a design team should be appointed who would work closely with EDAW, the Task Force team, and where appropriate adjacent landowners. Urban space design teams from around the world were thus targeted, with eight consultants being selected to go forward to the restricted tender stage. Three consultants were invited to present their scheme designs to the panel, with competitor interviews being held in mid-November 1997. The panel consisted of the EDAW team leader, representatives from the City Planning Department and the Task Force, together with a representative from the Landscape Institute.

The panel agreed that the second round of schemes presented a much greater understanding of the requirements, but the choice was not straightforward given some of those consulted suggested that many of the proposed solutions were impractical. It was felt, however, that Martha Schwartz Inc. (MSI), a landscape architect from Boston, Massachusetts, best demonstrated the vision, flair and enthusiasm required to take the project forward, as well as the technical expertise required to deliver a high-quality, innovative scheme. Thus, in December 1997 her practice (working in conjunction with Peter Walker and Partners), was appointed as concept designers for Exchange Square, and they were to work closely with MML and its consultants, and City Council officers to develop the project in distinct design phases. However, in order to achieve a balance between design and the practical and functional requirements of the square, further work was felt necessary on issues of maintenance, safety, accessibility, quality and use of materials, and cost. Following their appointment, MSI were issued with a revised brief, which took on board the jury's comments on their initial design, and mandated them to produce a scheme design that took into account the site's unique physical characteristics and programme requirements. Discussions were held with all relevant parties in attempting to ensure integration with surrounding development activity. A design report by MSI was presented to the Task Force in February 1998, and thereafter to the city-centre sub-committee. They both agreed to the outline design for Exchange Square, but fed in additional comments for the detailed design work.

In conjunction with the appointment of MSI as concept designers, Urban Solutions Manchester (USM) had been appointed as the design team leaders for both the first phase of public realm works and also for Exchange Square. Thus MSI and USM were brought together for the detailed design stage, with USM tasked with implementing the MSI scheme. Parallel to this process were the procedures associated with road closure orders, aimed at ensuring that once planning approval was gained all the necessary highway orders were in place. A traffic management plan for the area had also to be prepared in order to regulate traffic movement.

By July 1998, the proposals had been formally submitted for planning approval, with the design including the creation of pedestrian areas and routes, a water feature, seating, lighting, tree planting and highway works, and with an out-turn budget of £4 million. The solution to the change in levels involved a series of gently graded ramped walkways, and resulted in the creation of two primary spatial levels, an upper level outside the Marks & Spencer store, and a lower gently curved level relating more to the Millennium Quarter (Table 8.6).

The key landowners and occupiers of property in the vicinity of the square had been consulted over the proposals, with substantive objections being submitted on behalf of the breweries who argued that they would not have agreed to relocate their premises if they had known the intended format of the square's eventual design. Other organisations, such as English Heritage, whilst generally very supportive, were concerned at the detail of finishes where they impacted on listed buildings, and the likely quality of the necessary change of levels. The design solution contained a tall retaining wall (3.6 metres) at the end of New Cathedral Street, and was considered to represent a significant barrier to pedestrian movement, isolating the historic quarter and its listed buildings. The proposed flume was felt to add a further constraint on pedestrian flows, and was initially felt to be out of scale and context with the civic square. Further discussions with the breweries and utilities were to lead to a stepped-up design solution for the belvedere, with amendments being introduced to the original planning permission.

With the approval of road closure orders and utility diversion in September 1998, construction tender documentation was completed in November 1998, with the square to be delivered in phases due to the delivery dates of adjacent developments (Shambles West, Arndale build-out). Construction on site

Table 8.6 Key features of the detailed design for Exchange Square

---

- A belvedere balcony at the end of New Cathedral Street, overlooking the Millennium Quarter.
- A series of 'tracks' reflecting the importance of the railways to the industrial revolution, and surfaced in between with panels of coloured glass which would be illuminated at night.
- Moveable benches set within the tracks, and a row of embalmed palm trees adjacent to the new Marks & Spencer store.
- An abstract river or flume along the historic line of Hanging Ditch with flat-topped stones set flush with the surrounding paving.
- A bus service route together with a 'circus' connecting the Printworks and Exchange Square to the Millennium Quarter.
- Random tree planting of birch trees in order to reinforce the riverside feel, together with formal tree planting along the Arndale Centre frontage.

---

began in February 1999, with intended completion by the end of the year. Outstanding design issues were resolved, the only exception being the much-criticised embalmed palm trees (felt to be wholly at variance with the historical setting and seriousness of the site), which as a result of a further limited design were replaced by a set of windmills that have proved popular with the public.

> It was important to note that the brief states that the inclusion of any features within the square would be considered on their merits. It is difficult to see, even using the widest interpretation of the word 'merit', the benefits of artificial palm trees, which formed part of the winning schematic design.
>
> (Task Force officer)

Critics also felt that inclusion of seating in the form of small trolleys, whilst justified in terms of their reference to Manchester's industrial past, was poorly executed, having a 'plastic' appearance and with seating space limited by the large cartwheels, and these have subsequently been removed.

Case study 7: Urbis – the building

The winning masterplan for the bomb-damaged area incorporated a cultural quarter, which was to include the development of a significant new civic building. Given that this element of the programme was perceived from the outset as being beyond MML's timeframe, the City Council's Special Projects Team was mandated to deliver the Millennium Quarter and its flagship building.

> The original thinking was probably that I would take on Urbis as an arts capital project in its own right, but in the context of the masterplan that would never work because … there was this wider job to be done. And critically the money that we got from the Millennium Commission isn't just for Urbis.
>
> (Special Projects Team leader)

When the outline application to the Millennium Commission was submitted in late 1996, ideas for the flagship cultural centre were vague, and required a review of the city's existing cultural infrastructure. It was rapidly concluded that a theatre would be unlikely to be funded because the Royal Exchange was in the process of submitting their lottery application, the Millennium Commission does not fund theatres, and that such a proposal would be risky in revenue terms. The alternative idea was for a concept that started off as a centre for popular culture, built on the city's mushrooming reputation for popular music, and its evening economy. At the same time the North West Arts Board harboured a wish for a gallery of modern art in Manchester, complementing the City Art Gallery extension.

The Urbis concept was to be developed during autumn 1997 as a result of a consultation group of cultural interests being brought together to discuss both the building form and its cultural utility – 'the building will be one of the finest landmark buildings commissioned in the City' (City Council officer) – and forming a major visitor attraction. This group decided that the central theme of Urbis would be the celebration of cities, focusing on the growth and development of the modern city, and the challenges facing cities beyond the millennium. The facility, incorporating state-of-the-art and interactive technology, was intended to reinforce Manchester's role as an international visitor destination. Given its importance it was decided that it should be procured through a competitive process, and an international design competition was launched in January 1998. A competition brief for the building was produced in consultation with the Task Force and City Council officers, outlining the site and the design context for the development of the concept behind Urbis, and the design guidelines for the building.

The site is located within the original settlement of Manchester close to the city's cathedral, and is at the heart of a conservation area. At the time of the bombing it was used as a surface car park, was bounded by roads on all four sides, and was surrounded by a mix of land uses, some still evolving. The site for Urbis sat within the proposed Millennium Quarter, which included a number of components at different stages of realisation. Urbis would be bounded on two sides by the new Cathedral Gardens (City Park), which would be designed to provide an appropriate setting for the building as well as providing a central feature of the desire for an enhanced green space within the core and its specific historic setting.

The buildings surrounding the site reflected the historic significance of the area, and the design brief noted the importance of enhancing and reflecting upon such features. The objective behind the project was thus 'to create an attraction with local resonance and national/international appeal', and to 'educate while entertaining and entertain while educating'. The attraction was intended to be a new kind of museum with a radically different collection – one made up of the histories and experiences of the people who shaped urban spaces, through an archive of information, videotape and imagery.

The brief outlined the different elements of Urbis and their estimated floorspace requirements, these being expected to provide the starting point for the design process rather than representing a blueprint for development. The Urbis concept originally comprised a foyer containing shops/cafes and an interactive 'wonderwall'; a virtual tower displaying a panoramic/aerial view of Manchester and of other international cities; city galleries, containing a number of thematic exhibitions comparing and contrasting Manchester with other cities; community space and education and resource centres; and a space for a variety of exhibitions and events relating to different cities. However, these basic elements were 'open to the interpretation and presentation by individual design teams'.

Urbis – set
between the
Printworks and
Cathedral Gardens

Principles that were expected to be addressed through different aspects of the design related to the surrounding built heritage and urban form; distribution of uses and circulation; operational design issues; and car parking and vehicular access (Table 8.7). In terms of built heritage and urban form, the local authority was seeking a design that combined the best contemporary design with a respect for its historic setting. Additionally, the approach to the building lines of the development, particularly along Corporation Street and Fennel Street, would

Table 8.7 Detailed design principles for Urbis

- Urbis should be designed as a landmark building, which is of sufficient distinction to gain international renown, be imaginative and reflect the best in contemporary design.
- The design should reflect a compelling design vision, and an imaginative interpretation of both design and development aspirations.
- A practical approach to the delivery of Urbis should be demonstrated, and it must be fully accessible to all sectors of society.
- The design of Urbis should present a creative response to the site which integrates the new building within the urban surroundings, while providing a landmark building.
- Urbis should be designed in an innovative manner taking into account the technical and space requirements of the uses to be housed within it, with particular attention being given to exhibition design.
- Urbis should achieve value for money objectives, economy and justification of public expenditure that is in line with the construction budget set for the project, and consideration should also be given to the ongoing revenue implications.
- Urbis should be designed to address issues of energy efficiency, security, maintenance and levels of access for disabled people.
- Urbis should fit into its surroundings, with careful attention being given to its impact on the character of the conservation area and setting of listed buildings, without jeopardising design excellence and innovation.
- The design should address how visitors will move into, through and around Urbis, and how it will relate to its immediate environment, in accommodating seating areas, informal performance space and public art.
- The design should demonstrate an imaginative approach to the animation of the building and use of materials, including proposals for a lighting scheme, as the building should remain animated throughout the day and evening.

Source: MCC 1998: 23

be important in terms of how Urbis contributed to the surrounding streetscape in terms of scale and enclosure.

With regard to the scale of design proposals the brief specified site coverage, and argued that the mass of the building should be located along Corporation Street and on the eastern side of the site. Design teams were instructed to use the highest point of the Corn Exchange as the main reference point for maximum building heights, with the proposals expected to contain strong elements of vertical articulation. Finally, in terms of urban form, the brief specified that consideration should be given to the potential impact of design proposals on the microclimate of adjacent streets and spaces. In terms of distribution of uses and circulation, this related to both internal and external design elements, and proposals were required to consider the range of guiding principles. As part of the transport element of the renewal programme it was envisaged that Urbis would have its own car park, and would be served by a whole range of additional public and private transport modes as well as being highly accessible on foot.

The competition comprised two stages, with the initial pre-qualification stage involving submissions by 25 teams, of which 6 would be invited to prepare an outline design for the second stage, with the winner being announced in mid-March

Urbis – from Cathedral Gardens

1998. In parallel with this process meetings were held with utilities companies relating to utility maintenance and diversion, and with the established leaseholder with regard to site acquisition (NCP). Arising from the evaluation of submissions, Ian Simpson Associates, an innovative Manchester-based practice, was announced the winner, and following working-up of the detailed design work, submission for planning permission was forthcoming in summer 1999. The landmark building was expected to complete the 'circus' at the junction of Withy Grove and Corporation Street (the most northern section of Exchange Square), be set within its own public space, and linking Chetham's School, the cathedral and the Corn Exchange.

The £30 million construction and development of Urbis, managed by the Special Projects Team, was funded as part of the £42 million Millennium Quarter proposals by the Millennium Commission, ERDF, City Council and DETR. Financing was finally procured in autumn 1998, and the construction of the £23 million building began in early 2000. At the same time three exhibition designers were retained by Manchester City Council – At Large, Land Design Studio, and Event Communications – to transform the original concept into an interactive exploration of the metropolitan world that was to ultimately cost £7 million. The building and the exhibitions opened in June 2002, with the Millennium Quarter Trust being formed to oversee the development of the quarter and the management of Urbis (Table 8.8).

Table 8.8 Distribution of exhibition space within Urbis

- *Arrive* recreates the sights, sounds and emotions of arriving in a big city, looks at the reason why people travel to cities and explores the differing experiences of immigrants, inhabitants and commuters.
- *Change* explores how people influence and are influenced by the city, recreating examples from the developing and developed world, and bringing to life 200 years of Manchester's history.
- *Order* gives an insight both into how cities as living organisms function and into the blurring of lines between order and anarchy, fear and security, control and freedom as the dynamics of the city change.
- *Explore* explores how the city has been influenced and recorded by writers, architects, photographers, poets, painters film-makers and musicians.
- *Ground floor* the location of retail facilities, together with seminar, education and corporate entertainment spaces.

The 35-metre-tall building is contained on seven levels, enclosed within a glass skin that provides a sculptured surface for the building. It is accessed by a glass funicular (the 42-metre 'sky glide'), with the top level being the first of the exhibition levels. During its first year its visitor targets have been exceeded, and arrangements are firmly in place to handle its continuing revenue costs.

Case study 8: Corporation Street Bridge – the structure

Prior to the bombing, the Arndale and Marks & Spencer buildings were linked by an above-grade bridge across Corporation Street. This structure took the full force of the blast and had to be demolished, and the initial masterplan did not include a replacement bridge as part of its vision for the remodelled city centre. However, subsequent negotiations between P&O and the City Council over their interests within the core led to an agreement whereby the local authority would procure a replacement bridge to link the Arndale Centre with the new Marks & Spencer store.

It was decided that a design competition would help facilitate this, with the aim being to obtain a contemporary, innovative design. The brief for the bridge structure was prepared by EDAW in October 1997, outlining the built-form context, layout and technical standards that the design was expected to consider. The design challenge was to link two public areas (the Marks & Spencer atrium and the Arndale's mall), in order to facilitate clear and unobstructed pedestrian flows between the new Marks & Spencer store and the remodelled Arndale Centre at first-floor level, whilst contributing to the character of Corporation Street below. Since both building projects were at an early stage of development they gave limited insight into the end state of the built form that would attach the bridge.

The emerging physical context for the bridge presented challenges, in that the frontages of the two buildings were not parallel and the bridge would not intersect at right angles, with the first floors of the two buildings not at the same level. In addition to addressing these technical issues, it was expected that the bridge should make a positive contribution to the emerging streetscape of Corporation Street, whilst safeguarding the positive aspects of the existing built form, and established views. The structure was required to contribute to the design excellence of recently constructed bridges within the city, and become a significant design element in Manchester's urban fabric as a whole. This would involve the utilisation of contemporary materials and technologies; should be as transparent as possible, thus minimising the impact on Corporation Street; and should provide a dramatic experience for people using or passing under the bridge. Design teams were encouraged to use the opportunity to make an artistic statement, to use creative lighting, and facilitate coordination with the city's wider public art strategy.

It was expected that the bridge layout should be fully enclosed, with the structure's width to be kept to a minimum in order to reduce the overhead shadow. However, this requirement had to be balanced with the need to create a clear pedestrian flow between the two buildings, and unobstructed views across the bridge into each retail floor. Moreover, the width of the bridge had to complement the plan profile of the Marks & Spencer store and Arndale Centre, both still evolving. Furthermore, the different levels between the two connecting buildings had to be incorporated into the design of the bridge so that when viewed from Corporation Street the bridge appeared level, and would not seek to change the structure of the two buildings in any way.

Twenty companies expressed an interest in the design competition, five being invited to tender for the full design service for the project, and to submit indicative schemes. A final shortlist of two designers was selected, and Hodder Associates were selected as preferred designers in December 1997. Their dramatic glass tubular design offered a unique solution to pedestrian access across one of Manchester's busiest streets, utilising a range of innovative techniques, and setting new standards of structural and façade engineering. The structure, which cost £1 million, was completed in November 1999, tying in with the completion of the first phase of the renewal programme as a whole. It was fabricated off site, and lifted into place over one weekend.

Built-form quality and the core

The masterplanning process for the renewal programme was fairly distinctive in that it was largely predicated around an improved public realm, the development of built-form quality, and the enhanced permeability of the city centre. Whilst there had been attempts to improve the core's public realm prior to the bombing, and there were ongoing discussions with private developers over the possibilities of refurbishing the monolithic heart of the commercial core, the City Council was perceived as being insufficiently pro-active in ensuring the design quality of the built form, or the detail of new developments. The opportunity arising from the bombing was to radically change such perceptions, with design quality being at the core of the entire rebuilding and renewal programme, and this has transformed the character and sense of identity of the city centre. The biggest achievement has undoubtedly been that the urban framework provided by the masterplanning opportunity has helped provide the right structure for the commercial core, a radical change in development culture, and perceptions of Manchester as a place to invest.

Whilst all the civic spaces were paid for by public sector resources, responsibility for improvements to private buildings to further enhance the public realm were clearly laid at the feet of the private sector. The message to commercial operators was thus twofold. First, given the amount of public money being spent on civic spaces, private investment in the remodelled city centre would undoubtedly be hugely successful commercially. Once this premise was accepted, then it was inevitable that commercial operators would be expected to spend additional resources on their buildings to reinforce this commitment to quality. Tensions over such issues were inevitable, given perceptions by the private sector of the need to balance aesthetic improvements with commercial realism, and it is to the credit of the Task Force that in delivering the renewal

Corporation Street Bridge

Shambles pubs on receptor site next to cathedral

programme they managed to achieve design standards that are now considered the norm in relation to city-centre development more widely.

Ultimately, in some cases economic forces triumphed over design aspirations, and MML and its consultants had to adopt a pragmatic line to ensure that the private sector was kept fully on board. What is remarkable, however, is that so much has been achieved in transforming the qualities and potential of Manchester's city centre since 1998, and the centrality of built-form quality to such expression. The consequential effect has been a dramatic change of perception as to the qualities and attributes of the city centre as a whole, and a galvanising of the desire to encourage the city's renaissance that has had major economic and cultural ramifications.

Chapter 9

Urban consumption and cultural vitality

Over the past couple of decades we have seen the re-emergence of city centres as focal points for a specifically urban way of life, as they provide the prime context within which consumer experiences are both constructed and acted out. With the commodification of the city such consumption has become both an economic and a cultural touchstone of an urban society, seen as providing a bridge between the individual and experience of the urban environment. Over the past decade in particular, consumption has come to be seen as both a means and a motor of urban social change, with the increased commodification of culture perceived as central to our understanding of the postmodern city (Wynne & O'Connor 1998).

This chapter aims to focus on such concerns as they apply to city centres, initially considering such developments in terms of the use of urban space (sites and quarters) and of time (night-time economy), and to consider the role of the emergent residential dimension for such activity. Focusing on Manchester's experience, it reviews the evolution of cultural policy for the city centre and the recent boom in city-centre living as a dimension, before moving on to look at the cultural and residential elements of the renewal programme. Finally, it focuses on the strategic development of the Millennium Quarter as both a programme with major cultural objectives, and as a series of projects – Exchange Square, Cathedral Visitor Centre, Cathedral Gardens, Urbis – with a remit to unify and extend the city centre's cultural experience.

Policy and development context

The pro-active pursuit of cultural capital has encouraged a variety of forms of cultural consumption amongst individuals, and has stimulated cities to promote the growth of cultural industries and institutions. Such developments have been facilitated by structural economic changes – with lifestyle-specific industries seen to contribute to a city's economic growth – and to the creation of highly visible consumption spaces that are perceived to heighten urban competitiveness (Hannigan 1999). Indeed, cultural strategies have become central to image promotion and to innovative regeneration strategies, with investors motivated to create new spaces for urban consumption.

> Cities hit hard by long term decline of middle class residents and the erosion of commitment by business elites have gradually begun to view the diversity of 'urban lifestyle' as a source of cultural vitality and economic renewal.
>
> (Zukin 1995: 836)

Cultural policies and industries

Wynne & O'Connor (1998) argue that linking postmodern culture and urban form has centred around three processes of transformation associated with the contemporary city – the gentrification of formerly derelict and run-down areas, arts- and leisure-led regeneration programmes, and the re-imaging and partnership developments associated with place marketing – and signifies the increased commodification of culture in managing urban change. In addition, the timeframe for cultural consumption is not limited to the pattern of the working day, with the night-time economy generating increased employment (Bianchini 1995; Montgomery 1994). This has been perceived to be a positive feature of cultural consumption, not only in economic terms, but also in terms of safety and security within city centres, this being reinforced by the dramatic process of repopulation currently taking place within such areas.

Legitimation for the wider role of culture in urban policy reflects fundamental shifts in urban polity, with neo-liberal developments of the past two decades removing the traditional separation between 'high arts' and 'popular culture'. Indeed, the market context for such development has replaced the historic role of publicly funded projects, and has resulted in the explosive growth of popular culture at the expense of established institutions.

> While a thriving cultural industries sector may indicate a level of local creativity, it is the ability to nurture this sector and link its creativity to wider economic innovation and development which is a crucial test of the adaptability of cities to this global challenge.
>
> (Wynne & O'Connor 1998: 238)

In this context, the development of cultural strategies has been seen as strengthening local democracy through the expression of civic pride and community involvement. This has been reinforced by shifts in the mode of cultural consumption involving both a breakdown of barriers between diverse forms of culture, and the emergence of a new group of 'cultural intermediaries' to interpret the artefacts of cultural change and urban lifestyles (Evans 2001). Finally, the economic dimension associated with place-marketing activities and the growth of cultural industries are seen as central to re-imaging, to increase inter-city competitiveness, and to the attraction of investors. This is reinforced by the idea that the quality of urban life needs to be restored in post-industrial cities, with the aim of rediscovering the uniqueness of particular places and the promotion of cultural and civic development (Civic Trust 1994). Cultural industries are increasingly seen by policy makers as a source of new employment opportunities, with the emergence of the 'creative city' seen to bring together the best dimensions of both cultural and economic policy at the strategic level. Such cultural production can help create lively urban areas, be at the heart of the transformation and renovation of urban built form, and provide a vital component of the urban public realm with its diversity of spaces.

The residential dimension

City centres began diversifying their functional roles in the 1990s and, in addition to serving as focal points for employment, leisure and commercial activity, have once again become places to live. This has raised both academic and professional debate as to the role and benefit of city-centre residential populations. Increasingly seen by both policy makers and development interests as offering the opportunity to regenerate run-down areas of city centres, and the recycling of land uses, this element is now at the heart of revitalisation initiatives (Tiesdell *et al.* 1996). As demand for secondary office and tertiary commercial space has proved very volatile, property owners have increasingly realised the potential stability that exists in the conversion of property, and the promotion of mixed-use developments that are seen to be essential for the creation and maintenance of attractive liveable urban environments (Coupland 1997). There is general agreement that such residential development facilitates the wider objective of achieving urban vitality, by bringing together activity and diversity, and by creating a 'living heart' generating indigenous demand for facilities.

Others have seen city-centre housing as part of the wider debate relating to issues of urban capacity and sustainability, with town centres expected to play a crucial role in accommodating household growth, particularly that focused on one-person households (Jenks *et al.* 1996). A key aspect of such concerns relates both to the aspirations of households and to the profile of city-centre residents, with urban cores emerging as private housing-market niches for young professionals and childless couples, where the relationship between lifestyle stages and geographical location are particularly marked. Whilst the focus of such developments has been oriented towards the private sector – both for owner-occupation and for rental – there are small-scale social housing developments in evidence (primarily housing association) and a significant growth of student accommodation (increasingly provided by the private sector).

An important feature of such debate relates to the extent to which such housing schemes contribute to establishing new residential 'communities' within city centres. Although such residents may contribute significantly to the local economy through the consumption of leisure and entertainment facilities, attachment to such areas is often tenuous, and doesn't generally lead to robust social and community networks (Coupland 1997). Some debate has arisen, however, as to the extent to which the increasing propensity for mixed-use development schemes within city centres can facilitate the growth of 'village-like' communities, and questions remain as to the long-term sustainability of city-centre living (Oc & Tiesdell 1997).

The cultural dimension of city-centre residential communities has been the subject of considerable debate, with Montgomery (1995) arguing that – 'the key to successful city places is diversity, supported by relatively high numbers of people with different tastes and proclivities'. City-centre residents, by creating indigenous demand for facilities, stimulate the increasing number and mix of uses, and help extend the night-time economy and cultural diversity of the core (Lovatt & O'Connor 1995).

> In some senses a utopian exploration – a quest for 'the good life in the dirty old town' that once was Manchester … helping to distinguish oneself as a member of the fast moving vanguard of Manchester's cultural professional class.
>
> (Taylor *et al.* 1996: 295)

Questions have been asked concerning the suitability of city centres as places to live, and the possibilities of creating local environments that are conducive to the establishment of stable communities (Coupland 1997). Basic requirements are perceived to be the development of specific policies relating to safety and security, strategies for education and health, the provision of public space and environmental quality improvements, and the enhancement of service provision. In particular, the quality of the immediate environment and issues of personal safety are seen as paramount.

> What is preferable for the safety of the city centre as a whole are residential areas with a degree of integration, making a positive contribution to the peopling of the city's streets and creating more eyes on the street.
>
> (Oc & Tiesdell 1997: 169)

In urban development terms, the vast majority of city-centre residential developments have involved the conversion and recycling of existing building stock, as part of major regeneration strategies, often raising technical problems in the process (Barlow & Gan 1993). With the emergence of area-based master-planning within city centres a significant number of new-build schemes have also been approved, and these may throw up problems associated with the putting together of development parcels where a range of ownership and development interests may be involved. Restraints on the conversion of historic offices and warehousing facilities include the restrictions on viable conversion placed by the building and the restrictions placed by listed status, whilst more recent buildings are often aesthetically unattractive for residential use.

The rapid development of city-centre living over the past decade has both influenced and been affected by central government guidance. Current housing advice notes the opportunities for providing more housing in existing urban areas through conversion, improvement and redevelopment, whilst advice on transport advocates that an integrated and sustainable transport perspective would be reinforced by the recycling of existing building stock. Similarly, contemporary advice on town centres promotes residential and mixed-use developments as part of a wider concern with urban environmental quality. The URBED (1994) report argued that management strategies to improve the attractions, accessibility and amenity of Britain's town centres would be significantly helped by pro-active attempts to encourage more people to live within core areas, with the Urban White Paper (2000) reaffirming this commitment to city-centre living as part of a wider urban renaissance.

Developing and delivering a cultural perspective

Having discussed some of the conceptual themes behind the cultural and lifestyle dimensions of city centres, it is now appropriate to briefly look at the development of such concerns at the local level. This section will initially focus on the development of cultural policy within Manchester, and will then consider the lifestyles of city-centre residents.

Local cultural policy

Much of the early activity relating to the development of a distinctively local identity was promoted by agencies other than the City Council, with the Greater Manchester Council being particularly important in the early 1980s, acquiring Central Station and the Great Northern Warehouse complex (now G-Mex and the Great Northern Experience), and establishing the Museum of Science and Industry. In the late 1980s CMDC was to provide leadership in supporting the promotion of culturally significant developments, in stimulating residential development and a major programme of environmental enhancement, all aimed at improving the quality of the built environment and at providing a framework for establishing the city centre's cultural distinctiveness. It was to be a major stimulant in establishing the body that was later to become Marketing Manchester (1997), the establishment of the Castlefields Urban Heritage Park, and it strongly supported the city's Olympic bid. It was to see through the delivery of the city's main cultural landmark building, the Bridgewater Hall, and of the MEN Arena. In addition, during the late 1980s private sector initiative saw the emergence of two major cultural quarters – Chinatown, and the Gay Village – taking advantage of cheap property in the city's decayed warehouse zone, whilst at the other end of the city centre an urban theme park was opened as a major leisure attraction (Granada Studios Tours). At this stage Manchester's assets were 'heritage', a 'space for recreation' and an interest in 'spectacle and play'.

> An economy with the panache of a holiday camp, complementary to the business centre, was being promoted in the archaic shell of the old city centre.
>
> (Mellor 1997: 58)

During the 1980s the City Council was preoccupied with economic restructuring and concerns over social dislocation, seeing arts and culture policies as not requiring priority in funding terms, and it was not until the end of the decade that it began to recognise that a broader perspective was required to solve its urban problems. City Council interest in increasing the confidence of its cultural expression was initiated in the early 1990s by a major consultancy study. This was to assess the strength and weakness of the city's cultural economy, and draw up a strategy that would maximise the input and cost-effectiveness of investment in arts and culture; raise the profile of the city nationally and internationally; and ensure accessibility to the arts and culture of the city's inhabitants and users (Manchester Council 1992b). The report recognised the mixed economy of the city's cultural facilities, the need to work 'with the grain' of such activity, and commented on the 'overall lack of structures and resources ... capable of delivering an entrepreneurial approach to arts and cultural development'. The output from this exercise was a local authority Arts and Cultural Strategy (1992), which aimed to develop the city's cultural heritage and encourage its wider use; enhance a sense of place and promote wider participation in cultural activity; and develop opportunities for training and employment in the cultural industries.

This resulted in the restructuring of local authority departments specifically to accommodate the cultural profiling of the city, to coordinate policy and to manage culturally significant events, and to promote cultural policy and cultural industries at the heart of the city's entrepreneurial activities. The strategy

Table 9.1 Focus of the city's arts and cultural strategy

- *Arts and cultural heritage* to ensure secure development investment in the key organisations which act as cornerstones in Manchester's cultural economy and to enable other cultural initiatives in the private as well as the voluntary sector.
- *Sense of place and urban culture* to create an environment which reflects Manchester's objective to be recognised as a European Regional Capital, through new programmes for improved urban spaces, street life, cultural animation and public art.
- *Social cohesion* to break down barriers to access and encourage wider participation in arts and cultural activity; to recognise the distinctive culture of communities and diverse cultural and ethnic groups and the role that this can play in strengthening communities and neighbourhoods.
- *Economic development* to stimulate creativity and artistic development, affirming the role of culture in Manchester's future and taking a risk-positive approach to new ideas; to increase opportunities for training and employment in the cultural industries and to recognise the contribution of the cultural sector in the regeneration of the city.
- *Marketing and promotion* to increase both the numbers and range of arts audiences and cultural consumers, building up new audiences for the arts among both residents and visitors; to promote the role of arts and culture in projecting a more positive image of the city.

---

attempted to balance cultural production and consumption whilst placing emphasis on wider access and participation, and also aimed to integrate cultural policy with wider city-regeneration policies (Wansborough & Mageean 2000). A review of this strategy was carried out in 1997, and a new version published in 2000 (Table 9.1). In addition, the City Council began to actively push the notion of the '24-hour city' and the economic and cultural contribution of the night-time economy (Lovatt 1994). The planning philosophy of separating work, home and play was thus to be seriously challenged by a new philosophy of urbanity.

At the same time, other perspectives on cultural policy were developing, with Manchester's UDP promoting the strategic objectives of building upon and reinforcing the economic and cultural role of the regional centre, and fostering the development of the city's vibrant youth culture. Subsequent monitoring reports suggested the introduction of new development control policies to support the evening economy, whilst reducing potential conflicts between licensed activities and residential development. The UDP also promoted a need for a policy on urban art in the city centre as part of the wider concern with improvements to environmental quality. Similarly, the City Pride prospectus was committed to the international credentials of the regional centre, and its capacity to actively promote cultural identity and cultural enterprises. It noted that the regional centre already had a strong reputation for quality in both culture and sport, and a cultural diversity that had been of growing significance in transforming perceptions and images of the city.

Alongside the optimistic stance being taken by the City Council and its partners the cultural identity of Manchester was being strongly promoted by a variety of private actors and agencies who collectively identified a distinctive urban lifestyle within the city, and focused on aspects of popular culture dominated by youth. The largest contributors are discussed below.

'Madchester'

The club culture associated with music venues (notably the Hacienda) took off in the late 1980s, with local bands being nurtured to international success (New Order, The Smiths, Happy Mondays, Stone Roses), and with associated musical production facilities (Factory Records). The interaction between musicians, technicians, studio collaborators, DJs, fashion designers and graphic artists was to make the Hacienda 'the most creative venue in town' (Haslam 1999). Indeed, by the early 1990s Manchester's youth culture had acquired 'a rhythm which is governed as much by its music, fashion, sites, spaces and signs, as it is by its licensing hours' (Lovatt 1994). Increased and widespread use of drugs and associated gang violence led to attempts by the police to shut down the Hacienda (in 1994 ten clubs were closed or stopped running black music nights). This was initially resisted by the City Council, who realised its strategic significance in terms of the city's international credentials, and its economic value associated with the growth of cultural industries. However, it was to be permanently shut down in 1997, with the site being subsequently redeveloped for housing.

'Gunchester'

Strong media imagery that linked the city's cultural projection with crime, and focused on a couple of inner-city communities, drew international attention to the city in the early 1990s that was generally unfavourable, and increasingly took the gloss off the city's upbeat entrepreneurial face.

> Now Manchester is violence city UK, Moss Side is Britain's Bronx … one man shot dead, two others shot and injured in one weekend … nineteen serious woundings this year … shotguns and handguns, police body armour an issue … crack as well as heroin and softer. Moss Side, dangerous, exciting, gang war …
>
> (*Guardian Weekend* 15 June 1991)

'Gaychester'

Pride in the 'queer up North' tag evolved alongside youth and popular culture, increasingly as a sub-culture but reinforced by an emergent local authority policy framework (Taylor *et al.* 1996). In the early 1990s it was to become a major visitor/tourist attraction, with both a day-time and night-time economy, and with the commercial development of the 'pink pound' stimulating the wider regeneration of the 'village'. The Gay Village has now become an important economic asset for the city, as well as a marketing tool to sell the city's image as a progressive liberal city, welcoming a wide range of people and cultures (Quilley 1997; Hindle 1994).

'Sporting City'

The emergence of the city as a sporting venue has undoubtedly been a strong marketing tool, with the two Olympic bids giving the city self-confidence to over-haul its image of active local partnerships, and to sell itself internationally (Cochrane *et al.* 1996). In terms of cultural policy, the Olympic bid process required place-significant marketing and cultural commercialisation, and bequeathed a legacy of sport facilities and assets in and around the city centre. It paved the way for securing the Commonwealth Games, and their successful delivery in 2002, the culmination of a decade of activity in this field.

> In Manchester an urban bourgeoisie of merchants and local busi-nessmen who once worked and relaxed in the city centre has been replaced by a distinctive 'class fraction' which may work, relax and even live there.
>
> (Mellor 1997: 66)

Public–private partnerships involving established partnership linkages have been at the heart of such developments, which are increasingly based on developing leisure industries and tourism in order to attract further business investment to the city. More recently, however, questions have been raised as to the representational profiling of the city, with Marketing Manchester (with its rapidly abandoned 'we're up and going' logo) being challenged by a group of local cultural/leisure entrepreneurs (the McEnroe Group) who strongly backed 'Made in Manchester' as a benchmark for urban culture and lifestyle (Ward 2000). Furthermore, the city's growing reputation for the quality of its emerging built form is based on the development of several culturally significant buildings, and a new generation of culturally aware local architects (Mills 1997). Indeed, many of the city's influential cultural entrepreneurs and property developers are actively incor-porating urban design quality into their developments, in order to express certain cultural beliefs and attitudes relating to a vibrant city centre.

The current cultural profile

Recent estimates of cultural activity within the core noted that there were 350 licensed premises in the city centre, and that 5,000 people were employed in its night-time economy, with £250 million being spent annually on the entertainment business (MEN 8 August 1997). Law (2001) noted that the volume of tourism (both domestic and international) had increased significantly in the 1990s, as evidenced by the rapid expansion of hotels. Thus, whilst in 1980 the city centre had 7 hotels (982 beds), by 1990 it had increased to 13 (2,002), and by 2001 to 35 (5,197). At the same time, its city-centre population has increased dramatically, totalling around 250 in 1988, 10,000 by 2002, and is expected to be 15,000 by 2004. Whilst Manchester's experience of leisure- and lifestyle-led regeneration has been paralleled by other provincial cities, it is in some ways more pronounced in terms of the scale of its club scene, cafe culture, gay village and its residential development. What has been significant is that Manchester, unlike many other cities, had largely kept its decaying warehouse zone, this providing a cheap property resource that has underpinned such developments.

O'Connor (2000) took a critical look at the relationship of the cultural industry sector with agencies of local governance in Manchester, and assessed the importance of this sector for the material and symbolic restructuring of the city. He noted that networking, proximity and creative cooperation had added considerable value to the productivity, growth and rate of innovation in the sector, and that the city-centre housing market was closely associated with this upturn in cultural production and consumption. Indeed, much of the restoration and redevelopment of city-centre 'fringe' areas had been led by cultural firms and entrepreneurs. The study noted, however, that cultural firms were precarious and that social network support had proved vital. The researchers thus argued that new infrastructure – physical, communicative and organisational – was required if the cultural sector was to more markedly enhance city competitiveness. In addition, opening up of cultural industries to wider populations must be a priority for both social and economic reasons. Finally, cultural production had undoubtedly moved from the margins to occupy a more central role in the city's economic strategy, seen as integral to Manchester's claims for 'regional capital' and 'European City' status. The launch of a new strategic cultural development agency – Cultural Industries Development Service (1999) – did suggest the increasing vitality of this sector, and the need to promote its growth.

Urban consumption and city-centre residents

A central feature of the cultural dynamics of Manchester city centre has undoubtedly been the recent boom in residential development within the core. This has resulted in the completion of over a hundred schemes, providing homes for over 10,000 residents. This development has been closely associated with the development of postmodern lifestyles, and is closely linked to a culturally based urban regeneration strategy. Studies of the cultural dynamics of city-centre residents in Manchester have noted that three-quarters of such residents are under 40, less than a fifth are married, over half have degrees, and a substantial majority are in managerial/professional employment. The majority have moved from within the conurbation, trading living in the inner/outer suburbs for the city centre itself (Wynne & O'Connor 1998).

City-centre residents are perceived as enthusiastic consumers of central-area facilities, with upwards of a fifth of their respondents having a serious interest and regular participation in theatre, gallery or film. Attendance at classic music concerts was limited in comparison to other forms of cultural consumption, but such participation was still above the national average. Whilst the majority of respondents were regular consumers of bars and popular music venues, it was additionally noted that a significant minority had little contact or participation in such activities. Whilst respondents were generally 'middle brow' there were obvious divisions between consumers of 'high culture' and 'pop culture'. Social networks were also of interest in that respondents demonstrated 'leftish' politics associated with major issues rather than formal political party membership. Also, they were clear in the choice of friends, being in favour of 'sociable', 'amusing' and 'lively' acquaintances, and with relatively little support for 'refined', well-bred' and 'artistic' individuals. The researchers concluded that 'cultural awareness', 'activism and commitment' and 'style' were the main dimensions by which residents/respondents could be classified.

In Wynne and O'Connor's study, respondents generally revealed a high commitment to the use of cultural facilities and other forms of leisure activity, a relatively weak commitment to any traditional form of work ethic and the convenience of living close to one's workplace. Lifestyles showed a fluidity and openness with regard to non-traditional forms of sociability – the city centre being both an 'edge' and a 'stage', with a relatively weak commitment to tradi-tional urban lifestyles. For many of the younger respondents, their move to the city centre – 'where it's at', 'living at the heart of things' – was an attempt to 'open up and explore', taking a particular stand away from a perceived suburban lifestyle.

> Our respondents exhibit high degrees of reflexivity and a concern with image and presentation of the self over what might be described as more traditional concerns such as occupation, stability and career orientation … the centre is approached in terms of a sense of play, sociability and hedonism, but not one geared to the 'work hard, play hard' ethos of the yuppie.
>
> (Wynne & O'Connor 1998: 855)

Thus, for city-centre residents the process is essentially one of rene-gotiation of place and identity, and with 'cultural intermediaries' playing an increasingly active role in the definition of the cultural images to be presented, and the 'management of fluidity and uncertainty'.

Developing and delivering residential space

Manchester's City Centre Local Plan (1984) acknowledged that traditional city-centre uses could not be maintained at existing levels due to decentralising pressures and changing business practices. It recognised the opportunities offered by residential development – 'more housing would add to the quality and variety of the housing stock generally, promote greater diversity and activity, and bring back life to underused sites and buildings, especially where there is little or no pressure from other uses' – but was not in a position at that stage to facilitate such commitment.

The emergence of city-centre living

The work of the CMDC was to be the catalyst in developing and promoting such an agenda, within the context of improving central-area land and property markets. Its development strategy noted that bringing people back to the city centre, by encouraging and helping developers to create new housing schemes, many of them in restored buildings, was an essential part of its work, and it was able to announce at the termination of its remit that residential projects worth £140 million to build nearly 3,000 homes had been completed or approved. Two major developments were closely associated with the initial phase of the CMDC's activities, namely the developments along the Whitworth Street corridor ('Granby Village' refurbishment and new build) and the recycling of urban derelict land behind Piccadilly ('Piccadilly Village'). During this phase, where the market for city-centre living was unclear, grant assistance was necessary to reduce the risk for private investors, and CMDC administered £14 million for this purpose. However, by the mid-1990s no further grant aid was necessary, with investment opportunities and the buoyancy of the market already clear to private developers.

The city's UDP (1995) included two main policies encouraging housing within the city centre, dealing both with general housing development and with mixed-use developments. The housing policy component argued that – 'the city centre area as a whole is generally capable of accommodating further housing, set in an acceptable residential environment'. It noted that the authority was in a position to alert developers to opportunities offered by particular sites or buildings, carry out feasibility studies, undertake programmes of environmental improvement and traffic management to support residential use, and to provide grants for conversion. In terms of mixed-use development policies, the plan advocated the inclusion of a significant proportion of housing, where compatible. Concerns for environmental quality and the scope for potential conflict did however result in issues over the interface between residential and commercial developments, with this being tackled by the production of a code of practice. Such views and concerns were also reinforced by City Pride, one of whose key objectives was the repopulation of the conurbation's core. It noted that the value of enhancing residential opportunities within the city centre had already been demonstrated – in terms of its contribution to the centre's safety, interest and diversity – and argued that the range of available services and facilities must be improved if the regional centre was to develop further.

The consequence of all this for the city centre has been dramatic in that the booming market place has resulted in around 10,000 current residents, and with this expected to double by 2010 (Couch 1999). Indeed, 107 schemes had been completed, and a further 51 schemes had been granted planning permission by the end of 2001. Such development, whilst initially clustered in a number of key locations (Whitworth Street Corridor, Castlefield, Piccadilly), has in recent years spread comprehensively throughout the city centre (Table 9.2). Whilst largely being wholly residential, a number have been completed as components of mixed-development initiatives, and all are in close proximity to commercial activities. Of completed developments, three-quarters have been conversion schemes involving the recycling of tertiary offices, retail developments and warehousing, and with over 90 per cent of completed developments being private (either owner occupied or privately rented). With converted schemes, many of the properties have been listed buildings that have required sensitive and innovative approaches to their redevelopment.

In looking at the time phasing of such development, it is important to note that whilst there were a couple of developments in the city centre in the

Table 9.2 City-centre housing schemes

Scheme info	Pre-April 1994		May 1994 – Feb 1998		March 1998 – Dec 2001	
Completed	21		24		62	
new build	9		5		13	
conversion	12		17		46	
part both	–		2		4	
Units constructed	2367		1673		2921	
Size of scheme (units)	**New build**	**Conversion**	**New build**	**Conversion**	**New build**	**Conversion**
Under 20	–	–	1	8	2	21
20 – 70	3	6	3	7	6	17
Over 70	6	6	1	2	5	8

Planning application units	Total completions	Student bed spaces	Private dwellings	New build	Conversion	Mixed developments
5/91–4/94	2367	1003	1364	1351	1016	–
5/94–2/98	1673	1002	671	295	1377	1
3/98–7/01	1407	208	1886	545	519	–
At Aug 2001						
Under construction	–	–	2181	941	864	376
Planning approval	–	–	3573	2245	634	694

Source: Adapted from MCC 2001

1980s – St John's Garden (private) and the Smithfield development (local authority) – there was little further development until the early 1990s. At this stage a number of listed buildings in the Whitworth Street corridor were developed, a major area of contaminated vacant industrial land at Piccadilly was reclaimed (Syms 1993), and four new student halls of residence were completed. During this period converted accommodation largely occupied former warehousing and secondary office locations, but a number of the new-build schemes were also constructed on vacant land or former car parks.

The mid-1990s was marked by only 2 student developments (one being a 979-unit development on a former industrial site), a further 2 social renting schemes, and with the remaining 17 schemes being private developments (13 for sale, 4 for rent). Interestingly, however, during this stage, whilst the majority of refurbished schemes involved warehouses or warehousing/office/retail combinations (12), this period was also marked by the conversion of office blocks (7) and a hotel. For new-build schemes former car parks and light industrial units provided the basis for residential schemes. Finally, looking at the most recent period, land and building recycling is considerably more diverse, being particularly marked by office conversion (12), retail and retail storage conversions (11), warehouses (15), but also involving the conversion of a cinema, 2 hotels and 3 mills, and on cleared sites by 5 car parks and an industrial site. The vast majority of developments at this stage was for private ownership but it has included 10 rental schemes (4 private, 6 social). The remarkable boom in construction has meant that population density for the city centre – which has increased tenfold over the past decade – is expected to pass the city's average density in 2003 (95 per hectare). This has created a booming market in city-centre residential properties, with 400 being sold in 2000 at an average selling price of £117,000, nearly twice the city's average as a whole (Table 9.3).

It is important at this stage to briefly discuss the characteristics of Manchester's city-centre residents, with average household size being 1.4 (city as a whole 2.3), with 70 per cent of such residents being under 40, and with two-thirds of occupants living alone.

Table 9.3 Residential prices in Manchester city centre

Quarters	No. of properties	Average price
Q4/99	93	£102k
Q1/00	109	£113k
Q2/00	70	£114k
Q3/00	116	£115k
Q4/00	101	£127k
Q1/01	30	£140k

Source: Adapted from MCC 2001

The nature of city-centre residents

A major study of city-centre residents undertaken by Fitzsimmons (1998) focused on an analysis of 216 household respondents, four-fifths of whom were in private housing. In terms of the analysis of the socio-economic characteristics of respondents, he concluded that they had a distinctive profile, suggesting the existence of niche housing markets, and a polarisation of socio-economic profiles (Table 9.4).

Nearly two-thirds of all respondents were male, reflecting both professional and social lifestyles tied closely to the city centre, with two-thirds of all households either unmarried or cohabiting. The vast majority of respondents from

Table 9.4 Profile of city-centre respondents 1998

Respondent profiles %	Private owners	Private renters	Social housing
Age			
Under 16	—	—	—
Under 35	55	78	58
Under 55	24	18	28
Over 55	21	5	14
Sex – Male respondents	64	65	68
Marital status			
Single	46	54	61
Married	27	19	—
Cohabiting	18	14	14
Divorced	9	14	20
Widowed	—	—	5
Length of residence			
<1 year	15	48	17
1–3 years	31	33	19
3–5 years	27	11	17
Over 5 years	26	7	48
Previous residence			
Within city	40	30	74
Within conurbation	24	30	24
Elsewhere	36	40	2
Employment status			
Manual	4	—	23
Skilled non-manual	4	5	19
Professional/managerial	80	85	26
Unemployed/retired	7	3	33
Students	4	8	1
Location of employment			
Within city	58	65	72
Within conurbation	17	11	10
Elsewhere	25	24	18

Respondent profiles %	Private owners	Private renters	Social housing
Household income			
Under £10k	2	8	38
Under £30k	31	44	51
Under £50k	40	24	10
Over £50k	29	24	–
Size of accommodation			
Studio/1 bed	38	1	51
2 bed	58	45	38
Larger	4	15	11
Travel to work			
Foot/bicycle	42	52	52
Public transport	6	6	31
Car	52	42	17
Weekly use of facilities			
Shops	84	85	98
Pubs/bars	82	74	84
Cafes/restaurants	77	89	64
Libraries	16	11	5
Other leisure	60	60	56
Advantages (1st rank)			
Close to work	44	52	33
Close to shops	4	8	28
Close to cultural/social facilities	35	24	17
Disadvantage (1st rank)			
Quality of environment	10	8	5
Traffic congestion	17	19	16
Cost of property	7	23	–
Crime levels	13	27	24
Noise	6	8	6
Lack of open space	18	12	16

Source: Fitzsimmons 1998

private sector housing worked in professional or managerial positions – primarily business, financial and professional services, creative industries – supporting general assumptions made about the occupational profile of city-centre residents. The household incomes of respondents reinforced assumptions made as to the economic status of both private sector residents (a quarter of households earn over £50,000 annually) and those from social housing (half of all households earned under £15,000 annually).

In terms of accommodation type, 63 per cent of private sector respondents lived in one-person households with a further third in two-person households, accounting for the fact that almost all accommodation provided was two bedroomed or smaller. In addition, a fifth of private sector accommodation was a second home, this being particularly marked amongst respondents who were married/cohabiting, had household incomes of over £50,000, and were aged over 45. One-bedroom units were the largest accommodation category for social-housing respondents.

The high degree of mobility within the city-centre housing market was demonstrated by the fact that a fifth had lived centrally for less than a year, and with only a quarter of private sector respondents (and a half of social-housing respondents) having lived in the city centre for over five years. Indeed, a quarter of respondents intimated that they would move again within the year (a third of those married or cohabiting), a clear indication of the fairly high turnover of private sector properties. In the case of respondents with household income over £50,000, two-fifths were anticipating such a move in the following year. In terms of the reasons for moving from their present property, job-related moves and the need for larger property (usually outside the city centre) were important consider-ations, as was the focus on family life-cycle opportunities. Private sector renters were clearly much less committed to long-term city-centre residence, and would find it easier to move on, either based on job mobility or the wish to buy cheaper property in entering the housing market.

In assessing the reasons for moving into the city centre, the vast majority of respondents noted convenience to work and social activities. However, in the social rental sector, where all respondents were formally resident within the city, many had not moved there through choice, but had been rehoused or only offered city-centre accommodation. Whilst 40 per cent of private sector respon-dents previously lived within the city (a third of these being already resident in the city centre), over two-thirds had formerly lived within the conurbation. However, Fitzsimmons concluded that for those currently living in the city centre there were questions as to their sustainable development credentials in terms of their trans-port and travel behaviour, with 90 per cent of city-centre private sector residents being car owners (as against 20 per cent of social-housing respondents), and with considerable out-commuting by car being a feature of their existence.

Whilst respondents interacted to varying degrees with other residents of their housing schemes, in general community interaction was low. However, extensive use was made of city-centre cultural and leisure facilities, supporting the already-established notion that the residential population is creating an indige-nous source of demand for services. Virtually no difference existed in terms of the use of facilities between the residents who were owner-occupiers or were renters in the private sector, but there were significant differences in the range and type of services used, based on income.

In terms of the advantages of city-centre living, the main advantage perceived by private sector respondents was being close to work and to leisure facilities. For those over 45 the focus on work was central, but with theatres and restaurants additionally having significance. For social-housing respondents, access to shops and to public transport facilities was particularly significant. In terms of the disadvantages of city-centre living, traffic congestion, a lack of open space, and concern over crime levels were significant. Additionally, private sector households on low incomes, or renting their accommodation, saw the cost of property and of living in the city centre as being significant.

Respondents cited a number of ways in which the city centre could be improved as a residential location, focusing both on issues that affected the city centre as a whole, and on more immediate problems relating to the area immediately surrounding their development. The three main areas of concern were the need for improvements to their local environment, a reduction in crime, and an increased level of service provision. In relation to environmental concerns the main issue revolved around traffic pollution, with reducing the numbers of cars entering the city centre and the creation of traffic-free zones being popular responses. This was reinforced by a feeling that more urban green space within the central area would also be a positive benefit. Concern over security, reflected by the need for better policing and extension of CCTV facilities, was also perceived to be an important precursor for the continuing attraction of city-centre living. Finally, an increase in the number and range of local services and welfare facilities was also an important plea.

Residential elements of the renewal programme

The City Council's informal guidance framework for the renewal area viewed residential development as 'a key element in the process of regeneration', helping to create activity and vitality within the central area, natural surveillance through day and night, and contributing to the reduction of car use. This was perceived to reaffirm the Council's commitment to residential development, mixed use and sustainability within the city centre:

> The City Council wishes to promote genuine balance in residential communities, and to create real choice for residents of all income ranges through the creation of residential opportunities at all levels of the market, including an element of social housing provision.
>
> (MCC 1996a: 9)

As the masterplan firmed up details of the main development parcels, it was expected that a significant element of housing development would be included, to help sustain central-area services and amenities, and to take advantage of existing residential schemes. However, in reality, housing was to be squeezed out by the input of higher-value uses in the bomb-damaged core, with the original intention of 283 units being translated into 82 exclusive apartments, and with other housing development largely taking place on the fringes of the renewal area (Table 9.5). This was to prove equally valuable, however, in helping to sustain the boom in residential development within the core, with the overall

Table 9.5 Potential residential development sites in renewal area

---

- *Shudehill* originally perceived as a major contributor to housing development, but with the detail and scale of the Printworks leisure development and the transport interchange being publicised, the focus of residential development was to shift to the neighbouring Northern Quarter and to Smithfield, with the renewal programme being a major catalyst.
- *Shambles West* whilst the principle of a residential element of a mixed-use development block aiming to contribute to high-quality retailing within the core was agreed, final decisions were to await confirmation of the type of development that would contribute positively to the overall scheme. In addition, whilst the neighbouring Corn Exchange was not originally considered as a residential opportunity, it was subsequently considered (alongside the possibility of a hotel) as a possible contributor to a mixed-use development within the building.
- *Salford* an area adjacent to Salford Station (the western bank of the Irwell) was identified as offering potential in the original masterplan. It remained a major consideration, but was not identified by Salford MBC as a residential component of their renewal strategy for the Chapel Street corridor. It was argued that the longer-term removal of the Station Approach Bridge and the opening up of the river would offer an attractive living environment for future investment.

---

commercial and amenity benefits of the renewal programme undoubtedly enhancing the city centre's attractiveness for residential investment, and providing the momentum for further development.

By May 1998, the priority of the Task Force in relation to a housing strategy was to focus on creating a safer environment and an enhanced environmental setting, crucial for future housing development within the city centre as a whole; the determined marketing of investment opportunities and the pro-active development of private housing wherever it was feasible; and the strengthening of service infrastructure and amenities to underpin a 'living' city centre. In the event, the commercial success of the rebuilding programme and its tightly drawn boundary meant that implementation has focused on the Shambles West apartment scheme and the Smithfield development on the edge of the masterplan area. In relation to Shambles West, following market testing of the viability of high-quality housing on the site, proposals for 82 exclusive apartments on the upper floors of the Deansgate commercial frontage were agreed. The residential units, arranged on 14 floors, have been developed by a specialist residential developer (Crosby Homes) as a separate commercial arrangement to the retail development at ground level.

Whilst the scale of the Printworks/transport interchange developments precluded a residential component at Shudehill, they proved a major catalyst for bringing forward development opportunities on an adjacent site at Smithfield, led by the City Council and English Partnerships. This is intended to strengthen the links between the core area and the Northern Quarter, and has led to proposals for a £50-million mixed-use development at the Smithfield site, incorporating the phased development of 200 residential units, complemented by restaurants and retail units and a new public square.

Strategic development of the Millennium Quarter

Following the announcement of the winning masterplan, the City Council approached the Millennium Commission with initial proposals that reflected its ambition to recreate the linkages between the historic part of the city around the cathedral and the revitalised commercial core, to provide green and open public spaces, and to deliver a major landmark building as part of a distinctive cultural quarter to mark the new century. Previously obscured parts of the city's heritage – the cathedral and Chetham's School of Music – would be juxtaposed with the imaginative regeneration of older buildings into attractive new leisure and retail facilities. In addition, the quarter would feature a new city-centre green space and a major new cultural facility of inter-national standing. The quarter was to consist of several complementary components, with a genesis in the City Pride prospectus of the mid-1990s, and the opportunity presented by the renewal programme allowing the city to consider its further explora-tion. A working party of key interests – cultural industries, higher education, business – together with the Task Force and the City Council, concluded that open spaces dedicated to leisure, a landmark building that would attract by both its form and its content, and a centre close to the cathedral that would celebrate the significance of the medieval site, were what was required. Key elements of the proposed quarter were to be a new civic public space, a visitor centre for Manchester Cathedral, a major green space, and a landmark visitor attraction, which would celebrate 'the building and experience of the modern city' (MCC 1998).

It was felt that the scale and uniqueness of the Millennium Quarter proposals, and the fact that they fell outside the remit and scope of other public funding sources, meant that core funding could only be delivered by the Millennium Commission. The key factors that would make such proposals deliverable were that they were to be at the heart of the city centre's renewal, and that creation of this quarter would be dependent on strategic investment in the wider masterplan area. A major investment programme was necessary for the quarter itself, and had to be justified to the major funding agencies – 'a once in a lifetime opportunity to endow the city with valuable community assets in an area with enormous potential to benefit the people of Manchester and the wider region' (City Council officer). In its bid for Millennium Commission support, therefore, the City Council argued that its proposals were a defining moment in the city's history, and were symbolic of the creative energy being utilised to renew the core. It represented:

- high architectural design and environmental quality, the result of international design competitions – Masterplan, Exchange Square, Urbis – and the city's commitment to quality design in modern developments (Bridgewater Hall, Art Gallery extension);

- partnership contributions evident of community support, with evidence of a decade of public–private partnership already clear, and with community consultation identifying gaps in Manchester's cultural infrastructure. Interest group involvement and commitment was already evident in defining and refining the Urbis concept and the Cathedral Visitor Centre as part of a major new cultural quarter;

- the necessity for Commission funding due to the scale and uniqueness of the proposals, with public funding for the masterplan area not applicable for this unique project. Although significant public funding would be available to assist delivery, its creation as a millennium project was perceived as a unique opportunity;

- a substantial contribution to the community, at the heart of the city and regional capital, located in order to make a substantive contribution to quality of life and environment at the hub of the regional community. Designed to provide a valuable and lasting asset, it would capitalise on the opportunity to improve quality, operation, design and choice of lifestyle in the city centre;

- in millennium terms of looking both backwards and forwards, a visitor attraction on an international scale – 'dealing with the development of world cities in an interactive and exciting way, delivering an understanding of the way cities work, the people in them, their buildings, and public spaces' (MCC 1998). Built at the heart of medieval Manchester, the quarter was intended to reveal and revitalise the city's past by recreating its historic core in a contemporary manner, and take the visitor into the twenty-first century;

- for future generations, a significant point in the city's development, with the first city-centre park created in over a century, a reflection of its status as 'the first modern city of the industrial age', and of its importance as a visitor attraction.

Case study 9: Millennium Quarter concept and elements

The Millennium Quarter was expected to regenerate a sector of the city through the creation of a new civic space (Exchange Square), a visitor centre (Manchester Cathedral), a new green space (City Park subsequently named Cathedral Gardens), and a major new visitor attraction (Urbis Centre). The quarter extends over an area of 6.8 hectares and is bounded by Corporation Street to the east; Todd Street/Victoria Station Approach/Hunts Bank to the north; River Irwell to the west; and the cathedral/Cannon Street to the south. Located in one of the most historically significant areas of the city, it delineates the heart of medieval Manchester. The quarter, contiguous with the Cathedral conservation area, boasts an impressive archaeological and architectural heritage, including some of the city centre's most prestigious listed buildings (the cathedral, Chetham's School, Corn Exchange).

With major new developments being taken forward at the edge of the quarter as part of the renewal programme, and drawing in significant levels of commercial investment, it was argued that this would complement renewal activity, with the Millennium Quarter proposal being central to a vibrant city centre that was truly mixed in its uses and attractions. Millennium Commission support was forth-coming in January 2000, involving total project development costs for the quarter of £41.4 million, of which their grant was to be £20 million. The remainder of the funding requirements were to be provided by the renewal programme's public realm activities, the City Council (£6 million), a DETR special grant (£4 million), and EU funding (ERDF £12 million), and from private sector and other civic interests. All co-funding arrangements, however, had to be in a form satisfactory to the Millen-nium Commission, who set out detailed procedures for the delivery of project obli-gations and procurement procedures. By this stage all the necessary planning approvals had progressed, involving the granting of planning permission/conserva-tion area consents for Exchange Square (July 1998), City Park (July 1999) and Urbis (September 1999), and scheduled monument consent for the Cathedral Visitor Centre (December 1999). All elements of the quarter were in place by June 2002, with its longer-term management and maintenance to be guaranteed through the establishment of a Millennium Quarter Trust.

Running in parallel with this process, consultations and discussions were held with key landowners and contiguous land users to develop proposals for the Millennium Quarter, the Urbis site being acquired (March 1999) and archaeological investigations completed, with feasibility and business planning work being undertaken, and design briefs and design teams appointed. Road closure and traffic regulation orders were put in place and utility diversion works were completed. The completion of legal documentation and the appointment of the various contractors also took place at this stage, as did the appointment of a design coordinator for the range of galleries to be accommodated within Urbis.

The Millennium Quarter was perceived as a cohesive programme of activity which included interlinking public realm and building projects, involved the preparation of design briefs, and was developed through procurement processes that included international design competitions (Urbis, Exchange Square), context reports (City Park) and detailed concept design (Cathedral Visitor Centre).

Exchange Square

Promoted as one of the most prestigious new public spaces to be created in Britain to celebrate the millennium, it was intended to be design sensitive both to the city's new landmark buildings and to medieval Manchester, and to provide opportunities for both passive and active use by day and night. Created through the closure of an existing public highway, the square is intended to tie together both the oldest and newest aspects of Manchester, and to reconnect the medieval area of the city back to its retail core. Because of the existing site topography, the sculpting of level changes within the site was the major design factor that determined the use, aesthetic qualities, and accessibility of the space. It had thus to create variety in spatial and temporal terms, in providing a setting for surrounding buildings, make the square accessible to both people and activities, and provide strong pedestrian movements across and through the square drawing people into the Millennium Quarter.

Cathedral Visitor Centre

The city's pre-industrial history is rich, varied and relatively neglected, whilst its ecclesiastical history was untold due to the fact that the cathedral possessed little in the way of a 'public face' or facilities to inform and educate visitors. The new visitor centre, created in two adjoining buildings, and sitting above Hanging Bridge (hidden from view for a century), addresses both of these issues. Using displays, interactive models and exhibitions, it sets the scene for complementing Urbis. The centre is expected to become both a valid visitor destination in its own right, and an integral element of a visitor 'trail of discovery' helping to define and unify the quarter. It houses a small bookshop and 'living cathedral' exhibition, a medieval display and an educational resources centre. It is expected to revitalise the city's historic quarter, and in so doing play a vital role in telling the story both of how Manchester was born and of the focus for its future direction.

City Park/Cathedral Gardens

It is intended to provide a new tranquil public space (a feature of public consultation on city centre renewal), provide opportunities for activity and animation, improve the cathedral's environment and enhance the boundaries of Chetham's School. It is expected to stimulate the creation of riverside boardwalks and informal performance space, and is largely formed by the pedestrianisation of Fennel Street/Long Millgate. It provides a significant area of soft landscaping between Urbis, Chetham's School and the cathedral, significantly improves the setting of some of Manchester's most important historic buildings, and is a context for the landmark building. Links to the River Irwell are created through the provision of a promenade at street level along its east bank (with the potential closure of Victoria Street to general traffic arising from the completion of the IRR),

Millennium Quarter – Cathedral Gardens

and is connected to a lower-level boardwalk providing access to the Victoria Street arches. Finally, a range of public art initiatives were commissioned within its boundaries, in partnership with the North West Arts Board.

Urbis

The cultural focus of the Millennium Quarter, the 'museum of the modern city' chronicles and analyses the growth of cities and city cultures, highlighting present challenges and looking forward to how cities are reinventing themselves. These elements are considered internationally, but also look at the ramifications of Manchester's development on such processes. Intended to unwind the common strands that unite cities, and increase understanding of the ways in which cities are shaped and the complex issues they face, it is intended to attract 200,000 visitors annually.

In architectural form it symbolises the completion of a major new 'island' landmark within the city centre, completes the 'circus' at the junction of Withy Grove and Corporation Street, and sits in its own new public space. Intended to have an active street frontage, the glass-framed building gradually slopes upwards, within which a six-storey gallery structure has been set, with the reduced gallery floors on the upper levels providing a range of spaces for different

**Millennium
Quarter –
Cathedral
Visitor Centre**

exhibitions. Access to the galleries is through an internal funicular (the first of its kind in the world) that rises to the top, and the circulation then proceeds to the lower levels, with a prow space rising through a series of openings in the gallery floors. The external envelope of the building is a multi-layered glass skin, fitted to different degrees to produce a range of translucency appropriate to the spaces within. Two floors of the gallery explore a variety of themes where the starting point – Manchester the first modern city – is compared and contrasted with other cities both nationally and internationally. A number of thematic exhibitions radiate there-after from the central core – Arrive: the shock of the city; Change: the evolution of the city; Order: the challenge of the city; Explore: the city of your imagination. It is intended that the rigorous treatment of the modern city, with its virtual and interactive elements, will make Urbis a premier international destination entertaining to the widest cross-section of population in terms of both age and social profile, with a mission 'to educate while entertaining and entertain while educating'.

Reflecting on the impact of masterplan delivery

It is undoubtedly the case that delivery of the masterplan within the context of city-centre culture and leisure has been truly significant, with a major leisure development that promotes the creation of a new evening economy, civic spaces, and cultural and visitor attractions at the heart of the city centre's renewal and vitality. Additionally, it ties the core's northern edge to the commercial heart of the city, has enhanced the environmental and aesthetic qualities of the city centre, and has tied the most modern of the city's development to its historic past. Together with complementary developments elsewhere in the city centre – concert hall and art gallery extensions – it has greatly enhanced the city's cultural statement. Questions raised at the outset as to the capacity of competing leisure facilities to deliver an enlarged market for leisure and lifestyle activities are only now beginning to be addressed, with the profitability of the Great Northern Experience in question due to the success of the Printworks development. Indeed, the search by the owners of the former complex (only opened in 2001) for new owners, due to the disappointing trading figures, is reinforced by some rationalisation in the club/pub and restaurant markets, this being partly masked by the continuing boom in city-centre living.

The impact of the housing development on the renewal area is striking even if this is not significant in numerical terms, but the role of the masterplan's implementation as a catalyst for the continuing boom in city-centre residential development has been dramatic. This response is marked, both in relation to free-standing residential blocks and in terms of residential elements of mixed commercial developments extending into the Northern Quarter and the established city core.

Chapter 10

Enhancing city-centre access and mobility

Transport planning within the city aims to ensure maximum efficiency in terms of the movement of people and goods, and it has long been recognised that an efficient transport network is vital to the city's economic success. Increased awareness of the negative consequences of transport developments has brought into much sharper focus the tensions that exist between promoting physical development and enhancing environmental quality, with such issues as traffic congestion lying at the heart of the urban management challenge. Indeed, there is no simple solution to the problem of how to ensure access to and circulation within the urban core whilst creating and maintaining an attractive environment. Whilst over the last few decades government transport policy has served to reinforce a preference for private travel and movement of goods by road, there is now a growing awareness of the social, economic and environmental costs of such a focus.

Recent shifts in policy framework and focus have seen political and financial support becoming available for new sustainable transport initiatives, and in addition to revised planning policy guidance the requirement for integrated package bids lies at the heart of local transport plans. Integration is expected between the transport components of land use and environmental plans, between transport modes, and with the social, health and economic dimensions of local strategies. Government policy intentions may be helped by a change in attitude towards the future of city centres that has led to a growing demand for a higher-quality environment as an economic driver, the management of vehicular access and the promotion of sustainable transport modes, and the centrality of pedestrian mobility and accessibility to guarantee city-centre vitality. This chapter aims to consider the local policy context for such developments, looking at the established local transport policy context for Manchester city centre, the evolving transport strategy in response to the bombing and the management of its implementation, and with a focus on key transport projects that have recently been realised. Finally, it will consider the transport impact of the renewal programme, both on the bomb-damaged area and for the wider city and regional centre.

The established policy framework

The transport objectives of the renewal programme are set within the context of the development of an integrated transport strategy for the conurbation as a whole, and as such have their basis in a number of policy documents and established programmes. The overall thrust of such an approach has been to support the economy of the regional centre; to remove through traffic from the core, and to improve internal circulation within the centre; to encourage the greater use of public transport; and to provide a safe and pleasant environment for pedestrians and cyclists. However, different policy-making bodies have differing remits and agendas, this inevitably being reflected in the emphasis and interpretation placed on achieving these broad transport goals.

Development plans and development guidance

The key documents relating to transport planning aspects of the conurbation's core relate to the policies contained within local development plans. Manchester's UDP, adopted in 1995, focuses on:

- transport policies in relation to giving priority to future highway investment, to maintaining and improving the existing network, and to opening up suitable areas for economic development;
- the improvement of public transport in all its forms;
- making significant improvements for pedestrians and cyclists; and
- supporting the continued expansion of the airport in an environmentally sustainable manner.

With specific reference to the city centre, transport-focused policies relate to:

- environmental improvement programmes for major gateways and areas of major pedestrian activities, and improvements to public accessibility and amenity value of the core's waterways;
- targeted highway improvements and upgrading of the conurbation's bus and rail networks;

- the provision of safe, pleasant and convenient conditions for pedestrians and cyclists within the core, and the facilitating of improved public transport access and integration; and
- priority to be given to short- and medium-stay car parking within the core, and a diminishing of the public sector's role in such provision.

In terms of the plan's proposals for the renewal area, the focus on the Victoria Station/cathedral area was to promote the maintenance and improvement of the suburban rail network and the way it served the core; to maintain access by public transport, car and foot to the core, and to provide an appropriate level of car parking; and to enhance the character and environment of the Irwell and Corporation Street corridors. The area to the east (focusing on Shudehill) was already seen as a key location for the provision of a permanent long-stay public car park serving the commercial core, whilst the frontages to Corporation Street and Miller Street were considered high-priority environmental improvement corridors. The promotion of a better pedestrian environment was seen as imperative for the main retail area around the Arndale Centre and Shambles Square, as was improved accessibility to the commercial core through the provision of contiguous short-stay car-parking facilities. The second major retail area of the city – bounded by Deansgate, St Mary's Gate and John Dalton Street – was not seen as fundamentally important in terms of the problem created by through traffic, and the primary need in this area was to ensure its accessibility for service vehicles whilst enhancing the area's environmental character for pedestrian use. Thus the overall theme running through the plan's land-use policies is to promote central-area accessibility to the widest range of possible users, to enhance the environmental character of the central area, and to divert a significant element of through traffic from the core.

Salford's UDP, also adopted in 1995, focuses on the role of its transport policies in underpinning the drive for economic regeneration, acknowledging the local benefits to be achieved in contributing to the further development of the regional centre. The Central Salford planning area, lying adjacent to Manchester city centre, is seen to provide a focus for policy, offering the scope for redevelopment and regeneration, and having considerable economic potential. In this sense it is seen to capitalise on the proximity of Manchester city centre and the transformation of Salford Quays. It emphasises the need to improve rail and bus facilities to the regional centre, and to provide further parking opportunities to offset the extensive loss of long-stay provision due to redevelopment. Whilst this area had historically been planned as being entirely separate in land-use terms from Manchester, there was already evidence of its increasing incorporation into the dynamics of the regional centre.

Manchester's Development Guide (1996) sets out, as previously noted, the city's defining principles in relation to all new development, and it adopted the view that the city should contain a recognisable hierarchy of streets with a clear differentiation of roles, being seen as the public expression of the way people lived and interacted. The guide recognised that the use of private vehicles would not change significantly until there was a well-developed public transport infrastructure, but noted that new development proposals would be encouraged to respond to the future development of public infrastructure, particularly in the core.

Local transport plans

In the late 1960s a passenger transport authority was established for the conurbation (GMPTA, 1968), statutorily responsible for policy delivery in respect of public transport provision, with its executive body (GMPTE, 1974) responsible for securing the public transport services considered appropriate. For most of the 1980s and early 1990s capital-funding package bids were regularly submitted on behalf of the conurbation's local authorities, focusing on the main public and private transport infrastructure needs. After 1995, however, the emergence of a concern for broader-based and integrated transport packages came to the fore-front, and a new transport strategy was agreed with government, focusing on a greater commitment to public transport, and to interrelate such proposals with economic and community regeneration, and with sustainable development principles (GMPTA/AGMA 1998) (Table 10.1).

This package bidding system for the conurbation as a whole remained in place for five years, being replaced by the introduction of local transport plans in 2001. As well as traffic calming and traffic management measures, the main focus of the package bid directly affecting city-centre development related to inputs into the Inner Relief Road, city-centre works associated with Metrolink expansion, and the consequence for the core of implementing the conurbation's bus quality corridors.

City Pride agenda

This visioning exercise focused on the conurbation core, with the transport element expected to contribute to economic and employment growth as well as to reduce the impact of motorised traffic in sensitive areas. The social dimension of transport access and mobility was particularly stressed, with public transport users, pedestrians and cyclists expected to benefit from improved environmental conditions. Specific mention was also made of the need to ensure good links between the conurbation core, inner-city areas and gateway locations, with a focus on the need to enhance the Piccadilly Gateway and the extension of Metrolink.

In Manchester, where a whole range of transport 'experiments' had taken place over the previous half-century, the physical development of the core had been greatly influenced by transport planning, with each development phase leaving an indelible impression. Major transport planning exercises from the

Table 10.1 Greater Manchester's Transport Strategy and Investment Plan 1995

Transport Strategy
- *Public transport developments* to develop a strategic countywide network of high-quality public transport routes – to offer an attractive alternative to the car.
- *Economic and community regeneration* to make the regional centre and town and district centres more attractive – to prevent the dispersal of activity by making those places served by public transport the main areas of investment and activity.
- *Cycling and walking* to promote measures that make walking and cycling more attractive – to encourage more healthy and sustainable options for short trips.
- *Demand management* to promote demand management measures – to shift the balance of trip-making away from car use.
- *Accessible transport systems* to improve travel opportunities for people with mobility impairments – to ensure the transport system is accessible to all.
- *Promoting travel awareness* to use the 'hearts and minds' approach to persuade and promote the use of public transport, cycling and walking.
- *Selected road improvements* to promote selective road improvements – where these are the only means of achieving the objectives outlined.

Package investment plans
- To improve the environment, attractiveness and safety of the regional centre, together with the county's other urban centres and key employment nodes and to reduce the impact of motorised traffic.
- To increase the proportion of trips made to the regional centre, and other commercial and employment nodes by public transport, cycling and on foot, and to reduce the proportion made by car.
- To increase the proportion of short trips made on foot or by bicycle, and reduce the proportion made by car; and to reduce the number of longer trips to non-central locations.
- To reduce the impact of motorised traffic on residential areas and other sensitive areas.
- To make travel by public transport, cycling and walking as attractive as travel by private car; and to ensure that the county's transport system enables all our communities to lead a healthy lifestyle.
- To provide for the movement of freight which would support the economic development of the conurbation in ways which are consistent with the desire to reduce the impact of motorised traffic.
- To ensure that people can gain access to existing and potential employment and leisure sites, especially from within areas of economic and social deprivation, in ways which will help to reduce the number of longer trips to non-central locations.
- To provide for the movement of people and goods between Greater Manchester and the rest of the United Kingdom and Europe in ways which are consistent with the other objectives.

1940s to the end of the 1960s all proposed extensive road-building schemes to create a series of ring roads and radial routes around and into the city centre, the majority of which were not built or were scaled down due to cost constraints. For example, the Inner Ring Road, part of which was built in the 1960s as the Mancunian Way, has only now been completed as resources have been made available as part of the renewal programme (Inner Relief Road). In terms of increasing capacity and shorter journey times, they were intended to service the suburban-based motorist, even though they inevitably brought about social and economic dislocation to inner-city communities and businesses (Kitchen 1997).

Following a review of major road proposals in the mid-1970s, more costly elements were either abandoned or modified, and by the mid-1990s both the outer (M60) and inner (IRR) ring roads remained incomplete. Completion of these two routes was seen as imperative, with the IRR being regarded as the key to removing extraneous traffic from the city centre. The desire by the local authority to discourage commuter parking and to encourage visits by other users to the city centre, led it to shift from long-stay to short-stay parking in the mid-1990s, and to the city adopting a more commercial approach to the provision of parking facilities. At the same time a draft business plan aimed to improve the quality of parking facilities and information provided, in an attempt to counter the expected threat from the Trafford Centre.

Over the years numerous proposals had been advanced to improve public transport to and within the city, but it was not until the mid-1980s that the idea of a light rapid transit system was mooted. The first Metrolink line (Bury–Altrincham) became operational in 1992, and by the mid-1990s plans were in place (but not the finances secured) for a major expansion of the system to link up the conurbation's main centres. However, whilst Metrolink was expected to become a key component of Manchester's public transport system, it was accepted that it would not be the total solution to issues of city-centre accessibility. In this regard, the city's suburban rail network, which could help obviate such concerns, had suffered from poor linkages between the northern and southern components, attributed to the fact that each network was originally developed by different companies. Whilst under-utilised, it nevertheless provided the potential for carrying much larger numbers of people into the city centre.

The bus was expected to remain as the most important mode of public transport, even if its contemporary role was not fully effective, and it was not providing a competitive alternative to private motoring. In the late 1980s and early 1990s bus mileage increased whilst passenger numbers fell – the average numbers of passengers carried per bus-mile travelled halved between 1985 and 1994 – a symptom of the new deregulatory environment. Furthermore, bus users had historically been inadequately served in terms of terminal facilities, with Piccadilly Gardens being generally regarded as unattractive and unsafe after dark. The city's main covered bus station (Arndale bus station) was in a poor state of repair prior to the bombing, and the pedestrian environment was generally considered unfriendly.

Insufficient attention had been given to pedestrian modes of movement within the city – safety at crossings, the phasing of traffic signals, permeability within the centre – and the overall pedestrian ambience was considered poor. With the notable exceptions of King Street and Albert Square, the public realm was of poor quality, proving particularly challenging for the young, elderly and disabled. In addition, access across the city centre by bus was limited, due to restriction caused by the pedestrianisation of Market Street.

At the time of the bombing, therefore, the focus of transport planning had shifted significantly towards a major commitment to improving public transport in all its guises, and a reassertion of the central role of the public realm. However, the city centre was still faced with the fact that 60 per cent of all trips to and from the core were made by car and only 40 per cent by public transport. Whilst there was a commitment in place to change this modal split balance, the necessary mechanisms and resources were not in place to achieve this, and the transport intentions of the city-centre renewal plan were required to fit within a transport strategy with a much longer timeframe.

The masterplan's transport strategy

The development of an integrated transport strategy was a central component of the masterplanning framework from its inception, and it was acknowledged that a number of the city's overall transport weaknesses could be addressed as part of the reconstruction programme. In addition, a transport strategy was seen as vital in achieving the plan's objective of creating new public spaces free from vehicular traffic, rationing the dominance of the car on core city-centre streets, and substituting commercial floorspace in areas previously occupied by public highways. Ensuring easy access to and within the city centre was seen as essential if Manchester was to achieve its full potential as a strengthened, confident and forward-looking international city. With the publication of the initial masterplan in late 1996, transport proposals focused on the need to address modal integration and the arrangement of car-parking provision. These proposals were further developed and refined over the subsequent months, and by April 1997 the fundamental goals of the transport element were in place. This aimed:

- to ensure accessibility by all modes and users;
- to remove through traffic from the city centre by the completion of the IRR;
- to provide sufficient well-signed and good-quality short-stay car parking;
- to encourage greater use of all modes of public transport, and improved accessibility and movement within the city centre; and
- to provide a safe and pleasant environment for pedestrians and cyclists.

The strategy, comprising an integrated package of measures, was to be implemented over a ten-year period by a wide range of partners (principally the

Task Force, Manchester and Salford City Councils, GMPTA/GMPTE, public transport operators, GO NW and key landowners), with key city-centre elements to be delivered in the initial three-year rebuilding programme. It needed to be implemented in a planned and phased manner, however, in order to coordinate with development activities, and to minimise any disruption or reduction in accessibility during the rebuilding programme. This component of the renewal programme was thus set within the wider development of an integrated transport strategy for the conurbation as a whole, involving already well-established partnership activity, and a clear focus.

The primary objective of the transport strategy was to achieve a balance between ensuring good car access into the regional centre in combination with an enhanced role for public transport, with the goal being to facilitate a 50:50 modal split. The approach adopted to realise this goal involved the completion of the IRR and the improvement of public transport facilities. Completion of the IRR would, it was hoped, reduce the volume of through traffic in the city centre (nearly a third of the total), and act as an efficient distributor of traffic entering the city. Motorists would be directed to available parking facilities through the deployment of variable message signing (VMS) technology. It was felt that modal shift could be achieved if reliable, comfortable, safe and convenient forms of public transport were provided, with the early success of Metrolink providing evidence of this – a success that could be repeated on the extensive, but under-utilised suburban rail network, and on the bus network.

The general approach adopted towards the use of streets in the core area was to ensure that design facilitated pedestrian dominance once people had arrived in the city centre. It was felt that buses should have access during the day (subject to satisfactory management), and that light traffic should be allowed in during the evenings in order to create a sense of security and vibrancy, and to avoid 'dead' pedestrianised zones. The core elements of the transport objectives planned to be delivered within the initial funding programme were the IRR and its accompanying VMS system; a new transport interchange; a quality bus strategy and a Metrolink strategy; and a traffic and pedestrian management strategy – a package of activity that was to prove extremely challenging.

The Inner Relief Road

Removing extraneous traffic from the city centre was seen as the key to promoting other modes of movement into and within the city centre, and central to the objective of creating new public spaces within the commercial core. Much of the through traffic could be deflected from the city centre by completing the Inner Relief Road, and by giving drivers incentives to use it by giving it vehicle priority over radial routes. The completion of the Inner Relief Road, and upgrading of existing sections, involved the implementation of four individual elements, namely improvement of a section to form a dual carriageway (Dawson Street); the addition of a long-delayed missing section (Gore Street); the conversion of an existing element from a one-way route to a gyratory system (Addington Street); and alignment improvements to a key junction (Water Street).

As part of the plans to complete and upgrade the Inner Relief Road, new signs and signalling were proposed to ensure efficient use of the road, with priority being given to IRR movements over radial routes. This was to be connected to central-area car parks, with variable signage giving drivers up-to-date information around the whole route.

Bus and Metrolink strategy

The key to achieving the 50:50 modal split required a much greater use of bus travel, and it was recognised that increased use could only be achieved through significant improvements in the quality of vehicles, infrastructure and service. In order to achieve these improvements a Bus Quality Partnership was formed between the bus operators, the local authority and GMPTA/GMPTE. The work of this partnership focused on the city centre (and was separate from the established conurbation-wide partnership), with the agreement aiming to provide a commitment to invest in new vehicles, bus priority measures and integrated ticketing, alongside the rebuilding programme's established timetable. A bus strategy for the core was to be developed by MML in consultation with the key interests involved, this focusing on investment in high-specification, low-emission vehicles, with bus priority measures and an integrated ticketing strategy; the development of a coherent, rational and easy to understand network that maintained and improved access to key employment, retail and leisure centres; and allowing buses to penetrate key pedestrian-dominated streets from which other traffic was excluded, but limiting the numbers and type of vehicles being used.

A central component of the strategy to improve and encourage greater use of public transport was the development of a transport interchange that would incorporate a bus terminal to replace the one decommissioned by the bombing (Arndale bus station); a multi-storey car park to meet the functional and geographical needs of the city centre, and any additional demands that might arise from the implementation of the renewal programme's commercial strategy; and new Metrolink stations in recognition of the additional demands on the system.

A package of bus priority measures were proposed in order to improve services and reduce journey times, and two 'bus super stops' were planned in order to provide high-quality facilities at major stopping points within the commercial core. To enable greater movement within the city centre by public transport, a bus routing strategy for low-emission buses was also developed. Provision was to be made in the design of the public realm to accommodate the route of such a 'metroshuttle', which would ferry passengers around the city centre as a free service. Finally, a ten-year

Metrolink strategy for the city centre was envisaged, intended to form a city-centre loop, and considered to be part of the vision for completion of the network as a whole. Within the timescale of the renewal programme, however, proposals were more modest, being restricted to the construction of two new Metrolink stations within the core (Market Street, Shudehill).

Traffic and pedestrian management strategy

A traffic management strategy for the centre was developed by MML in consultation with key user groups, and was intended to accord with the overall transport aim of removing extraneous traffic, to enhance and extend pedestrian space, and to improve permeability. It aimed to ensure that facilities were designed that were pedestrian dominant, and that no 'dead' pedestrianised zones would be created; that during the day buses would be enabled to penetrate pedestrian-dominated areas, subject to controls on both bus numbers and quality; and that light traffic be allowed back into pedestrian-dominated areas in the evening in order to generate more activity and to create a greater sense of security.

The general intention was to keep general traffic out of core city-centre streets in order to promote a high-quality pedestrian environment, subject to satisfactory circulation arrangements for cars. Furthermore, it was recognised that major developments aimed at strengthening and diversifying the city's economic base would lead to additional evening activity, and that certain routes that were closed during the day would be opened up from late evening to early morning. Although one of the masterplan's aims was to reduce the number of cars entering the city centre, it was accepted that the new leisure, retail and commercial uses proposed for the redeveloped core would create additional travel demands. It was anticipated that around a thousand spaces would be required, largely to be provided by the multi-storey car park within the transport interchange, but also through replacement underground parking facilities at flagship projects (Shambles block). In addition, it was acknowledged that existing car-parking provision, both in the redeveloped area and beyond, needed refurbishing and upgrading, if the hoped-for step change in the city centre's environmental quality was to be achieved. The scope for this work included improvements to the internal layout of parking areas, entry/exit arrangements, pedestrian access and security, lighting, surface finishes, external appearance and landscaping.

Managing implementation

As already noted, the conurbation's evolving transport strategy envisaged an integrated programme of initiatives that would be implemented over a ten-year timescale, whilst MML's more focused transport strategy aimed to ensure that specific elements could be delivered within the initial three-year renewal programme. This was one area, however, that required a timescale beyond that of the Task Force mandate, with key elements underpinning the masterplan being delivered long after MML's demise.

The city-centre transport strategy was produced in November 1997, its key objectives being the diversion of a substantial amount of through traffic from the central area, rebalancing the street environment in favour of pedestrians, and the active promotion of policies supporting public transport whilst maintaining general accessibility. Such objectives were to be achieved by the completion of the IRR and its complementary signing and signalling strategy; an enhanced bus and Metrolink role in the core; a programme of roadworks and closures to facilitate development; and improved car parking to cater for changing commercial and leisure demands (Table 10.2).

Table 10.2 Masterplan transportation outputs

Overall strategy
- 50:50 public/private transport share
- Reduction of through traffic
- Pedestrian dominance within central area
- Routing and signage strategy
- Planned and phased approach

Inner Relief Route (IRR)
- Dawson Street section
- Swan/Addington Street gyratory
- Water Street improvements
- Gore Street 'missing link'

IRR signing and signalling
- Route-signing strategy
- Car-park signing strategy

Metrolink
- Market Street island station
- Initial design for possible new city-centre route
- Shudehill station

Bus strategy
- Bus Quality Partnership
- Investment in new vehicles
- Coherent, rational bus routes
- Bus priority measures
- Integrated ticketing strategy
- New high-quality bus station
- Metroshuttle buses
- Restricted bus penetration within city centre

Street Closures
- Road closure procedures
- Traffic regulation orders
- Surface treatment works
- Upgrade and refurbishment of existing car-parking spaces

Cycling
- Dedicated cycle routes
- Secure cycle-parking facilities

Intended to be completed during MML's mandate were elements of the IRR and its associated signage, the new Metrolink stations and bus super stop, metroshuttle and bus priority measures, the transport interchange, and a range of traffic management measures. In financial terms, of the £28.5 million required to implement the transport elements of the masterplan, £24 million was to come through supplementary credit approval, 'ring fenced' but managed through the Transport Plans and Programmes (TPP) process, and with the other element mainly funded by other public sector sources (ERDF). In addition to this funding and improvement package, two key elements of the conurbation's transport plan were seen as crucial to the long-term sustainability of the renewal programme: namely, the completion of the IRR and the city-centre Metrolink loop. MML delivered its contribution to the completion of the IRR to time and to budget. In addition, a solution to the 'missing link' problem was identified and funding secured in order to complete the whole IRR before the Commonwealth Games. The transport interchange – at the heart of the masterplan – was delayed for over three years arising from issues related to CPO challenges, and will not be fully completed until late 2004.

In terms of overall construction management, implementation of the masterplan strategy was to require a complex programme of street closures and restrictions, with proposals to restrain traffic varying from complete closure of roads to simple traffic calming measures. Additionally, certain streets were closed to different kinds of vehicles at different times of day. The transport strategy had to be implemented in a planned and phased manner so as to coordinate with the main redevelopment activities taking place within the core, and by the maintenance of coherent and well-signed routes into and out of the city during the rebuilding process. A routing strategy for construction traffic was produced, based on individual contractors obtaining access from the IRR with minimal encroachment into other areas of work. The construction vehicle strategy also addressed the need for continuing detailed liaison with those undertaking major renewal projects, attempting to coordinate not only each phase of construction, but also the wider implementation of the strategy. It was produced in consultation with the local authority, landowners and contractors, and emergency services.

Oscar Faber's role as transport advisers was to develop an integrated transport strategy in consultation with the key local partners, with the strategy aiming to ensure that accessibility was maintained and improved for all trips, by all modes, to and from the city centre. The objective was to facilitate a significant switch to public transport, and to encourage through traffic to use other routes so that significant environmental improvements and a much safer environment could be created. In order to achieve these elements, detailed consultations were entered into with a range of bodies, facilitated by established Task Force networks –

landowners and developers, contractors, civic and other pressure groups, central and local government and GMPTA/GMPTE, with city-centre business and Marketing Manchester, and with the bus operators and the Bus Quality Partnership.

The project dimension

In looking at the delivery of the transport strategy and its impact on the wider renewal programme, this chapter will now consider the experience of a number of discrete projects, focusing on the development history and framework of the site, considerations relating to project feasibility, and the process of development realisation.

Case study 10: the Inner Relief Road

The Manchester/Salford Inner Relief Road (IRR) had always been of central importance for the transport strategies of both cities, and had survived the rationalisation of major road projects by government in the mid-1970s. Completion of the route remained a priority for funding in the conurbation's transport package bids throughout the 1990s despite a shift in national transport policy away from road building. It was seen as vital in freeing up road space in the city centre, and in facilitating much-needed improvements for pedestrian movement and for public transport. The first section of the road was built in 1980, and the project was three-quarters complete by the time of the bombing, at a cost to central government of around £18 million. It was argued that its completion would benefit the core by:

- accommodating through traffic displaced from the city centre;
- improving road safety for all road users;
- assisting in the regeneration of derelict industrial areas on the fringes of the regional centre;
- improving conditions in the commercial and business heart of the region by removing unnecessary traffic, whilst improving access to locations around the relief road;
- enabling improvements in bus circulation and the management of traffic in sensitive areas, and releasing capacity to accommodate more frequent Metrolink services;
- improving conditions for pedestrians, cyclists and disabled travellers within the city centre; and
- safeguarding and improving the environment, and minimising the adverse effects of traffic congestion in terms of noise and pollution.

The first implementation plan identified four individual components to IRR development: namely, the Dawson Street section, the Addington Street gyratory, Water Street improvements, and the Gore Street section. Dawson Street was a single-carriageway stretch of road linking the long-established Mancunian Way to Regent Road and to the region's motorway network. As both Mancunian Way and Regent Road were dual carriageways, the Dawson Street link had become a traffic bottleneck that the programme was to specifically address in a £12.3-million scheme. The construction of extra lanes by building demolition and a new carriageway alignment was expected to substantially increase the road's capacity, help with the continuing regeneration of the Castlefield area and environmentally improve the Bridgewater Canal, whilst at the same time take pressure off the city centre. The first phase of the route was completed in September 1998 with the final section being completed in July 1999.

Swan Street (the stretch of the IRR between Oldham Road and Rochdale Road) was a one-way route, and in order to enable traffic to move around this stretch of the IRR in both directions it was decided that a gyratory system should be constructed along a parallel route at Addington Street. The £2.7-million scheme was started in April 1999 and completed in August 1999, and included the widening of Addington Street, together with pedestrian facilities at the Swan Street junction. These improvements cured the traffic bottleneck, and were to play a vital role in easing traffic flow around the city's core.

Improvements to the junction at Water Street were promoted as a way of encouraging traffic to use the route as part of the IRR in the absence of the missing link. This £500,000 scheme, initially resisted by Salford due to the fear that it could undermine the case for the Gore Street 'missing link', was however to proceed, with the detailed design and land acquisition completed by spring 1998, and with junction improvements completed by early 1999.

The Gore Street 'missing link' had, for a long time, been the key to completing the IRR, and whilst the original alignment was promoted in Salford's UDP, it was perceived to be over-complex and expensive, and unlikely to be funded. Hence a cheaper alternative alignment was advanced that did not require major investment in bridge-works, with the £12-million scheme being at the heart of masterplan's delivery. The scheme would make the best use of existing railway bridge arches, and possessed considerable development and regeneration potential for the local area, opening up new sites and improving visibility, accessibility and status for the route. More widely it would underpin the transport strategy for the core area, improve traffic management along Deansgate, and would have major longer-term implications for the success of the Millennium Quarter.

Acquiring funding for the scheme was always going to be difficult given the general presumption against major highway schemes in the conurbation's transport package bids, and government requested that the option of a

**Inner Relief Route
– new bridge
crossing the
River Irwell**

possible Private Finance Intiative (PFI) be considered. This was not to prove
feasible, and the Council decided to put in a new submission for conventional
funding as part of the emerging local transport plan. With the success of the application, work on the route was to commence in early 2001, with full completion of
the 'missing link' being accomplished in July 2002, in time for the additional transport pressures generated by the Commonwealth Games.

**Site of the much
delayed transport
interchange**

As part of the plan to complete and upgrade the IRR, new signage and signalling were proposed to ensure the efficient use of the new route. Hence a £2-million route and car park signalling availability strategy was put in place, to be developed and introduced to coincide with the completion of the works on the IRR. In particular, the strategy worked to ensure that the IRR functioned as an effective by pass for traffic wishing to avoid the city centre, as well as an efficient distributor of traffic entering the centre. VMS signage was installed, and was linked to car parks to give drivers up-to-date information on the availability of space.

Case study 11: transport interchange

A central component of the strategy to improve, and thus encourage greater use of, public transport was the development of a new transport interchange. The facility would incorporate a bus terminal (to replace the former Arndale bus station), multi-storey car park (to accommodate both established and any additional traffic pressures generated by the Printworks development), and a new Metrolink station. It was expected to provide high-quality passenger waiting and information facilities, together with a retail concourse. A number of routing strategies were considered for the provision of the bus-centre component, with alternate locations at Withy Grove, Whitworth Street and Greengate in Salford (the former Victoria bus station) being evaluated as possibilities.

A key feature in the final choice of site was to be the extent to which the bus centre and attendant routing strategies informed the overall masterplan. The transport benefits of the options, availability of land, views of operators, and the impact of a bus centre on adjacent development were also key considerations. An area of land at Shudehill facing Withy Grove was identified as the preferred option of the GMPTA/GMPTE and the operators, regarded as the most convenient site for passengers, and the location best able to secure optimal bus penetration of the city centre. In relation to the masterplan's integrated transport vision, the Shudehill area was perceived to be a prominent location for improving regional transport provision, and acquiring the site through a CPO was viewed as necessary if agreement to release the land was not forthcoming.

Established land covenants and design issues were to prove critical in the realisation of proposals, with the site owned by the Co-operative Insurance Society (CIS) and the Co-operative Wholesale Society (CWS). As the site had been the location of its headquarter operations over the previous half-century, the company aimed to ensure that all proposed developments were in keeping with the area and its own activities. CIS had obtained planning consent for a mixed-use scheme on the proposed interchange site in the early 1990s, although this did not go ahead due to market conditions. In addition, the site was located in the Shudehill conservation area, and possessed a number of historically significant buildings on its eastern side. However, many original buildings in the area had been demolished, and there was general uncertainty as to the area's future.

Manchester's UDP noted that any developments in this location would require a high standard of design since it was at the heart of an environmental improvement corridor, and the plan suggested that a mixed commercial development, a residential mixed-use development or a long-stay car park might be appropriate. In addition, the SPG for the bomb-damaged area noted that development had to be of high-quality design, appearance and materials, and conservation area and listed building procedures had to be followed. The landmark and high-profile corners characteristic of the area needed to be addressed, and the frontage of each block had to be of high-quality design and appearance; and buildings providing end views had to be visually prominent and attractive rather than being part of the street wall.

As part of the proposed development of the transport interchange project it was expected that the developers of the Printworks and GMPTE would assume leasehold interest to the land, since Richardsons already had permission for a 1,000-space car park to underpin the Printworks development. They were persuaded to be content with a somewhat lower figure given that the integrated transport strategy was intended to provide excellent public transport to the core of the renewal programme. The programme was expected to bring new activity into the area and to regenerate vacant land and derelict buildings, provide a quality 'back of pavement' development along Shudehill, whilst at the same time retaining the key historic street pattern. It was also recognised that the development of the interchange would have positive effects on the adjoining Smithfield conservation area, both in terms of the visible quality of the proposed development, and in assisting the securing of ongoing economic investment. Since the site was owned by CIS it was necessary to get their agreement, and they appeared content to allow an outline planning application for the proposed development to be submitted. Indeed, the Task Force and its consultants worked up a preferred scheme with Richardsons in summer 1997 for presentation to CIS/CWS for consideration. In this scheme CIS/CWS (the freeholder) would grant a lease to Richardson Developments for the overall development (Printworks and the interchange), with covenants relating to the overall performance of the interchange. Richardsons would sub-let the interchange to the City Council at a peppercorn rent, with covenants requiring them to work within specified constraints; and the City Council would grant an under-lease to the interchange operator (assumed to be GMPTE), who would manage the facility with the same obligations. In the event CIS/CWS retained a prohibition on the lease granted to Richardsons, removal of which required the offer of a number of dedicated private parking spaces to the landowner, strict controls on the operation of the interchange, restriction on the height and construction of the building for visual reasons, and a number of highway requirements.

This was a precursor for the initiation of the detailed design and development work associated with the proposed development, for which a Transport Interchange Project Group was established – Richardsons, City Council, Task Force, GMPTA/GMPTE and Altram (Metrolink operator). In early 1998 the available budget for the development stood at £7.1 million (£4 million from Richardsons and £3.1 from the Task Force) to provide 780 parking spaces to service the Printworks, and to provide a quality transport interchange.

A full planning application for the transport interchange was submitted in October 1998 for a proposal that included a bus/coach station, multi-storey car park and retail concourse, and the demolition of existing buildings on a site bounded by Dantzic and Bradshaw Streets and Shudehill. This was for a 49,000-square-metre interchange extending over seven levels, to include a bus station capable of accommodating 154 buses per hour (18 stands), 780 parking spaces on six levels, and a concourse of offices and retail units. This was approved in January 1999 subject to a range of conditions relating to materials and elevation drawings; satisfactory lighting, acoustic and vapour abstraction and ventilation; details of vehicle access and parking layout, pedestrian priority works and traffic management measures; and of archaeological investigation, ground investigation and landscaping needs prior to development. A parallel conservation area consent was also submitted in December 1998, together with an application to demolish buildings on site to make way for the proposed change.

These proposals had already begun to raise serious concerns, both from the perspective of the established landowner and from conservation interests within the city. The principal reasoning behind the sustained objection of CIS related to their preference for alternative sites for the interchange, focusing specifically on land adjacent to Victoria Station. They argued that in design, functionality, transport and passenger provision terms it was a superior location to Shudehill. The scheme's proponents – City Council, Task Force, PTE and bus operators – were however in complete agreement that this suggestion did not present a realistic alternative in either bus routing or passenger provision terms, and that the Shudehill site presented by far the preferred location. Indeed, they argued that the Victoria Station option had been considered and rejected at an early stage in the planning process.

CIS also argued that the local authority had not fully recognised the importance of the site as part of a conservation area, the constraints imposed as a result of the listed buildings contiguous to the site, and that the proposed design would break away from the traditional solid building interface. The City Council's view, backed by the Task Force, was that if agreement in principle could not be reached with CIS/CWS, then it would immediately declare a CPO in order to acquire the site. Negotiations with CIS/CWS continued over the next six months in an attempt to overcome their objections, alongside parallel preparations for a possible CPO inquiry.

During the autumn CIS/CWS were major objectors to the planning application for the interchange, perceiving the futuristic design as paying little attention to the character of Shudehill, and as failing the criteria of local authority guidance for the area. It was seen to be inappropriate to adjacent listed buildings and perceived to fundamentally damage the conservation area. They were also concerned with highway and traffic management aspects of the proposal, and the noise and pollution issues raised by such a major development. Concerns were also expressed by English Heritage and Manchester Civic Society about the design quality, loss of buildings contributing to the character of the Shudehill conservation area, and the erosion of the historic grain of the area. In addition, conservation interests were also opposed, arguing that approval would destroy the integrity of large parts of the conservation area and the traditional street pattern.

As a result of negotiations between the Task Force and CWS (and the removal of Danztic Street access and egress proposals) they withdrew their objections to the scheme prior to the CPO inquiry. However, CIS were unwilling to follow suit and the inquiry took place in January 1999. The main argument advanced by the local authority for granting the CPO was the strategic contribution that the transport interchange would make to the continued revival of the regional centre, its role in reviving the Shudehill area as a major gateway route, and the removal of the area's current uncertainties. Indeed, the transport facility would replace the outdated Arndale bus station and bus stops along Cannon Street with an accessible 'state of the art' facility that would also improve the setting for the conservation area along Withy Grove, enable the redevelopment of Arndale North, and modernise the area through the introduction of new activity. It provided no significant conflict with the UDP, was in accord with the framework established by the SPG for the bomb-damaged area, and with Manchester's development guide.

Although actively encouraged to do so as a result of discussions held with them in the month leading up to the CPO, English Heritage did not submit either written or oral comments. The city's Civic Society were to argue, however, that the importance of the conservation area had been underplayed by the local authority, and that any proposed development should take account of the existing building footprints and historic street patterns. They argued that the interchange proposals contradicted UDP policies and the SPG, and did not fulfil conservation area development criteria. In addition, the demolition of buildings within a conservation area had not been justified by a thorough consideration of alternative options and the effects of the proposal on neighbouring areas. It was perceived to be out of scale, replacing a wide range of existing land uses, leading to the destruction of vistas, and a substantial increase in the flow of traffic. Altogether, it had not been proved that the land was suitable or required for the development of the interchange. Whilst such conservation arguments were supported and also propounded by CIS, a major aspect of their concern related to their frustration at not being in a position to capitalise on development opportunities offered by the wider renewal programme.

The inspector's report (March 1999) – whilst arguing that the proposal would greatly benefit regeneration proposals within the area, and would improve Manchester's public transport strategy – concluded that the proposed scheme failed to accord to local/national policy guidance concerning development in conservation areas. He argued that the importance of the conservation area was an element that surpassed all the scheme's proposed benefits, and recommended that the CPO order should not be confirmed.

> A massive structure would be located on a unsuitable site, effectively splitting off one part of the city from the rest. In design terms it will be a disaster to rank with the exterior of the Arndale Centre. The site is too small for the combination of a bus station/interchange and car park and leads to a damaging building in a Conservation Area.

> The threatened streets are typical of the intimate streetscape which is a distinctive characteristic of this part of the conservation area … The historically dominant red brick is entirely absent from the building … regeneration was played as a 'trump card' because it was a paramount consideration overriding everything else.

> (Brier 1999: 22, 26–28)

Following the initial failure by the City Council to gain approval for the CPO, the inspector's report was considered by the Secretary of State (DETR) to assess whether there was a sufficiently compelling case, in the public interest, to justify authorising the CPO. Central government was mindful that the scheme had planning permission, and that delay over the interchange proposals would have a destabilising effect on the whole renewal programme. The Secretary of State as confirming authority, had to consider whether the land was *suitable* for and *required* for development, and that it accorded with both central and local policy guidance. In particular, whilst the masterplan was not part of the UDP, and had been revised in mid-1998 in consultation with government as part of the annual review process, the Secretary of State was mindful of the fact that government had not previously given any indication of serious concerns with the interchange proposal. The Secretary of State was clear that the proposal would offer considerable regeneration benefits, but was concerned (as was the inspector) with the extent to which the quality of the proposed development offered scope for preserving the character and appearance of the Shudehill conservation area. Indeed, in the Secretary of State's view, the proposal as it stood did not represent 'the controlled and positive management of change' envisaged in PPG15, with its scale and character threatening to harm the conservation area.

The need for a new bus station was not perceived to be an issue, and the car-parking proposals would balance the loss of spaces elsewhere in the city centre, and would reduce the acreage devoted to surface-level car parking in the city's historic areas. The Secretary of State concluded he was not convinced that the inspector had sufficient evidence before him in ruling out the Victoria Station site, and he required more information before coming to a final conclusion. He also differed from the inspector in relation to the justification for the number of car-parking spaces; the weight to be attached to the UDP Small Area Policy; the effects of the development on the setting of listed buildings; and conclusive evidence that the land was reasonably necessary and/or required for the purposes for which the orders were made. He thus invited the parties to submit additional information concerning:

- the scope for and practicality of siting an interchange with similar elements to that proposed, in whole or part, and/or alongside Victoria Station;
- the relative advantages of locating such an interchange or parts thereof at the Victoria Station and Shudehill sites, in terms of transport integration and ease of pedestrian access to and from city-centre facilities and attractions;
- the scope for reducing the scale, physical bulk and above-ground visual impact of the car-parking element; and
- alternative designs for the proposed redevelopment of the site such as would further enhance the city centre, and seek to address all the concerns about design, visual impact, landscaping and the character of the conservation area.

Responses were made to DETR in January 2000, primarily by the City Council (supported by MML), but also by English Heritage and by CIS. The Council's response argued that there were compelling reasons for siting the proposed development at Shudehill, even if a site at or alongside Victoria Station were available or affordable; that there was no scope for further reduction in car-parking spaces beyond the significant reduction achieved since the original planning permission and conservation area consent; and that the design improvements achieved since the Local Inquiry would fully meet the Secretary of State's concerns. In addition, if the Shudehill interchange was not approved, the Printworks developer would proceed with a scheme for a separate multi-storey car park with no bus facilities, and characterised by both bulk and a bigger footplate.

In September 2000, the Secretary of State had considered the responses to his 'minded to approve' letter, and decided that the inquiry should be reopened. The deadlock was finally broken in March 2001, with an agreement by CIS to withdraw and not to force a second inquiry, as a result of the promotion of a revised scheme with new elevations. Thereafter, detailed legal and financial procedures could be undertaken to commence purchase of the site and transfer of the land, and to confirm conservation area consent for the revised proposals. The £21-million interchange will cater for 2,000 buses a day, form an integral part of the Metrolink network with a new tram stop, and incorporate 770 new car-parking spaces to serve the developments around Exchange Square and the city centre more widely. Work on the new tram stop and the enabling works for the new interchange building started in summer 2002, with the interchange expected to be fully operational by late 2004. Since it was a condition of the original plan-ning permission for the Printworks that it should not be used until the interchange was operational, it is understandable that this condition has subsequently been varied, with this initiative to be completed four years after the Printwork's launch. Established public transport links and car-parking facilities have inevitably had to take the load in the meantime, but a major threat to the delivery of the programme has been lifted.

The agreement on progressing the interchange has been the key to unlocking regeneration plans for Arndale North facing on to Corporation Street and Withy Grove. In spring 2002 Prudential was thus in a position to unveil plans for an £125-million redevelopment and upgrading of the Arndale Centre, the vast bulk of which is to be investment in the redevelopment of Arndale North. This will add 28,000 square metres of new retail space (making a total of 130,000 square metres), spread over 60 shop units, including a four-level department store fronting Exchange Square. The area that was previously occupied by Cannon Street, currently a bus stopping street dividing the northern and southern halves of the centre, is to find a new life as 'New Cannon Street': a mixed-use glass-covered mall (the Wintergarden in the original masterplan). A single-storey hall will replace the existing market. The Arndale North redevelopment programme is expected to start following the completion of the transport interchange, to be completed in 2005.

The transport impact of the renewal programme

The study's focus group discussion reinforced the views that the transport elements of the masterplan had been the most challenging aspect of the renewal programme during the lifetime of MML, arising from the sheer complexity of the task, resource and legal difficulties, and the need to implement a panoply of regulatory measures and procedures. However, by the summer of 2002 the IRR was completed, and expected to have an immediate effect on traffic congestion within the centre. The new transport interchange project was on site, expected to transform both the physical and regeneration prospects of Shudehill and its surrounding area, and to contribute towards a more integrated transport policy for the city centre. The new Metrolink stations were delivered – Market Street (late 1998) and the Shudehill station (late 2002) – and had been incorporated into the interchange designs. The signage strategy had been completed, as was the phased introduction of bus priority measures on radial routes, integrated ticketing and public information, and the bus super stop on Cross Street. All traffic management measures in line with public realm development had been completed by the end of 1999, and the pedestrian management strategy was in place. It had also facili-tated the early establishment of the Bus Quality Partnership, and the linkage and coordination of private sector interests that would not otherwise have taken place.

There is a feeling, however, that the medium-term impacts of the transport elements will be mixed, in that whilst improvements to transport infra-structure undoubtedly 'contribute to the current competitiveness of the city', and have helped fend off competition from the Trafford Centre, they will lead to increased private and commercial traffic volumes overall. Many of the transport and traffic improvements are very localised even within the city centre, and have facilitated greater improvements to accessibility amongst some groups than for others. Whilst the IRR will inevitably switch some capacity to other parts of the system, it will require backing up by measures that ensure that motorists use it in preference to travelling through the city centre. Current enforcement problems in preventing cars using Cross Street during the day reinforce such concerns.

Following the resolution of the CPO issue over the interchange and the successful redesign of specific elements of the project, delays to construction contracts have resulted in continuing problems of established terminal capacity, with the major bus operators concerned at the rate of progress. Indeed, there remains some questioning of the rationale of the interchange, in that as the centre continues to expand and becomes increasingly differentiated in its various quar-ters there will be a need for more cross-centre links with multiple linear termini rather than two central interchanges (Shudehill, Piccadilly). However, it is clear that, from a public interest viewpoint, the coordinated management of city-centre bus density was long overdue in terms of both safety and pollution considerations, but it is premature to assess the medium-term effects of present intentions. The recent launch of the free metroshuttle bus that connects the interchanges to all key locations across the city centre and the Metrolink network undoubtedly provides good multi-linear linkages.

Whilst the Bus Quality Partnership is perceived to have accelerated the process of transport integration, there remain questions as to the extent to which it has fundamentally changed perceptions of public transport or will facilitate significant modal shift. Whilst considerable scope remains for extending 'park and ride' schemes, and making greater use of the local rail network to ease central-area congestion, some concern is already being expressed at likely tram congestion within the core as the full Metrolink system is put in place over the next decade. The recent introduction of free bus travel within a city-centre loop, creating better links between the main rail stations and areas within the commercial core, is however seen to provide a further element of integration within this wider vision.

Many commentators feel that in spite of the increased capacity and improved signage, issues of parking and access have still not been fully addressed, and that it will take some time for people to become familiar with the new layout of the centre. There have undoubtedly been improvements to car parking quality and security, involving a switch from surface and on-street parking to multi-storey capacity within the core, but a range of issues remain. In particular, the rapidly growing demand for additional parking facilities from the city centre's booming residential market has begun to raise concerns, as has the increasingly commercial nature of short-term parking capacity. In terms of access issues within the core, there is a firm commitment that improvements to the quality of the public realm need to be rolled out to other parts of the city centre, and an awareness of the need to ensure long-term maintenance – 'if revenue for maintenance doesn't follow capital investment, areas soon deteriorate'. In addition, there remain concerns as to general access to the city centre, particularly in relation to the evening economy, with the need to ensure that the new central area is not 'just for those wanting pubbing and clubbing'.

Finally, whilst there are undoubted regrets that the transport elements have proved the most intractable elements to deliver, the rebuilding programme is ultimately seen as a small step in the continually evolving process addressing the city's transport problems. Indeed, what is seen as critically important is that the city's transport interests see the experience gained as part of the renewal programme as capable of being rolled out for the city centre as a whole, thereby enhancing the city's overall sustainability and competitiveness.

Part 4

New opportunities and challenges

The final section of the book attempts to bring together the main conclusions arising from the study, to briefly discuss current efforts to sustain city-centre competitiveness, and to consider such experience within the framework of the wider urban management agenda. It reflects on concerns discussed in the first part of the book, namely the emerging challenges for urban governance arising from increasing competition for resources and the scope for policy innovation, and considers this within the context of a continuing commitment by local policy makers to enhance the scope and vitality of the city centre.

By looking at Manchester's current development trajectory, and its post-millennium development aspirations, it reinforces discussions relating to the centrality of a distinctive local policy environment, the focus of the second part of the book. The continuing entrepreneurial narrative and its associated partnership culture is reasserted, and brief commentary made of its sustained mobilisation of regeneration capacity for collaborative action. That this has involved, and continues to involve, a dynamic programme management dimension reflects a very distinctive local policy culture, worthy of wider discussion. This has already been commented on in the third part of the book, where the focus lay with development implementation and the process of programme management and project delivery.

In the longer term, however, Manchester's contemporary experience still raises questions as to the enduring nature of the city centre's transformation for the city as a whole, and emerging evidence of increasing social and economic polarisation within the wider urban realm. This raises fundamental questions for urban policy management, and the future renaissance of Britain's core cities.

Chapter 11

Continuing city-centre competitiveness

The main body of the study has considered the urban management framework for considering an entrepreneurial agenda, focusing on the city-centre dimension of such debate. It has then progressed to consider the local context within Manchester for city-centre development, and the delivery of local capacity for a major renewal programme following the dramatic effects of the bombing of its commercial core. Finally, it has considered the distinctive institutional focus and the complexity of programme management arrangements and processes of project delivery in facilitating a transformed city centre for the new millennium. It is thus opportune at this stage to attempt to tie such discussions together, in terms of the relationship between the renewal area and the wider city centre, and to the management of the city as a whole.

Since the early 1990s Manchester city centre has seen a dramatic upturn in its fortunes under a stable political leadership, a creative entrepreneurial partnership between public and private sector interests, and a clear reinforcement of its regional capital aspirations. Indeed, the profile and achievements of the renewal programme following the bombing have had a major effect on both the agenda and working methods associated with regeneration activities elsewhere in the city centre and beyond. The experiential learning associated with masterplan delivery that has been compressed into a five-year period of intense activity has proved unique, facilitating new perspectives in 'rolling out' such experience through other regeneration initiatives.

The present chapter thus briefly considers wider city-centre development initiatives over the past five years, running in parallel and following on from the renewal programme for the bomb-damaged area, and the influence that this may have on renewal programmes over the next decade. It sets this within the wider context of policy developments for the city centre – Manchester City Centre

Strategic Plan (2002) – and for the city as a whole – Local Strategic Partnership (LSP, 2002), Community Strategy (2002) – attempting to tie in the experience of the study with emerging policy developments. Finally, it attempts to set the Manchester experience within the wider context relating to management challenges to the entrepreneurial agenda, namely the increasing social and economic polarisation of our core cities, and the need for a dynamic programme of urban renaissance that addresses the aspirations of local communities as a whole.

City-centre development 1996–2002

It is important at this stage to look briefly at a number of key developments in the wider city centre and beyond that have been the focus of development activity over the past five years. These have both impacted on the progress made with the renewal programme within the bomb-damaged area, and been influenced by the programme's achievements and outputs. Key amongst these have been the out-of-town Trafford Centre and the East Manchester initiatives, both outside the regional centre's boundaries but having major impacts on and being impacted by the progress within the city centre. Within the core, the main post-bomb development activity has spatially concentrated on the Piccadilly regeneration initiative, an area with immense development potential between Deansgate and the River Irwell (Spinningfields/Left Bank), and the new urban quarter that has emerged around the former Central Station site (Petersfield). In addition, an emerging location that has received a great deal of attention but has proved extremely challenging to realise major development has been the Northern Quarter, on the fringes of the core's primary commercial zone.

The Trafford Centre, a £600-million development that opened in autumn 1998, threatened from the outset the fragile commercial rebirth of the city centre, with major department stores as anchor tenants, a full range of retail and leisure facilities, and extensive free parking (Lambert Smith Hampton 1999). Indeed, retailers in the city centre were to experience an initial downturn in their business in the period immediately following the centre's opening, but retail sales were to fight back strongly over the next 18 months as the inconvenience of the reconstruction programme lessened and the completion of the first phase of renewal provided new opportunities for commercial investment. As the Trafford Centre has matured and Manchester city centre has strongly bounced back, a more mature relationship has evolved between the two. Indeed, it is expected that retailing within the city centre (£1.5 billion annually) will settle down at around three times that envisaged for the Trafford Centre.

A more recent focus for policy attention has been East Manchester, for which a major regeneration strategy was published in 2001, and which if fully realised over the following 15 years will undoubtedly have a major impact on the commercial health of the city centre as a focus for investment. The £2-billion strategy, being coordinated by the East Manchester Urban Regeneration Company, envisages the establishment of a new district shopping centre and a strategic business park (160 hectares) less than two miles from the city centre, and is committed to the development of 12,500 new homes, improvements to a further 7,000 houses, and the doubling of the area's population to 60,000. The focus of the full panoply of central government and EU regeneration initiatives – and the site of the recent Commonwealth Games – its rapidly changing relationship within the core will inevitably have an impact on city-centre activity and performance over the next decade (MCC 2001).

Within the existing city centre the main strategic developments over the past few years have been associated with the Piccadilly Initiative, the Petersfield Quarter, and the Spinningfields masterplan, these being underpinned by the vision set out in the city's initial local transport plan.

Piccadilly Initiative

Prior to the bombing, the Piccadilly area of the centre had been the city's main priority for strategic investment, having long suffered from a poor-quality environment, providing poor linkages with the commercial core and an inappropriate gateway for the city, and characterised by a significant range of underused and derelict buildings. Following the initiation of the bomb-damaged core's renewal programme it became possible for the local authority and its main partners to refocus attention on this neglected area, and to implement a regeneration framework that would give the city centre a greater coherence. This was to focus on four main elements – the refurbishment of Piccadilly Station; the remodelling of Piccadilly Gardens; the reconfiguration and renewal of Piccadilly Plaza; and the development of the Rochdale Canal Basin.

Railtrack's £55-million investment during the period 2000–02 was to provide a new roof and lighting for the railway station, the provision of a new two-level concourse and a multi-storey car park, the refurbishing and recladding of the station's existing office tower, and the relocation of the station's main entrance. This was to stimulate investment in the immediately adjacent area, primarily focused on a new hotel development (Malmaison) and a major mixed-use proposal (Piccadilly Triangle). A parallel development on the other side of Piccadilly Gardens was to see the transformation of Chorlton Street Coach Station with new facilities, recladding and modernisation (2001–02). Piccadilly Gardens was recreated as a prime public open space within the city centre, involving the remodelling and landscaping of the park and the construction of a recreational pavilion. Funding for such improvements was to be partly provided by the sale of part of the site for a major office building offering 14,000 square metres of office space and with ground-floor restaurants. This was also to act as a shield for the park from traffic noise, and together with the pavilion building to provide the framework for a dramatic upgrade of the immediately adjacent bus interchange and pedestrian area.

Overlooking the gardens, Piccadilly Plaza – a major retail, office and hotel development of the 1960s, sorely in need of redevelopment following a collapse in development and maintenance investment – was significantly under-occupied. It was bought for refurbishment in 1998, and a major £100-million investment programme is currently in place (in 2003). Its three-phase redevelopment envisages a new two-level shopping arcade with a cut-through route linking Piccadilly Gardens to China Town; the refurbishment and recladding of a major office tower (Sunley Building); the refurbishment and improvement of facilities at one of the city's premier hotels (Piccadilly); and the demolition of an existing office building to its podium to make way for a major new health and fitness centre. When fully refurbished, the 'Piccadilly Exchange' will comprise 31,000 square metres of office space, 17,000 square metres of retailing, and a 19,000-square-metre hotel. The scheme will also revitalise the current streetscape, enhance the retail and leisure facilities throughout the development, and improve both lighting and general accessibility.

The final element in this major regeneration strategy relates to the Rochdale Canal Basin, where the intention is to provide a major new residential and office development around a new marina setting. This scheme ties the Piccadilly redevelopment more specifically to the long-established intentions of rejuvenating the historic warehouse-dominated Northern Quarter.

The Petersfield Quarter

On the edge of the retail core, a new mixed-development quarter – retail, leisure, tourism and office development area – has begun to gel over the past few years, anchored by the G-Mex Exhibition Centre (1986) and the Bridgewater Initiative of the early 1990s. It has emerged as the Petersfield Quarter, and its late-1990s development trajectory focused on the Great Northern Experience, the Convention Centre and hotel development associated with the Free Trade Hall building. The £100-million Great Northern Experience, mooted for a decade (a priority with CMDC) but only realised in 2001, houses a cinema, megaplex complex, active fitness centre, restaurants, bars and speciality retail space (33,000 square metres, together with a 1,400-space car park). It has involved the transformation of a railway goods warehouse and an old Victorian terrace of associated offices, and the creation of a new public square and pavilion building.

Manchester's Convention Centre was to open in 2001 in an 8,600-square-metre building housing a multi-purpose exhibition space capable of seating 1,200, together with an 800-seat auditorium, seminar rooms and media facilities. It is directly linked to the G-Mex Exhibition Centre, and both facilities are managed jointly. Finally, facing these facilities a major new hotel for business use is currently being constructed in the form of a 16-storey tower development with a central atrium linking this to the public aspects of the development, which lie within the listed front façade of the Free Trade Hall.

Spinningfield development

Mooted in 2000, a strategic new mixed-use development has been proposed in a masterplan for an 8.9-hectare site between Deansgate and the River Irwell. This £500-million Spinningfields complex of 245,000 square metres is expected to feature ten major new office buildings, two luxury hotels and several residential apartment buildings. It is also to house a new regional headquarters for the court service, a new City Magistrates' Court, a college site and an array of shops, restaurants and bars. In the period up to 2010 it is intended to open up this area of the city centre, to lead to the formation of two new public squares, and to create a new pedestrian footbridge across the River Irwell. As a direct consequence of this initiative (the first phase of which was begun in 2001), and the completion of a major bridge element to the IRR, a regeneration framework for a contiguous site – The Left Bank – has now been identified as a potential site for 'clustering' media, creative industries and high-tech business within the city centre. Its increasing accessibility makes it a prime investment site, leapfrogging the Irwell and including Salford City Council in the proposed development partnership.

Transport developments

Metropolitan Manchester's first Local Transport Plan (LTP, 2001) aimed at integrating transport at a county level, with a vision to support the conurbation's development as a creative and distinctive European regional capital. The aim was to help strengthen, modernise and diversify the local economy, to support urban regeneration measures, and to focus such improvements on major employment centres such as the regional centre. In Manchester's LTP there is an emphasis on the continuing revitalisation of the regional centre, the continued growth of the airport, and the renewal and improvement of urban neighbourhoods. Focusing specifically on the city centre as a whole, the plan details transport initiatives beyond the bomb-damaged areas – Piccadilly, Northern Quarter, Spinningfields, the Petersfield Quarter, Castlefields and the major gateway areas to the city centre. There is also a recognised need to enhance pedestrian safety, and to improve links to public transport stations and interchanges, as well as providing more and better-quality space for people walking within the centre. It also reinforces the city's extensive programme of city-centre car park improvements in contributing to the enhancement of the economy and environmental quality of the regional centre. The pricing structure for central-area parking is geared in favour of short-stay, off-peak parking, again to discourage commuting and to support trading activity. This is supported by Salford's LTP for the area within its boundary contiguous to the regional centre (Chapel Street Corridor).

By the turn of the millennium, plans were well advanced for the rapid expansion of Metrolink, with a 'big bang' approach being proposed, with the clear intention to deliver major transit extensions to Rochdale and Oldham, Manchester

Airport and Ashton-under-Lyne. This programme, to be fully delivered before 2010, was approved as a single investment package by central government in mid-2002. It will transform the city centre's accessibility for public transport, and to the wider coherence of the entire metropolitan area. A Manchester cross-rail development is also proposed as part of the bidding process for the Trans-Pennine Express franchise.

The city's contemporary policy framework

The key to understanding the city's current policy preoccupations with its city centre have been brought together in the recently issued city-centre strategic plan, and the local authority leadership of the city-wide LSP and Community Strategy agendas. It is important to briefly reflect at this stage on the consequence of these initiatives for both the city centre and the wider city.

City-centre strategic plan 2000–05
In a report to the City Council in March 2000, it was proposed that a non-statutory strategic plan should be prepared for the city centre by the City Centre Management Company that was intended to act as an exit strategy for MML at the completion of its remit. Building on the strengths of previous action, and expected to influence the UDP review then being initiated, it was intended to provide a basis for future policy that sustained the momentum of city-centre development.

The purpose of the city-centre strategic plan is to develop an agreed framework for continued regeneration, investment and service improvement in the city centre over the coming years. Through strong civic leadership and dynamic partnership action, the creation of a world-class city centre will help maintain Manchester's position as the nation's leading regional centre, but more importantly it will enable the city to successfully compete as an international investment and visitor destination (MCC 2002c: 2).

It is intended to provide an agreed framework for regeneration, investment and service improvement in the city centre to 2005, reflecting the needs and aspirations of the range of stakeholders involved, in what is one of the key economic generators for both the city and the wider region. Designed to complement existing statutory documents, it is to be used to inform the development and delivery of the city's Community Strategy and LSP as the vehicle for partnership action. It notes that the vision of the city centre has progressed through a decade of City Pride strategic frameworks that have continuously attempted to improve the competitiveness of the 'nation's leading regional capital', whilst enabling its local communities to share in that success (Table 11.1).

To address strategic targeting and evaluation of the performance of the plan, the document notes that its success is to be measured by its ability to create

Table 11:1 Key city-centre assets and priorities for action 2002/03

Assets

- The highly acclaimed rebuilding programme after the 1996 bomb, which has seen significant retail, leisure and public realm developments, with private investment of over £750m.
- A city-centre economy that provides employment for 120,000 people, and improved investor confidence that has helped to create more than 10,000 new jobs in recent years.
- An improved visitor infrastructure and cultural and sporting facilities, which have made Manchester the nation's most important destination outside London for overseas visitors.
- A strong and expanding retail market, with sustained interest from both the UK and overseas, quality retailers, and high rental values of up to £300 per square foot.
- Enormous growth in residential development, which has resulted in the population growing from a few hundred in the mid-1980s to a projected 15,000 by 2005.
- Continued investment in transport, including the completion of the Inner Relief Route in 2002, £10m of improvements to car parks, quality buses and passenger facilities, and the continued expansion of Metrolink.
- One of the largest concentrations of higher-education activity in Europe, which is working to unlock academic excellence to strengthen the competitiveness of the city and region, and to increase the city's employment base through expanding knowledge-based industries.
- The establishment of a pioneering City Centre Management Company, driven by the private sector with council backing, with an annual budget of £500,000.

Priorities for action

- The need to build on the linkages between the city centre and key adjacent areas – Hulme, Moss Side, Ancoats and Miles Platting, and East Manchester – to maximise regeneration opportunities and address local needs.
- The need to ensure that the city centre remains the key focus for regeneration strategies in the wider regional centre, including the Chapel Street area, Salford Quays, Pomona.
- The need to address the office market in Manchester, at a time when industries are undergoing fundamental changes. The needs of users in terms of footplates and access – especially in relation to Manchester's competitiveness with other UK and European cities – are crucial, not least in terms of planning and transport policies.
- The need to further strengthen the range and quality of the retail, leisure and hotel offer in the city centre to remain competitive, and to meet the needs of residents, shoppers and visitors.
- The need to ensure that Manchester builds on its success in supporting knowledge-based industries through its innovative partnerships with its higher-education institutions, and is able to meet the development needs of new and growth sectors through initiatives such as Spinningfields and the Southern Gateway.
- The need to improve the quality, management and maintenance of the public realm in the city centre, and to develop new arrangements to secure ongoing improvements.
- The need to improve public transport access and availability.
- The need to reduce crime and improve safety and security.
- The need to provide a growing city-centre population with access to schools, health care, and local shopping facilities.
- The need to improve visitor facilities, for both leisure and business visitors. The Commonwealth Games provides a valuable focus for this, but more important is the need to build on its ongoing legacy.
- The need to focus marketing strategies and events programmes to support the objectives of the plan, whilst exploiting the opportunities provided by the Commonwealth Games to achieve real synergy.
- The need to address the long-term issues of the funding and governance of major cities like Manchester which have regional responsibilities and a key role to play in both regional and UK economies.

Source: Adapted from MCC 2002a: 7–8

7,500 new jobs in key economic sectors within the core by 2005, and to improve the ability of the city's residents to access such opportunities. It is also intended to attract £1.5 billion of new private sector investment in development initiatives, and to facilitate infrastructural improvements underpinned by developments in mainstream public investment and services. It is expected to generate a significant reduction in recorded crime, and an overwhelming public satisfaction with both the management and standard of public spaces and on-street services within the city centre. Finally, it is expected to effect a positive change in modal split in favour of public transport, the completion of car park improvements, the delivery of the new transport interchange and bus priority measures, and improved signage for both pedestrians and drivers. It accepts, however, that a number of these ambitious improvements to the city centre's competitiveness may be delivered beyond the timescale of this initial plan.

The plan then proceeds to detail the component parts, themes and service issues that will contribute to its overall achievement, setting out key actions within each theme or service area. It summarises the constituent spatial elements of the city centre, identifying their distinctive contribution to the profile of the city centre as a whole, and outlining long-term area-specific regeneration objectives (Table 11.2).

Overall, it is thus clear that the City Council, its agents and its partners appear committed to continue the entrepreneurial agenda and the cooperative action that is well embedded in the city centre, attempting to provide a clear basis for general acceptance by both policy makers and investors of the city's rapid rise as a major European regional capital.

Local Strategic Partnership and Community Strategy
Under the Local Government Act 2000 local government has been given new powers to establish LSPs to promote the well-being of their communities. Whilst

Table 11.2 Component elements of the city-centre strategic plan

Sectoral objectives

• Performance of the city centre	• Marketing, events, visitor services
• Managing the public realm	• Residential infrastructure
• Transport strategy and services	• Planning frameworks and services
• Security management	• Funding and governance

Area profiles

• Millennium Quarter	• Spinningfield
• Northern Quarter	• Retail and Commercial Core
• Piccadilly Gateway	• Chinatown
• Eastern Gateway	• The Village
• Higher Education Precinct	• Petersfield
• Southern Gateway	• Strategic Waterways
• Castlefield	

Manchester has noted its traditional strength in partnership working, it has accepted that much more needs to be done to improve the wider economic performance of the city, and the quality of life of its residents. In essence, the main remit is to demonstrate that the success of city-centre activity over the past decade can be translated to handle the much more intractable problems facing the majority of Manchester's local neighbourhoods and communities. In framing its LSP structure, that city envisages that this new approach to cooperative partnership and action will:

- reinforce the city's status as the regional capital and bring together the different parties who influence its economic and social well-being;
- help develop a 'strategic direction' for the city in a coordinated manner, and drive forward its overall social and economic regeneration;
- help introduce new and innovative methods for agencies to work together, and make sure that this focus is linked to the actual delivery of improvement programmes that meet the priorities of the city's residents; and
- stimulate the formation of a Manchester Regeneration Fund, make sure it makes the best use of the financial contributions by the variety of agencies involved, and help fund the Community Strategy

(Source: MCC 2002a).

Its proposals to establish the LSP were formally published in September 2001, aiming to build on the existing framework of local partnerships to tackle the city's chronic social and economic problems. It accepts that with 27 of the city's 33 electoral wards firmly entrenched within the highest decile of policy concerns nationally – as measured by the national index of deprivation – that the new emphasis on integrated approaches to regeneration and renewal, rooted in the communities affected, presents a real opportunity for a fresh start to tackle the issues that contribute to these dramatic statistics. Whilst the Community Strategy, Public Service Agreements (PSA) and the Neighbourhood Renewal Strategy provide the mechanisms for a front-line attack on these concerns, the LSP is intended to provide the base from which these are driven, refined, adapted and monitored (Table 11.3).

In delivering their commitment to establish the LSP, a major Manchester conference was held in early 2002 for community organisations, and public and private sector interests, to agree a format for the promotion of a local community strategy and of ways for involving residents in the LSP. This was intended to agree content, set priorities and monitor progress; to agree PSA targets for public agencies operating across the city; to confirm membership of the proposed LSP's steering group and executive; and to become a forum where central government, regional

Table 11.3 Manchester's Local Strategic Partnership (LSP)

Action Plan 2002/2003

Strategic	• Develop a Manchester renewal strategy. • Establish a Manchester Regeneration Fund. • Develop a strategy to raise the LSP's profile and generate a commitment to its work.
Inclusive	• Review the structure, operation and membership of the LSP. • Develop a strategy for community and resident engagement within the LSP structure.
Action focused and performance managed	• Determine if further strategy should be set to progress the Community Strategy.. • Review progress on the implementation of the Public Service Agreement. • Develop a series of measurable baselines associated with indicators included in the Community Strategy. • Develop a common performance management system. • Develop an investment programme for Neighbourhood Renewal and EU Objective 2 funding.
Efficient	• Instigate a rolling programme of review of local partnerships. • Review of thematic structures required to take forward the Community Strategy. • Establish a code of practice.
Learning and developmental	• Establish a learning and development programme that seeks to develop shared vision and understanding, partnership working, and that promotes integrated programmes and delivery vehicles.

Source: Adapted from MCC 2002a

agencies and local organisations can meet to discuss issues affecting the city's regeneration as a whole. An LSP steering group was subsequently established to supervise the delivery of the Community Strategy and PSA; to agree local initiatives and set priorities for tackling social and economic exclusion, and for improving local quality of life; to review established partnership arrangements across the city; and to develop new ways for mainstream public service providers to work together.

This was additionally expected to establish guidelines for working groups to address specific areas of community concern; to oversee the establishment and supervision of the Manchester Regeneration Fund; and to approve the way resources from this fund were spent on the Community Strategy and the Neighbourhood Renewal Strategy. Specific LSP working groups were also established to carry forward specific initiatives and themes arising from the Manchester conference and the work involved in preparing the Community Strategy. Finally, established local partnerships were encouraged to integrate the activities of all agencies working within the same geographical area, and ward coordination meetings were facilitated to oversee the way in which council services were delivered, and to measure their success against targets set in annual ward performance plans.

An LSP executive group, made up of senior officers of the main delivery agencies, was established to ensure that stakeholders remained committed to the objectives set by the Manchester Conference and the LSP steering group, and to ensure that such decisions were converted into action. Since they controlled the resources of the main implementing bodies, they were perceived to have a central role in ensuring the delivery of both partnership activity and delivery frameworks.

Whilst the city's Community Strategy is to be delivered through the LSP's structures, thematic and area-based partnerships, and by individual action by partners, its neighbourhood renewal strategy is expected to translate the direction and priorities of the Community Strategy at the neighbourhood level (Table 11.4). The local authority is to continue to use its existing powers and policies to reinforce such a commitment, with the strategy additionally providing an overall vision, a thematic focus for action, and a vehicle for handling cross-cutting policy concerns. Each theme within the Community Strategy – the majority of which are likely to impact on the city centre as well as on local communities – is being developed by a thematic partnership within the LSP structure, who are also expected to develop action plans for its eventual delivery. A number of cross-cutting themes – poverty, inequality, environment, impact of new technology – are also being developed, to inform such activity.

Table 11.4 Manchester's Community Strategy

The vision
- Coordinate improvements in public services so that they do more to improve the life of Manchester's people.
- Integrate the improvement of public services within a comprehensive programme for the regeneration of the city.
- Provide an agreed framework for the future direction of public investment within the city.
- Encourage and enable partners to use their powers to the full in support of the priorities of the community strategy for the benefit of the city and its people.
- Address issues extending beyond the boundaries of Manchester, as appropriate, to reflect the city's significance to the national economy, and its role as the regional capital of the North West.

Thematic focus for action
- Competing in a global economy.
- Investing in children, young people and families.
- Housing and sustainable communities.
- Making Manchester safer.
- Tackling health inequalities.
- Creating a modern transport infrastructure.
- Enhancing the cultural base.

Source: Adapted from MCC 2002b, 5–6

Delivery of Manchester's Community Strategy is expected to depend first and foremost on the development of excellent working relationships between partners through the structures of the LSP. However, whilst this will inevitably build on a decade of focused partnership activity, it will undoubtedly require new ways of working and investing in the mainstream delivery of services and activities. It is expected to pilot new ways of dealing with problems that the city's residents face on a daily basis, and will also lead to the establishment of a range of baseline indicators that will enable the City Council and its partners to identify the extent to which both outputs and outcomes help narrow the gap between the city and national averages. Short and medium targets will also need to accord with national priorities and the funding focus of major implementing agencies, and will provide a substantial challenge if local partners are to successfully move the city forward as a whole (MCC 2002b).

A continuing challenge for the entrepreneurial agenda

This study has reflected on the emergent political economy of the city, focusing on entrepreneurial agendas and the complexity of partnership working in developing and delivering urban governance at the local level. It has attempted to consider the scope for local collaborative action in delivering enterprising and innovative responses to specific local policy concerns and challenges, and has focused on the role and pro-active management of the urban core. Setting this within the context of a detailed empirical study of Manchester, it has considered its distinctive governance and the experience of policy development and delivery within its city centre.

The study has been concerned with the mobilisation of regeneration capacity for collaborative action and the local scope for policy innovation, looking in particular at the institutional structures and procedures put in place to produce a recovery plan and programme following the crisis faced by the city as a result of bombing of its core. It has then proceeded to focus centrally on delivery of the vision, looking specifically at the management of programme and project implementation. The key focus of such implementation experience has been to enhance the commercial vitality and competitiveness of the core, to facilitate significant improvements to the quality of its built environment, to reinforce its cultural and lifestyle dynamic, and to improve access and mobility both to and within the city centre.

It is now opportune to briefly consider continuing challenges to such an entrepreneurial agenda within a wider consideration of urban change processes. Central amongst these have been the contemporary commitment to a competitive urban policy, creating pressures on cities to remain at the forefront of the global economy, whilst addressing the cumulative legacy of urban restructuring and change that have major socio-cultural dimensions. Such tensions have generated significant challenges for changing patterns of urban governance, and have demanded the creation of new structures of local interest representation and leadership. An emblematic feature of such urban policy concerns has been the emergence of entrepreneurialism, with localities engaged in a competitive search for new sources of development resources in response to the ceaseless process of economic and social restructuring.

In addition to the economic dimensions of such approaches, entrepreneurial discourses have been articulated spatially, resulting in complex interactions between key players that may vary from city to city and across individual local communities. This has contributed to major changes in the institutional basis for local governance, creating pressures for inter-agency working and collaborative partnership activity, and the adoption of more business-like approaches to decision making. An examination of how entrepreneurial cultures are produced and consumed at the local level reveals an important shift, however, away from global concerns of urban dynamics to views on the distinctiveness of local policy environments, with a variety of alternative perspectives competing for dominance.

The real challenge for urban management, therefore, is to ensure that notions of entrepreneurial governance do not become the stock response to the process of economic and social restructuring, and a belief that only a particular range of externally oriented growth policies can address such problems. In the search for new urban policy solutions this may require the consideration of alternative policy directions, given that distributional inequity may be produced or exacerbated by many such entrepreneurial actions. Indeed, increased social and spatial polarisation and the selective regeneration experienced within cities have led to the growing realisation of the interdependence between economic competition and social inequality and exclusion.

The evidence suggests that cities with well-developed social networks, or those characterised by greater social cohesion, tend to have better prospects, and that the failure to nurture social capital increases economic vulnerability. However, the relationship between social cohesion and competitiveness is complex, involving a consideration of governance at a variety of scales, and is not easy to translate into proposals for action. But notions of 'creative potential' and 'community capacity building' may be at the heart of such concerns, and may provide an alternative vision to entrepreneurialism as the dominant mode of urban management over the next decade.

Whilst urban policy has tended to focus on the regeneration of individual cities, or to deal with particular urban spaces or sectors, often in a piecemeal way, lasting solutions can only come by looking at such concerns within the context of changes within the wider urban system. Single-policy formulae are not the answer, and the evidence suggests that the interplay between competitiveness and social exclusion requires both coherent economic policies and inclusive social perspectives. There is undoubtedly a need to foster partnership and consensus building between hitherto competing agendas – economic, environmental, social – and a pooling of funding and expertise, to ensure the development of a more integrated policy response at the local level.

The translation of such concerns into policy prescriptions remains elusive, however, and lies at the heart of the government's recent Urban White Paper (DETR 2000). Its concerns lie not only with strengthening local economies and increasing economic opportunities for deprived areas, but also with transforming urban environments to ensure increased security and enhanced quality of life within cities, and a commitment to rebuild neighbourhoods and communities that are currently excluded. Such an urban policy perspective seeks to deliver a strategic approach to policy integration, to strengthen the role of local governance, to harness the commitment and capacities of local communities, and to encourage and facilitate partnership working to deliver sustainable futures.

Finally, in addressing such issues within the context of Manchester's experience, there is little doubt that the period since the early 1990s has seen radical changes in the form and content of the city's policies, the transformation of its city centre, and a major re-imaging of its profile. The sustained leadership of the city's political elite and its senior officers has provided a stable and unchallenged vision at the heart of local governance. It has instinctively tapped into the vision of the entrepreneurial city, not only as an opportunistic and pragmatic response to central government policies and to funding regimes, but also bringing a distinctive local conception of the city's problems and prospects. Thus it has been both pragmatic and innovatory in its approach to development and regeneration, and has been at the cutting edge of such practice within the UK.

The sheer depth of the city's economic and social problems facilitated the political space during the late 1980s to launch a fairly radical form of policy innovation, and the ability to develop imaginative and even risky projects. Indeed, the ability of Manchester to procure new and ever more impressive development opportunities during the 1990s has become part of the legend of the success of its leadership, and reflects well on its capacities to develop fruitful local partnerships. That this was underpinned by a stable national economy, and a number of core economic drivers at the local level, was strengthened by the absence of any major policy failures in its playing of the 'regeneration game'. When disaster did strike – in the form of the bombing of its core – established partnership activity and existing development frameworks were well placed to provide an opportunistic response. Such collaborative partnerships undoubtedly underpinned, and continue to facilitate, a politically successful form of governance in handling strategic urban regeneration concerns, and have been the city's main contribution to the national debate on urban policy.

Despite the material and political success of the enterprising narrative, and the promotion of an urban 'trickle-down' thesis affecting the wider city and conurbation, there are concerns that the long-term consequences of these policies may facilitate economic and social polarisation. Indeed, critics have argued that the same radicalism and innovation are now required to handle the structural problems of social inequality and exclusion within the city as have been adopted in relation to its main economic drivers, namely the city centre and its airport.

> Many of the city's underlying social and economic problems have been displaced rather than solved ... that for all the manifest progress which has been made in turning around the city centre ... the effect of this activity on the socio-economic 'fundamentals' has been extremely modest.
>
> (Peck & Ward 2002: 5)

The city has long languished near the bottom of the league tables relating to issues of social deprivation and inequality, and there is no doubt that the underlying task of regeneration and sustaining the city's neighbourhoods and communities as a whole has become harder. Thus current preoccupations with developing and delivering the Local Strategic Partnership and Community Strategy are at the heart of attempts to develop and deliver a more integrated and holistic vision for the city as a whole, and to enable the transformation of the city's aspirations to be rolled out to influence the lives of all its residents.

Bibliography

Ambrose, P. (1994) *Urban Process and Power*, London: Routledge.

Amin, A. and Thrift, N. (eds) (1995) *Globalisation, Institutions and Regional Development in Europe*, Oxford: Oxford University Press.

Architect's Journal (1996) *Comment*, 1 August: 10.

ATCM (1994) *The Effectiveness of Town Centre Management*, London: Association of Town Centre Management.

ATCM (1996) *Managing Urban Spaces in Town Centres: A Good Practice Guide*, London: Association of Town Centre Management.

ATCM (2000) *Entrepreneurial Management of our Town and City Centres*, London: Association of Town Centre Management.

ATCM (2002) *Sustainable Funding for Town Centre Management*, London: Association of Town Centre Management.

Audit Commission (1989) *Urban Regeneration and Economic Development: The Local Authority Dimension*, London: HMSO.

Audit Commission (1996) *Just Capital – Local Authority Management of Capital Projects*, London: HMSO.

Audit Commission (1997) *Rome Wasn't Built in a Day – A Management Handbook on Getting Value for Money from Capital Programmes and Construction Projects*, London: HMSO.

Audit Commission (1999) *A Life's Work: Local Authorities, Economic Development and Economic Regeneration*, London: Stationery Office.

Averley, J. (1997) 'Remaking Manchester', *Town and Country Planning*, January: 14–15.

Bailey, N. (1995) *Partnership Agencies in British Urban Policy*, London: UCL Press.

Barlow, I. M. (1997) 'Administrative systems and metropolitan regions', *Environment and Planning C: Government and Policy*, 15, 4: 399–411.

Barlow, J. and Gann, D. (1993) *Offices into Flats*, York: Joseph Rowntree Foundation.

Bassett, K. (1996) 'Partnerships, business elites and urban politics: new forms of governance in an English city', *Urban Studies*, 35: 539–55.

Batho, S., Williams, G. and Russell, L. (1999) 'From crisis management to controlled recovery: the emergency planning response to the bombing of Manchester City Centre', *The Journal of Disaster Studies, Policy and Management*, 23, 217–34.

Begg, I. (1999) 'Cities and competitiveness', *Urban Studies*, 36: 795–809.

Begg, I. (ed.) (2002) *Urban Competitiveness – Policies for Dynamic Cities*, Bristol: Policy Press.

Begg, I., Moore, B. and Altunbas, Y. (2002), 'Long run trends in the competitiveness of British cities', in I. Begg (ed.), *Urban Competitiveness – Policies for Dynamic Cities*, Bristol: Policy Press.

Berridge, J. (1997) *Reflections* – personal communication, Toronto.

Berry, J., McGreal, S. and Deddis, B. (eds) (1993) *Urban Regeneration, Property Investment and Development*, London: E & F N Spon.

Beynon, H., Elson, D., Howell, D., Peck, J. and Shaw, L. (1993) *The Remaking of Economy and Society: Manchester, Salford and Trafford 1945–92*, WP1 University of Manchester: Manchester International Centre for Labour Studies.

Bianchini, F. (1995) 'Night cultures, night economies', *Planning Practice and Research*, 10, 2: 121–6.

Blackman, T. (1995) *Urban Policy in Practice*, London: Routledge.

Bibliography

Boddy, M. (2002) 'Linking competitiveness and cohesion', in I. Begg (ed.), *Urban Competitiveness – Policies for Dynamic Cities*, Bristol: Policy Press.

Boddy, M. and Fudge, C. (eds) (1984) *Local Socialism? Labour Councils and the New Left Alternative*, Basingstoke: Macmillan.

Bogason, P. and Tooney, T. A. J. (1998) 'Networks in public administration', *Public Administration*, 76: 205–28.

Bramley, G. and Lambert, C. (2002) 'Managing urban development: land use planning and city competitiveness', in I. Begg (ed.), *Urban Competitiveness – Policies for Dynamic Cities*, Bristol: Policy Press.

Breheny, M. (ed.), (1992) *Sustainable Development and Urban Form*, London: Pion.

Brier D. H. (1999) *Inspector's Report on the Transport Interchange CPO*, Bristol: Planning Inspectorate.

Buchanan Report (1963) *Traffic in Towns*, London: HMSO.

Burton, P. and O'Toole, M. (1993) 'Urban development corporations: post fordism in action or fordism in retrenchment', in R. Imrie and H. Thomas (eds), *British Urban Policy and the Urban Development Corporations*, London: Paul Chapman Publishing.

Castells, M. (1977) *The Urban Question*, Cambridge, MA: MIT Press.

Castells, M. (1989) *The Informational City: Information Technology, Economic Restructuring, and the Urban-Regional Process*, Oxford: Basil Blackwell.

Castells, M. and Hall, P. (1993) *Technopoles of the World: The Making of the 21st Century Industrial Complexes*, London: Routledge.

CIOB (1996) *Code of Practice for Project Management for Construction and Development*, London: Longman.

Civic Trust (1994) *Liveable Towns and Cities*, London: Civic Trust.

CMDC (1990) *Development Strategy*, Manchester: Central Manchester Development Corporation.

CMDC (1996) *Eight Years of Achievement*, Manchester: Central Manchester Development Corporation.

Cochrane, A. (1993) *Whatever Happened to Local Government?* Buckingham: Open University Press.

Cochrane, A. (1996) 'Redefining urban politics for the 21st century', in A. Jonas and D. Wilson (eds), *Urban Growth Machines – Twenty Years On*, Albany, NY: State University of New York.

Cochrane, A., Peck, J. and Tickell, A. (1996) 'Manchester plays games: exploring the local politics of globalisation', *Urban Studies*, 33: 1319–36.

Cochrane, A., Peck, J. and Tickell, A. (2002) 'Olympic dreams: visions of partnership', in J. Peck and K. Ward (eds), *City of Revolution: Restructuring Manchester*, Manchester: Manchester University Press.

Cockburn, C. (1977) *The Local State: Management of Cities and People*, London: Pluto Press.

Collinge, C. and Hall, S. (1997) 'Hegemony and regime in urban governance, towards a theory of the locally networked state', in N. Jewson, and S. MacGregor (eds), *Transforming Cities: Contested Governance and New Spatial Divisions*, London: Routledge.

Cooke, P. (1990) *Localities: The Changing Face of Urban Britain*, London: Unwin Hyman.

Cooke, P., Davies, C. and Wilson, R. (2002) 'Urban networks and the new economy: the impact of clusters in planning for growth', in I. Begg (ed.), *Urban Competitiveness – Policies for Dynamic Cities*, Bristol: Policy Press.

Couch, C. (1999) 'Housing development in the city centre', *Planning Practice and Research*, 14, 1: 69–86.

Coupland, A. (ed.) (1997) *Reclaiming the City: Mixed Use Developments*, London: E & F N Spon.

CURS (1985) *Local Economic Initiatives Study: Manchester City Council*, Birmingham: Centre for Urban and Regional Studies, University of Birmingham.

D'Arcy, E. and Keogh, G. (2002) 'The market context of property development and activity', in S. Guy and J. Henneberry (eds), *Development and Developers*, Oxford: Blackwell.

Deakin, N. and Edwards, J. (1993) *The Enterprise Culture and the Inner City*, London: Routledge.

Dearlove, J. (1973) *The Politics and Policy of English Local Government*, Cambridge: Cambridge University Press.

Deas, I. and Giordano, B. (2001) 'Conceptualising and measurement of urban competitiveness in major English cities: an exploratory approach', *Environment and Planning A*, 33: 1411–29.

Deas, I. and Giordano, B. (2002) 'Locating the competitive city in England', in I. Begg (ed.), *Urban Competitiveness – Policies for Dynamic Cities*, Bristol: Policy Press.

Deas, I. and Ward, K. G. (2000a) 'From the "new localism" to the "new regionalism?" The implications of regional development agencies for city-regional relations', *Political Geography*, 19: 273–92.

Deas, I. and Ward, K. G. (eds) (2002) 'Metropolitan manoeuvres: making Greater Manchester', in Peck, J. and Ward, K. (eds), *City of revolution: restructuring Manchester,* Manchester: Manchester University Press.

Deas, I., Peck, J., Tickell, A., Ward, K. and Bradford, M. (1999) 'Rescripting urban regeneration the Mancunian way', in R. Imrie and H. Thomas (eds), *British Urban Policy and the UDCs*, 2nd edition, London: Paul Chapman Publishing.

Deas, I., Robson, B. and Bradford, M. (2000) 'Rethinking the UDC experiment: the case of Central Manchester, Leeds and Bristol', *Progress in Planning*, 54, 1, Amsterdam: Elsevier Science.

DETR (1996) *Town Centres and Retail Development*, PPG6, London: HMSO.

DETR (1997) *General Policy and Principles*, PPG1, London: HMSO.

DETR (2000) *Our Towns and Cities: The Future – Delivering an Urban Renaissance*, London: Stationery Office.

DETR (2001) *Transport*, PPG13, London: Stationery Office.

DETR/ATCM (1997) *Town Centre Partnerships*, London: DETR.

Duffy, H. (1995) *Competitive Cities: Succeeding in the Global Economy*, London: E & F N Spon.

Duncan, S. and Goodwin, M. (1988) *The Local State and Uneven Development: Behind the Local Government Crisis*, Cambridge: Polity Press.

Eisenschitz, A. and Gough, J. (1993) *The Politics of Local Economic Policy*, Basingstoke: Macmillan.

Evans, G. (2001) *Cultural Planning – An Urban Renaissance*, London: Routledge.

Evans, R. (1997) *Regenerating Town Centres*, Manchester: Manchester University Press.

Fitzsimmons, J. (1998) 'City centre living: a study of residents of central Manchester', unpublished MTPI dissertation, School of Planning and Landscape, Manchester University.

Gibb, K., Mackay, D. and White, M. (2002) 'The property sector, and its role in shaping urban competitiveness', in I. Begg (ed.), *Urban Competitiveness – Policies for Dynamic Cities*, Bristol: Policy Press.

Giddens, A. (1998) *The Third Way*, Cambridge: Polity Press.

Giordano, B. and Twomey, L. (2002) 'Economic transition: restructuring local labour markets', in Peck, J. and Ward, K. (eds), *City of revolution: restructuring Manchester*, Manchester: Manchester University Press.

GMPTA/AGMA (1998) *The Greater Manchester Transport Package*, Manchester: Greater Manchester Passenger Transport Executive.

Goodwin, M. and Painter, J. (1997) 'Concrete research, urban regimes and regulation theory', in M. Lauria (ed.), *Reconstructing Urban Regime Theory: Regulating Urban Politics in a Global Economy*, Thousand Oaks, CA: Sage.

Gordon, A. (1997) 'Issues and problems in conducting economic impact analysis: a case study of the IRA bombing of Manchester city centre', unpublished MA thesis, Faculty of Environment, Leeds Metropolitan University.

Graham, C. (1998) 'Disaster!', *British Journal of Administrative Management*, Nov/Dec: 9–13.

Bibliography

Graham, S. (1998) 'The end of geography or the explosion of place? Conceptualising space, time and information technology', *Progress in Human Geography*, 22, 2: 165–85.

Graham, S. and Marvin, S. (1996) *Telecommunications and the City: Electronic Places, Urban Spaces*, London: Routledge.

Grail, J. (2000) 'Town centre management', in P. Allmendinger, A. Prior and J. Raemaker (eds), *Introduction to Planning Practice*, Chichester: Wiley.

Griffiths, R. (1995) 'Cultural strategies and new modes of urban intervention', *Cities*, 12, 4: 253–65.

Griffiths, R. (1998) 'Making sameness: place marketing and the new urban entrepreneurialism', in N. Oatley (ed.), *Cities, Economic Competition and Urban Policy*, London: Paul Chapman Publishing.

Griffiths, S. (1998) 'A profile of poverty and health in Manchester', executive summary, Manchester: Manchester City Council.

Hall, T. (1997) '(Re)placing the city: cultural relocation and the city centre', in S. Westwood and J. Williams (eds), *Imagining Cities: Scripts, Signs and Memory*, London: Routledge.

Hall, T. (1998) 'Introduction – entrepreneurial governance, policy and practice', in T. Hall and P. Hubbard (eds), *The Entrepreneurial City: Geographies of Politics, Regimes and Representation*, Chichester: Wiley.

Hall, T. and Hubbard, P. (1996) 'The entrepreneurial city: new urban politics, new urban geographies', *Progress in Human Geography*, 20: 153–74.

Hall, T. and Hubbard, P. (eds) (1998) *The Entrepreneurial City: Geographies of Politics, Regimes and Representation*, Chichester: Wiley.

Hannigan, J. (1999) *Fantasy City*, London: Routledge.

Harding, A. (1995) 'Elite theory and growth machines', in D. Judge, G. Stoker and H. Wolman, *Theories of Urban Politics*, London: Sage.

Harding, A. (1998) *Hulme City Challenge: Did it Work?* Liverpool: Liverpool John Moores University.

Harrison, M. (1981) 'Housing and town planning in Manchester before 1914', in A. Sutcliffe (ed.), *British Town Planning, The Formative Years*, Leicester: Leicester University Press.

Hartwell, C. (2001) *Manchester – Pevsner Architectural Guides*, London: Penguin Books.

Harvey, D. (1989a) *The Urban Experience*, Oxford: Basil Blackwell.

Harvey, D. (1989b) *The Condition of Postmodernity*, Oxford: Basil Blackwell.

Harvey, D. (1989c) 'From managerialism to entrepreneurialism: the transformation of urban governance in late capitalism', *Geografiska Annaler, B: Human Geography*, 71: 3–17.

Haslam, D. (1999) *Manchester, England: The Story of the Pop Cult City*, London: Fourth Estate.

Hastings, A. (1996) *Less than Equal: Community Organisations and Estate Regeneration Partnerships*, Bristol: Policy Press.

Hastings, A. (1999) 'Analysing power relations in partnerships: is there a role for discourse analysis?' *Urban Studies*, 36: 91–106.

Hay, C. (1996) *Re-stating Social and Political Change*, Buckingham: Open University Press.

Hayward, R. and McGlynn, S. (1995) 'The town centre we deserve?' *Town Planning Review*, 66, 3: 321–8.

Healey, P. (1997a) *Collaborative Planning: Shaping Places in Fragmented Societies*, Basingstoke: Macmillan.

Healey, P. (1997b) *Project Management – Getting the Job Done on Time and on Budget*, London: Butterworth Heinemann.

Healey, P. (1998a) 'Building institutional capacity through collaborative approaches to urban planning', *Environment and Planning A*, 30: 1531–46.

Healey, P. (1998b) 'Collaborative planning in a stakeholder society', *Town Planning Review*, 69: 1–22.

Healey, P., Davoudi, S., O'Toole, M., Tavsanoglu, S. and Usher, D. (1992) *Rebuilding the City – Property Led Urban Regeneration*, London: E & F N Spon.

Healey, P., Cameron, S., Davoudi, S., Graham, S. and Madanipour, A. (eds) (1995) *Managing Cities: The New Urban Context*, London: Wiley.

Hebbert, M. and Deas, I. (2000) 'Greater Manchester – "up and going"', *Policy and Politics*, 28: 79–92.

Herd, D. and Patterson, T. (2002) 'Poor Manchester: old problems and new deals', in J. Peck and K. Ward (eds), *City of Revolution: Restructuring Manchester*, Manchester: Manchester University Press.

Hill, D. (2000) *Urban Policy and Politics in Britain*, Basingstoke: Macmillan.

Hillier Parker (1994) *Quality of the Public Realm in Town and City Centres*, London: Hillier Parker.

Hindle, P. (1994) 'Gay communities and gay space in the city', in S. Whittle (ed.), *The Margins of the City – Gay Men's Urban Lives*, Newcastle: Athenium Press.

Holden, A. (1996) 'Re-building Manchester: the discursive construction of the urban', unpublished MA dissertation, University of Manchester.

Holden, A. (1999) 'Manchester first! entrepreneurial strategies and enterprising narratives in the construction of a local economic hegemonic project', unpublished PhD thesis, University of Manchester.

Holliday, J. (1973) *City Centre Redevelopment*, London: Charles Knight & Co.

Hubbard, P. (1998) 'Introduction – representation culture and identities', in T. Hall and P. Hubbard (eds), *The Entrepreneurial City: Geographies of Politics, Regimes and Representation*, Chichester: Wiley.

Hutchinson, J. (1995) 'Can partnerships which fail succeed? The case of city challenge', *Local Government Policy Making*, 22: 41–51.

Huxham, G. (ed.) (1996) *Creating Collaborative Advantage*, London: Sage.

Imrie, R. and Thomas, H. (1993) 'The limits of property-led regeneration', *Environment and Planning C*, 11: 87–102.

Innes, J. E. (1999) 'Evaluating consensus building', in L. Susskind, S. McKearnan and J. Thomas-Larner (eds), *The Consensus Building Handbook*, Thousand Oaks, CA: Sage.

Jencks, C. and Peterson, P. E. (1991) *The Urban Underclass*, Washington, DC: Brookings Institute.

Jenks, M., Burton, E. and Williams, K. (eds) (1996) *The Compact City: A Sustainable Urban Form?* London: E & F N Spon.

Jensen-Butler, C., Schacher, A. and van Weestop, J. (eds) (1997) *European Cities in Competition*, Aldershot: Avebury.

Jessop, B. (1997a) 'The entrepreneurial city: re-imaging localities, redesigning economic governance, or restructuring capital?', in N. Jewson and S. MacGregor (eds), *Transforming Cities: Contested Governance and New Spatial Divisions*, London: Routledge.

Jessop, B. (1997b) 'The governance of complexity and the complexity of governance', in A. Amin and J. Hausner (eds), *Beyond Markets and Hierarchies: Third Way Approaches to Transformation*, Edward Elgar: Aldershot.

Jessop, B. (1998) 'The enterprise of narrative, and the narrative of enterprise: place marketing and the entrepreneurial city', in T. Hall and P. Hubbard (eds), *The Entrepreneurial City: Geographies of Politics, Regimes and Representation*, Chichester: Wiley.

Jewson, N. and MacGregor, S. (1997) *Transforming Cities: Contested Governance and New Spatial Divisions*, London: Routledge.

Jones, M. (1997) 'Spatial selectivity of the state? The regulationist enigma and local struggles over economic governance', *Environment and Planning A*, 29: 831–64.

Jones, M. (1998) 'Restructuring the local state: economic governance or social regulation', *Political Geography*, 17: 959–88.

Jones, M. and Ward, K. (1998) 'Grabbing grants? The role of coalitions in urban economic development', *Local Economy*, May: 28–38.

Judge, D., Stoker, G. and Wolman, H. (1995) *Theories of Urban Politics*, London: Sage.

Kellie, E. (2002) www.regeneration-manchester.co.uk

Kidd, A. (1993) *Manchester*, Keele: Ryburn Publishing.

Kitchen, T. (1996) 'The future of development plans: reflections on Manchester's experience 1945–1995', *Town Planning Review*, 67: 331–53.

Kitchen, T. (1997) *People, Politics, Policies and Plans: The City Planning Process in Contemporary Britain*, London: Paul Chapman Publishing.

Kitchen, T. (2001) 'Planning in response to terrorism: the case of Manchester, England', *Journal of Architectural and Planning Research*, 18, 4: 326–40.

Knox, P. and Taylor, P. J. (eds) (1995) *World Cities in a World System*, Cambridge: Cambridge University Press.

Kresl, P. (1995) 'The determinants of urban competitiveness', in P. Kresl and G. Gappert (eds), *North American Cities and the Global Economy*, Urban Affairs Annual Review, 44, London: Sage Publications.

Krugman, P. (1996) 'Making sense of the competitiveness debate', *Oxford Review of Economic Policy*, 12: 17–25.

Kwakye, A. A. (1997) *Construction Project Administration in Practice*, London: Longman.

Lambert Smith Hampton (1999) *The Effects of the Trafford Centre*, Manchester: Lambert Smith Hampton.

Law, C. (1988) 'From Manchester docks to Salford Quays: a progress report on a redevelopment project', *Manchester Geographer*, 9: 2–15.

Law, C. (1992) 'Property-led urban regeneration in inner Manchester', in P. Healey, S. Davoudi, M. O'Toole, S. Tavsanoglu and D. Usher (eds), *Rebuilding the City – Property-led Urban Regeneration*, London: E & F N Spon.

Law, C. (1994) 'Manchester's bid for the Millennium Olympic Games', *Geography*, 79: 222–31.

Law, C. (2001) *Discovering Cities – Manchester*, Sheffield: Geographical Association.

Lawless, P. (1991) *Public-Private Sector Partnerships in the United Kingdom*, Sheffield: Sheffield Hallam University, CRESR.

Lawless, P. (1994) 'Partnership in urban regeneration in the UK: the Sheffield Central Area Study', *Urban Studies*, 31, 8: 1303–24.

Lawless, P. (1996) 'The inner cities: towards a new agenda?' *Town Planning Review*, 67: 21–43.

Leach, R. and Percy-Smith, J. (2001) *Local Governance in Britain*, Basingstoke: Palgrave.

Leach, S. and Davis, H. (eds) (1996) *Enabling or Disabling Local Governance*, Buckingham: Open University Press.

Leese, R. (1996) 'New labour, new local government', *Renewal*, 30–3.

Lever, J. (1997) 'The service sector in the centre of Manchester', in S. Liszewski and C. Young (eds), *A Comparative Study of Lodz and Manchester: Geographies of European Cities in Transition*, Lodz, Poland: Lodz University Press.

Lever, W. (2002) 'The knowledge base and the competitive city', in I. Begg (ed.), *Urban Competitiveness – Policies for Dynamic Cities*, Bristol: Policy Press.

Lever, W. F. and Turok, I. (1999) 'Competitive cities: introduction to the review', *Urban Studies*, 36, 5/6: 791–4.

Leverhulme Trust (1998) 'Managing urban development partnerships: the recovery of Manchester city centre', Grant F/120/BC, 1998–2000.

Lichfield, D (2000) 'Organisation and management', in P. Robert and H. Sykes (eds), *Urban Regeneration – A Handbook*, London: Sage.

Lloyd, P. (1980) 'Manchester: a study of industrial decline and economic restructuring', in H. White (ed.), *The Continuing Conurbation: Change and Development in Greater Manchester*, Farnborough: Gower.

Loftman, P. and Nevin, B. (1996) 'Going for growth: prestige projects in three British cities', *Urban Studies*, 33: 991–1019.

Loftman, P. and Nevin, B. (1998) 'Pro-growth local economic development strategies: civic promotion and local needs in Britain's second city, 1981–1996', in T. Hall and P. Hubbard (eds), *The Entrepreneurial City: Geographies of Politics, Regimes and Representation*, Chichester: Wiley.

Logan, J. and Molotch, H. (1987) *Urban Fortunes: The Political Economy of Place*, Berkeley, CA: University of California Press.

Lovatt, A. (1994) 'The 24-hour city: proceedings of the First National Conference on the Night Time Economy', Manchester: Manchester Metropolitan University.

Lovatt, A. and O'Connor, J. (1995) 'Cities and the night-time economy', *Planning Practice and Research*, 10: 2, 127–33.

Lowndes, V., Nanton, P., McCabe, A. and Skelcher, C. (1997) 'Networks, partnerships and urban regeneration', *Local Economy*, 11: 333–42.

Lowndes, V. and Skelcher, C. (1998) 'The dynamics of multi-organisational partnerships: an analysis of changing modes of governance', *Public Administration*, 76: 313–33.

Mackintosh, M. (1992) 'Partnerships: issues of policy and negotiation', *Local Economy*, 7: 210–24.

Malone, P. (1997) 'The mending of Manchester', *Urban Design Quarterly*, 61, January: 11–13.

Manchester City Council (1984a) *Review of the Corporate Economic Strategy*, Manchester, MCC.

Manchester City Council (1984b) *City Centre Local Plan*, Manchester, MCC.

Manchester City Council (1992a) *Economic Development Strategy*, Manchester: MCC.

Manchester City Council (1992b) *Arts and Cultural Strategy*, Manchester: MCC.

Manchester City Council (1994) *City Pride: A Focus for the Future*, Manchester: MCC.

Manchester City Council (1995a) *Unitary Development Plan for Manchester*, Manchester: MCC.

Manchester City Council (1995b) *Manchester Housing Strategy*, Manchester: MCC.

Manchester City Council (1996a) *A Guide to Development in Manchester*, Manchester: MCC.

Manchester City Council (1996b) *Supplementary Planning Guidance for the Bomb Damaged Area*, Manchester: MCC.

Manchester City Council (1997a) *City Pride 2: Partnerships for a Successful Future*, Manchester: MCC.

Manchester City Council (1997b) *An Arts and Cultural Strategy for Manchester*, Manchester: MCC.

Manchester City Council (1998) *Millennium Quarter Proposals*, Manchester: MCC.

Manchester City Council (2001) *City Pride Partnership – Economic Development Plan 2001–04*, Manchester: MCC.

Manchester City Council (2002a) *Manchester Local Strategic Partnership*, Manchester: MCC.

Manchester City Council (2002b) *The Manchester Community Strategy 2002–2012*, Manchester: MCC.

Manchester City Council (2002c) *Manchester City Centre Strategic Plan*, Manchester: MCC/ Manchester City Centre Management Company Ltd.

Manchester City Council/Newsco (1996–2002) *Update Manchester*: the bulletin of economic development issues, quarterly, Manchester: MCC.

Manchester Millennium Ltd (1996a) *Competition Brief – Stage 1, Competition Brief – Stage 2*, Manchester: MML.

Manchester Millennium Ltd (1996b) *International Urban Design Competition*, Manchester: MML.

Manchester Millennium Ltd (1996c) *Framework for the Future: City Centre Masterplan*, Manchester: MML.

Manchester Millennium Ltd (1997) *First Implementation Plan*, Manchester: MML.

Manchester Millennium Ltd (1998) *Second Implementation Plan*, Manchester: MML.

Manchester Millennium Ltd (1999) *Third Implementation Plan*, Manchester: MML.

Manchester Millennium Ltd (1997–99) *Millennium: News on the Rebuilding of Manchester City Centre*, issues 1–9, Manchester: MML.

Marketing Manchester (1997) *A New Image for the Manchester City Region*, Manchester: Marketing Manchester.

Marshall, W. (1994) 'Urban design in Manchester', *Urban Design Quarterly*, April: 18–21.

Meadowcroft, J. (1998) 'Cooperative management regimes: a way forward', in R. Glasbergen (ed.),
 Cooperative Environmental Governance: Public-Private Agreements as a Policy Strategy,
 Dordrecht: Kluwer Academic Publishers.
Mellor, R. (1997) 'Cool times for a changing city', in N. Jewson and S. MacGregor (eds),
 Transforming Cities: Contested Governance and New Spatial Divisions, London: Routledge.
Mellor, R. (2002) 'Hypocritical city: cycles of urban exclusion', in J. Peck and K. Ward (eds), *City of
 Revolution: Restructuring Manchester*, Manchester: Manchester University Press.
Millington, S. (1997) 'Local governance and local economic development in Manchester', in S.
 Liszewski and C. Young (eds), *A Comparative Study of Lodz and Manchester: Geographies of
 European Cities in Transition*, Lodz, Poland: Lodz University Press.
Mills, G. (1997) 'Embracing the new – focus on architecture in Manchester', *Architect's Journal*, 3
 April: 29–36.
Montgomery, J. (1994) 'The night time economy of cities', *Town and Country Planning*, November:
 302–7.
Montgomery, J. (1995) 'Urban vitality and the culture of cities', *Planning Practice and Research*, 10,
 2: 101–9.
Myles, J. and Taylor, I. (1998) *After the 1996 Bomb: Public Consultation in the 'Rebuilding' of
 Manchester*, Salford Papers in Sociology 24, Salford: Salford University.

New East Manchester (2001) *Regeneration Framework*, Manchester: MCC.
Newman, P. and Verpraet, G. (1999) 'The impacts of partnership in urban governance: conclusions
 from recent European research', *Regional Studies*, 33: 487–91.

Oatley, N. (ed.), (1998) *Cities, Economic Competition and Urban Policy*, London: Paul Chapman
 Publishing.
Oc, T. and Tiesdell, S. (1997) *Safer Town Centres – Reviewing the Public Realm*, London: Paul
 Chapman Publishing.
O'Connor, J. (1973) *The Fiscal Crisis of the State*, New York: St Martin's Press.
O'Connor, J. (2000) *The Cultural Production Sector in Manchester*, Manchester: Manchester
 Metropolitan University.
O'Connor, J. and Wynne, D. (eds) (1996) *From the Margins to the Centre: Cultural Production and
 Consumption in the Post Industrial City*, Basingstoke: Arena.

Painter, J. (1997) 'Regulation, regimes, and practice in urban politics', in M. Lauria (ed.), *Reconstructing
 Urban Regime Theory: Regulating Urban Politics in a Global Economy*, Thousand Oaks, CA: Sage.
Painter, J. (1998) 'Entrepreneurs are made, not born: learning and urban regimes in the production
 of the entrepreneurial city', in T. Hall and P. Hubbard (eds), *The Entrepreneurial City:
 Geographies of Politics, Regimes and Representation*, Chichester: Wiley.
Painter, J. and Goodwin, M. (1995) 'Local governance and concrete research: investigating the
 uneven development of regulation', *Economy and Society*, 24: 334–56.
Parkinson, M. (1996) '25 years of urban policy in Britain – partnership, entrepreneurialism or
 competition', *Public Money and Management*, July–September: 7–14.
Parkinson, M. and Robson, B. (2000) *Urban Regeneration Companies: A Process Evaluation*,
 London: DETR.
Parkinson-Bailey, J. (2000) *Manchester – An Architectural History*, Manchester: Manchester
 University Press.
Peck, J. (1995) 'Moving and shaking: business elites, state localism and urban privatism', *Progress
 in Human Geography*, 19: 16–46.
Peck, J. and Emmerich, M. (1992) 'Recession, restructuring and the Greater Manchester labour market:
 an empirical overview', *SPA Working Paper 17*, School of Geography: University of Manchester.

Peck, J. and Tickell, A. (1994) 'Too many partnerships … the future of regeneration partnerships', *Local Economy*, 9: 251–65.

Peck, J. and Tickell, A. (1995) 'Business goes local: dissecting the business agenda in Manchester', *International Journal of Urban and Regional Research*, 19: 55–78.

Peck, J. and Ward, K. (eds) (2002) *City of revolution: restructuring Manchester*, Manchester: Manchester University Press.

Peters, B. G. (1997) '"With a little help from our friends": public-private partnerships as institutions and instruments', in J. Pierre (ed.), *Partnerships in Urban Governance – European and American Experience*, London: Macmillan.

Pierre, J. and Stoker, G. (2000) *Towards Multi-Level Governance: Developments in British Politics*, London: Macmillan.

Porter, M. (1995) 'The competitive advantage of the inner city', *Harvard Business Review*, May–June: 55–71.

Porter, M. (1997) 'New strategies for inner-city economic development', *Economic Development Quarterly*, 11, 1: 11–27.

Porter, M. (1998) *The Competitive Advantage of Nations*, London: Macmillan.

Potts, G. (2002) 'Competitiveness and social fabric: links and tensions in cities', in I. Begg (ed.), *Urban Competitiveness – Policies for Dynamic Cities*, Bristol: Policy Press.

Powell, W. (1991) 'Neither market nor hierarchy: network forms of organisation', in G. Thompson, J. Frances, R. Levacic and J. Mitchell (eds), *Markets, Hierarchies and Networks: The Coordination of Social Life*, London: Sage.

Putnam, R. (1993) *Making Democracy Work: Civic Traditions in Italy*, Princeton, NJ: Princeton University Press.

Quilley, S. (1995) 'Economic transformation and local strategy in Manchester', unpublished PhD thesis, University of Manchester.

Quilley, S. (1997) 'Constructing Manchester's new urban village: gay space and the entrepreneurial city', in G. Brent-Ingram (ed.), *Queers in Space: Landscapes of Marginalized Sexualities and Communities*, Washington, DC: Bay Press.

Quilley, S. (1999) 'Entrepreneurial Manchester: the genesis of elite consensus', *Antipode*, 31: 185–211.

Quilley, S. (2000) 'Manchester First: from municipal socialism to the entrepreneurial city', *International Journal of Urban and Regional Research*, 24, 3: 601–15.

Quilley, S. (2002) 'Entrepreneurial turns, municipal socialism and after', in J. Peck and K. Ward (eds), *City of revolution: restructuring Manchester*, Manchester: Manchester University Press.

Quilley, S. and Ward, K. (1999) 'Global "system" and local "personality" in urban politics', *Environment and Planning D*, 3, 1: 5–34.

Randall, S. (1995) 'City Pride – from "municipal socialism" to "municipal capitalism"?' *Critical Social Policy*, 15: 40–59.

Rapkin, D. and Strand, D. (1995) 'Competitiveness – useful concept, political slogan or dangerous obsession', in D. Rapkin and W. Avery (eds), *National Competitiveness in a Global Economy*, London: Lynne Rienner.

Rattenburg, K. (1997) 'Making the best out of the bomb', *Design*, spring: 54–7.

Reiss, G. (1996a) *Programme Management Demystified – Managing Multiple Projects Successfully*, London: E & F N Spon.

Reiss, G. (1996b) *Project Management Demystified – Today's Tools and Techniques*, London: E & F N Spon.

Rhodes, R. (1997) *Understanding Governance*, Buckingham: Open University Press.

Roberts, P. and Sykes, H. (2000) *Urban Regeneration – A Handbook*, London: Sage.

Bibliography

Robson, B. (2002) 'Mancunian ways: the politics of regeneration', in J. Peck and K. Ward (eds), *City of revolution: restructuring Manchester*, Manchester: Manchester University Press.

Robson, B., Bradford, M. and Deas, I. (1999) 'Beyond the boundaries: vacancy chains and the evaluation of urban development corporations', *Environment and Planning A*, 31: 647–64.

Robson, B., Bradford, M., Deas, I., Hall, E., Harrison, E., Parkinson, M., Evans, R., Garside, P., Harding, A. and Robinson, F. (1994) *Assessing the Impact of Urban Policy*, London: HMSO.

Rodgers, H. B. (1986) 'Manchester: metropolitan planning by collaboration and consent, or civic hope frustrated', in G. Gordon (ed.), *Regional Cities in the UK 1890–1980*, London: Harper and Row.

Rogers, R. (1999) *Towards an Urban Renaissence: The Urban Task Force*, London: E & F N Spon.

Rogerson, R. (1999) 'Quality of life and city competitiveness', *Urban Studies*, 36, 5/6: 969–86.

Rowley, A. (1996) 'Mixed use development: ambiguous concept, simplistic analysis and wishful thinking', *Planning Policy and Research*, 11, 1: 85–97.

RTPI (1998) *Planning in Partnership: A Guide for Planners*, London: Royal Town Planning Institute.

Russell, L. (1998) *The Recovery of Manchester City Centre: Reflecting on Experience* (Report to Manchester Millennium Ltd), Manchester University.

Saunders, P. (1980) *Social Theory and the Urban Question*, London: Hutchinson.

Shaw, K. and Robinson, F. (1998) 'Learning from experience? Reflections on two decades of British urban policy', *Town Planning Review*, 69, 1: 49–63.

Simmie, J. (ed.), (2001) *Innovative Cities*, London: E & F N Spon.

Simmie, J., Sennett, J. and Wood, P. (2002) 'Innovation and clustering in the London Metropolitan region', in I. Begg (ed.), *Urban Competitiveness – Policies for Dynamic Cities*, Bristol: Policy Press.

Skelcher, C., McCabe, A., Lowndes, V. and Nanton, P. (1996) *Community Networks in Urban Regeneration*, Bristol: Policy Press.

Sorkin, M. and Zukin, S. (eds) (2002) *After the World Trade Center: Rethinking New York*, New York: Routledge.

Stewart, M. (1994) 'Between Whitehall and townhall: the realignment of urban regeneration policy in England', *Policy and Politics*, 22: 133–45.

Stewart, M. (1996) 'Competition and competitiveness in urban policy', *Public Money and Management*, July–September: 21–6.

Stoker, G. (1995) 'Regime theory and urban politics', in D. Judge, G. Stoker and H. Wolman (eds), *Theories of Urban Politics*, London: Sage.

Stoker, G. (1997) 'Public-private partnership and urban governance', in J. Pierre (ed.), *Partnerships in Urban Governance – European and American Experience*, London: Macmillan.

Stone, C. (1993) 'Urban regimes and the capacity to govern, a political-economy approach', *Journal of Urban Affairs*, 15: 1–28.

Sullivan, H. and Lowndes, V. (1996) *City Challenge Succession Strategies: Governance through Partnership*, INLOGOV, Birmingham University.

Syms, P. (1993) 'Piccadilly Village: property investment and development', in J. Berry, S. McGreal and B. Deddis (eds), *Urban Regeneration, Property Investment and Development*, London: E & F N Spon.

Taylor, A. (2000) '"Hollowing out or filling in?" Task forces and the management of cross cutting issues in British government', *British Journal of Politics and International Relations*, 2, 1: 46–71.

Taylor, I., Evans, K. and Fraser, P. (1996) *A Tale of Two Cities*, London: Routledge.

Tewdwr-Jones, M. and Allmendinger, P. (1998) 'Deconstructing communicative rationality: a critique of Habermasion collaborative planning', *Environmental and Planning A*, 30: 1975–89.

Thompson, G., Frances, J., Levacic, R. and Mitchell, J. (eds) (1991) *Markets, Hierarchies and Networks: The Coordination of Social Life*, London: Sage.

Thornley, A. (1993) *Urban Planning under Thatcherism. The Challenge of the Market*, 2nd edn, London: Routledge.

Tibbalds, F. (1992) *Making People-Friendly Towns, Improving the Public Environment in Towns and Cities*, Harlow: Longman.

Tickell, A. and Peck, J. (1996) 'The return of the Manchester Men: men's words and men's deeds in the remaking of the local state', *Transactions (T.I.B.G.)* 21, 595–616.

Tiesdell, S., Oc, T. and Heath, T. (1996) *Revitalising Historic Urban Quarters*, London: Butterworth-Heinemann.

Turok, I. (1992) 'Property led regeneration: panacea or placebo?' *Environment and Planning A*, 24: 361–80.

Tye, R. and Williams, G. (1994) 'Urban regeneration and centre-local government relations – the case of east Manchester', *Progress in Planning*, 42: 1, Oxford, Pergamon Press.

Urban Studies (2001) *Special Issue – Urban Neighbourhoods*, 38, 12: 2103–316.

URBED (1994) *Vital and Viable Town Centres – Meeting the Challenge*, London: HMSO.

Wansborough, M. and Mageean, A. (2000) 'The role of urban design in cultural regeneration', *Journal of Urban Design*, 5, 2: 181–97.

Ward, K. G. (1996) 'Rereading urban regime theory: a sympathetic critique', *Geoforum*, 27: 427–38.

Ward, K. G. (1998) 'Governing the city: a regime approach', unpublished PhD thesis, University of Manchester.

Ward, K. G. (2000) 'From rentiers to rantiers: active entrepreneurs, structural speculators and the politics of marketing the city', *Urban Studies*, 37, 7: 1093–107.

Wilks-Heegs, S. (1996) 'Urban Experiments Ltd revisited: urban policy comes full circle?' *Urban Studies*, 33: 1263–79.

Williams, G. (1983) *Inner City Policy – A Partnership with the Voluntary Sector*? London: National Council for Voluntary Organisations.

Williams, G. (1995) 'Prospecting for gold: Manchester's City Pride experience', *Planning Practice & Research*, 10: 345–58.

Williams, G. (1996) 'City profile: Manchester', *Cities*, 13: 203–12.

Williams, G. (1998) 'City vision and strategic regeneration: the role of City Pride', in N. Oatley (ed.), *Cities, Economic Competition and Urban Policy*, London: Paul Chapman Publishing.

Williams, G. (1999) 'Greater Manchester', in P. Roberts, K. Thomas and G. Williams (eds), *Metropolitan Planning in Britain: A Comparative Study*, London: Jessica Kingsley.

Williams, G. (2000) 'Rebuilding the entrepreneurial city: masterplanning responses to the bombing of Manchester city centre', *Environment & Planning B*, 27: 485–505.

Williams, G. (2002) 'City building – developing Manchester's core', in J. Peck and K. Ward (eds), *City of revolution: restructuring Manchester*, Manchester: Manchester University Press.

Williams, G., Batho, S. and Russell, R. (2000) 'Responding to urban crisis: the emergency planning response to the bombing of Manchester city centre', *Cities*, 17, 4: 293–304.

Williams, K. and Green, S. (2001) *Literature Review of Public Space and Local Environments*, Oxford: Oxford Brookes University.

Wilson, D. and Game, C. (2002) *Local Government in the United Kingdom*, 3rd edition, Basingstoke: Palgrave Macmillan.

Worpole, K. and Greenhalgh, L. (1999) *The Richness of Cities: Urban Policy in a New Landscape*, London: Comedia and Demos.

Wynne, D. and O'Connor, J. (1998) 'Consumption and the postmodern city', *Urban Studies*, 35, 5/6: 841–64.

Zukin, S. (1988) *Loft Living*, London: Hutchinson.

Zukin, S. (1995) *The Culture of Cities*, Cambridge, MA: Blackwell.

Appendix 1
Individual interviews

Manchester Millennium Ltd Task Force Board Chair, Chief Executive, Project Director, Procurement Manager, Project Manager, Recovery Coordinator.

Manchester City Council Council Leader, Deputy Leader, Chair of Finance Committee, Chair of City Centre Sub-Committee, Chief Executive, Head of Policy Unit, Head of Special Projects, City Centre Manager, Head of Planning, Chief Building Surveyor, Divisional Engineer, City Treasurers Department, Emergency Planning Officer, Head of Parking Services, Head of Markets, Head of Press Office, Head of Building Services.

Government Office North West Regional Director, Head of Urban Initiatives Team, Director of Infrastructure and Planning, Head of European Programmes Secretariat.

Landowners and commercial interests P&O, Prudential Assurance, Frogmore Estates, Co-operative Insurance Services, Marks & Spencer, First Bus.

Consultants EDAW, Oscar Faber, Ian Simpson Associates, Jim Chapman Architects, Urban Solutions, Poole Stokes Wood, Joe Berridge.

Other interests Lord Mayor's Appeal Fund Administrator, Greater Manchester Police, Greater Manchester Passenger Transport Executive, Chetham's School, Dean of Manchester Cathedral, Manchester Evening News, Property Consultants, Manchester Civic Society.

Appendix 2
Focus group meetings

These involved a range of public, private and community interests, with each meeting consisting of around 8–12 participants, and lasting 2–3 hours. They were held at a neutral venue within the city centre during January/February 2000, with a standard thematic approach being adopted in facilitating discussion and debate.

Focus group 1: economic competitiveness

- Commercial surveying firms – GVA Grimley, Lambert Smith Hampton, Dunlop Heywood.
- Private development interests – Peel Holdings, Crosby Homes, Urban Splash.
- Other agencies – North West Development Agency, Training and Enterprise Council, Marketing Manchester, Chamber of Commerce.
- Local authority – Valuation and Property Department, City Centre Manager.

Focus group 2: built environment

- Local architectural practices – Chapman Robinson, Simpson Associates.
- Government interests – GO NW, Manchester City Council Environment and Development Department, City Architects.
- Other interests – EDAW, Greater Manchester Pedestrians Association.

Focus group 3: transport, access and mobility

- Transport operators – Stagecoach, Railtrack.
- Government interests – GO NW, Manchester City Council Traffic and Transport Division.
- Other interests – Manchester Parking, Greater Manchester Transport Action Group, GMCVS.

Index

Index

Index